Test Authors: Alyssa Coburn, Nicole Burmingham, Daniel Melko, and Julia Dopp

Test editors: Sarah Phillips, Jenna Brightwell, Amanda Ratzloff, Julia Dopp, Erin Doyle, and Taylor Hanson

ISBN: 978-1-7323159-0-7
Library of Congress Control Number: 2018947213

Nurturing Wisdom Tutoring's Practice Tests: The HSPT

By Nurturing Wisdom Tutoring, Inc.®

www.nurturingwisdom.com

Table of Contents

HSPT Test 5

HSPT Test 6

HSPT Test 7

HSPT Test 8

Overview of the HSPT

We'll give it to you straight: the High School Placement Test is challenging. But that doesn't mean you can't do well on it! Becoming familiar with the test format, question types, skills tested, and timing restraints will help you achieve competitive scores.

Used for admissions to many Catholic high schools, the HSPT assesses eighth graders' math, reading, verbal, and language arts skills. Often, students find that the skills tested are unfamiliar or rusty, and that the questions are tricky. In addition, many students have difficulty finishing each section within the time limits - even kids who don't typically struggle with timing issues.

Working through the eight practice tests in this book, you'll improve your skills, speed up your pacing, and build your confidence. Don't be surprised if the HSPT feels a lot easier after completing this book!

Before diving into the practice tests, learn more about the HSPT below. When you have an understanding of the parts of the test, you'll be able to maximize your practice time.

Timing

The HSPT is divided into five sections and contains a total of 298 multiple choice questions. You'll have 2.5 hours total, broken down as outlined in this chart.

Section	Number of Questions	Time Allotted
Verbal Skills	60	16 minutes
Quantitative Skills	52	30 minutes
Reading	62	25 minutes
Mathematics	64	45 minutes
Language	60	25 minutes

Sections

The five sections of the HSPT test a variety of skills, some you'll recognize, others may be new to you. Below are descriptions of the question types and some notes about what what makes each section challenging. While the purpose of this book is not to teach test prep strategies, these tips will give you some direction.

Verbal

The verbal section tests vocabulary and verbal reasoning skills. It contains five question types.

Synonyms: Each question presents a word, and you have to choose a word from the answer choices that most closely matches the original word's meaning.

Antonyms: These items look like the synonym type, but you must select the word that has the *opposite* meaning of the given word. Many students make the mistake of selecting the synonym rather than the antonym because they don't read directions carefully!

Analogies: For this question type, you have to determine the relationship between two words and then pair a second set of words with a similar relationship.

Classifications: For these questions, you're provided with a list of four words and asked to select the word that doesn't belong. The word that doesn't belong may not fit with the other words, or may be the word that defines the overall category of the rest of the list.

Logic: These items include three statements. You must determine whether the third statement is true, false, or uncertain based on the first two statements.

What makes this section challenging?

Timing: You'll have to answer 60 questions in 16 minutes! Most students do not finish on time the first time they take the test, so don't panic if that's the case for you.

Vocabulary: Most of the words are at an eighth grade level. The testmakers don't pull the words from a set vocabulary list, so building up a strong vocabulary through reading will go a long way on this section!

Quantitative

The quantitative section is the first of two math sections and includes a variety of math and number sense questions.

Series reasoning: You're given a list of numbers with one or two missing and must identify a pattern to figure out the missing number(s).

Algebraic Comparison: For this question type, you're given three separate math problems. The multiple choice component then offers four options comparing them, and you must choose the correct comparison.

Geometric Comparison: The structure of these questions resembles Algebraic Comparison Questions. You're presented with one or more geometric figures and asked to draw a conclusion based on that figure(s).

Math Translation: These questions provide a mathematical statement in words for you to translate into a number equation - and then find the solution. Skills tested may include fractions, percents, square roots, exponents, and averages.

What makes this section challenging?

Timing: It's tight, and the comparison questions require more time than other question types.

No calculator allowed: Ugh, not what you want to hear, we know. You'll need to get comfortable rattling off your math facts, as well as working out problems mentally and with pencil and paper.

Reading

The reading section contains four or five passages that are each a few paragraphs long. Typically, three or four passages are non-fiction and one or two passages are fiction. The section contains two types of questions.

Reading: Usually there are 40 reading questions total, about eight to ten per passage. The questions ask you to identify details, draw conclusions, define vocabulary in context, and determine the main idea.

Vocabulary: The reading section also includes 22 additional vocabulary questions. You're given a three- or four-word phrase, with one of the words underlined. You must choose a word with a meaning most similar to the underlined word.

What makes this section challenging?

Pacing: Don't spend too much time reading the passages or deliberating the answer choices. Understanding what the different types of questions are looking for will help you move through the test more quickly, but you may also need to do some extra reading fluency work apart from this book.

Vocabulary: Students are often surprised by the vocabulary questions at the end of this section. Some find it helpful to do the vocab questions first since they can do them relatively quickly, and then move on to the reading questions.

Math

The math section involves more traditional math problem-solving and is more challenging than the quantitative section. The questions test a large variety of math skills such as place value, ratios, probability, algebra, and geometry. You'll also need to be familiar with math terms such as remainder, prime numbers, and consecutive numbers.

What makes this section challenging?

Timing: We weren't kidding when we said timing is one of the reasons the HSPT is a tough test! To perform well on this section, you must have a solid foundation in the skills tested (through pre-algebra) so that you don't waste time on the basics.

Word Problems: There are a lot of word problems on this section, so learn how to break them down and answer what is being asked.

No calculator allowed: You know the drill: work on those mental math skills and don't be afraid to write things down!

Language

The language section tests a student's knowledge of effective writing. This section is divided into three parts.

Punctuation, capitalization, and usage: Typically, this part includes 40 questions that test very picky rules. You're given three sentences, one of which may contain an error. You must choose the sentence with the error, or indicate that none of the sentences contain mistakes.

Spelling: Similar to the first part of the language section, each spelling multiple choice item presents three sentences, one of which may contain an error. You're asked to identify the sentence with the error, or choose the option "No mistakes."

Composition: The final part of the language section includes questions which ask you to identify the best writing. There are a variety of question types, including word choice, topic sentences, and clarity and conciseness.

What makes this section challenging?

The "No mistake" option: Students often have trouble identifying errors, so they choose "No mistake" too quickly. Always double check before choosing that answer!

HSPT Test 1

Verbal Section 1

60 Questions, 16 Minutes

Instructions: Select the best answer.

1. Which word does not belong with the others?

   a. lion
   b. moose
   c. kangaroo
   d. bear

2. Sam is taller than Ranuk. Kevin is shorter than Ranuk. Sam is taller than Kevin. If the first two statements are true, the third statement is

   a. true
   b. false
   c. uncertain

3. Which word does not belong with the others?

   a. inch
   b. kilometer
   c. mile
   d. yard

4. Impassive most nearly means

   a. inexpressive
   b. passive
   c. active
   d. immature

5. Amateur is to expert as student is to

   a. school
   b. professor
   c. parent
   d. peer

6. Rudimentary means the *opposite* of

   a. simple
   b. easy
   c. sophisticated
   d. rustic

7. Marcus hits more home runs than Nicholas. Nicholas hits fewer home runs than Andre. Andre hits more home runs than Marcus. If the first two statements are true, the third statement is

   a. true
   b. false
   c. uncertain

8. Which word does *not* belong with the others?

   a. lamp
   b. candle
   c. flashlight
   d. sun

9. Benevolent most nearly means

   a. kind
   b. unhappy
   c. friendly
   d. violent

10. Malfunction most nearly means

    a. malaise
    b. worried
    c. failure
    d. uncertain

11. Which word does *not* belong with the others?

    a. plane
    b. wing
    c. cockpit
    d. engine

12. Cabinet is to kitchen as glovebox is to

    a. gloves
    b. car
    c. house
    d. dresser

13. Equality means the *opposite* of

    a. equity
    b. rights
    c. admonishment
    d. difference

14. Which word does *not* belong with the others?

    a. delighted
    b. devoted
    c. cheerful
    d. joyful

15. Which word does *not* belong with the others?

    a. jazz
    b. rock and roll
    c. rap
    d. music

16. Apprehend most nearly means

    a. scuffle
    b. comprehend
    c. recognize
    d. capture

17. Rigid means the opposite of

    a. light
    b. static
    c. flexible
    d. wrong

18. Fan is to cool as car is to

    a. heat
    b. drive
    c. stop
    d. highway

19. Cake is to cupcake as bread is to

    a. bake
    b. crust
    c. roll
    d. butter

20. Avenue A is longer than Avenue B and C. Avenue D is longer than Avenue A. Avenue D is longer than Avenue C. If the first two statements are true, the third statement is

    a. true
    b. false
    c. uncertain

21. Hypnotic most nearly means

    a. captivating
    b. drug
    c. magic
    d. intense

22. Scarcity means the *opposite* of

    a. few
    b. scary
    c. happy
    d. plenty

23. Procure most nearly means

    a. positive
    b. resist
    c. obtain
    d. cure

24. Equilateral is to triangle as bus is to

    a. car
    b. vehicle
    c. wheel
    d. speed

25. Which word does *not* belong with the others?

    a. portrait
    b. still life
    c. sculpture
    d. landscape

26. Lana scores more goals than Tyler and Samson. Patrick scores fewer goals than Tyler. Samson scored the least amount of goals. If the first two statements are true, the third statement is

    a. true
    b. false
    c. uncertain

27. Period is to stop as comma is to
    a. continue
    b. list
    c. pause
    d. grammar

28. Generator N lasts longer than generator T. Generator T doesn't last as long as generator O. Generator O lasts longer than generator N. If the first two statements are true, the third statement is
    a. true
    b. false
    c. uncertain

29. Obtuse most nearly means
    a. unintelligent
    b. smart
    c. blunt
    d. large

30. There were more German shepherds at the dog park than chihuahuas or daschunds. There are more daschunds than chihuahuas at the dog park. There are the least amount of chihuahuas. If the first two statements are true, the third statement is
    a. true
    b. false
    c. uncertain

31. Liters are to milliliters as gallons are to
    a. pounds
    b. barrels
    c. grams
    d. cups

32. Julien is older than Noelle. Eleanor is older than Julien. Noelle is older than Eleanor. If the first two statements are true, the third statement is
    a. true
    b. false
    c. uncertain

33. Which word does *not* belong with the others?
    a. juvenile
    b. child
    c. youth
    d. play

34. Boast means the *opposite* of
    a. blunt
    b. brave
    c. humility
    d. pride

35. Which word does *not* belong with the others?
    a. teal
    b. purple
    c. magenta
    d. burgundy

36. Which word does *not* belong with the others?
    a. partial
    b. bias
    c. open
    d. prejudice

37. Patriot most nearly means
    a. American
    b. nationalist
    c. collaborator
    d. supporter

38. Peterstown is northwest of Centerville. Centerville is south of Johnsburg and Peterstown. Johnsburg is north of Centerville. If the first two statements are true, the third statement is
    a. true
    b. false
    c. uncertain

39. Which word does *not* belong with the others?
    a. Minnesota
    b. California
    c. Ontario
    d. Delaware

40. Novel means the *opposite* of

    a. old
    b. new
    c. used
    d. story

41. Tedious most nearly means

    a. unexciting
    b. hilarious
    c. intellectual
    d. ancient

42. Sordid means the *opposite* of

    a. trashy
    b. slow
    c. respectable
    d. educated

43. Michael ate fewer hot dogs than Dan. Dan ate more hot dogs than Courtney. Michael ate more hot dogs than Courtney. If the first two statements are true, the third statement is

    a. true
    b. false
    c. uncertain

44. Tonya is standing in front of Hazel and Guy in line. Guy is standing behind Hazel. Hazel is standing in between Tonya and Guy. If the first two statements are true, the third statement is

    a. true
    b. false
    c. uncertain

45. Which word does *not* belong with the others?

    a. whisk
    b. spatula
    c. kitchen
    d. pot

46. Which word does *not* belong with the others?

    a. wood
    b. brick
    c. steel
    d. building

47. Happy is to ecstatic as sad is to

    a. joyful
    b. woeful
    c. indifferent
    d. rage

48. Which word does *not* belong with the others?

    a. poodle
    b. dog
    c. beagle
    d. dalmatian

49. All blergs are snorts. No snorts are flibbits. Blergs can be flibbits. If the first two statements are true, the third statement is

    a. true
    b. false
    c. uncertain

50. Pompous most nearly means

    a. cheerful
    b. phony
    c. modest
    d. arrogant

51. Feasible most nearly means

    a. possible
    b. implausible
    c. profitable
    d. eventful

52. Which word does *not* belong with the others?

    a. broccoli
    b. apple
    c. peach
    d. orange

53. Pragmatic means the *opposite* of

    a. loyal
    b. logical
    c. impractical
    d. advanced

54. Intrepid most nearly means

    a. brave
    b. cowardly
    c. important
    d. sleepy

55. Max baked more cakes for the bake sale than Fiona. Andrew baked more cakes for the bake sale than Fiona. Max baked more cakes for the bake sale than Andrew. If the first two statements are true, the third statement is

    a. true
    b. false
    c. uncertain

56. Which word does *not* belong with the others?

    a. oatmeal
    b. eggs
    c. fruit
    d. cake

57. Tyranny means the *opposite* of

    a. oppression
    b. democracy
    c. isolation
    d. argument

58. Watercolor is to paint as sourdough is to

    a. art
    b. soup
    c. bread
    d. drawing

59. Which word does *not* belong with the others?

    a. vehicle
    b. stagecoach
    c. carriage
    d. sleigh

60. Foolhardy is to careful as wise is to

    a. afraid
    b. cunning
    c. ignorant
    d. blissful

Quantitative Section 1

52 Questions, 30 minutes

Instructions: Select the best answer.

61. Review the series: 4, 2, 5, 3, 6, __. What number should come next?

    a. 9
    b. 3
    c. 4
    d. 8

62. Examine (A), (B), and (C) and find the best answer.

    (A) 5% of 60
    (B) $\frac{5}{6}$ of 6
    (C) .05 × 600

    a. (A) is smaller than (C) but larger than (B)
    b. (C) is larger than (A) and (B)
    c. (B) is smaller than (A) but larger than (C)
    d. (B) is equal to (A) but smaller than (C)

63. What is eight plus $\frac{1}{4}$ of 16?

    a. 12
    b. 24
    c. 18
    d. 16

64. The circle below has center A. Find the best answer.

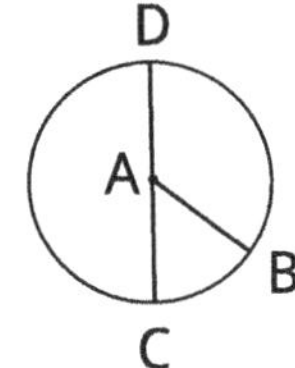

    a. AB < AD
    b. DC - AC = AB
    c. DC > AB + AC
    d. DC < AD

65. What is the next number in the following series: 80, 40, 20, 10, ___?

    a. 2
    b. 2.5
    c. 4
    d. 5

66. Look at this series: 4, 5, 7, 10, 14, ___. What number should come next?

    a. 18
    b. 19
    c. 16
    d. 20

67. What is 30% of 120?

    a. 40
    b. 36
    c. 30
    d. 12

68. Examine (A), (B), and (C) and find the best answer.

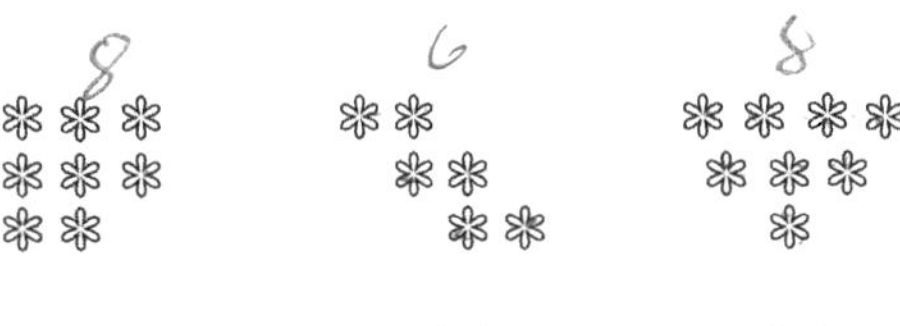

(A) (B) (C)

    a. (A) and (C) are equal and have fewer flowers than (B)
    b. (B) has fewer flowers than (A) and more flowers than (C)
    c. (A) has more flowers than (C) and less flowers than (B)
    d. (A) and (C) are equal and have more flowers than (B)

69. Examine (A), (B), and (C) and find the best answer.

(A) 2^2
(B) 3^2
(C) 4^1

a. (A) is larger than (B) but smaller than (C)
b. (A) is equal to (C) and smaller than (B)
c. (C) is smaller than (A) but larger than (B)
d. (A) is larger than (C) and equal to (B)

70. Review the series: 3, 2, 9, 4, 27, ____. What number should come next?

a. 54
b. 16
c. 8
d. 4

71. What is the next number in the following series: $\frac{1}{5}$, $\frac{3}{5}$, 1, $\frac{7}{5}$, ____?

a. $\frac{5}{5}$
b. 2
c. $\frac{8}{5}$
d. $\frac{9}{5}$

72. What is 8 more than the mean of 6, 16, and 14?

a. 20
b. 13
c. 40
d. 21

73. Examine (A), (B), and (C) and find the best answer.

(A) (15 - 3) - 6
(B) 6 - (3 - 15)
(C) 15 - (6 - 3)

a. $(A) + (B) < (C)$
b. $(B) - (C) < (A)$
c. $(C) > (B)$
d. $(A) + (C) = (B)$

74. Review the series: 3, 6, 2, 4, 0, ____. What number should come next?

a. 2
b. 0
c. -4
d. -2

75. Look at this series: 16, A, 8, D, 4, ____. What number or letter should come next?

a. 2
b. F
c. G
d. 0

76. What is 4 more than the product of 8 and 12?

a. 96
b. 100
c. 104
d. 92

77. The figure below is made up of an isosceles triangle and a square. In it, y = 7, z = 6, x = 5. Examine (A), (B), and (C) and find the best answer.

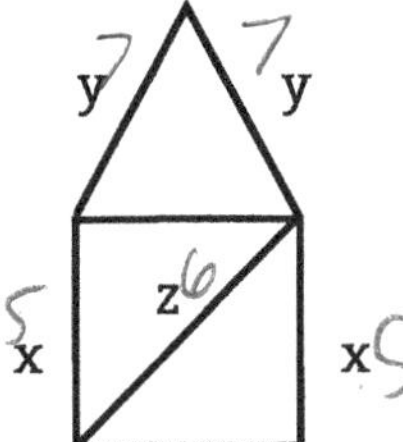

(A) The area of the square
(B) The perimeter of the figure
(C) x + y + z

a. (A) + (C) < (B)
b. (A) < (C)
c. (B) - (C) < (A)
d. (B) < (A)

78. What is the next number in the following series: 40, 7, 20, 11, 10, ___?

a. 15
b. 7
c. 5
d. 16

79. 3 less than 40% of 60 is what number?

a. 24
b. 21
c. 27
d. 30

80. Review the series: 72, 63, 54, 45, 36, ___. What number should come next?

a. 20
b. 26
c. 30
d. 27

81. Examine (A), (B), and (C) and find the best answer.

(A) The area of a square with side 6
(B) The perimeter of a square with side 8
(C) The perimeter of an equilateral triangle with a side of 10

a. (A) is smaller than (C) but greater than (B)
b. (B) is smaller than (A) but larger than (C)
c. (A) is larger than (C) but smaller than (B)
d. (A) and (C) are equal but larger than (B)

82. What number is 2 less than $\frac{1}{6}$ of 24?

a. 1
b. 2
c. 3
d. 4.

83. What is the missing number in the following series: 4, 2, ___ , 3, 2, 4?

a. 1
b. 2
c. 3
d. 4

84. Review the series: 3, 1, 6, 2, 9, ___. What number should come next?

a. 2
b. 3
c. 12
d. 10

85. What numbers should come next in the series: 32, 23, 16, 8, 23, 4, ___ , ___?

a. 8, 23
b. 23, 2
c. 2, 23
d. 23, 8

86. Examine (A), (B), and (C) and find the best answer.

    (A) 13% of 65
    (B) $\frac{1}{4}$` of 36
    (C) 10

    a. (A) is smaller than (C) but greater than (B)
    b. (B) is smaller than (A) but larger than (C)
    c. (A) is larger than (C) but smaller than (B)
    d. (B) is larger than (A) but smaller than (C)

87. Look at this series: 36, 12, 18, 6, ___, 4. What number is missing?

    a. 2
    b. 12
    c. 3
    d. 18

88. The square of what number is ten more than the product of two and three?

    a. 2
    b. 4
    c. 5
    d. 6

89. Examine (A), (B), and (C) and find the best answer.

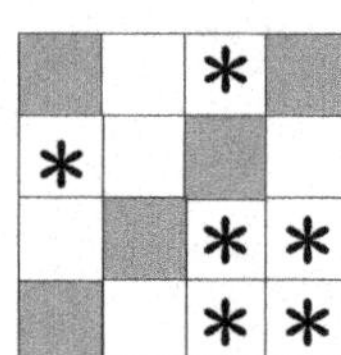

    a. Total ■ > Total *
    b. Total * + Total ■ > Total □
    c. Total □ - Total * > Total ■
    d. Total * - Total □ = Total ■

90. If you purchase a burger, french fries, ice cream, and milk, and hand the cashier a $20 bill, how much change would you receive?

    a. $8.94
    b. $8.90
    c. $7.95
    d. $9.03

91. What is 30% of 15% of 600?

    a. 27
    b. 28
    c. 30
    d. 33

92. Review the series: 12, 4, 28, ___, 140, 132. What number is missing?

    a. 84
    b. 133
    c. 196
    d. 20

93. Review the series: $\frac{1}{4}$, $\frac{1}{2}$ ___, 1, $\frac{5}{4}$, Find the missing number.

    a. $\frac{3}{4}$
    b. $\frac{3}{8}$
    c. $\frac{1}{6}$
    d. $\frac{2}{3}$

94. $\frac{3}{4}$ of $\frac{1}{8}$ of 32 is what number?

a. 2
b. 3
c. 6
d. 12

95. What is the missing number in the following series: 20, 4, ___, 6, 5, 8?

a. 10
b. 17
c. 3
d. 12

96. Examine the figure below and select the best answer.

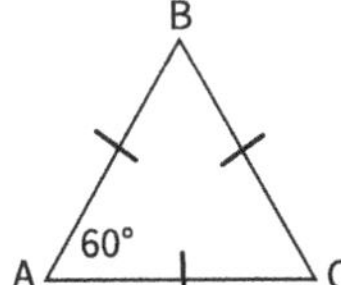

a. $\angle A > \angle B$
b. $\angle B > \angle C < \angle A$
c. $\angle A = \angle B = \angle C$
d. $\angle C > \angle B$.

97. What is the missing number in the following series: 58, 51, ___, 37, 30, 23?

a. 38
b. 49
c. 44
d. 47

98. The sum of 58 and 13 minus 24 is what number?

a. 57
b. 95
c. 21
d. 47

99. 2 cubed less than 3 cubed is what number?

a. 3
b. 19
c. -19
d. 27

100. Examine (A), (B), and (C) and find the best answer.

(A) The area of a circle with radius 3
(B) The circumference of a circle with radius 3
(C) The area of a circle with radius 4

a. (C) is larger than both (A) and (B)
b. (B) is smaller than (A) but larger than (C)
c. (A) is smaller than (B) but larger than (C)
d. (C) is larger than (A) but smaller than (B)

101. Review the series: I, III, V, VII, ___, XI. What number is missing?

a. X
b. IX
c. XII
d. VIII

102. $\frac{3}{4}$ of 36 is 5 more than what number?

a. 18
b. 22
c. 32
d. 27

103. Look at this series: 15, 11, 13, 9, 11, ___. What number should come next?

a. 7
b. 13
c. 10
d. 6

104. Examine (A), (B), and (C) and find the best answer.

(A) $(\sqrt{25}) \times 5$
(B) 5^2
(C) 12.5×2

a. (A) = (B) = (C)
b. (B) < (A) < (C)
c. (C) > (B) < (A)
d. (A) + (C) = (B)

105. Look at this series: 32, 30, 26, ____, 12, 2. What number is missing?

a. 24
b. 22
c. 20
d. 18

106. 18 is what percent of 72?

a. 4%
b. 16%
c. 25%
d. 32%

107. Consider the following figure and find the best answer.

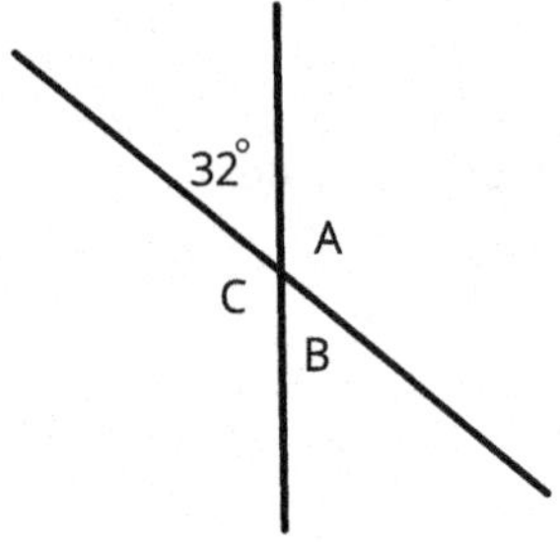

a. Angle A is larger than Angle B, but equal to Angle C
b. Angle C is equal to 32 degrees
c. Angle A plus Angle C equals Angle B plus 32 degrees
d. Angle C is larger than both Angle A and Angle B

108. Review the series: 12.5, $\frac{47}{4}$, 11.0, $\frac{41}{4}$, 9.5, ____. What number should come next?

a. 7.5
b. $\frac{37}{4}$
c. 8.75
d. $\frac{35}{4}$

109. Examine (A), (B), and (C) and find the best answer.

(A) $\frac{7}{10}$
(B) $\frac{35}{50}$
(C) $\frac{7}{20}$

a. (A) < (C) > (B)
b. (B) > (A) > (C)
c. (A) = (B) < (C)
d. (A) = (B) > (C)

110. Examine (A), (B), and (C) and find the best answer.

(A) 7.2×10^3
(B) 0.0072×10^6
(C) 7200

a. (B) < (A) > (C)
b. (C) > (A) > (B)
c. (A), (B), and (C) are equal
d. (A) = (B) < (C)

111. Look at this series: 3, 6, 8, 16, 18, ____. What number should come next?

a. 20
b. 24
c. 36
d. 38

112. Given (A), (B) and (C), select the best answer.

(A) $\frac{2}{3}$ of 36

(B) $\frac{4}{5}$ of 20

(C) $\frac{2}{7}$ of 49

a. (A) is less than (B) and less than (C)
b. (B) is greater than (C) and greater than (A)
c. (C) is less than (B) and less than (A)
d. (A) is less than (C) and greater than (B)

Reading Section 1

62 Questions, 25 Minutes

Reading Comprehension

Instructions: Read each passage carefully and mark one answer for each question.

Questions 113 - 122 refer to the passage below.

Rome was not built in a day, nor did it fall in one. Historians often cite the year AD 476 as the end of Rome. This is only partially accurate. Although Rome's last emperor Romulus was overthrown in AD 476 , Rome's decline actually lasted for over one hundred years. Just as it took more than one day for Rome to fall, there was not a single reason that the empire crumbled.

Centuries before Rome fell the appeal of working in government was waning. On many occasions, politicians had to pay out of pocket to finance public works like bridges, roads, and aqueducts. Citizens no longer wanted the job of helping to govern the empire.

To further complicate governmental matters, there was no clear means of succession when an emperor died or resigned. The lack of official rules regarding succession resulted in civil wars. In a reorganization attempt in AD 285, Emperor Diocletian divided the large Roman Empire in half, allowing for two men to rule. The capital for both empires, Rome, was located in the west portion of the empire. In AD 330 , Emperor Constantine moved the capital to the eastern city of Constantinople, causing Rome to lose prestige, power, and money.

Economically speaking, Rome was a struggling. Trade was often disrupted by civil wars, invasions from Germanic tribes, and pirates in the Mediterranean. Fighting these battles was also costly. Inflation plagued the empire as the prices for items rose dramatically. In order to pay for these wars and public works, high taxes were levied against frustrated Roman citizens.

Perhaps the most important cause for the fall of Rome was the people themselves. Population was declining. Citizens no longer felt loyal to the Roman Empire and were apathetic towards public issues. Christianity also changed citizens' views of the empire, and the emperor was no longer viewed as a diety. Popes and religious leaders soon took more of an active role in politics and civic life.

The short term causes for Rome's fall are just as complex and build upon many of the issues discussed here. Germanic tribes had taken over much of what had been Rome's large empire, and by AD 400 only the Italian peninsula was left under Roman control.

113. Considering the passage, which would not be an example of a "public work"?

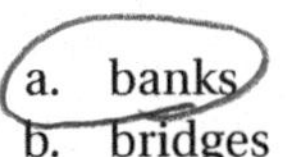

a. banks
b. bridges
c. roads
d. aqueducts

114. The author of this passage most likely believes

a. that the United States is doomed for failure like Rome
b. people often take a too-simplistic view of Rome's downfall
c. if the Roman people had been more determined, Rome would not have fallen
d. only the western half of the Roman Empire fell

115. Which of the following would be the best title for this passage?

a. "The Rise and Fall of the Roman Empire"
b. "Be Careful What You Reap"
c. "Complex Causation that Ended an Empire"
d. "Chaos, Cholera, and Climate Destroy Rome"

116. How did the changing economy directly impact the citizens?

a. Dicoletian moved the capital.
b. Taxes were increased.
c. Politicians had to pay out of pocket for public goods.
d. Their population was declining.

117. Which of the following options would most likely follow the last paragraph?

a. A discussion of the immediate actions that led to Rome's fall.
b. A discussion on what happened to the other half of Rome's empire.
c. A discussion on who the Germanic tribes were and why they invaded.
d. A discussion that compares two historians' interpretations on Rome's fall.

118. What does the word waning as used in this reading passage mean?

a. wandering
b. terrible
c. lessening
d. problematic

119. In which of the following would you expect to find this passage?

a. a social science textbook
b. a psychology journal
c. a news report
d. a Roman soldier's diary entry

120. Which of the following was a NOT a reason taxes increased?

a. to pay for roads
b. to pay church leaders
c. to pay soldiers
d. to pay for weapons

121. Why was it problematic not to have a plan for succession?

a. leaders fought for power
b. no one wanted the job of emperor
c. citizens grew frustrated
d. Germanic tribesmen filled the vacuum left by the last leader

122. Based on the passage one can likely infer that

a. if the Roman Empire had governed more efficiently, they'd still be around today
b. Roman contributions to civilization are all around us
c. life for an average Roman citizen was difficult
d. from its founding Rome was destined for failure

Questions 123 - 132 refer to the passage below.

North American rabbits belong to two classes easily distinguished by their size and habits. The larger form includes the varying hares (or snowshoe rabbits) and the jackrabbits. They are found throughout nearly all of Alaska and Canada and in all the states west of the Mississippi except Arkansas and Louisiana. The smaller form, generally called cottontail rabbits, are present in most states, but are absent from most of Maine, New Hampshire, New York, and Minnesota.

In habits, the cottontail rabbits differ greatly from the larger rabbits. They live in copses and thickets rather than in open fields. The young are born blind, without fur, and helpless, while those of the larger rabbits have the eyes open, are partially furred, and are active when born.

Cottontail rabbits breed several times a year during the warmer months, the litters averaging five or six young. The nest is usually placed in a hollow or depression in the ground. It is composed of dead grass and warmly lined with fur which the female pulls from her own body. The male rabbit takes no part in caring for the young. These animals breed so rapidly that despite their many natural enemies they often become numerous enough to inflict serious losses on farmers and fruit growers.

Cottontail rabbits eat all sorts of herbage — leaves, stems, flowers, seeds, leaves, buds, bark, and fruits. They usually prefer the most succulent foods, including tender garden vegetables, clover, alfalfa, and fallen ripe fruits; but they also exhibit a remarkable delicacy of taste by eating certain varieties of a plant species and neglecting other plants of the same species. Prof. C. V. Piper reports that in Oregon, rabbits ate Arabian alfalfa down to the ground, while they did little damage to other varieties grown in surrounding areas. When favorite foods are absent, rabbits resort to whatever is available. During summer droughts or when deep snows cut off ordinary supplies, the animals attack the bark of growing trees or shrubs.

123. Which type of rabbit is born without fur?

   a. snowshoe rabbit
   b. varying hare
   c. cottontail rabbit
   d. arctic rabbit

124. An appropriate title for this passage would be

   a. "Rabbits around the World"
   b. "The Breeding Habits of Cottontail Rabbits"
   c. "Why Rabbits Make Good Pets"
   d. "Rabbits of North America"

125. According to the author, in which of these states would snowshoe rabbits be found?

   a. California
   b. New York
   c. Michigan
   d. Louisiana

126. Which of the following do cottontail rabbits like to eat the least?

   a. buds
   b. bark
   c. alfalfa
   d. flowers

127. Rabbits are considered a pest by farmers because

   a. they breed on their land
   b. they introduce disease
   c. they eat their crops
   d. they chase away other animals

128. Cottontail rabbits are similar to larger breeds of rabbits in that they

   a. are born blind
   b. are small
   c. live in thickets
   d. are found in North America

129. As it is used in the passage, the word <u>delicacy</u> most nearly means

a. robustness
b. subtlety
c. sweetness
d. breakable

130. This passage would most likely be found in a

a. chemistry textbook
b. Canadian wildlife guide
c. animal science textbook
d. newspaper

131. Based on the information in the passage, what would happen if a farmer were able to prevent cottontail rabbits from entering their farm?

a. fewer plants would grow to full size
b. there would be no effect on plant growth
c. more plants would grow to full size
d. fewer insects would harm the plants

132. The author of this passage is most likely a

a. biologist
b. farmer
c. physicist
d. geography teacher

Questions 133 - 142 refer to the passage below.

The sun set as Sarika jumped onto her bike and began her journey home. She rode quickly, the leaves under her tires crackling like sparklers on a summer day. Dinner would be ready soon, and if she wasn't there on time, there'd be an exchange of furtive glances between her siblings. She knew it was hard for them to keep her secret, and Sarika was frustrated that she needed to keep this a secret at all. It wasn't like she was skipping school, hanging out with the "bad" kids, or talking back to her parents like her sister, Anika.

She wished she could be more like Anika, who didn't care if she disappointed her parents. But that wasn't Sarika, who hated confrontation of any kind. So when she got the lead in the school play, she didn't tell her parents. She wished that she could keep it from her siblings, too; however, Sarika needed their help once rehearsals started. She convinced her brother, Abram, to join his school's book club on Thursdays so that she didn't have to care for him while her parents worked late. Anika, of course, took no convincing at all. She even offered to help with Sarika's chores, though Sarika was sure that Anika would prefer to go to battle for her against their parents.

When she confided in her best friend, Jade, Sarika couldn't get her to understand. Jade thought Sarika could reason with her parents. She couldn't fathom why Sarika didn't just tell her parents that she was the lead in the play, and she would have to kiss a boy.

"Just tell them!" Jade argued, "It's not like you'll really kiss him anyway!" All Sarika and Michael had to do was get their faces close enough to look like a kiss. But try telling that to her parents. They were incredibly strict and had never even allowed her to attend a boy-girl party. In fact, her dad had told her a million times that she couldn't date until she was twenty-two! Sarika knew that if she asked for her parents' permission she would be forbidden from participating.

And so, here she was riding her bike home at lightning speed from her middle school play rehearsal. She left so quickly that she hadn't even realized her backpack was still in the school's auditorium.

133. According to the passage, which of the following is a correct characterization of the siblings?

    a. Sarika and Anika are just alike.
    b. Sarika and Abram have similar views on their parents.
    c. Michael doesn't want to help his sister Sarika.
    d. With some persuading, the siblings all care about helping Sarika.

134. The line "crackling like sparklers on a summer day" is an example of which literary technique?

    a. simile
    b. foreshadowing
    c. metaphor
    d. personification

135. The author presents Sarika as

    a. confident
    b. determined
    c. naive
    d. foolish

136. Why would Sarika's parents be upset if they knew her secret?

    a. They had forbidden her from participating in the play.
    b. She was not supposed to date until she was twenty-two.
    c. There was a kissing scene in the play.
    d. They did not like her riding her bike home in the dark.

137. What is likely to happen when Sarika gets home?

    a. Her siblings will tell Sarika's parents because it has been so difficult keeping the secret.
    b. Jade will try to lie for her if she is late to dinner.
    c. Sarika will be forced to quit the play.
    d. Sarika will have to explain where her backpack is.

138. Who is Michael?

a. an actor in the play
b. Sarika's boyfriend
c. Sarika's brother
d. a friend from school

139. It is likely that this story takes place

a. in the winter
b. in the fall
c. in the summer
d. any time of the year

140. By saying, " Anika would prefer to go to battle for her," the author is suggesting that

a. Anika wants to get into a fight with Sarika
b. the sisters have an antagonistic relationship
c. Anika wants to stand up for her sister to her parents
d. Anika thinks Sarika should be more like her and argue with their parents

141. Why do you think the author has Sarika forget her backpack?

a. to indicate how difficult it is for Sarika to keep a secret from her parents
b. to show how recklessly Sarika is behaving
c. to teach the reader a lesson
d. to warn the reader

142. When did Sarika tell her siblings the secret?

a. as soon as she made the play
b. once rehearsals started
c. once her parents suspected her secret
d. one of the them found out, so they all had to know

Questions 143 - 152 refer to the passage below.

On April 9, 1939, Marian Anderson, an African American singer, performed at the Lincoln Memorial, bringing unprecedented attention to the nation's racial barriers and discrimination.

In the years prior to the concert, Anderson had been performing throughout Europe. This changed in 1935 when she performed at New York's Town Hall and was invited to perform at the White House. There, she met the first lady, Eleanor Roosevelt, who would become a lifelong friend. In 1936, Anderson's career in America widened when she began to sing annual concerts to benefit Howard University School of Music in Washington, D.C. In January 1939, Howard University requested permission from the Daughters of the American Revolution (DAR) to use Constitution Hall for a concert on Easter weekend. Constitution Hall was the largest auditorium in Washington, D.C. and seated over 4,000 people.

At the time, the DAR was an exclusively white heritage association, and they followed an aggressive form of patriotism that aligned with the racial <u>segregation</u> of Washington, D.C. in 1939. When black patrons attended events, they would be seated in a different section of the hall, and the DAR had an unwritten policy of allowing only white performers. Those organizing Miss Anderson's concert hoped that her fame and reputation would inspire the DAR to make an exception, but their request to use Constitution Hall was denied. Despite pressure from the press, great artists, and politicians, the DAR maintained their position. Thousands of DAR members resigned in protest, including First Lady Eleanor Roosevelt.

Mrs. Roosevelt and others continued to work to find a <u>venue</u> for the concert, and they eventually persuaded Secretary of the Interior Harold L. Ickes to arrange an outdoor concert at the Lincoln Memorial. Ickes was excited to have a display of democracy on this scale, and he met with President Roosevelt for his approval. On March 30th, it was announced that Marian Anderson would officially perform at the Lincoln Memorial on Sunday, April 9, 1939.

The crowd of 75,000 people that attended the Easter Sunday concert included dignitaries and everyday citizens of all races and ages. The concert was broadcast over the radio, allowing hundreds of thousands of listeners across the nation to hear the concert as well.

143. In what year did Marian Anderson meet Eleanor Roosevelt?

   a. 1939
   b. 1937
   c. 1936
   d. 1935

144. As it is used in the passage, <u>segregation</u> most closely means

   a. difference
   b. support
   c. seperation
   d. inclusion

145. Eleanor Roosevelt and the Daughters of American Revolution disagreed about whether

   a. Marian Anderson should perform at the White House
   b. African Americans should be able to attend concerts at Constitution Hall
   c. there should be Easter Sunday performances at Constitution Hall
   d. African Americans should be allowed to perform at Constitution Hall

146. As it is used in the passage, <u>venue</u> most closely means

   a. date
   b. site
   c. audience
   d. sponsor

147. This passage is primarily about

a. Marian Anderson's career
b. The events that led to Marian Anderson's concert at the Lincoln Memorial
c. The discrimination enacted by the Daughters of the American Revolution
d. American musicians of the 1930s

148. Howard University initially believed that the Daughters of the American Revolution would allow Anderson to perform because

a. Anderson was famous and well respected
b. the press put pressure on the DAR
c. Anderson was an African American singer
d. Eleanor Roosevelt was a member of the DAR

149. The Lincoln Memorial was different than Constitution Hall in that the Lincoln Memorial

a. was outdoors and could not accommodate as many people
b. was indoors and could not accommodate as many people
c. was outdoors and could accommodate more people
d. was indoors and could accommodate more people

150. Who did NOT pressure the Daughters of the American Revolution to allow Anderson to perform?

a. the press
b. Eleanor Roosevelt
c. artists
d. Secretary Ickes

151. Why did the author include the information provided in the last paragraph?

a. to demonstrate that the concert was a success
b. to explain why the Daughters of the American Revolution were concerned
c. to persuade the reader that Marian Anderson was a skilled singer
d. to show that people like attending concerts on Easter Sunday

152. One can infer that Secretary Ickes

a. was supportive of the DAR's decision
b. loved listening to music
c. did not agree with racial segregation
d. felt that racial discrimination was justified

Vocabulary

Instructions: Choose the word that means the same, or about the same, as the underlined word.

153. A bashful person

a. sweet
b. shy
c. angry
d. older

154. A deliberate act

a. purposeful
b. delicate
c. uncertain
d. sly

155. To collate papers

a. throw away
b. pull apart
c. neaten
d. assemble

156. The lenient judge

a. tough
b. intelligent
c. merciful
d. experienced

157. The immaculate dress

a. flawless
b. dirty
c. beautiful
d. tiny

158. The optimistic leader

a. pessimistic
b. strong
c. helpful
d. hopeful

159. The studious student

a. serious
b. bookish
c. easygoing
d. disinterested

160. An atypical idea

a. deceitful
b. ordinary
c. unusual
d. calculated

161. A dubious claim

a. suspicious
b. unlikely
c. strong
d. clear

162. A cryptic answer

a. obscure
b. interesting
c. unlikely
d. careful

163. The embellished story

a. interesting
b. boring
c. truthful
d. exaggerated

164. The punctual employee

a. dishonest
b. prompt
c. hardworking
d. easygoing

165. To surpass a goal

a. exceed
b. overcome
c. stall
d. undermine

166. A feasible solution

a. easy
b. uncomfortable
c. difficult
d. attainable

167. An omniscient narrator

   a. fascinating
   b. reticent
   c. all-knowing
   d. unhelpful

168. The ebullient child

   a. sweet
   b. cheerful
   c. shy
   d. beautiful

169. The gossamer fabric

   a. gaudy
   b. pretty
   c. delicate
   d. thick

170. A malevolent man

   a. magnanimous
   b. lazy
   c. malicious
   d. military

171. A plausible explanation

   a. believable
   b. incoherent
   c. fascinating
   d. worthy

172. The bucolic scenery

   a. interesting
   b. rural
   c. bustling
   d. golden

173. An indignant citizen

   a. unhappy
   b. homeless
   c. eager
   d. resentful

174. His dilapidated home

   a. interesting
   b. delicate
   c. ramshackle
   d. sturdy

Math Section 1

64 Questions, 45 Minutes

Instructions: Select the best answer.

175. Round 342.7163 to the nearest hundredth.

a. 342
b. 342.72
c. 342.716
d. 342.7

176. What is the remainder of $\frac{214}{3}$?

a. 0
b. 1
c. 2
d. 3

177. The prime factorization of 18 is

a. 3×6
b. $9 + 9$
c. $2 \times 2 \times 3$
d. $2 \times 3 \times 3$

178. Solve: $5(2 - 4) + 7 =$

a. 17
b. 3
c. -3
d. -17

179. Which is the greatest amount?

a. 5 quarts
b. 1 gallon
c. 8 pints
d. 15 cups

180. What is the area of a circle with radius 6?

a. 12
b. 12π
c. 36
d. 36π

181. Which of the following is true?

a. $7 + 2 \geq 10$
b. $4 - 6 < 2$
c. $9 - 4 > 6$
d. $5 - 4 \leq -1$

182. Simplify: $4(-3)^2$

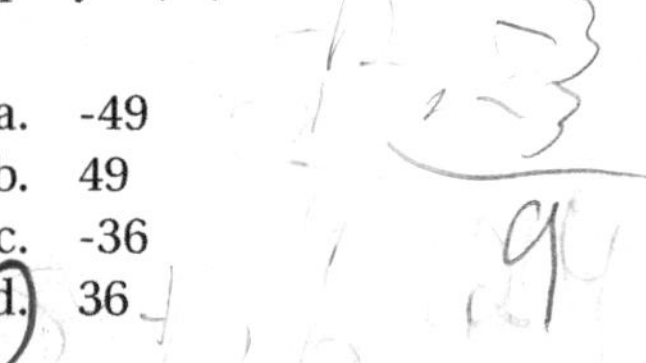

a. -49
b. 49
c. -36
d. 36

183. Which of the following is a pair of reciprocals?

a. $(4, \frac{1}{4})$
b. $(-5, 5)$
c. $(0, 2)$
d. $(5, 10)$

184. The measure of angle A is

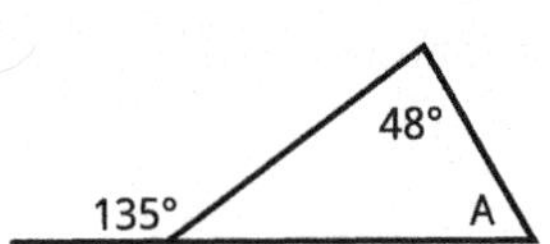

a. 87°
b. 73°
c. 67°
d. 78°

185. Which property is illustrated by the following: $3(4 \times 2) = (3 \times 4)2$?

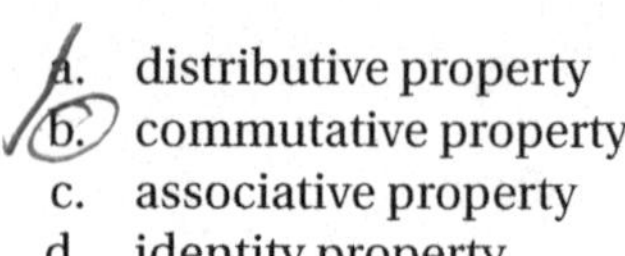

a. distributive property
b. commutative property
c. associative property
d. identity property

186. The square root of 56 is between

a. 5 and 6
b. 6 and 7
c. 7 and 8
d. 8 and 9

187. What is the perimeter of a square with area 49?

a. 49
b. 28
c. 24
d. 27

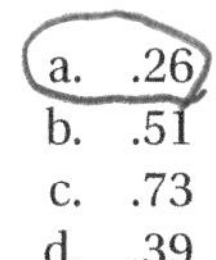

188. Solve: $\frac{(4 + 2)}{(3 - 5)}$

a. 1
b. -3
c. 2
d. -4

189. An equilateral triangle has side 5. What is its perimeter?

a. 10
b. 30
c. 15
d. 12.5

190. Given the two sets of numbers A = {1, 4, 5, 6} and B = {1, 2, 5, 7}, what is A ∩ B?

a. {1, 2, 4, 5, 6, 7}
b. {1, 6, 7}
c. {4, 6, 7}
d. {1, 5}

191. Solve: $\frac{\frac{9}{5}}{\frac{3}{5}}$

a. 3
b. $\frac{27}{5}$
c. 27
d. 2

192. 35° and 145° are which types of angles?

a. consecutive
b. complementary
c. supplementary
d. congruent

193. What number is 16 more than 30% of 80?

a. 40
b. 24
c. 50
d. 30

194. Which decimal is between $\frac{2}{5}$ and $\frac{3}{5}$?

a. .26
b. .51
c. .73
d. .39

195. What is the volume of a cube with side 5?

a. 25
b. 100
c. 125
d. 225

196. Which of the following has approximately the same value as $\frac{6}{7}$?

a. 83%
b. 91%
c. 88%
d. 86%

197. What is shown below?

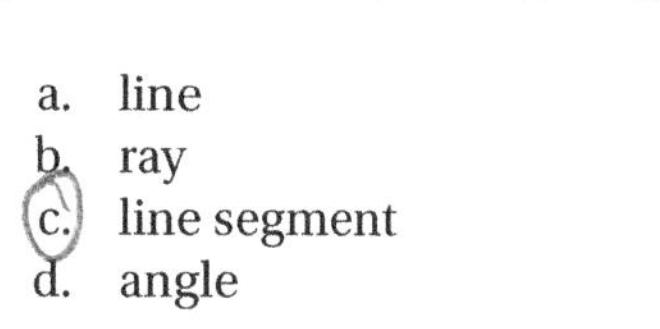

a. line
b. ray
c. line segment
d. angle

198. A three-dimensional version of a square is called a

a. cube
b. prism
c. cone
d. sphere

199. What is the place value of the number 2 in the number 9,382.14?

a. tens
b. hundreds
c. ones
d. tenth

200. Solve for a: 3a - 5 =10.

a. $\frac{5}{3}$
b. 5
c. 3
d. 2

201. The high school bowling team has an average of 10, 8, 7, 6, 9, and 10 strikes in their last 6 games. If they want to attain an average of 8 strikes per game how many strikes must they get in their next game?

a. 4
b. 6
c. 8
d. 10

202. The pie chart below represents the final science grades for the 8th grade students at Anytown Middle School. If there are 150 students total, how many students received an A in science?

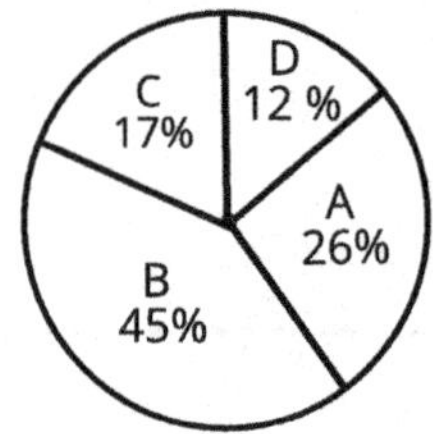

a. 39
b. 26
c. 25
d. 36

203. What is 40,532 in scientific notation?

a. 4.0532×10^3
b. 4.0532×10^4
c. 40.532×10^4
d. 405.32×10^2

204. Samuel is three times as old as Callie, who is half as old as Ebony. If Ebony is 42 years old, how old is Samuel?

a. 21
b. 78
c. 63
d. 7

205. Patrick is buying a new tablecloth for his dining room table. If his table is 8 feet long and 4 feet 6 inches wide, at minimum, how many square feet does his tablecloth need to be to cover the entire table?

a. 36 square feet
b. 25 square feet
c. 32 square feet
d. 40 square feet

206. A local department store is discounting all of their clearance items by $5. Stephanie selects a sweater that was originally $80 and brings it to the register. When she gets there, she learns that she will receive an additional 40% off the clearance price of her sweater. How much will Stephanie pay, not including taxes?

a. $30
b. $32
c. $45
d. $48

207. A concert hall sold 150 student tickets at $3.25 each and 320 adult tickets at $6.50 each. How much money was collected?

a. $1,462.50
b. $975.00
c. $2,567.50
d. $2,245.75

208. Ingrid had a fever every day of Thanksgiving break. On Wednesday she had a fever of 100.9°, on Thursday it was 101.2°, and on Friday it was 102.4°. Over the weekend it dropped to 100.3°. What was the range of her temperature?

a. 101.2°
b. 100.9°
c. 0.6°
d. 2.1°

209. Kelly and Cori both sell magazine subscriptions. If they sold 70 subscriptions one day, and Kelly sold 2 less than twice Cori's total, how many subscriptions did Cori sell?

a. 46
b. 24
c. 35
d. 22

210. The graph below represents the average yearly income of employees of an office supply company.

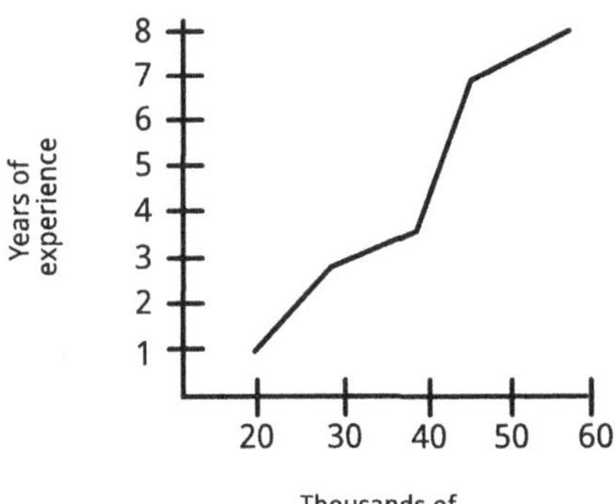

What is the best estimate of an employee's salary who has worked at the company for seven years?

a. \$40,000
b. \$45,000
c. \$35,000
d. \$55,000

211. How many $3\frac{3}{4}$ inch ribbons can be cut from a spool of ribbon containing $4\frac{1}{2}$ feet of ribbon?

a. 14
b. 15
c. 33
d. 34

212. Solve for z: $\frac{3z}{10} = \frac{2}{15}$

a. 4
b. 9
c. $\frac{4}{9}$
d. $\frac{9}{4}$

213. Chloe wants to do an art project using construction paper. She has 4 sheets of purple paper, 3 sheets of green paper, and 1 sheet of red paper. If she selected a sheet of paper at random, what is the probability that it would be green?

a. $\frac{3}{8}$
b. $\frac{1}{2}$
c. $\frac{1}{8}$
d. $\frac{5}{8}$

214. Which of the following values for x satisfies the following inequality: $x + 3 < 12 - 2x$

a. $x < -3$
b. $x < 3$
c. $x < 6$
d. $x > 3$

215. Greta scored 3 points total in her last 9 games. How many points will she score in the next 12 games if she continues to score points at the same rate?

a. 3
b. 4
c. 7
d. 9

216. A seamstress needs to purchase enough fabric for five panels that are 3 feet 6 inches long. If the fabric is sold by the foot, how many feet must she buy?

a. 17
b. 18
c. 19
d. 20

217. Simplify: $\sqrt{120}$

a. $2\sqrt{20}$
b. $2\sqrt{30}$
c. $4\sqrt{15}$
d. $4\sqrt{30}$

218. It took Raul 5 hours to drive to his parents' house, which is 260 miles away. How fast was Raul driving?

a. 55 mph
b. 58 mph
c. 52 mph
d. 47 mph

219. Holly can walk 3 miles in 45 minutes. If she keeps up this pace, how many miles could she walk in 3 hours?

a. 6.75 miles
b. 10 miles
c. 12 miles
d. 16 miles

220. Due to a clerical error, a flight to Los Angeles was extremely overbooked. An announcement was made that only 55% of those who bought a ticket would be able to board the plane. If 220 people purchased tickets, how many would not be able to board the plane?

a. 99
b. 110
c. 121
d. 140

221. If a triangle's height is 7 and area is 70, what is its base?

a. 5
b. 20
c. 10
d. 7

222. How many ounces are in 16 pounds?

a. 1 oz
b. 2 oz
c. 128 oz
d. 256 oz

223. Dan is following a recipe for sugar cookies which calls for 3 tablespoons of baking soda. Unfortunately, he has misplaced his tablespoon and can only find a teaspoon. If there are 3 teaspoons per tablespoon, how many teaspoons of baking soda should he use?

a. 1 teaspoon
b. 6 teaspoons
c. 9 teaspoons
d. 12 teaspoons

224. Solve for y: $5y - 7 = 3(2y + 3)$

a. -16
b. -1
c. 10
d. -8

225. What is the value of c in the triangle below?

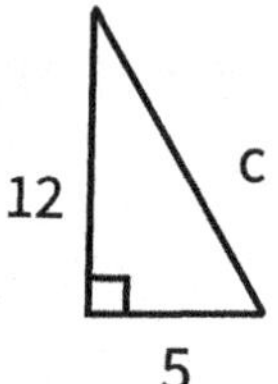

a. 15
b. 17
c. 13
d. 10

226. On a restaurant's menu, the ratio of appetizers to entrees to desserts is 3:6:2. If there are 33 items total, how many are entrees?

a. 66
b. 11
c. 24
d. 18

227. The figure below is made up of three squares, each of which has an area of 9. What is the figure's exterior perimeter?

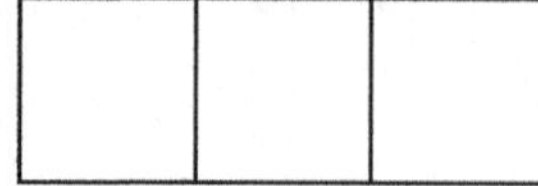

a. 27
b. 24
c. 36
d. 33

228. Mason purchased 2 tickets to a concert which cost $60 each. However, the ticket seller he used to purchase the tickets charged a processing fee of 7.5% of the total cost of the tickets. How much in total did Mason need to pay?

a. $4.50
b. $9.00
c. $64.50
d. $129.00

229. The table below shows how many students at a high school enrolled in performing arts classes over the course of three years.

	2016	2017	2018
Theater	44	56	48
Music	45	35	39
Dance	29	39	42
Total	118	130	129

In 2017, what percentage of these students enrolled in theater classes?

a. 37%
b. 30%
c. 41%
d. 43%

230. How many miles are in 15 kilometers if there are 0.62 miles in 1 kilometer? Round your answer to the nearest hundredth.

a. 9.30 km
b. 17.84 km
c. 24.19 km
d. 29.23 km

231. Nia paid $789.60 for her cell phone bills last year. How much did she pay on average per month?

a. $66.72
b. $68.20
c. $78.90
d. $65.80

232. The cube of 3 is equal to 9 times what number?

a. 2
b. 1
c. 3
d. 4

233. In the equation below a = 3 and b = 2. What is c?

$3b - 2a = c$

a. 5
b. 0
c. -5
d. 14

234. Sophia began volunteering at the animal shelter at 10:45 AM and finished at 4:15 PM. How much time did she spend volunteering?

a. 4 hours and 30 minutes
b. 5 hours and 30 minutes
c. 5 hours and 15 minutes
d. 4 hours and 45 minutes

235. What three dimensional figure can be made by folding this paper pattern:

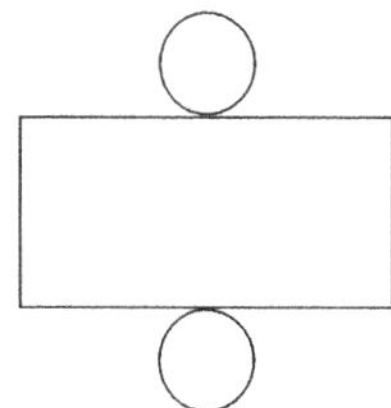

a. cone
b. sphere
c. rectangular prism
d. cylinder

236. Marco is painting his bedroom, which has 475 sq ft of wall surface area. One can of paint can cover 75 sq ft of wall. How many cans of paint will Marco need to finish painting his bedroom?

a. 4
b. 5
c. 6
d. 7

237. A school that teaches only 7th and 8th grade had a total student population of 280. If 155 of the students are in 8th grade, what percent of the total student population is in 7th grade? Please round to the nearest tenth.

a. 44%
b. 44.6%
c. 55.4%
d. 58.3%

238. The figure below can be classified as a

a. quadrilateral
b. parallelogram
c. diamond
d. nonagon

Language Section 1

60 Questions, 25 Minutes

Usage and Mechanics

Instructions: For questions 239-278, check the sentences for errors of usage, capitalization, or punctuation. If there is no error, choose D.

239.

a. It's fun to go to the pool, especially when the weather is nice.
b. Your eating all of my Halloween candy.
c. Italy is beautiful in September and October.
d. No mistakes.

240.

a. Sadie gave Luisa and I the keys to your house.
b. Although it is warmer out today than yesterday, you should still wear a hat.
c. Have you seen Melanie today?
d. No mistakes.

241.

a. Imani and her sister went to Disney World last year and had an amazing time.
b. That is the friendliest dog I've ever seen.
c. Next Spring, I want to grow broccoli, lettuce, and tomatoes in our garden.
d. No mistakes.

242.

a. The kids' playpen is filled with toys they never use.
b. Kayla doesn't understand why she failed her math test.
c. "What's the weather like today?" Mary asked.
d. No mistakes.

243.

a. Ashley took guitar classes last year but never practiced between lessons.
b. Thats the strangest thing I've ever seen!
c. Raul told me that his friends saw the movie already.
d. No mistakes.

244.

a. Asia is the larger continent in the world.
b. Even though I've never played a musical instrument, I'd like to go to the symphony one day.
c. Sleep affects your ability to stay focused throughout the day.
d. No mistakes.

245.

a. If he were allowed, Ivan would eat pizza, pasta, and candy all day.
b. My little sister admitted that she lost my favorite shirt.
c. Most city parks, except Eastern Park, is littered with trash.
d. No mistakes.

246.

a. It started raining so Mohammad and I walked home from the park.
b. "Susan eat your lunch", said my mother.
c. That's the scariest movie I've ever seen!
d. No mistakes.

247.

a. Between you and me, I've never liked Grandma's oatmeal cookies.

b. Lake Hammond has several picnic tables that we can use for the family reunion.

c. My sister who loves anything made with chocolate ate the entire German chocolate cake.

d. No mistakes.

248.

a. When taking vacations to different parts of the country, alot of people travel by airplane.

b. Until taking Algebra 101 I always had earned good grades in math.

c. The school's playground needs to be repaired and repainted.

d. No mistakes.

249.

a. "I'm going to lie down after practice," said my brother.

b. Cal wore his Halloween costume all day today.

c. I like going to school after.

d. No mistakes.

250.

a. I could of spent all weekend at the beach.

b. I don't feel very well today, so I think I'm going to go home early.

c. Lorenzo walked quickly down the hall to get to his French class on time.

d. No mistakes.

251.

a. At the convenience store, I bought folders, pens, and pencils.

b. Aside from France, the country I'd like to visit most is south Africa.

c. Bobbi asked, "Have you seen the new Star Wars movie yet?"

d. No mistakes.

252.

a. Aside from Tricia, everyone was excited to have a snow day.

b. My mom surprised my dad with a trip to the Grand Canyon.

c. The toddler nearly tripped over his untied shoelaces.

d. No mistakes.

253.

a. Mehan and Mikalya want to go to the library after school.

b. I've never seen anyone as excited as Selma.

c. After art class, the girls clothing was splattered with paint.

d. No mistakes.

254.

a. Although I practiced for weeks, I still lost the race.

b. "Watch out! she exclaimed.

c. When Zach and Samantha feel how cold it is, they're going to regret not wearing coats today.

d. No mistakes.

255.

a. Carlos likes playing basketball but I like playing baseball.

b. Every Saturday morning Trent takes the bus to his cousin's house.

c. Whose car is parked in my driveway?

d. No mistakes.

256.

a. After we got back from vacation, I had to stay up all night to catch up on my school work.

b. Every Easter I color eggs with my mom, sister, and brother.

c. Why did you forget to study for your test.

d. No mistakes.

257.

a. Although I had more classes, I had less books in my backpack than Sheri.
b. "Okay," I sighed.
c. Near the end of my vacation, I sent you a postcard from Houston, Texas.
d. No mistakes.

258.

a. The book had a scratch on its cover.
b. Although Ian is from Chicago, his favorite football team is the Philadelphia Eagles.
c. Everyone in the town had their own car.
d. No mistakes.

259.

a. My dad is usually in a foul mood after work.
b. I love snow but I don't like driving in it.
c. I played well at the game last weekend.
d. No mistakes.

260.

a. Jonah lost his sister's hamster again!
b. My favorite expression is "everything in moderation."
c. Have you read The Adventures of Tom Sawyer?
d. No mistakes.

261.

a. One must stand by his or her principals when making a serious decision.
b. Everyone brought his jersey to the basketball game.
c. The toys at the Chicago Children's Museum belong to everyone.
d. No mistakes.

262.

a. The dog is lying in the sun.
b. Truth be told, I don't think I enjoy social media.
c. When you finish reading the book, give it back to Karlee or me.
d. No mistakes.

263.

a. Rottweilers and German Shepherds often get a bad reputation.
b. The coach yelled, "Get out there and score some goals!"
c. Valentine's Day is my least favorite holiday.
d. No mistakes.

264.

a. The lion ate his kill before any hyenas could steal it.
b. A ride on a hot air balloon is rather expensive.
c. The cupcakes Noelle baked were delicious.
d. No mistakes.

265.

a. Learning a second language should be mandatory in all elementary schools.
b. Espionage is punishable by death in some countries.
c. The students lost the game on the B team.
d. No mistakes.

266.

a. Valentina sold fewer cookies than Luisa.
b. Will you sit this box on the counter?
c. A note was given to me.
d. No mistakes.

267.

a. Neither the cheese nor the ham was part of her diet.
b. Pavol is the smaller of the three brothers.
c. I prefer to arrive on time.
d. No mistakes.

268.

a. Aunt Sherry is coming tomorrow.
b. There's nothing we can say to help.
c. The swimsuit with the yellow polka dots is her's.
d. No mistakes.

269.

a. The teapot is cracked; she needs replaced.

b. Let's leave before we're late.

c. Do you know if Jerome plays soccer?

d. No mistakes.

270.

a. I always eat breakfast, brush my teeth, and go walking my dog before school starts.

b. We requested fries with our meal.

c. Which class do you like better?

d. No mistakes.

271.

a. The president requested a meeting with the legislature.

b. Felicity hanged the photo of her friend's dog in her locker.

c. Marco arrived on Tuesday, January 20th.

d. No mistakes.

272.

a. Sanae's sister is three years old.

b. Christmas Day will be on Sunday next year.

c. It was more smart of Dexter to schedule his surgery early in the morning.

d. No mistakes.

273.

a. Can you please take my dark, red dress to the cleaners.

b. You and I both know she lied to the teacher.

c. In order to effect change, the manager gave all his employees bonuses.

d. No mistakes.

274.

a. The Girl Scouts are selling cookies in my neighborhood.

b. What will you say to mom when she finds out you missed class?

c. Dr. Bernard gave a speech at the university.

d. No mistakes.

275.

a. Pablo said, "It's getting hot in here."

b. I wonder if Selma will make it on time.

c. "I'm not sure," said Elizabeth, who I will invite to my quinceanera.

d. No mistakes.

276.

a. Seamus asked if he might stay for dinner.

b. I like playing tennis; it's such a good workout.

c. Thomas was asking for trouble, right?

d. No mistakes.

277.

a. "Fire," Igor yelled.

b. Don't lie down on the floor.

c. Vacation starts the first day of spring.

d. No mistakes.

278.

a. "Take this book home," Mrs. Hamilton said.

b. Bring me some soup, pretzels, and orange juice.

c. Heading out to the store Julien forgot to grab his backpack.

d. No mistakes.

Spelling

Directions: For questions 279-288, look for errors in spelling. If there is no mistake, choose D.

279.

a. I highly reccommend the new diner on Main Street.

b. The Sahara is the largest hot desert in the world.

c. Jamie cut the pie into eight pieces.

d. No mistakes.

280.

a. My dog Rover reacts excitedly whenever he meets someone new.
b. Armond is practically an expert at dodgeball.
c. Billy and Sasha got into an arguement at school on Tuesday.
d. No mistakes.

281.

a. Groundhog Day is celebrated every year on February 2nd.
b. Coach Williams apreciates all the hard work her team puts in at practice.
c. The beginning of the movie was confusing to many viewers.
d. No mistakes.

282.

a. Victor enjoys orange juice with his breakfast.
b. The calender I bought for this year features pictures of adorable kittens from across the world.
c. One of Don's favorite recipes to prepare is chicken with forty cloves of garlic.
d. No mistakes.

283.

a. Evan dreams of studying abroad in a foriegn country.
b. Jade found the comedian quite humorous.
c. Penelope could sense that something was wrong.
d. No mistakes.

284.

a. Sanaa joined a commitee to help overhaul her school's lunch program.
b. Lima is the capital city of Peru.
c. Miguel was asked to take his dog for a walk immediately.
d. No mistakes.

285.

a. Morgan buys a souvenir keychain from every new country he visits.
b. I believe tomorrow will be a splendid day.
c. Dana is very passionate about conservation and protecting the enviroment.
d. No mistakes.

286.

a. Anna has had a stubborn popcorn kernel stuck between her teeth all afternoon.
b. Bob's fuel gauge read as nearly empty, so he began searching for a gas station.
c. Monica's mini-golf score Saturday night far exceded her expectations.
d. No mistakes.

287.

a. Leslie and Ron have been neighbors for over two decades.
b. Jared has been looking forward to getting his driver's lisence all year.
c. William Shakespeare is my favorite playwright.
d. No mistakes.

288.

a. Tina guarranteed that her portion of the project will be finished by Thursday.
b. Homer came back from lunch with a noticeable ketchup stain on his shirt.
c. Claude is in charge of planning the summer schedule at the recreation center.
d. No mistakes.

Composition

Directions: For questions 289-298, read the question and select the best answer.

289. Choose the best word to join the thoughts together.

Mark practiced at the batting cages more than any of his teammates; __________ he was the team leader in home runs.

a. nevertheless,
b. surprisingly,
c. consequently,
d. unusually,

290. Choose the best word(s) to join the thoughts together.

Ancient Egyptian civilization was responsible for some truly awe-inspiring architectural marvels. __________ the Great Pyramid of Giza was built using only Bronze Age technology but has stood for over 4,000 years!

a. However,
b. For example,
c. Despite this,
d. Additionally,

291. Choose the group of words that best completes the sentence.

When baking chocolate chip cookies from scratch for the first time, __________.

a. you must follow a good cookie recipe because that is very important.
b. following a good chocolate chip cookie recipe is an important thing to do.
c. it is important to follow a good homemade chocolate chip cookie recipe.
d. it is important to follow a good recipe.

292. Which of these expresses the idea most clearly?

a. Although Mario ended up not enjoying it, Mario was happy that he tried sushi for the first time, which is something he had never tried before.
b. Even though Mario didn't like it, he is glad that he tried it.
c. Although he didn't enjoy it, he is glad that he tried sushi.
d. Although he ended up not enjoying it, Mario was happy that he gave sushi a try.

293. Which of these expresses the idea most clearly?

a. The play *Hamlet* is Renee's favorite play.
b. *Hamlet*, which is Renee's favorite, is a play.
c. Renee's favorite play is *Hamlet*.
d. *Hamlet* is the play that is Renee's favorite.

294. Which of these sentences fits best under the topic "A Brief History of Video Games"?

a. Video games can provide entertainment and are an interesting hobby.
b. The SNES home video game console was released in North America in 1991.
c. Many people prefer playing tabletop board games to video games.
d. There are many educational video games available for purchase.

295. Which of the following topics is best for a one-page essay?

a. How to Plan Three Healthy Meals a Day
b. The Battles of the American Revolutionary War
c. An In-Depth Look at the Human Nervous System
d. English Literature of the Seventeenth and Eighteenth Centuries

296. Which of the following topics is best for a five-page essay?

    a. An Analysis of All the Works of William Shakespeare
    b. A Brief History of American Vegetable Gardens
    c. Quick Tips for Organizing Your Closet
    d. How to Make Scrambled Eggs

297. Which sentence does NOT belong in the paragraph?

    (1) There are many signs that the planet Mars was once home to abundant liquid water, just like on Earth. (2) Mars is the fourth planet of our solar system. (3) For example, on the surface of Mars, there are many landforms that suggest that there were once rivers and lakes that have since dried up. (4) There is even evidence that almost a third of the planet was covered by a large, liquid ocean.

    a. 1
    b. 2
    c. 3
    d. 4

298. Where should the sentence "Ingrid especially loves it when she gives her students time to write in their journals at the end of class" be placed in the following paragraph?

    (1) Ingrid's favorite class this year is English. (2) She believes that Ms. Miller, her creative and engaging teacher, is who makes it truly special. (3) If it were up to Ingrid, she wouldn't ever leave for her next class when the bell rings!

    a. Before sentence 1
    b. After sentence 1
    c. Between sentences 2 and 3
    d. After sentence 3

Answer Key

Verbal

1. C
2. A
3. B
4. A
5. B
6. C
7. C
8. D
9. A
10. C
11. A
12. B
13. D
14. B
15. D
16. D
17. C
18. B
19. C
20. A
21. A
22. D
23. C
24. B
25. C
26. C
27. C
28. C
29. A
30. A
31. D
32. B
33. D
34. C
35. A
36. C
37. B
38. A
39. C
40. A
41. A
42. C
43. C
44. A
45. C
46. D
47. B
48. B
49. B
50. D
51. A
52. A
53. C
54. A
55. C
56. D
57. B
58. C
59. A
60. C

Quantitative

61. C
62. B
63. A
64. B
65. D
66. B
67. B
68. D
69. B
70. C
71. D
72. A
73. D
74. B
75. C
76. B
77. C
78. A
79. B
80. D
81. B
82. B
83. C
84. B
85. C
86. D
87. B
88. B
89. B
90. A
91. A
92. D
93. A
94. B
95. A
96. C
97. C
98. D
99. B
100. A
101. B
102. B
103. A
104. A
105. C
106. C
107. A
108. D
109. D
110. C
111. C
112. C

Reading

113. A
114. B
115. C
116. B
117. A
118. C
119. A
120. B
121. A
122. C
123. C
124. D
125. A
126. B
127. C
128. D
129. B
130. C
131. C
132. A
133. D
134. A
135. B
136. C
137. D
138. A
139. B
140. C
141. A
142. B
143. D
144. C
145. D
146. B
147. B
148. A
149. C
150. D
151. A
152. C
153. B
154. A
155. D
156. C
157. A
158. D
159. B
160. C
161. A
162. A
163. D
164. B
165. A
166. D
167. C
168. B
169. C
170. C
171. A
172. B
173. B
174. C

Math

175. B
176. B
177. D
178. C
179. A
180. D
181. B
182. D
183. A
184. A
185. C
186. C
187. B
188. B
189. C
190. D
191. A
192. C
193. A
194. B
195. C
196. D
197. C
198. A
199. C
200. B
201. b
202. A
203. B
204. C
205. A
206. C
207. C
208. D
209. B
210. B
211. A
212. C
213. A
214. B
215. B
216. B
217. B
218. C
219. C
220. A
221. B
222. D
223. C
224. A
225. C
226. D
227. B
228. D
229. D
230. A
231. D
232. C
233. B
234. B
235. D
236. D
237. B
238. A

Language

239. B
240. A
241. C
242. D
243. B
244. A
245. C
246. B
247. C
248. A
249. C
250. A
251. B
252. D
253. C
254. B
255. A
256. C
257. A
258. C
259. B
260. C
261. A
262. D
263. D
264. A
265. C
266. B
267. B
268. C
269. A
270. A
271. B
272. C
273. A
274. B
275. C
276. D
277. A
278. C
279. A
280. C
281. B
282. B
283. A
284. A
285. C
286. C
287. B
288. A
289. C
290. B
291. D
292. D
293. C
294. B
295. A
296. B
297. B
298. C

HSPT Test 2

Verbal Section 2

60 Questions, 16 Minutes

Instructions: Select the best answer.

1. Convene most nearly means to

   a. close
   b. repel
   c. dissolve
   d. assemble

2. Dormant means the *opposite of*

   a. awake
   b. asleep
   c. winter
   d. inert

3. The temperature in April was warmer than the temperature in May. The temperature in June was cooler than in May. The temperature in June was cooler than in April. If the first two statements are true, the third statement is

   a. true
   b. false
   c. uncertain

4. Cat is to mammal as bonnet is to

   a. hat
   b. hair
   c. summer
   d. contain

5. Which word does *not* belong with the others?

   a. ravenous
   b. hungry
   c. empty
   d. satisfied

6. Hurricane is to breeze as yell is to

   a. talk
   b. speak
   c. whisper
   d. whimper

7. Which word does *not* belong with the others?

   a. stamen
   b. pistil
   c. petal
   d. rose

8. Ridicule means the *opposite* of

   a. joke
   b. hurt
   c. laugh
   d. praise

9. Which word does *not* belong with the others?

   a. language
   b. French
   c. Swahili
   d. Arabic

10. Which word does *not* belong with the others?

    a. Santa Claus
    b. The Easter Bunny
    c. The Tooth Fairy
    d. Dracula

11. Atrophy most nearly means

    a. incline
    b. better
    c. slow
    d. deteriorate

12. Eric played video games longer than Jamal and Marissa. Jamal played video games longer than Tyrel. Eric played video games for less time than Tyrel. If the first two statements are true, the third statement is

    a. true
    b. false
    c. uncertain

13. All of the homes in Brickton have fences made of wood. No wood fences are black. None of the homes in Brickton have black fences. If the first two statements are true, the third statement is

    a. true
    b. false
    c. uncertain

14. Which word does *not* belong with the others?

    a. run
    b. jump
    c. walk
    d. sleep

15. Placid most nearly means

    a. true
    b. warm
    c. sedate
    d. lake

16. Ramble is to prattle as grace is to

    a. clumsy
    b. eloquence
    c. aloof
    d. temperament

17. Which word does *not* belong with the others?

    a. film
    b. television
    c. show
    d. movie

18. Verbatim means the *opposite* of

    a. Literally
    b. Different
    c. Precise
    d. Verbosely

19. Multilingual most nearly means

    a. polyglot
    b. polygamous
    c. language
    d. transcriber

20. Sarah has more friends than Julio. Julio has fewer friends that Anika. Sarah has fewer friends than Anika. If the first two statements are true, the third statement is

    a. true
    b. false
    c. uncertain

21. Formidable most nearly means

    a. fashionable
    b. laughable
    c. powerful
    d. small

22. Callous most nearly means

    a. nice
    b. insensitive
    c. smooth
    d. cowardly

23. Which word does *not* belong with the others?

    a. curling
    b. snowboarding
    c. skiing
    d. tennis

24. Car is to engine as bicycle is to

    a. muscle
    b. wheel
    c. tread
    d. transport

25. The grocery store is north of the hardware store. The barber shop is south of the grocery store. The hardware store is north of the barber shop. If the first two statements are true, the third statement is

    a. true
    b. false
    c. uncertain

26. Lackadaisical means the *opposite* of

    a. careless
    b. enthusiastic
    c. minimal
    d. grand

27. Which word does *not* belong with the others?

    a. circle
    b. cube
    c. sphere
    d. cylinder

28. Delectable most nearly means

    a. tasty
    b. detestable
    c. democratic
    d. muted

29. Immaculate means the *opposite* of

    a. flawed
    b. perfect
    c. heroic
    d. calculated

30. Jamal works from home more often than both April and Britta. April works from home more often than Britta. Britta works from home less often than both Jamal and April. If the first two statements are true, the third statement is

    a. true
    b. false
    c. uncertain

31. Serene most nearly means

    a. tiresome
    b. shaky
    c. chaotic
    d. peaceful

32. Which word does *not* belong with the others?

    a. physics
    b. chemistry
    c. biology
    d. science

33. Mad is to infuriated as glad is to

    a. cheerless
    b. overjoyed
    c. gloomy
    d. confused

34. Which word does not belong with the others?

    a. sandal
    b. sneaker
    c. fedora
    d. loafer

35. Emilio scored more points at the game than Martin. Charlie scored fewer points than Martin. Emilio scored fewer points than Charlie. If the first two statements are true, the third statement is

    a. true
    b. false
    c. uncertain

36. Which word does *not* belong with the others?

    a. sparrow
    b. falcon
    c. penguin
    d. robin

37. Bewilder most nearly means

    a. comfort
    b. destroy
    c. confuse
    d. tame

38. Meek means the *opposite* of

    a. watchful
    b. shy
    c. bold
    d. mild

39. Which word does *not* belong with the others?

    a. sonnet
    b. haiku
    c. limerick
    d. poem

40. Sunny is to dim as humid is to

    a. cloud
    b. shining
    c. wet
    d. arid

41. Which word does *not* belong with the others?

  a. gold
  b. diamond
  c. silver
  d. bronze

42. Jovial means the *opposite* of

  a. happy
  b. wasteful
  c. miserable
  d. glad

43. Despise means the *opposite* of

  a. adore
  b. hurtful
  c. hate
  d. sweet

44. Tyler's house is north of Alaina's house. Alaina's house is west of Emma's house and south of Vihaan's house. Tyler's house is north of Vihaan's house. If the first two statements are true, the third statement is

  a. true
  b. false
  c. uncertain

45. Which word does *not* belong with the others?

  a. coffee
  b. tea
  c. hot chocolate
  d. chocolate milk

46. Rational most nearly means

  a. wise
  b. logical
  c. absurd
  d. apathetic

47. Broccoli is to vegetable as mango is to

  a. food
  b. eat
  c. sweet
  d. fruit

48. Phobia most nearly means

  a. morose
  b. despise
  c. haste
  d. fear

49. Which word does *not* belong with the others?

  a. car
  b. minivan
  c. vehicle
  d. SUV

50. Which word does *not* belong with the others?

  a. plate
  b. fork
  c. spoon
  d. knife

51. Tatiana sells more lemonade than Kiersten and Raven. Raven sells more lemonade than Jackson. Jackson sells the most lemonade. If the first two statements are true, the third statement is

  a. true
  b. false
  c. uncertain

52. Bird is to nest as bear is to

  a. hole
  b. house
  c. den
  d. cub

53. Boat is to captain as train is to

  a. mechanic
  b. engineer
  c. passenger
  d. rail

54. Perilous means the *opposite* of

  a. risky
  b. uncertain
  c. easy
  d. safe

55. Desterville has fewer residents than Happyville. Destertville has more residents than Waterville. Waterville has the fewest residents. If the first two statements are true, the third statement is

    a. true
    b. false
    c. uncertain

56. Google is to search as textbooks is to

    a. learn
    b. teacher
    c. class
    d. memorize

57. Shrewd most nearly means

    a. clever
    b. mean
    c. unhappy
    d. witch

58. All green-eyed toobles have pink hair. No pink haired toobles have purple feet. All green-eyed toobles have purple feet. If the first two statements are true, the third statement is

    a. true
    b. false
    c. uncertain

59. Mateo reads more books than Ariana and Cai. Cai reads more books than Conor. Conor reads fewer books than Ariana. If the first two statements are true, the third statement is

    a. true
    b. false
    c. uncertain

60. Which word does *not* belong with the others?

    a. freshman
    b. high school
    c. sophomore
    d. senior

Quantitative Section 2

52 Questions, 30 Minutes

Instructions: Select the best answer.

61. The square root of 36 is 4 more than what number?

    a. 2
    b. 10
    c. 12
    d. 68

62. Review the following series: 27, ___, 23, 17, 19, 13, 15. What number should fill the blank?

    a. 29
    b. 21
    c. 26
    d. 20

63. 2 more than twice a number is 22. What is that number?

    a. 10
    b. 20
    c. 5
    d. 15

64. Examine the following series: 13, 12, 14, 11, 15, ___. What number should come next?

    a. 9
    b. 12
    c. 10
    d. 14

65. What is $\frac{2}{5}$ of $\frac{1}{4}$ of 200?

    a. 30
    b. 20
    c. 10
    d. 5

66. What number should come next in the following series: 17, 14, 11, 8, 5, ___?

    a. 1
    b. 4
    c. 3
    d. 2

67. 25% of 40% of 90 is what number?

    a. 36
    b. 9
    c. 18
    d. 22.5

68. Examine the figure below in which a= 5 and c= 9

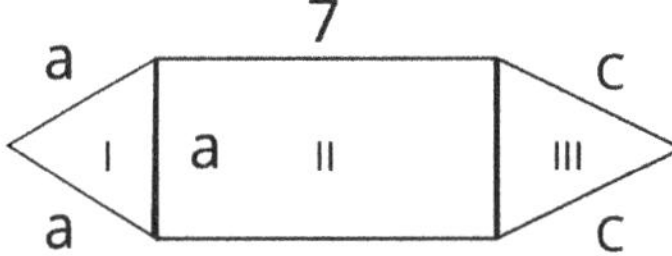

    a. The perimeter of shape I is greater than the perimeter of shape II
    b. The perimeter of shape II is greater than the perimeter of shape III
    c. The area of shape II is greater than the sum of the perimeters of shape I and shape II
    d. The perimeter of shape II is equal to the perimeter of shape III

69. Look at the series: 3.69, 3.79, 3.89, 3.99, ___. What number should come next?

    a. 3.109
    b. 4.09
    c. 3.09
    d. 4.10

70. Review the following series: 24, 36, 6, ___, 3, 15. What number is missing?

    a. 18
    b. 1
    c. 15
    d. 2

71. Examine (A), (B), and (C) and find the best answer.

(A) 3.06×10^5
(B) 2.98×10^6
(C) 4×10^4

a. (B) < (A) and (B) < (C)
b. (A) >(B) and (A) > (C)
c. (C) < (A) and (C) >(B)
d. (A) < (B) and (C) < (B)

72. Examine the figures below and find the best answer.

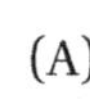

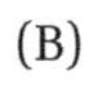

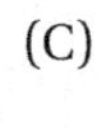

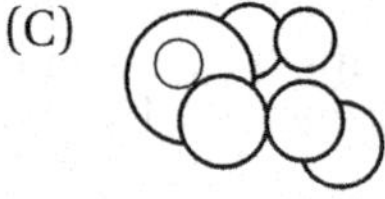

a. Figure (A) contains one less circle than figure (C)
b. Figure (B) contains one more circle than figure (C)
c. Figure (C) contains two more circles than figure (A)
d. Figure (B) contains two less circles than figure (C)

73. Review the series: 36, 9, 6, 27, 1, ____. Find the next number.

a. .16
b. 9
c. 81
d. 54

74. Examine (A), (B), and (C) and find the best answer.

(A) $7 + 5\,(2 - 6) - 3$
(B) $(7 + 5)\,2 - 6 - 3$
(C) $7 + 5 \times 2 - (6 - 3)$

a. (A) = (B) = (C)
b. (A) < (C) > (B)
c. (C) < (A) and (C) > (B)
d. (B) > (C) > (A)

75. E is the center of the circle. Select the best answer.

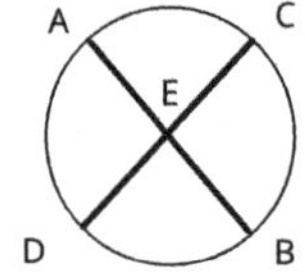

a. $\overline{AB} > \overline{CD}$
b. $\overline{EC} < \overline{EB}$
c. $\overline{AB} - \overline{EB} = \overline{EC}$
d. $\overline{EB} > \overline{AB}$

76. Examine (A), (B), and (C) and find the best answer.

(A) $\sqrt{4}$
(B) $2\sqrt{3}$
(C) 2

a. (A) is greater than (B)
b. (A) is equal to (C) but less than (B)
c. (A) is less than (B) and greater than (C)
d. (A) is equal to (B) and (C)

77. What number is missing in the following series: 28, 26, 22, ____ , 8, -2?

a. 20
b. 18
c. 16
d. 12

78. Examine this series: 3, 9 ,6,____, 15, 45. What number is missing?

a. 3
b. 18
c. 12
d. 30

79. What letter or number should come next in the series: 1, B, 3, D, 5, ___?

a. E
b. F
c. 6
d. 7

80. What number is 3 less than 14% of 50?

a. 4
b. 7
c. 10
d. 12

81. Examine the triangles below and find the best answer.

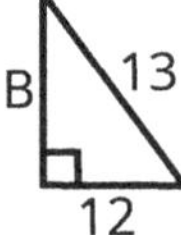

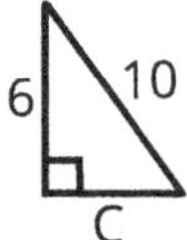

a. Side A is longer than side B but shorter than side C
b. Side C is longer than the sum of sides A and B
c. Side A is equal in length to side B but shorter than side C
d. Side B is longer than both side A and side C

82. What is the next number in the following series: 8, 3, 11, 9, 14, ___?

a. 10
b. 12
c. 17
d. 27

83. What number is 5 more than the average of 16, 22, 8, and 10?

a. 9
b. 14
c. 19
d. 61

84. Examine the series: 50, 52, 26, 28, ___, 16. What number is missing?

a. 10
b. 14
c. 24
d. 30

85. Examine (A), (B), and (C) and find the best answer.

(A) $(3 \times 3)^2$
(B) $3^2 \times 3^2$
(C) 81

a. (B) is larger than (A) but smaller than (C)
b. (A) is larger than (B) but smaller than (C)
c. (C) is larger than (A) and (B)
d. (A), (B), and (C) are equal

86. 45 is $\frac{5}{8}$ of what number?

a. 9
b. 36
c. 60
d. 72

87. Examine the figure below and find the best answer.

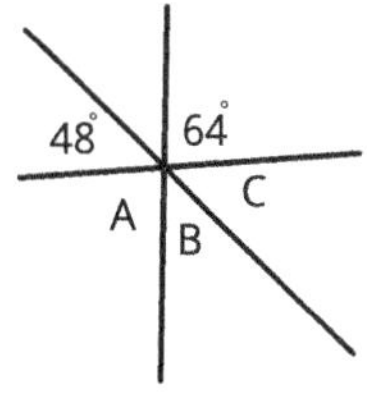

a. Angle A is smaller than both Angle B and Angle C
b. Angle B is larger than Angle C but smaller than Angle A
c. Angle B is larger than either Angle A or Angle C
d. Angle C is larger than Angle A but smaller than Angle B

88. Review the series: 3, 12, 10, ___, 38, 152. What number is missing?

a. 8
b. 15
c. 40
d. 48

89. What is the next number in the following series: 18, 22, 26, 30, 34, ___?

a. 35
b. 36
c. 37
d. 38

90. Examine the figures below and find the best answer.

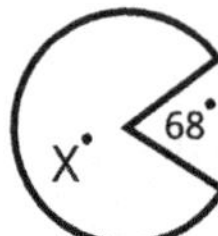

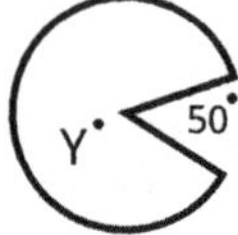

a. X° + Y° > Z° + 283°
b. Z° + Y° < X° + 335°
c. Z° + X° < Y° + 302°
d. X° + Y° < Z° - 20°

91. Examine (A), (B), and (C) and find the best answer.

(A) $\frac{1}{2} \times \frac{1}{4} + 3$
(B) $\frac{1}{2} \div \frac{1}{4} + 3$
(C) $\frac{1}{2} + \frac{1}{4} + 3$

a. (A) is larger than both (B) and (C)
b. (B) is larger than both (A) and C)
c. (C) is larger than (B) but smaller than (A)
d. (B) is smaller than (A) but larger than (C)

92. Review the series: 3.125, $3\frac{1}{4}$, 3.375, ___, 3.625, $3\frac{3}{4}$. What number is missing?

a. $3\frac{1}{2}$
b. 3.5
c. 3.525
d. 3.4

93. Solve for x for (A), (B), and (C). Find the best answer.

(A) $0.75x - 6 = 6$
(B) $0.5x - 3 = 7$
(C) $0.25x - 2 = 4$

a. (C) > (A) > (B)
b. (A) < (C) < (B)
c. (B) > (A) and (A) < (C)
d. (A) = (B) < (C)

94. What percent of 80 is 48?

a. 60%
b. 65%
c. 70%
d. 75%

95. Examine (A), (B), and (C) and find the best answer.

(A) $(\frac{64}{4}) \times 2$
(B) 2^4
(C) $4 \times 2 + 8$

a. (B) + (C) = (A)
b. (A) = (B) - (C)
c. (B) × (C) = (A)
d. (A) + (B) = (C)

96. What are the next two numbers in this series: 2, 3, 5, 8, 12, ___, ___?

a. 16, 22
b. 17, 22
c. 17, 23
d. 18, 23

97. What number should come next in the series: 15, 12, 14, 11, 13, ___?

a. 11
b. 14
c. 16
d. 10

98. What is the quotient of $\frac{1}{4}$ and $\frac{2}{3}$?

a. $\frac{1}{6}$
b. $\frac{3}{8}$
c. $\frac{3}{7}$
d. $\frac{1}{2}$

99. Examine the rectangles below and find the best answer.

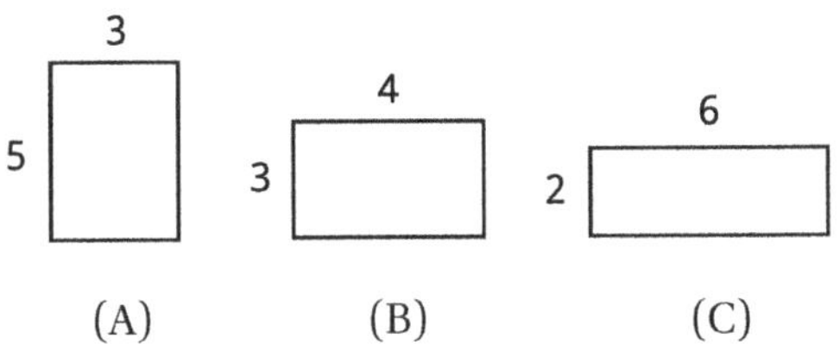

(A) (B) (C)

a. The area of (B) is larger than the area of (A)
b. The areas of (A) and (C) are equal
c. The areas of (B) and (C) are equal
d. The area of (A) is smaller than the area of (C)

100. What is 8 plus the quotient of 12 and 3?

a. 23
b. 12
c. 7
d. 16

101. Examine (A), (B), and (C) and find the best answer.

(A) 30% of 60
(B) 20
(C) 25% of 70

a. (A) is larger than (B) but smaller than (C)
b. (A) is equal to (C) and larger than (B)
c. (C) is smaller than (A) but larger than (B)
d. (A) is larger than (C) but smaller than (B)

102. Look at the series: 6, 4, 7, 2, 8, ___. What number should come next?

a. 0
b. 6
c. 2
d. 4

103. Examine (A), (B), (C) and find the best answer.

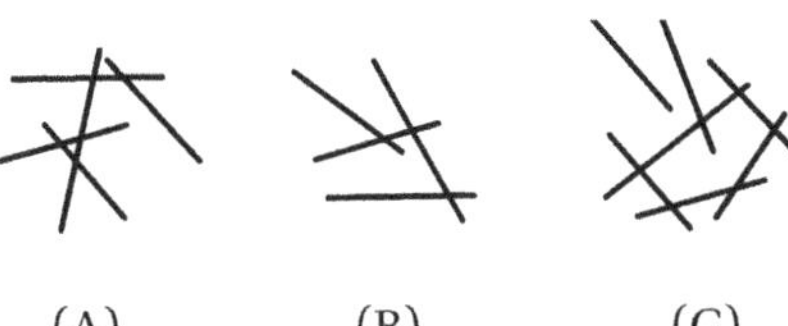

(A) (B) (C)

a. (A) + (B) < (C)
b. (C) - (B) > (A)
c. (C) - (A) < (B)
d. (C) - (B) < (C) - (A)

104. What number should come next in this series: 64, 32, 16, 8, ___?

a. 8
b. 6
c. 2
d. 4

105. The product of 4 squared and 2 is what number?

a. 18
b. 36
c. 32
d. 8

106. What is 5 less than the product of $\frac{4}{3}$ and $\frac{3}{4}$?

a. 6
b. -4
c. -1
d. 4

107. Examine this series: 16, 8, 12, 6, 10, ___. What number should come next?

a. 5
b. 14
c. 12
d. 3

108. What number should come next in this series: 3.2, 4.2 1.6, 3.2, .8, ___ , ___?

a. 2.2, .4
b. .4, .2
c. 1.6, .4
d. 2.2, .6

109. Look at the series: 4, IV, 6, VI, 8, ___. What number should come next?

a. VII
b. IIIX
c. XII
d. VIII

110. Examine (A), (B), and (C) and find the best answer.

(A) 5^2
(B) 2^4
(C) 4^2

a. (A) - (B) = (C)
b. (C) - (B) = (B) - (C)
c. (C) + (B) < (A)
d. (A) + (B) < (A) + (C)

111. 3 less than 40% of 60 is what number?

a. 24
b. 21
c. 27
d. 30

112. What letter should come next in this series: C, F, I, L, O ___?

a. Q
b. R
c. S
d. P

Reading Section 2

62 Questions, 25 Minutes

Reading Comprehension

Instructions: Read each passage carefully and mark one answer for each question.

Questions 113 - 122 refer to the passage below.

Spanning over 3,256 kilometers, Australia's rabbit-proof fence is the longest continuous fence in the world. It stretches from south to north, splitting the entire continent into two uneven parts. Built in the early 1900s, this fence was designed to keep rabbits from spreading to Australia's western farmlands from the eastern regions.

Rabbits were originally brought to Australia by settlers in the 1780s. Initially, they were kept in captivity and bred for meat. However, in 1859, an English settler named Thomas Austin decided to release 24 rabbits into the wild to be hunted. Other settlers, inspired by Austin, soon followed suit. At the time, Austin thought that "the introduction of a few rabbits could do little harm." He was wrong. Australia was the the ideal breeding ground for rabbits. The countryside's farms provided a plethora of food, and the warm climate meant that rabbits could breed year round. As a result, the rabbit population grew exponentially over the next decade, even though hunters killed over 2 million rabbits each year.

Australia's disquieted citizens became desperate to find a solution to the rapidly spreading invasion. One day in 1896, a surveyor named Arthur Mason suggested that a fence be constructed to contain the rabbits. This led to the creation of the first rabbit-proof fence, which was completed in 1907. Unfortunately, the fence could not be constructed fast enough to be fully effective, and rabbits crossed over it while it was still being built. Therefore, a second fence and eventually a third fence were added to attempt to more successfully enclose the rabbits.

Today, the rabbit-proof fence remains an imperfect barrier for all sorts of wild animals, such as dingoes, kangaroos, and, of course, rabbits.

113. When was the idea of the rabbit proof fence proposed?

a. 1859
b. 1780
c. 1896
d. 1907

114. Multiple versions of the rabbit proof fence were constructed because

a. rabbits are a huge nuisance
b. Arthur Mason insisted on it
c. other parts of Australia were being destroyed by rabbits
d. rabbits were able to cross through the fence while it was being built

115. As it is used in the passage, plethora most nearly means

a. scarcity
b. barn
c. abundance
d. trough

116. Based on the information provided in the passage, what must have happened to some of the rabbits released for hunting?

a. They were all successfully hunted.
b. They escaped and eventually died off.
c. They fought with other rabbits.
d. They survived and bred with other rabbits.

117. Australia's rabbit problem was caused by

  a. settlers bringing rabbits into the country for meat
  b. Thomas Austin releasing 24 rabbits onto his farm
  c. settlers breeding rabbits on their farms
  d. Thomas Austin and other settlers releasing rabbits into the wild

118. This passage might be found in

  a. an encyclopedia entry on Europe
  b. an Australian history textbook
  c. a newspaper
  d. an Australian settler's journal

119. As it is used in the passage, <u>disquieted</u> most nearly means

  a. loud
  b. excited
  c. whispering
  d. worried

120. Based on the information in the passage, why were rabbits such a nuisance in Australia?

  a. The rabbits ate the crops from farms.
  b. The rabbits ate the food of other native animal species.
  c. The settlers did not like seeing so many rabbits in their farms.
  d. The rabbits carried diseases.

121. A good title for this passage would be

  a. "The Longest Fences in the World"
  b. "The Origins of the Rabbit-Proof Fence"
  c. "Rabbits: A Nuisance!"
  d. "Thomas Austin: An Australian Settler"

122. Was the rabbit-proof fence able to contain the rabbits?

  a. Yes, although it had to be constructed multiple times, it was able to contain the rabbits.
  b. At first it was able to contain the rabbits, but today the rabbit proof fence is ineffective.
  c. No, despite being built multiple times, it was not able to completely contain the rabbits.
  d. Yes, it was able to contain the rabbits immediately.

Questions 123 - 132 refer to the passage below.

While Tom was eating his supper, and stealing sugar as opportunity offered, Aunt Polly asked him questions that were full of guile, for she wanted to trap him into damaging revealments. Like many other simple-hearted souls, it was her pet vanity to believe she was given a talent for dark and mysterious cunning. Said she:

"Tom, it was middling warm in school, wasn't it?"

"Yes'm."

"Powerful warm, warn't it?"

"Yes'm."

"Didn't you want to go a-swimming, Tom?"

A bit of a scare shot through Tom—a touch of uncomfortable suspicion. He searched Aunt Polly's face, but it told him nothing. So he said:

"No—well, not very much."

The old lady reached out her hand, felt Tom's shirt, and said:

"But you ain't too warm now, though." And it flattered her to reflect that she had discovered that his shirt was dry without him knowing that that was what she had in her mind. But in spite of her, Tom knew where the wind lay, now. So he predicted what might be the next move:

"Some of us pumped on our heads—mine's damp yet. See?"

Aunt Polly was vexed to think she had overlooked that bit of evidence. Then she had a new inspiration:

"Tom, you didn't have to undo your shirt collar where I sewed it, to pump on your head, did you? Unbutton your jacket!"

The trouble vanished out of Tom's face. He opened his jacket. His shirt collar was securely sewed.

"Bother! Well, go 'long with you. I'd made sure you'd played hookey and been swimming. But I forgive ye, Tom. I reckon you're a kind of a singed cat, as the saying is—better'n you look. This time."

She was half sorry her sagacity had miscarried, and half glad that Tom had stumbled into obedient conduct for once.

But Sidney said:

"Well, now, I thought you sewed his collar with white thread, but it's black."

"Why, I did sew it with white! Tom!"

But Tom did not wait for the rest. As he went out at the door he said:

"Sidney, I'll lick you for that."

In a safe place Tom examined two large needles which were thrust into the lapels of his jacket, and had thread bound about them—one needle carried white thread and the other black. He said:

"She'd never noticed if it hadn't been for Sid. Confound it! Sometimes she sews it with white, and sometimes she sews it with black. I wish she'd stick to one or t'other—I can't keep the run of 'em. But I bet you I'll lam Sid for that. I'll learn him!"

He was not the model boy of the village. He knew the model boy very well though—and loathed him.

123. What is the most likely relationship between-Tom and Sid?

  a. amicable, because they have an honest friendship
  b. hostile, because Sid is trying to get Tom into trouble
  c. neutral, because they do not interact much
  d. supportive

124. Which of the following describes Aunt Polly's reaction when she believed Tom hadn't skipped school?

  a. disappointed, because she was hoping to catch Tom in a lie
  b. relieved that for once Tom was being obedient
  c. shocked that he had behaved so well
  d. she felt both a little sorry and glad

125. When Aunt Polly says, "Bother! Well, go 'long with you. I'd made sure you'd played hookey and been swimming. But I forgive ye, Tom. I reckon you're a kind of a singed cat, as the saying is—better'n you look. This time," she means

  a. that she's very sorry for not trusting him
  b. that she may be wrong about him playing hooky, but she knows he's lied in the past
  c. that she will soon find out he's actually lying
  d. that she will try and be more fair in the future to Tom

126. From whose point of the view is this story told?

  a. Tom's
  b. Aunt Polly's
  c. a third person's
  d. Sidney's

127. When Aunt Polly compares Tom to a "singed cat, as the saying is - better'n you look." She is using

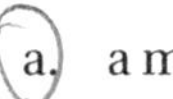

  a. a metaphor
  b. irony
  c. personification
  d. symbolism

128. This story most likely takes place

  a. immediately after school
  b. over the weekend
  c. in the evening
  d. in the morning

129. Tom and Aunt Polly

  a. do not like one another
  b. have a trusting and open relationship
  c. both try to trick each other at dinner
  d. do not enjoy Sid's company

130. It can be reasonably inferred from this line, "He was not the model boy of the village. He knew the model boy very well though—and loathed him," that Tom

  a. was close friends with the model boy
  b. has no ambition to be perfect
  c. wants to be better, but he will never be a model boy
  d. would like to be the model boy

131. What does the black thread symbolize?

  a. Aunt Polly's care of Tom
  b. Aunt Polly's ruthlessness
  c. Tom's innocence
  d. Tom's guilt

132. Which of the following explains the real reason why Tom's head is wet?

  a. He had pumped water on his head.
  b. He had gotten in a quarrel with Sid.
  c. He went swimming.
  d. He pretended to have wet hair to confuse Aunt Polly.

Questions 133 - 142 refer to the passage below.

The discipline of sociology describes socialization as the ways in which people learn the norms (rules) and beliefs of the society they live in. Socialization begins from the time one is born and continues throughout one's life. In the United States, the four most important factors of socialization are family, school, peer groups, and mass media.

A child's family is their primary world for the first few years of life. Family has the most profound impact on how the child understands the world around him or her. This is often why children share more than just physical traits with their parents. Several factors impact the way in which families socialize their children: religion, ethnicity, social class, and even parental occupation. For instance, most middle-class parents have "white-collar" jobs that value creativity and independence. Not surprisingly, these are the same values that many middle-class families teach their children.

School is next major agent of socialization. Students typically spend at least twelve years in school, where they learn from formal curriculum and from interactions with peers. Additionally, for most children, school is the first place they learn to engage with authority figures other than their own parents. In the United States, schools teach students to be neat, patient, and obedient. Students are also encouraged to compete for good grades and other rewards. All of these attitudes are things students carry with them to some degree into adulthood.

A third major factor of socialization is the peer group. Peers become increasingly important in socialization as a child approaches adolescence. As children age, they spend a great deal of time with their peers, both in and out of school. At this stage, peers' influence is often greater than any other socialization factor. This is particularly true when it comes to lifestyle preferences like music and clothing. More importantly, peers provide emotional support, companionship, and fun. However, not all effects of peer socialization are positive. Peer pressure can cause children to misbehave, make poor decisions, and break rules that they would not otherwise disobey..
As people age, peer groups may become less important, especially as one begins a career, marries, and starts a family of his or her own.

133. Which of the following options would be most likely to follow the last paragraph?

a. an analysis of why peer groups are less important to adults
b. a summary of the four ways children are socialized
c. a discussion of the negative side effects of peer pressure
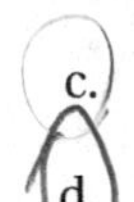
d. a discussion of how mass media impacts socialization

134. According to this passage, what would likely have the biggest impact on which movie a thirteen-year-old chooses to watch?

a. family

b. peers
c. school
d. mass media

135. The author's purpose in writing this passage is

a. to explain why students succumb to peer pressure
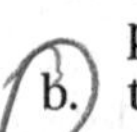
b. to explain how children and ultimately all people learn about their society
c. to analyze the social interactions children have with their peers and parents
d. to encourage people to closely examine the types of relationships they have

136. According to the passage, what is the difference between peer groups and schools?

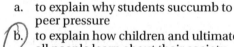

a. Schools are a bigger influence than peer groups on socialization.
b. Schools provide a different type of socialization than peer groups.
c. Schools are far more important in the socialization process.
d. Schools are not nearly as important as peer groups are.

137. A good title for the passage would be

a. “The Dangers of Peer Pressure”
b. “How People are Socialized Around the World”
c. “In Nature vs. Nurture, Nurture Wins!”
d. “How We Become Us: Socialization”

138. As it is used in the passage, <u>peer</u> most nearly means

a. look
b. adults
c. companions
d. students

139. Unlike family, the peer group

a. remains an important socialization factor throughout a person’s life
b. is most powerful during adolescence
c. helps children interact with authority figures
d. is a major factor of socialization

140. Based on the passage, which of the following is a correct inference regarding socialization?

a. Because the United States has freedom of religion, faith plays no role in socialization.
b. In the United States, competition is an important value.
c. Societies around the world have similar norms and beliefs.
d. The social interactions children have with authority figures in schools are usually punitive.

141. Why might peer groups become less important over time?

a. As people age, they do not have as much time as they used to for their friends.
b. As people age, they no longer care about music, movies, or clothing.
c. As people age, the downsides of peer pressure become too great.
d. As people age, they have no need for friends.

142. According to the passage, which of the following would be an example of how schools socialize students?

a. Everybody gets a prize for participating in a Young Writers’ contest.
b. Students wait in line to order lunch.
c. Students take a bus home from basketball practice.
d. Teachers collaborate on curriculum projects.

Questions 143 - 152 refer to the passage below.

While World War II and the Nazi regime have been studied extensively, their effect on the arts and artists of the age are sometimes overlooked. Some musicians were harmed directly by the Nazis and their policies, while others suffered because of their associations with the Nazi party.

Kurt Weill was a German composer of Jewish descent that stood for everything the Nazis opposed. He was one of the earliest and most obvious targets of artistic oppression in the Third Reich. In 1930, Weill's opera Aufstieg und Fall der Stadt Mahagonny premiered at a time when the growing power of the right wing brought increased scrutiny and censorship to his work. Weill eventually realized that he and his wife were on the Nazi blacklist and would be arrested; so they fled to France in 1933, hoping the stay would be temporary. In September of 1935, Weill went to New York to work on a production of The Eternal Road. Afterwards, Weill chose to stay in the United States, where he lived until his death in 1950.

Other musicians, such as the Austrian conductor Herbert von Karajan, profited from the Third Reich's reorganization of the musical world. When a Jewish conductor was removed from his position due to his heritage, von Karajan stepped in as the symphony's new conductor. He became increasingly popular among Nazi elites, and was selected as the leader of the Berlin State Opera in 1935. However, von Karajan did not stay in the Third Reich's good graces forever. When he married Anita Gütermann, the heiress to a textile fortune, he was stripped of all but one of his positions within the Reich because of her Jewish lineage. After the war, the Soviets issued a ban on von Karajan's performances because of his voluntary association with the Nazi party.

Similarly, Germaine Lubin was a French soprano who suffered for her perceived German sympathies after the war. In 1939, Lubin became the first French soprano to appear at the Bayreuth Festival in Germany, gaining considerable fame. She regularly associated with known Nazis and performed in Paris throughout the German occupation. Her career came to an abrupt end in 1944 when she was arrested by the French government for her alleged collaboration with the Nazis. Although she was ultimately acquitted of this charge, she was condemned to five years of 'dégredation nationale' (i.e. second-class citizenship). By 1953, she had completely stopped publicly performing.

143. Why was Kurt Weill targeted by the Nazi party?

a. They disliked his music.
b. He was Austrian.
c. He was a Nazi sympathizer.
d. He was Jewish.

144. As it is used in the passage, oppression most nearly means

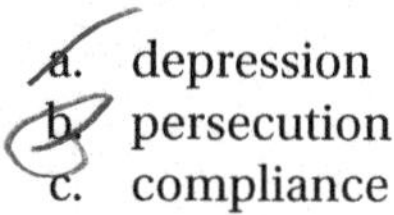

a. depression
b. persecution
c. compliance
d. demands

145. How did Weill's and von Karajan's experiences with the Nazi regime differ?

a. Weill was a Nazi sympathizer, whereas von Karajan was not.
b. Von Karajan profited from the Nazi regime because he married an heiress, whereas Weill's lack of Nazi connections caused him to suffer.
c. Von Karajan and Weill were both censored by the Nazi regime, but Weill was censored more heavily.
d. Weill was targeted by the Nazis, whereas von Karajan temporarily profited from the Nazi regime.

146. This passage is primarily about

a. why musicians cooperated with the Nazi regime
b. the impact of Herbert von Karajan's marriage on his professional life
c. how different musicians and composers were impacted by the Nazi regime
d. the impact of the Nazi regime on German life

147. According to the passage, Kurt Weill moved away from Germany. When did he move back to Germany?

  a. 1933
  b. 1935
  c. 1950
  d. he never moved back to Germany

148. You can infer from the passage that after the war, von Karajan's career

  a. suffered because of his association with the Nazi party
  b. temporarily suffered, but eventually rebounded
  c. blossomed
  d. stayed about the same as it had during the Nazi regime

149. According to the passage, which musicians lived in France at some point?

  a. Lubin and von Karajan
  b. Lubin
  c. Weill and Lubin
  d. Weill and von Karajan

150. The author most likely included the line "When a Jewish conductor was removed from his position due to his heritage, von Karajan stepped in as the symphony's new conductor" in order to

  a. show that von Karajan was helpful during the war
  b. explain why von Karajan supported the Nazi regime
  c. defend von Karajan's decision to associate the Nazis
  d. prove that von Karajan benefited professionally during the war

151. One can infer that Lubin was suspected of being a Nazi sympathizer because she

  a. was a member of the Nazi party
  b. performed in Germany and associated with Nazis
  c. was the conductor for German symphonies
  d. performed in Paris before the war

152. Which of the following would be the LEAST appropriate topic for the next paragraph?

  a. an explanation of how scientists were affected by the Nazi regime
  b. a description of another musician negatively affected by the Nazi regime
  c. an explanation of what happened to Lubin in the 1950s
  d. a profile of a musician positively affected by the Nazi regime

Vocabulary

Instructions: Choose the word that means the same, or about the same, as the underlined word.

153. A colossal mistake

a. unintentional
b. immense
c. insignificant
d. important

154. A rational decision

a. smart
b. illogical
c. weak
d. sensible

155. An unprecedented action

a. neutral
b. interesting
c. groundbreaking
d. fantastic

156. The pampered child

a. happy
b. spoiled
c. soft-spoken
d. wealthy

157. The worldly woman

a. elderly
b. sophisticated
c. businesslike
d. important

158. A daily chronicle

a. record
b. decision
c. schedule
d. routine

159. To hinder progress

a. allow
b. dislike
c. encourage
d. impede

160. The company's inception

a. concept
b. progress
c. beginning
d. goals

161. The translucent fabric

a. dull
b. opaque
c. gaudy
d. sheer

162. An abstract idea

a. conceptual
b. concrete
c. beautiful
d. smart

163. To concede defeat

a. believe
b. admit
c. reject
d. dislike

164. His meager salary

a. insufficient
b. enormous
c. acceptable
d. rising

165. The fraudulent seller

a. overpriced
b. unhelpful
c. dishonest
d. pushy

166. To feign interest

a. show
b. pretend
c. debate
d. describe

167. Honored <u>posthumously</u>

a. after hours
b. financially
c. after death
d. belatedly

168. The <u>subordinate</u> officer

a. junior
b. ranking
c. superior
d. inexperienced

169. The <u>malleable</u> substance

a. rigid
b. delicate
c. soft
d. pliable

170. She felt <u>ambivalent</u>

a. worried
b. uncertain
c. encouraged
d. nothing

171. The <u>bombastic</u> speech

a. insane
b. extraordinary
c. pompous
d. exciting

172. The <u>impartial</u> jury

a. objective
b. biased
c. subjective
d. wavering

173. He <u>plodded</u> upstairs

a. stomped
b. trudged
c. ran
d. eased

174. The <u>churlish</u> man

a. religious
b. tired
c. sad
d. rude

Math Section 2

64 Questions, 45 Minutes

Instructions: Select the best answer.

175. Solve: $\frac{4}{7} + \frac{3}{4}$

a. $1\frac{1}{4}$
b. $\frac{27}{28}$
c. $1\frac{9}{28}$
d. $1\frac{1}{3}$

176. 129 is evenly divisible by what number?

a. 2
b. 3
c. 9
d. 6

177. 62 is what percent of 1,400? Round to the nearest tenth.

a. 4.5%
b. 4.4%
c. .4%
d. .5%

178. Which of the following are consecutive numbers?

a. 2, $\frac{1}{2}$
b. 3, -3
c. 8, 9
d. 4, 6

179. What is the least common multiple of 8 and 12?

a. 84
b. 12
c. 48
d. 24

180. A grocery store is selling grapes at $3.49 a pound. How much would 2.5 pounds of grapes cost?

a. $12.73
b. $6.98
c. $87.30
d. $8.73

181. Solve: 137.14 - 119.67

a. 19.07
b. 18.36
c. 18.44
d. 17.47

182. Round 4,568,510 to the nearest thousand.

a. 4,568,500
b. 4,569,000
c. 4,568,000
d. 4,570,000

183. Simplify: $\sqrt{a^4b^5c^3}$

a. $a^2b^2c\sqrt{bc}$
b. $a^4b^4c^2\sqrt{bc}$
c. $a^2b^2c\sqrt{b^3c}$
d. It can not be simplified.

184. What symbol should go in the circle:

3.28 ○ 11/4?

a. >
b. <
c. =
d. ≤

185. Write out thirty million four hundred and twenty thousand thirteen in numerals.

a. 3, 420, 113
b. 30, 420, 130
c. 30, 420, 013
d. 30, 400, 213

186. Which point is on a line?

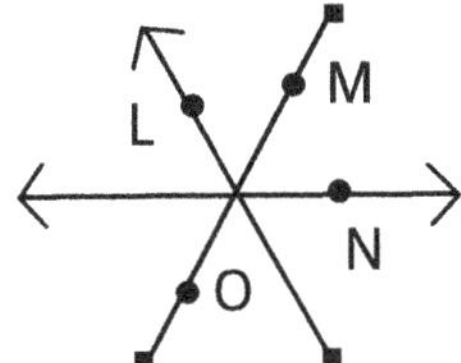

a. N
b. L
c. M
d. O

187. What is the median of the following group of numbers 6, 9, 3, 12, 14, 2, and 9.

a. 7
b. 7.8
c. 8.5
d. 9

188. What is the area of a square with side x?

a. 2x
b. x^3
c. x^2
d. 4x

189. Solve: $|4 - 6| + 12 =$

a. 10
b. 14
c. 2
d. 22

190. Which property is illustrated by:

$(3 \times 4)\,8 = 3\,(4 \times 8)$

a. commutative property
b. identity property
c. associative property
d. distributive property

191. What is 5% of 170?

a. 8
b. 9
c. 9.5
d. 8.5

192. The sum of a number and its double is 36. What is the number?

a. 24
b. 16
c. 12
d. 8

193. Angle A is supplementary to angle B. If angle B is 37°, what is the measure of angle A?

a. 53°
b. 143°
c. 43°
d. 153°

194. Given the two sets of numbers A = {1, 8, 9} and B = {1, 4, 5, 8}, what is $A \cup B$?

a. {1, 4, 5, 8, 9}
b. {1, 8}
c. {9, 4, 5}
d. {1, 4, 8, 9}

195. Solve: 2^4

a. 4
b. 8
c. 16
d. 32

196. Caleb has to read 15 poems for homework. It takes him between 3 and 5 minutes to read each poem. Which choice below is the best approximation of how long it will take Caleb to read all 15 of his poems?

a. 30 minutes
b. 45 minutes
c. 60 minutes
d. 75 minutes

197. How many 1 inch cubes will fit in a cube with a side 4?

a. 16
b. 64
c. 8
d. 128

198. What is the place value of the number 5 in the number 8.6591?

a. tens
b. hundreds
c. tenths
d. hundredths

199. Mary is making lemonade using a container of lemonade mix. The container's instructions say to add $\frac{3}{4}$ of a cup of mix to 3 cups of water. If Mary uses 4.5 cups of mix, much water will she use?

a. 9.5 cups
b. 11 cups
c. 13.5 cups
d. 18 cups

200. Eduardo and his two friends went out to dinner and evenly split their bill. If each of them paid $15.21, what was the total bill?

a. $30.42
b. $45.63
c. $3.07
d. $38.51

201. The table below shows the year of birth of the first five US presidents.

President	Year of Birth
George Washington	1732
John Adams	1735
Thomas Jefferson	1743
James Madison	1751
James Monroe	1758

How many years older was George Washington than James Madison?

a. 21 years
b. 25 years
c. 19 years
d. 11 years

202. Michael is preparing a recipe from a British cookbook that gives all measurements in metric units, but his kitchen scale only measures weight in pounds. If the recipe calls for 1.7 kilograms of an ingredient and there are 2.2 pounds per kilogram, how many pounds of the ingredient does Michael need? Round your answer to the nearest hundredth.

a. 0.77 lbs
b. 1.54 lbs
c. 3.74 lbs
d. 3.89 lbs

203. Solve for y: $2y + 8 = 2$

a. -3
b. -4
c. 5
d. 4

204. What is the diameter of a circle whose area is 144π?

a. 24
b. 12π
c. 12
d. 24π

205. Anna is three times as old as Catherine, who is half as old as Karen. If Karen is 20 years old, what is the sum of their ages?

a. 10
b. 20
c. 30
d. 60

206. How many sides does a heptagon have?

a. 9
b. 5
c. 6
d. 7

207. What is the name of the following shape?

a. cylinder
b. cone
c. prism
d. cube

208. If there are 2.54 centimeters in an inch, how many meters are in 42 inches? Round your answer to the nearest hundredth.

a. 1.07 meters
b. 16.53 meters
c. 106.68 meters
d. 1653.00 meters

209. 1 large pizza from the local pizzeria feeds 6 people. If Carl hosts a pizza party for 41 people, how many pizzas will he need to buy?

a. 5
b. 6
c. 7
d. 8

210. Arjun decided to watch a movie. He owns 4 action movies, 6 comedies, and 5 dramas. If he selected a movie at random, what is the probability that it would not be a drama?

a. $\frac{1}{3}$
b. $\frac{2}{3}$
c. $\frac{1}{2}$
d. $\frac{3}{4}$

211. In the coordinate plane below, in which quadrant is (-2, -5)?

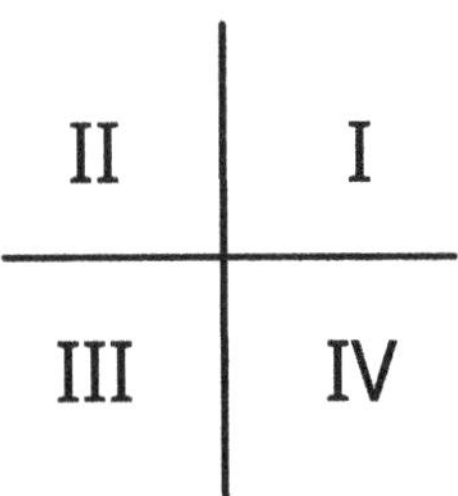

a. I
b. II
c. III
d. IV

212. The table below shows the number of goals scored by a hockey team in their 10 pre-season games.

Number of Goals	Number of Games
1	2
2	1
3	4
4	3

What is the average number of goals scored?

a. 7
b. 2.5
c. 2.8
d. 3

213. How many pints are in 2 gallons?

 a. 8
 b. 12
 c. 16
 d. 20

214. What is the value of c in the triangle below?

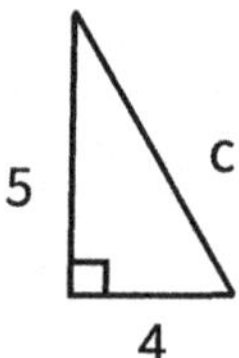

 a. 3
 b. $\sqrt{41}$
 c. $2\sqrt{5}$
 d. 6

215. A summer camp typically has a capacity of 250 campers. To increase their capacity, the camp sets up tents that allow them to accommodate 12% more campers. How many total campers can now attend the camp?

 a. 30
 b. 220
 c. 280
 d. 310

216. Jon sold 85 cell phones and 30 phone chargers last week. Twenty customers purchased both a cell phone and phone charger. If each customer can only purchase one of each item, how many customers purchased only cell phones?

 a. 20
 b. 65
 c. 85
 d. 105

217. What is the area of the shaded region?

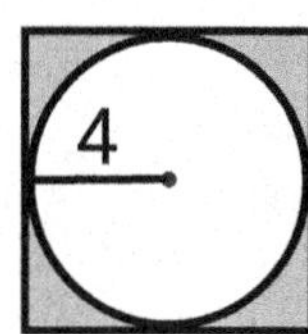

 a. $64 - 16\pi$
 b. $16 - 8\pi$
 c. $64 - 8\pi$
 d. $16\pi - 16$

218. If $5x - 7 = 38$, what does $2x$ equal?

 a. 9
 b. 6
 c. 12
 d. 18

219. A candy store charges $3 for 8 pieces of chocolate. How much will it cost Rosalie to purchase 20 pieces of candy?

 a. $6.00
 b. $7.50
 c. $7.00
 d. $8.50

220. Mariska earns $11.24 an hour and Alexi earns $10.73 and hour. If they both work 8 hours, how much more money does Mariska earn?

 a. $3.08
 b. $3.12
 c. $4.08
 d. $4.12

221. Mrs. Amin's cat ran to the top of a 24 foot tree. To reach her cat, she leaned a 26 foot ladder against the tree. How far from the bottom of the tree did she place the base of her ladder?

 a. 22 feet
 b. 10 feet
 c. 12 feet
 d. 5 feet

222. In Summersville Middle School, the ratio of sixth to seventh to eighth grade students is 3: 2: 1. If there are 96 students total, how many of them are in seventh grade?

 a. 16
 b. 24
 c. 32
 d. 48

223. What is the volume of the rectangular prism below?

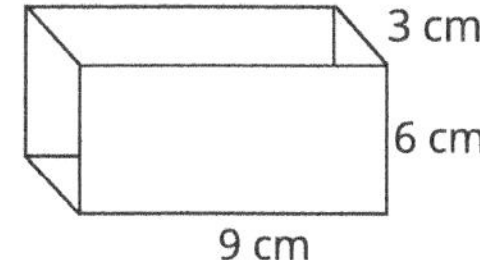

a. 162 cm^3
b. 168 cm^3
c. 196 cm^3
d. 198 cm^3

224. Solve $2x^2 - 4y + 7$ if $x = 2$ and $y = 3$.

a. 2
b. 17
c. 18
d. 3

225. The graph below shows the daily sales of three different types of cars. How many total cars were sold after two days?

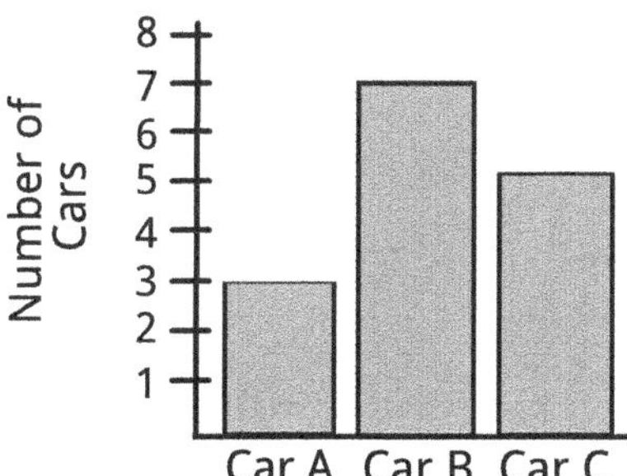

a. 14
b. 15
c. 30
d. 45

226. Solve: $(4 + 2)^3$

a. 36
b. 216
c. 126
d. 25

227. Three students in a class score 69%, 78%, and 92% on a test, respectively. What would a fourth student need to score for the students' average to be 82%?

a. 89
b. 92
c. 87
d. 93

228. A factory ships 420 bags of rice to Greenville Grocery Store in boxes. Each box can hold up to 18 bags of rice. What are the minimum number of boxes that the factory can use to ship the rice?

a. 22
b. 23
c. 24
d. 25

229. Evan took the train to his grandmother's house. The train was travelling at 54 miles per hour for the entire 135 mile trip. How long was the train ride?

a. 3 hours
b. 2.5 hours
c. 2.75 hours
d. 3.25 hours

230. Marshawn arrives at school at 7:45 AM. He has to leave at 1:30 PM for a doctor's appointment. How long will Marshawn be at school?

a. 6 hours and 15 minutes
b. 5 hours and 15 minutes
c. 5 hours and 45 minutes
d. 6 hours and 45 minutes

231. Maia bought a $70 purse on sale for $56. What percent discount did she receive on the purse?

a. 84%
b. 20%
c. 16%
d. 80%

232. Solve for x: $\sqrt{25} + x = 12$

a. 5
b. 6
c. .5
d. 7

233. Select the statement which must ALWAYS be true for the trapezoid below:

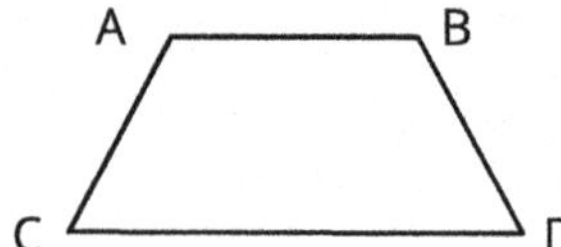

a. $\overline{AB}$ is parallel to $\overline{CD}$
b. angle A is equal to $\angle$ D
c. $\overline{AC}$ is parallel to $\overline{BD}$
d. $\overline{AC}$ is equal to $\overline{BD}$

234. Which of the following choices will satisfy the inequality: $-4 < x < 3.2$?

a. -4.1
b. 4
c. 3.2
d. 3.1

235. Using the figure below, solve for x.

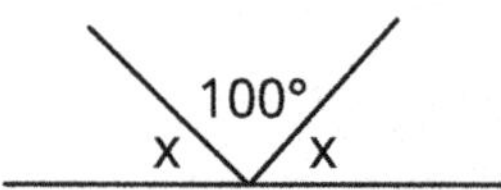

a. 80°
b. 40°
c. 60°
d. 20°

236. Jeanne is cutting a piece of wood. How many 5 inch segments can she cut from a piece of wood that is 1 yard, 4 inches long?

a. 6
b. 12
c. 8
d. 10

237. An animal shelter has 36 cats and 24 dogs. If these are the only pets in the shelter, what percent of the pets in the shelter are dogs?

a. 40%
b. 60%
c. 44%
d. 38%

238. If the area of a triangle is 40 and it's height is 8, what is its base?

a. 5
b. 10
c. 8
d. 20

Language Section 2

60 Questions, 25 Minutes

Usage and Mechanics

Instructions: For questions 239-278, check the sentences for errors of usage, capitalization, or punctuation. If there is no error, choose D.

239.

a. Everyone must remember their place in line for tomorrow's rehearsal.
b. Neither Patrick nor Henry enjoyed tutoring with me.
c. It's high time you took your school work seriously.
d. No mistakes.

240.

a. Please hand that book to Sanali and me.
b. Tricia, I'd like you to meet my mother.
c. Running late to the game.
d. No mistakes.

241.

a. Troy knew I wouldn't be happy with his decision.
b. Please clean up the childrens' toys.
c. She and I are best friends and teammates.
d. No mistakes.

242.

a. My absolute favorite book is *Night of the Twisters*.
b. Because you lost my necklace, I'll have to replace it.
c. Why don't you except his apology .
d. No mistakes.

243.

a. I could have received a better grade if I had tried harder.
b. Keep off the grass until the fertilizer dries.
c. When you see Marco, can you tell him to come to my office?
d. No mistakes.

244.

a. The brownies with chocolate frosting are my favorite.
b. I lost interest after the play had begun.
c. I played terrible in yesterday's concert.
d. No mistakes.

245.

a. Without any hesitation, I asked my best friend to the homecoming dance.
b. Which of the backpacks is mine?
c. Of all my teammates he is the better one at free throws.
d. No mistakes.

246.

a. Can you explain yourself, Ritu?
b. I need to pack three shirts, two pairs of socks, and shoes, and jeans.
c. I'll never be a morning person no matter how hard I try.
d. No mistakes.

247.

a. Joel or his friends orders the food.
b. Can you bring the leftover meatloaf home to Grandpa?
c. The spring flowers are my favorite part of May.
d. No mistakes.

248.

a. A lot of us are going out after the basketball game.
b. "I prefer pizza with mushrooms." Gerald remarked.
c. Edie likes to dance, but Nora prefers gymnastics.
d. No mistakes.

249.

a. Everyone knows he has to check his grades daily.
b. It's up to Dad whether I can leave the house.
c. She gracefully danced over to the podium.
d. No mistakes.

250.

a. The old, oak grandfather clock in my parents' house chimes every fifteen minutes.
b. The days go by far too slowly with you gone.
c. Arzu's favorite class is Sociology.
d. No mistakes.

251.

a. My grandpa had an eclectic taste in music; he listened to both ABBA and Johnny Cash.
b. Between my friends, I'm the happiest about school starting later.
c. Winston played nicely with the other dogs at the dog park.
d. No mistakes.

252.

a. Neither Julien nor Noelle could wait for Christmas morning.
b. Jenna started school last week and is a bit nervous about the workload.
c. Please buy: milk, butter, and eggs at the grocery store.
d. No mistakes.

253.

a. The Cherokees ritual's of stomp dancing attract large crowds.
b. We three have been in the same class since preschool.
c. The route that I took was faster than I expected.
d. No mistakes.

254.

a. Rosalind lives three miles farther down the road.
b. Both Mrs. Huff and Mrs. Easler are my social studies teachers; she shares an office.
c. Kelly, my best friend, makes everyone laugh.
d. No mistakes.

255.

a. Belgrade is the only capital city I've ever lived in.
b. "Have you studied enough?" Sanja inquired.
c. Will you provide free council to my client?
d. No mistakes.

256.

a. Both of them are welcome to visit anytime.
b. The temperature outside never varies this time of year.
c. The sides of the house was damaged in the hail storm last week.
d. No mistakes.

257.

a. My teacher doesn't like me, because I am often late to class and disruptive.
b. Due to my illness, I had to drop the class.
c. I'm really enjoying the biography of Queen Elizabeth.
d. No mistakes.

258.

a. "Who is going to watch the children while I work, " my mom asked?
b. I avoid social media at all times; I prefer face-to-face interactions.
c. Kristi has a terrible temper when she doesn't get enough sleep.
d. No mistakes.

259.

a. "The assignment is due on Friday, March 4th," Mr. Wilson said.
b. I love all of my classes this year except geometry.
c. Their going to be late to the wedding.
d. No mistakes.

260.

a. It's important to consistently get plenty of rest.
b. One of Molly's favorite desserts are pie.
c. President Lincoln was elected on November 6, 1860.
d. No mistakes.

261.

a. Mike's lost notebook was found several weeks later in his room.
b. Of the two sisters, Beth was the fastest runner.
c. Dan is not known for the cleanliness of his locker.
d. No mistakes.

262.

a. Each person should do their own work.
b. My dog, Ollie, is the absolute best at catching tennis balls.
c. Thanksgiving is celebrated in America on the fourth Thursday of November every year.
d. No mistakes.

263.

a. Mercury is the planet closest to the Sun.
b. Ginger the cat loves it's scratching post.
c. "Set the table for dinner," Billy ordered.
d. No mistakes.

264.

a. Stephanie who is the youngest of three children is also the funniest.
b. Don't forget to pack a towel, swimsuit, and sunglasses for our beach trip tomorrow.
c. Margaret dreams of visiting the city of Nice, France at least once in her life.
d. No mistakes.

265.

a. Did you put away the groceries like I asked you to.
b. *Of Mice and Men* by John Steinbeck is one of Trina's favorite books.
c. I would like my birthday cake to be marble cake with chocolate frosting, please!
d. No mistakes.

266.

a. Malcolm is trying to limit his intake of sugary sodas.
b. David has always been interested in sleight of hand magic.
c. Marty thinks that hiking is a great way to get exercise and interact with nature and also it's a lot of fun!
d. No mistakes.

267.

a. Make sure to wear your hat and gloves during the snowstorm to avoid frostbite!
b. Chicago sits on the coast of lake Michigan.
c. Roseanne found the quality of the produce to be unacceptable.
d. No mistakes.

268.

a. The storm effected everyone who lived in the tri-county area.
b. "Millie, can you call your brother and tell him I'm coming over?" Uncle John asked.
c. It took Evan over an hour to dig his car out of the snow.
d. No mistakes.

269.

a. "To whom am I speaking?" Mary asked.
b. When Martin goes on vacation, he likes to swim, to hike, and shopping.
c. I have never been to Salt Lake City, Utah.
d. No mistakes.

270.

a. The Declaration of Independence was signed on July 4, 1776.
b. Billy was instructed to lay the book down on the table.
c. Plants use photosynthesis to create sugar and oxygen out of carbon dioxide and water.
d. No mistakes.

271.

a. The squirrel attempted an ambitious jump to a tree branch that was fifteen feet away.
b. I prefer sweet to savory breakfasts.
c. The frisbee was thrown by aunt Jodi to Christina.
d. No mistakes.

272.

a. Cheri brought a sleeping bag, pajamas, and a flashlight to the slumber party.
b. Maya fiercely argued for an extended curfew.
c. Tim baked less cookies for the bake sale than Brad.
d. No mistakes.

273.

a. Meera and me went running after school.
b. "I would do anything to see that concert!" Marlee exclaimed.
c. I can't decide if I enjoy Halloween or Valentine's Day candy more.
d. No mistakes.

274.

a. I am going to lie down for a while because I have a headache.
b. Isabella wanted to go to the park but she was told to finish her homework first.
c. The 2006 Winter Olympics were held in Turin, Italy.
d. No mistakes.

275.

a. Marcia and Maureen went sledding over the weekend.
b. The original Ferris Wheel was unveiled at Chicago's World's Columbian Exhibition in 1893.
c. "Let's go fly a kite! Melinda exclaimed."
d. No mistakes.

276.

a. Adrian loves to dance as a form of exercise.
b. Jessies dog Checkers loves to jump in puddles.
c. The class loves to re-enact fairy tales like *Cinderella*.
d. No mistakes.

277.

a. "May I be excused?" William asked politely.
b. As a consequence of parking in a no parking zone, Megan's car was towed away.
c. It was so foggy this morning that it was impossible to see anything more than six inches away from you.
d. No mistakes.

278.

a. Despite the hot and humid summer day, it was still pleasant outside in the shade.
b. The room full of families.
c. Disappointingly, the fireworks were cancelled due to poor weather conditions.
d. No mistakes.

Spelling

Directions: For questions 279-288, look for errors in spelling. If there is no error, choose D.

279.

a. I'm hoping to go shopping tomorrow.
b. I was really embarrassed when I forgot my teacher's name.
c. The horse galloped through the prarie.
d. No mistakes.

280.

a. The mischievous cat knocked the glass of milk off the table.
b. I'm going to fill out an application for the job at the restaurant.
c. Kahil and Charlotte finished their science project early.
d. No mistakes.

281.

a. We don't have school on Presidents' Day.
b. I never recieved the package from Ebony.
c. Aidan carried the television up a flight of stairs.
d. No mistakes.

282.

a. Apparantly, the roads are too icy to drive on right now.
b. Yesterday my sister bought all the materials she needed for her college art class.
c. I had an amazing dessert at the Lakehouse Restaurant.
d. No mistakes.

283.

a. I won't be going to school for the foreseeable future.
b. Our neighbor is getting a new dog tomorrow.
c. A new buisness opened over Labor Day weekend.
d. No mistakes.

284.

a. In the documentary, the senator was apologizing profusely.
b. The location of the wedding ceremony was beautiful and serene.
c. My aunt's tree was hit by lightening last night.
d. No mistakes.

285.

a. I counted out the change in my pocket: two nickels, three quarters, and eighteen pennies.
b. I'll be dissapointed if I don't get to go to the concert tomorrow night.
c. Is it appropriate for me to ask if I can bring my cousin to Jason's party?
d. No mistakes.

286.

a. I ate only one peice of birthday cake.
b. My dad's signature is often illegible, making it impossible to read.
c. The bookkeeper got the figures wrong on our financial statements.
d. No mistakes.

287.

a. My best friend learned to speak Spanish when her sister moved to Mexico.
b. The princess wore an exquisite, beaded tiara to the ball.
c. The pronunciation of the word "zebra" is different in the US and England.
d. No mistakes.

288.

a. My parents threw me the best surprise party.
b. The mathematical procedures needed to solve the problem were beyond my ability.
c. Brandi had a really sucessful school year.
d. No mistakes.

Composition

Directions: For questions 289-298, read the question and select the best answer.

289. Choose the best word to join the thoughts together.

I forgot to water the garden; __________ most of my plants were wilted.

a. nevertheless,
b. conversely,
c. therefore,
d. however,

290. Choose the best word to join the thoughts together.

Amazingly, __________ I forgot to study for my test, I still got an A.

a. although
b. whereas
c. besides
d. none of these

291. Choose the group of words that best completes the sentence.

a. When my history teacher assigns us a test, __________.
b. she is always helping us complete the study guide.
c. we complete the study guide with my history teacher's help.
d. she helps us complete the study guide.
e. we complete the history study guide with my teacher's help.

292. Which of these expresses the idea most clearly?

a. My mom called the front office on my first day of school to make sure that I was okay five times.
b. On my first day of school, the front office was called by mom five times to make sure that I was okay.
c. My mom, on my first day of school, to make sure that I was okay called the front office five times.
d. On my first day of school, my mom called the front office five times to make sure that I was okay.

293. Which of these expresses the idea most clearly?

a. I wanted to get chosen for the competitive basketball team, so I made a plan: practice every day, watch videos of myself playing, and ask the coach for tips.
b. I made a plan to practice every day, ask the coach for tips, and watch videos of myself playing so could be I chosen to be on the competitive basketball team.
c. I wanted to get chosen for the competitive basketball team, so I made a plan: practice every day, watching videos of myself playing, and making sure to ask the coach for tips.
d. Since I wanted to get chosen for the competitive basketball team, I made a plan to be practicing every day, watching videos of myself playing, and asking the coach for tips.

294. Which of these expresses the idea most clearly?

a. Although we were tired, before sunset we wanted to find our campground so we hiked through the mountains.
b. We hiked through the mountains until sunset although we were tired to find our campground.
c. Although we were tired, we hiked through the mountains until sunset to find our campground.
d. We wanted to find our campground, so we hiked through the mountains, although we were tired, until sunset.

295. Which of these sentences fits best under the topic "How to Mow Your Lawn"?

   a. Mowing your lawn is hard work.
   b. Always hire someone else to mow your lawn.
   c. When mowing your lawn, make sure to mow in rows so you don't miss any grass.
   d. You don't need to mow your lawn in winter.

296. Which of the following topics is best for a one-page essay?

   a. Dinosaurs of the Cretaceous Period
   b. The Eating Habits of the Brachiosaurus
   c. An In-Depth Analysis of the Extinction of Dinosaurs
   d. An Exploration of How Birds Evolved from Dinosaurs

297. Which sentence does NOT belong in the paragraph?

   Willa had always been interested in moving to Phoenix. (2) When she lost her job in New York, she decided that it was the perfect time to make the move. (3) Arizona is beautiful in the winter months. (4) Willa packed up her bags the next week and boarded a bus to Phoenix.

   a. 1
   b. 2
   c. 3
   d. 4

298. Where should the sentence "When traveling to Italy, consider staying in the countryside" be placed in the following paragraph?

   The scenery is stunning, with beautiful ruins, rolling hills, and more grape vines than you can imagine. (2) The small, local towns are full of charm and history, and you can easily occupy most of your day wandering through their winding streets. (3) From the countryside, you can also can easily access larger, nearby towns such as Florence, Lucca, and Pisa.

   a. Before sentence 1
   b. Between sentences 2 and 3
   c. After sentence 1
   d. After sentence 4

Answer Key

Verbal

1. D
2. A
3. A
4. A
5. D
6. C
7. D
8. D
9. A
10. D
11. D
12. B
13. A
14. D
15. C
16. B
17. B
18. B
19. A
20. C
21. C
22. B
23. D
24. A
25. C
26. B
27. A
28. A
29. A
30. A
31. D
32. D
33. B
34. C
35. B
36. C
37. C
38. C
39. D
40. D
41. B
42. C
43. A
44. C
45. D
46. B
47. D
48. D
49. C
50. A
51. B
52. C
53. B
54. D
55. A
56. A
57. A
58. B
59. C
60. B

Quantitative

61. A
62. B
63. A
64. C
65. B
66. D
67. B
68. B
69. B
70. A
71. D
72. C
73. C
74. D
75. C
76. B
77. C
78. B
79. B
80. A
81. C
82. D
83. C
84. B
85. D
86. D
87. C
88. C
89. D
90. C
91. B
92. A
93. C
94. A
95. A
96. C
97. D
98. B
99. C
100. B
101. D
102. A
103. C
104. D
105. C
106. B
107. A
108. A
109. D
110. B
111. B
112. B

Reading

113. C
114. D
115. C
116. D
117. D
118. B
119. D
120. A
121. B
122. C
123. B
124. D
125. B
126. C
127. A
128. C
129. C
130. B
131. D
132. C
133. D
134. B
135. B
136. B
137. D
138. C
139. B
140. B
141. A
142. B
143. D
144. B
145. D
146. C
147. D
148. A
149. C
150. D
151. B
152. A
153. B
154. D
155. C
156. B
157. B
158. A
159. D
160. C
161. D
162. A
163. B
164. A
165. C
166. B
167. C
168. A
169. D
170. B
171. C
172. A
173. B
174. D

Math

175. C
176. B
177. B
178. C
179. D
180. D
181. D
182. B
183. A
184. A
185. C
186. A
187. D
188. C
189. B
190. C
191. D
192. C
193. B
194. A
195. C
196. C
197. B
198. D
199. D
200. B
201. C
202. C
203. A
204. A
205. D
206. D
207. B
208. A
209. C
210. B
211. C
212. C
213. C
214. B
215. C
216. B
217. A
218. D
219. B
220. C
221. B
222. C
223. A
224. D
225. C
226. B
227. A
228. C
229. B
230. C
231. B
232. D
233. A
234. D
235. B
236. C
237. A
238. B

Language

239. A
240. C
241. B
242. C
243. D
244. C
245. C
246. B
247. A
248. B
249. D
250. C
251. B
252. C
253. A
254. B
255. C
256. C
257. A
258. A
259. C
260. B
261. B
262. A
263. B
264. A
265. A
266. C
267. B
268. A
269. B
270. D
271. C
272. C
273. A
274. B
275. C
276. B
277. D
278. B
279. C
280. D
281. B
282. A
283. C
284. C
285. B
286. A
287. D
288. C
289. C
290. A
291. C
292. D
293. A
294. C
295. C
296. B
297. C
298. A

HSPT Test 3

Verbal Section 3

60 Questions, 16 Minutes

Instructions: Select the best answer.

1. Parched most nearly means

   a. fixed
   b. torn
   c. papery
   d. thirsty

2. Politician is to govern as professor is to

   a. school
   b. state
   c. president
   d. educate

3. Swelter means the *opposite* of

   a. flood
   b. bruise
   c. freeze
   d. wilt

4. Which word does *not* belong with the others?

   a. page
   b. book
   c. cover
   d. spine

5. Haley is taller than Tiffany. Seema is shorter than Haley. Seema is taller than Tiffany. If the first two statements are true, the third statement is

   a. true
   b. false
   c. uncertain

6. Gullible most nearly means

   a. trusting
   b. suspicious
   c. birdlike
   d. savage

7. Which word does *not* belong with the others?

   a. polyester
   b. cotton
   c. wool
   d. silk

8. Flurry is to blizzard as drizzle is to

   a. downpour
   b. sprinkle
   c. weather
   d. fog

9. Plunder most nearly means

   a. slip
   b. steal
   c. give
   d. dive

10. Agile most nearly means

    a. scary
    b. joyous
    c. slow
    d. nimble

11. Maya is older than Amy. Kristen is older than Maya. Amy is younger than Kristen. If the first two statements are true, the third statement is

    a. true
    b. false
    c. uncertain

12. Excruciating means the *opposite* of

    a. icy
    b. pleasant
    c. painful
    d. annoying

13. Which word does *not* belong with the others?
   a. lyrics
   b. melody
   c. harmony
   d. song

14. Which word does *not* belong with the others?
   a. computer
   b. calculator
   c. abacus
   d. smartphone

15. Wizard is to magic as knight is to
   a. castle
   b. medieval
   c. sword
   d. horse

16. Which word does *not* belong with the others?
   a. vision
   b. sense
   c. hearing
   d. touch

17. Desolate most nearly means
   a. barren
   b. sweet
   c. populated
   d. tardy

18. Articulate means the opposite of
   a. coherent
   b. unclear
   c. painted
   d. smartly

19. Moon is to Earth as Mars is to
   a. Phobos
   b. space
   c. planet
   d. Sun

20. Trent runs more quickly than Luiz. Alex runs more slowly than Luiz. Alex runs more quickly than Trent. If the first two statements are true, the third statement is
   a. true
   b. false
   c. uncertain

21. Coffee is to mug as gas is to
   a. tank
   b. car
   c. truck
   d. gas station

22. Which word does *not* belong with the others?
   a. elegant
   b. stately
   c. grand
   d. unrefined

23. The Springfield hockey team scores more goals than the Franklin hockey team. The Franklin hockey team scores more goals than the Greenville hockey team. The Greenville hockey team scores the fewest goals. If the first two statements are true, the third statement is
   a. true
   b. false
   c. uncertain

24. Luciana is standing in front of Kevin and Chen. Carter is standing behind Chen. Carter is standing in front of Kevin. If the first two statements are true, the third statement is
   a. true
   b. false
   c. uncertain

25. Cursory means the *opposite* of
   a. perfunctory
   b. easy
   c. meticulous
   d. swear

26. Coerce most nearly means

    a. allow
    b. limit
    c. meld
    d. force

27. Sun is to cloud as face is to

    a. nose
    b. eyes
    c. body
    d. mask

28. Which word does *not* belong with the others?

    a. dinosaur
    b. tiger
    c. bear
    d. lion

29. Serene most nearly means

    a. sweet
    b. tranquil
    c. sleepy
    d. happy

30. Carmen's backpack is lighter than Emilia's backpack. Janice's backpack is heavier than Emilia's backpack. Carmen's backpack is the heaviest backpack. If the first two statements are true, the third statement is

    a. true
    b. false
    c. uncertain

31. Controversial most nearly means

    a. contentious
    b. important
    c. contrary
    d. intelligent

32. Bus is to car as department store is to

    a. clothes
    b. boutique
    c. mall
    d. shoes

33. Which word does *not* belong with the others?

    a. hail
    b. rain
    c. storm
    d. sleet

34. Garish means the *opposite* of

    a. modest
    b. flashy
    c. ornate
    d. small

35. All white-tailed horses and spotted horses live in the big stable. All brown tailed horses live in the small stable. Some grey tailed horses live in the small stable. If the first two statements are true, the third statement is

    a. true
    b. false
    c. uncertain

36. Which word does *not* belong with the others?

    a. aunt
    b. great-aunt
    c. uncle
    d. grandmother

37. Which word does *not* belong with the others?

    a. Spanish
    b. Japanese
    c. French
    d. Portuguese

38. Frail means the *opposite* of

    a. energetic
    b. flimsy
    c. vulnerable
    d. strong

39. Which word does *not* belong with the others?

    a. desk
    b. office
    c. chair
    d. computer

40. Izzy grows more flowers than Marshall, Alice, and Ranuk. Ranuk grows more flowers than Chloe. Chloe grows more flowers than Izzy. If the first two statements are true, the third statement is

a. true
b. false
c. uncertain

41. Lasso is to wrangle as ruler is to

a. measure
b. leader
c. school
d. tool

42. Subliminal most nearly means

a. underground
b. message
c. imperceptible
d. visible

43. Subjugate means the *opposite* of

a. defeat
b. surrender
c. conquer
d. control

44. Credible means the *opposite* of

a. sincere
b. dishonest
c. playful
d. thoughtful

45. Vociferous most nearly means

a. brandish
b. peaceful
c. quiet
d. noisy

46. All puggles are muggles. No puggles wear collars. No muggles wear collars.If the first two statements are true, the third statement is

a. true
b. false
c. uncertain

47. Which word does *not* belong with the others?

a. period
b. comma
c. exclamation point
d. question mark

48. Epics are bigger than novels but not as big as trilogies. Dictionaries are bigger than epics but not as big as encyclopedias. Trilogies are the smallest. If the first two statements are true, the third statement is

a. true
b. false
c. uncertain

49. Which word does *not* belong with the others?

a. religious
b. sacred
c. secular
d. spiritual

50. Ethnocentric most nearly means

a. free
b. open
c. tribal
d. biased

51. Precocious most nearly means

a. quick
b. dimwitted
c. verbal
d. paranoid

52. Mr. Starz has more students than Ms. Pilsen. Mr. Santos has more students than Ms. Poretti, but not as many as Mr. Starz. Ms. Pilsen has the more students than Mr. Santos. If the first two statements are true, the third statement is

a. true
b. false
c. uncertain

53. Which word does *not* belong with the others?

    a. breakfast
    b. toast
    c. oatmeal
    d. orange juice

54. Which word does *not* belong with the others?

    a. Greece
    b. Italy
    c. Mexico
    d. Denmark

55. Adroit is to clumsy as passive is to

    a. peaceful
    b. war
    c. aggressive
    d. astute

56. Acumen means the *opposite* of

    a. sensitive
    b. smart
    c. ignorant
    d. sharp

57. Bike route W is longer than bike route J. Bike route J is longer than route N. Bike route W is longer than route N. If the first two statements are true, the third statement is

    a. true
    b. false
    c. uncertain

58. Which word does *not* belong with the others?

    a. spring
    b. summer
    c. winter
    d. season

59. Which word does *not* belong with the others?

    a. drill
    b. wrench
    c. laptop
    d. saw

60. Play is to stage as trial is to

    a. verdict
    b. test
    c. lawyer
    d. courtroom

Quantitative Section 3

52 Questions, 30 Minutes

Instructions: Select the best answer.

61. What number should come next in this series: 58, 54, 50, 46, 42, ___?

 a. 40
 b. 38
 c. 36
 d. 34

62. 18 is 4 more than the product of 2 and what number?

 a. 7
 b. 11
 c. 14
 d. 22

63. Examine (A), (B), and (C) and find the best answer.

 (A) $(4 + 8) \times 3 + 2$
 (B) $4 + 8 \times 3 + 2$
 (C) $4 + 8 \times (3 + 2)$

 a. (A) = (B) = (C)
 b. (A) > (B) > (C)
 c. (A) > (B) < (C)
 d. (C) > (A) < (B)

64. $\frac{3}{4}$ of 24 is 4 less than what number?

 a. 14
 b. 18
 c. 22
 d. 28

65. The average of 4, 16, 12, and 10 is 5 more than what number?

 a. 5.5
 b. 10.5
 c. 15.5
 d. 37

66. Review the following series: 7, 14, ___, 34, 37, 74. What number is missing?

 a. 16
 b. 17
 c. 21
 d. 28

67. Examine the figure below and find the best answer.

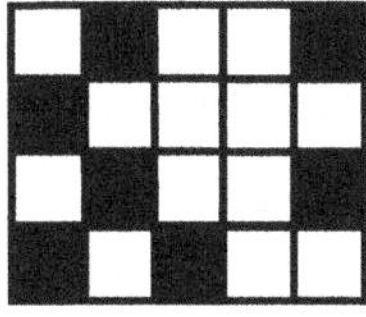

 a. The number of black squares is 4 less than the number of white squares.
 b. The number of black squares plus 7 is one more than the number of white squares.
 c. The number of white squares is half the product of the number of black squares and 3.
 d. The number of white squares squared is 144.

68. What number is 5 less than 20% of 108?

 a. -16.6
 b. 16.6
 c. 21.6
 d. 26.6

69. Examine (A), (B), and (C) and find the best answer.

(A) $y = \frac{1}{2}x + 4$

(B) $y = \frac{1}{2}x + 3$

(C) $y = -2x + 4$

a. Lines (A) and (B) are parallel to each other but perpendicular to line (C)
b. Line (C) is parallel to line (A) but perpendicular to line (B)
c. When x = 2, y is 5 for line (A), 4 for line (B), and 8 for line (C)
d. Lines (A) and (C) have the same slope

70. What number should come next in this series: 10, 10, 20, 60, 240, ___?

a. 300
b. 500
c. 1000
d. 1200

71. Examine (A), (B), and (C) and find the best answer.

(A) $(x + 4)(x - 3)$

(B) $(4x + 2)(x + 5)$

(C) $(x + 6)(x - 2)$

a. (A) is equal to $x^2 + x - 7$
b. (A) and (C) both equal $x^2 + 4x - 12$
c. (B) is equal to $4x^2 + 22x + 10$
d. (B) is equal to $5x + 7$

72. What number is 3 times $\frac{1}{2}$ of $\frac{1}{4}$ of 64?

a. 8
b. 16
c. 24
d. 32

73. Examine (A), (B), and (C) and find the best answer.

(A) The circumference of a circle with a diameter of 10

(B) The area of a circle with a radius of 4

(C) A area of a circle with a circumference of 8

a. (A) > (B) > (C)
b. (C) = (B) > (A)
c. (C) > (A) > (B)
d. (A) + (B) = (C)

74. Review the following series: 5, 12, ___, 9, 9, 6, 11. What number is missing?

a. 7
b. 10
c. 12
d. 15

75. Examine (A), (B), and (C) and find the best answer.

(A) $\sqrt{45}$

(B) $3\sqrt{5}$

(C) $(\sqrt{(\sqrt{25})}) \times 3$

a. (A) = (C) < (B)
b. (C) < (A) > (B)
c. (A) > (C) > (B)
d. (A) = (B) = (C)

76. What number should come next in this series: $1, \frac{7}{8}, \frac{3}{4}, \frac{5}{8}, \frac{1}{2}$, ___?

a. $\frac{1}{4}$
b. 0.5
c. $\frac{3}{8}$
d. 0.375

77. Examine (A), (B), and (C) and find the best answer.

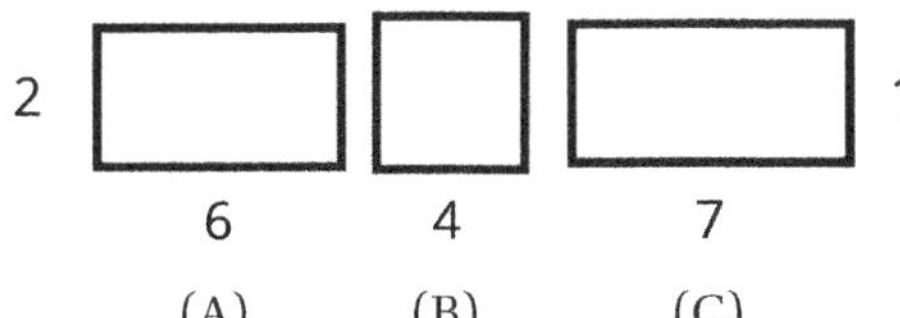

(A) (B) (C)

a. Rectangle (A), square (B), and rectangle (C) all have the same perimeter, but square (B) has the largest area of the three figures
b. Rectangle (A) has a larger area and smaller perimeter than rectangle (C)
c. Square (B) has a larger area than rectangle (C), but a smaller area than rectangle (A)
d. Square (B) has the smallest perimeter of the three figures

78. 8 is 32% of what number?

a. 4
b. 10
c. 16
d. 25

79. Look at this series: 3, 9, 7, 13, 11, ____. What number should come next?

a. 9
b. 17
c. 5
d. 16

80. The sum of 8 and what number is equal to the product of 2 and 12?

a. 16
b. 24
c. 32
d. 6

81. What number should come next in this series: 30, 20, 25, 10, 20, ___?

a. 15
b. 5
c. 0
d. 25

82. Examine (A), (B), and (C) and find the best answer.

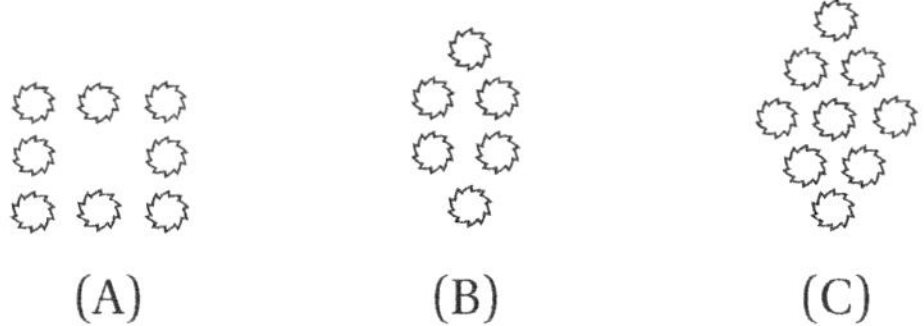

(A) (B) (C)

a. (C) - (A) < (C) - (B)
b. (C) - (A) > (B)
c. (C) + (B) > (C) + (A)
d. (A) - (B) < (C) - (A)

83. What is the sum of 5 and 30% of 60?

a. 18
b. 22
c. 13
d. 23

84. Examine (A), (B), and (C) and find the best answer.

(A) $\frac{1}{4}$ of 120
(B) $\frac{1}{6}$ of 150
(C) $\frac{1}{5}$ of 125

a. (A) + (B) = (C) + (B)
b. (A) - (C) = (B)
c. (A) - (B) < (B) - (C)
d. (C) + (B) < (A) + (C)

85. What number is $\frac{2}{3}$ of the sum of 8 and 7?

a. 10
b. 30
c. 15
d. 25

86. Review the following series: 12, 6, 10, 5, 9, ____. What number is missing?

a. 4.5
b. 4
c. 13
d. 12.5

87. The square of 4 is equal to the product of 2 and what number?

a. 16
b. 32
c. 6
d. 8

88. Examine (A), (B), and (C) and find the best answer.

(A) 2 quarters, 1 dime, and 3 pennies
(B) 1 quarter, 3 dimes, and 2 pennies
(C) 2 quarters, 1 nickel, and 6 pennies

a. (A) is larger than (B) but smaller than (C)
b. (A) is equal to (C) and smaller than (B)
c. (C) is larger than (B) but smaller than (A)
d. (B) is larger than (A) but smaller than (C)

89. Examine the figure below and select the largest answer.

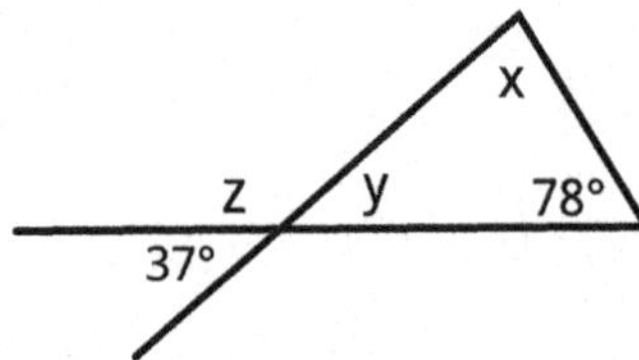

a. x
b. y
c. z
d. 78°

90. What number should come next in this series: 2.1, 1.7, 1.9, 1.5, 1.7, ___?

a. 1.2
b. 2.1
c. 1.3
d. 1.4

91. Look at this series: 97, 93, 89, 85, 81, ___. What number should come next?

a. 78
b. 77
c. 76
d. 75

92. Examine (A), (B), and (C) and find the best answer.

(A) $20 - (5 + 11)$
(B) $12 - 2 \times 4 + 1$
(C) $3 \times 4 - 5 \times 2$

a. $(A) - (C) < (B) - (A)$
b. $(A) + (C) > (B)$
c. $(A) + (C) > (B) + (A)$
d. $(A) - (B) > (C)$

93. Look at this series: 5, 7, 10, 14, 19, ___. What number should come next?

a. 24
b. 21
c. 25
d. 26

94. What is 40% of 25% of 120?

a. 12
b. 30
c. 48
d. 18

95. What is the next number in the following series: 8, 5, 6, 5, 4, 5, ___?

a. 3
b. 6
c. 5
d. 2

96. Look at the series: 45, 50, 40, 45, 35, ___. What number should come next?

a. 30
b. 40
c. 55
d. 45

97. What number should come next in this series: 38, 39, 93, 40, 41, 93, ____?

a. 41
b. 94
c. 42
d. 39

98. Seven times what number equals the difference of six squared and eight?

a. 2
b. 3
c. 4
d. 5

99. Review the following series: 144, 72, ____ , 38, 42, 21. What number is missing?

a. 36
b. 76
c. 42
d. 48

100. Examine (A), (B), and (C) and find the best answer.

(A) 3^5
(B) 2^4
(C) 1^{10}

a. (A) > (B) < (C)
b. (A) > (B) and (A) > (C)
c. (C) < (A) and (C) >(B)
d. (A) < (B) < (C)

101. What number should come next in this series: 4, 6, 18, 20, 60, 62, ___?

a. 64
b. 124
c. 186
d. 180

102. Given (A), (B), and (C), select the best answer.

(A) 36%
(B) $\frac{2}{5}$
(C) .43

a. (A) is greater than (B) and less than (C)
b. (B) is equal to (C)
c. (C) is greater than (A) and (B)
d. (B) is less than (A) and greater than (C)

103. What is the next number in the following series: 39, 38 , 30, 47, 21, ___?

a. 40
b. 56
c. 12
d. 37

104. Examine the figure below and select the best answer.

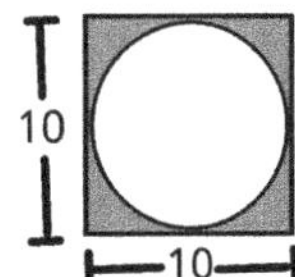

a. The radius of the circle is 5
b. The radius of circle is 10
c. The area of the circle is greater than the area of the square
d. The area of the circle is equal to the area of the square

105. Review the series: $\frac{1}{16}$, $\frac{1}{8}$, $\frac{1}{4}$, $\frac{1}{2}$, 1, ____. Find the next number.

a. $1\frac{1}{2}$
b. 2
c. 3
d. $\frac{30}{16}$

106. Look at this series: 200, 100, ____ , 70, 110, 55. What number is missing?

   a. 140
   b. 90
   c. 50
   d. 85

107. Examine the equilateral triangle and regular pentagon below and select the best answer.

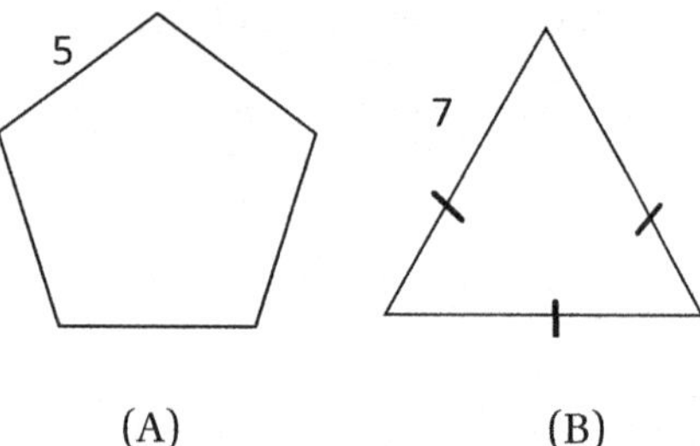

   a. (A) has a larger perimeter than (B)
   b. (B) has a larger perimeter than (A)
   c. (A) and (B) have equal perimeters
   d. The perimeter of (A) can not be determined

108. What is the missing number in the following series: I, 2,___IV, 5, 6, VII

   a. III
   b. VI
   c. 3
   d. 4

109. What number is 12 less than $\frac{2}{3}$ of 9?

   a. 3
   b. 6
   c. -4
   d. -6

110. Review the following series: 8, 10, ____ , 9, 6, 8. What number is missing?

   a. 13
   b. 8
   c. 12
   d. 7

111. Examine the rectangle and select the correct answer.

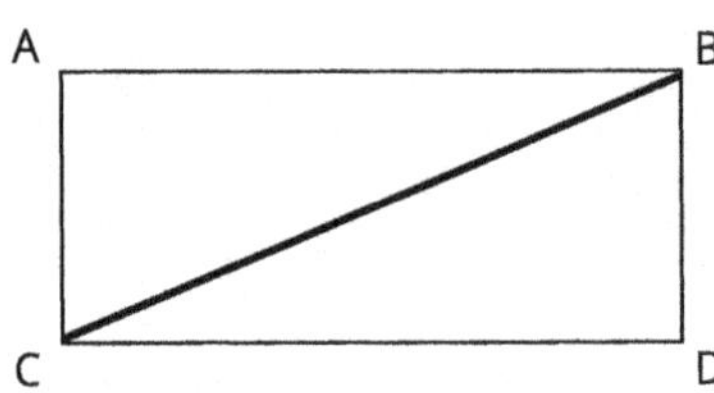

   a. AB > BC
   b. AC < BD
   c. BC = CD
   d. BC > BD

112. What number is missing from this series: 103, 2, 106, 10, ____, 50?

   a. 25
   b. 109
   c. 103
   d. 5

Reading Section 3

62 Questions, 25 Minutes

Reading Comprehension

Instructions: Read each passage carefully and mark one answer for each question.

Questions 113 - 120 refer to the passage below.

Melodrama is a form of theatre that was popular in the early 19th century. It is characterized by overly dramatic plots, exaggerated characters, and happy endings.

In its early days, melodrama attracted primarily lower and middle class audiences who used theatre to escape from the hardships of everyday life. They wanted to see a play full of suspense and intrigue, but in the end, wanted good to win over evil. Therefore, melodramas tend to have fantastically complicated plots, in which the hero saves the day at the last minute.

A typical melodrama starts with a provocation, which sets the plot in motion. This provocation usually involves a wicked character doing something cruel to a good character. Next, comes pangs, which are the hardships that an innocent character experiences at the hands of the evil character. Finally, the play ends with a penalty, which is suffered by the evil character in the play.

Audience expectations also influenced how characters were created. The audience did not want to have to try to understand intricate and deep characters. Therefore, easily identifiable <u>stock</u> characters, such as the hero, heroine, and villain were created and used in every melodrama.

Today, elements of melodrama can be found in soap operas and many television shows and movies.

113. According to the author, which element(s) of melodrama did the audiences impact?

    a. the plot
    b. the characters and plot
    c. the setting
    d. the characters and setting

114. In chronological order, a standard plot of a melodrama includes

    a. provocation, penalty, pangs
    b. penalty, pangs, provocation
    c. penalty, provocation, pangs
    d. provocation, pangs, penalty

115. As it is used in the passage, the word <u>stock</u> most nearly means

    a. stereotypical
    b. complex
    c. unique
    d. likable

116. Based on what you read in this excerpt, melodrama audiences would enjoy which type of plot?

    a. A heroine suffers at the hands of an evil villain. She is forced to marry the villain at the end of the play.
    b. A hero and heroine fall in love and get engaged. The play ends with their wedding.
    c. A villain robs the heroine of her inheritance. The hero tries to get her inheritance back, and almost fails, but succeeds at the last minute.
    d. A hero gets thrown into prison for a crime he didn't commit by the villain. The heroine tries to save the hero, but fails.

117. A good title for this passage would be

    a. "An Introduction to Melodrama"
    b. "A History of the Theatre"
    c. "An Exploration of Melodrama's Stock Characters"
    d. "Theatre Audiences"

118. According to the passage, in which century was melodrama popular?

    a. the 1900s
    b. the 1800s
    c. the 21st century
    d. the 20th century

119. If the article continued, what would the author discuss next?

    a. melodrama's stock characters
    b. another form of theatre
    c. American movies and tv shows
    d. modern day versions of melodrama

120. A typical melodrama audience member would likely have included

    a. the queen
    b. a wealthy landowner
    c. a maid
    d. a nobleman

Questions 121 - 128 refer to the passage below.

Oh, Michael! A squeezing, wrenching, grasping, scraping, clutching, covetous, old sinner! Hard and sharp as flint, from which no steel had ever struck out generous fire. The cold within him froze his old features, nipped his pointed nose, shrivelled his cheek, stiffened his gait; made his eyes red, his thin lips blue; and spoke out shrewdly in his grating voice. A frosty ice was on his head, and on his eyebrows, and his wiry chin. He carried his own low temperature always about with him; he iced his office in the summer; and didn't thaw it one degree at Christmas.

External heat and cold had little influence on Michael. No warmth could warm, no wintry weather chill him. No wind that blew was bitterer than he, no falling snow was more intent upon its purpose, no pelting rain less open to entreaty. Foul weather didn't know where to have him.

Nobody ever stopped him in the street to say, with gladsome looks, "My dear Michael, how are you? When will you come to see me?" No beggars implored him to bestow a trifle, no children asked him what it was o'clock, no man or woman ever once in all his life inquired the way to such-and-such a place. Even the blind men's dogs appeared to know him, and when they saw him coming on, would tug their owners into doorways and then wag their tails as though they said, "No eye at all is better than an evil eye, dark master!"

121. In describing Michael as "sharp as flint," the author is utilizing which literary technique?

   a. personification
   b. simile
   c. irony
   d. foreshadow

122. What does the author mean when he says, "he iced his office in the summer"?

   a. Michael turned off the heat in his office on cold days.
   b. Michael did not like the warmth.
   c. Michael's office was "cold" simply because of Michael's presence.
   d. Michael brought ice into his office to keep it cold.

123. According to the passage, people avoided Michael because

   a. he was wealthy
   b. his actions were harsh
   c. he avoided all people
   d. he was blind

124. Based on the description of Michael in the passage, one can assume

   a. Michael was as changeable as the weather.
   b. Michael hated summer.
   c. Michael wished he were different.
   d. Michael was determined and set in his ways.

125. What is the author's purpose in this passage?

   a. to introduce the character of Michael
   b. to describe the setting in which the story takes place
   c. to foreshadow an action
   d. to resolve a conflict

126. Michael is like the weather in all ways EXCEPT

   a. he is colder
   b. he is harsher
   c. he is more determined
   d. he is more bountiful

127. When the dogs of the blind men wag their tails as if to say, "No eye at all is better than an evil eye, dark master!" who might the "dark master" they are referring to be?

   a. Michael
   b. a beggar
   c. the devil
   d. a character we have not yet met

128. From whose point of view is this story told?

   a. a friend of Michael's
   b. Michael himself
   c. a beggar's
   d. someone who is familiar with Michael's habits

Questions 129 – 136 refer to the passage below.

The peacock mantis shrimp is arguably one of the most compelling and beautiful sea creatures known to man. This hard-shelled creature is difficult to miss: its multicolored shell is bursting with vibrant reds, oranges, greens, and blues. A pair of eyes, each moving independently of the other, protrude from its head. Although these eyes may look primitive, they are more complex than they seem. While the human eye has only three color-receptive cones (red, green, and blue), the mantis shrimp has sixteen. This means that it can see colors, including ultraviolet light, that humans cannot even imagine.

Typically measuring only two to seven inches in length, the peacock mantis shrimp may seem <u>innocuous</u> at first glance. However, it is a fierce predator, with the ability to strike prey with its clubs at a speed of 50 miles per hour – the fastest strike of any animal! This extraordinary speed allows the peacock mantis shrimp to break the shell of its prey with only one punch. Even more unbelievably, this quick strike produces superheated pockets of air which cause an implosion of light, sound, and heat, typically killing or disabling prey.

Remarkably, the peacock mantis shrimp does not get injured while hitting its prey. This is mainly due to the composition of its resilient clubs. These clubs are being closely studied by engineers and scientists, who are using what they learn to improve soldiers' body armor.

129. How many color-receptive cones does a mantis shrimp have?

   a. 3
   b. 2
   c. 7
   d. 16

130. Why do you think the word peacock is used in the name "peacock mantis shrimp"?

   a. because the shrimp is distinctly related to peacocks
   b. because the shrimp can see so many different colors
   c. because of the shrimp's colorful exterior
   d. because peacocks are also aggressive predators

131. As it is used in the passage, <u>innocuous</u> most nearly means

   a. strong
   b. harmless
   c. aggressive
   d. friendly

132. It can reasonably be inferred that the "implosion of light, sound, and heat" produced when the peacock mantis shrimp strikes prey

   a. injures the peacock mantis shrimp
   b. scares away other animals
   c. stuns or injures the prey
   d. is the only reason the peacock mantis shrimp is so powerful

133. You would expect to find the kind of information in this passage in a

   a. newspaper editorial
   b. college microbiology textbook
   c. scientific research paper
   d. online science magazine

134. Why do you think the author included the detail about the shrimp's size?

   a. to illustrate why the shrimp may not look dangerous at first
   b. to help the reader identify the shrimp in the wild
   c. to explain how shrimp are classified
   d. to explain why the shrimp is dangerous

135. What is the author's attitude toward the peacock mantis shrimp?

   a. neutral
   b. critical
   c. admiring
   d. sympathetic

136. What do you think the author will write about in the next paragraph?

   a. a description of another type of shrimp
   b. an explanation of what scientists are learning about the shrimp's body armor
   c. an analysis of the shrimp's strike
   d. a description of a different scientific discovery

Questions 137 - 144 refer to the passage below.

Almost all languages, from English to Mandarin, form naturally over thousands of years. One notable exception is Esperanto, a language invented by Dr. Ludovik Lazarus Zamenhof in 1887. Zamenhof created Esperanto because he felt that many misunderstandings between different countries and cultures were caused by the inability to communicate through a shared language. Despite his concern, Zamenhof had no desire to <u>eradicate</u> native languages such as English or Mandarin; in fact, he felt that native languages were necessary to preserve culture. Therefore, he envisioned that Esparento would be used as a second language by people throughout the world. This would facilitate communication between different countries and, he hoped, ultimately achieve world peace.

Since Esperanto is a constructed language, Zamenhof was able to purposefully design it to be easy to learn and speak. In fact, studies have shown that Esperanto can be learned up to 20 times faster than many native languages! Esperanto has only 16 grammatical rules, unlike the hundreds of grammatical rules found in the English language. Esparanto's words are also easy to spell and pronounce, as they follow regular phonetic spelling patterns. For example, in Esperanto, all nouns end in -o, adverbs end in -e, and adjectives end in -a.

Zamenholf hoped that Esperanto would become <u>ubiquitous</u>. Although Esperanto hasn't become as widespread as he had hoped, it's estimated that up to two million people speak Esperanto today.

137. A good title for this passage would be

  a. "Interesting World Languages"
  b. "How to Learn Esperanto"
  c. "What is Esperanto?"
  d. "The Superiority of Native Languages"

138. As it is used in the passage, <u>eradicate</u> most closely means

  a. maintain
  b. destroy
  c. share
  d. sell

139. How is Esperanto different from other languages?

  a. It's harder to learn.
  b. It's spoken more widely.
  c. It's very similar to other languages.
  d. It's not a native language.

140. According to the information provided in the passage, so far, has Esperanto achieved Zamenhof's original goals?

  a. Yes, Esperanto has become a universal second language.
  b. Yes, Esperanto is now used to foster discussions of world peace.
  c. No, Esperanto has not yet achieved Zamenhof's goals of universal usage or world peace.
  d. No, Esperanto has not achieved its goal of world peace, but it has become a universal second language.

141. Based on its usage of the passage, what is the meaning of the word <u>ubiquitous</u>?

  a. omnipresent
  b. used
  c. well-received
  d. respected

142. Why is Esperanto easy to learn?

  a. It has fewer words to learn to spell.
  b. It has fewer grammatical rules and consistent spelling rules.
  c. It is similar to other widely spoken languages.
  d. It has fewer pronunciation rules.

143. What problem did Zamenhof notice that caused him to create Esperanto?

   a. Different languages made it difficult to travel.
   b. Native languages were all too complicated.
   c. Native languages took too long to learn.
   d. People miscommunicated because they spoke different languages.

144. What do you think the next paragraph will focus on?

   a. other invented languages
   b. Zamenhof's successes in making Esperanto widespread
   c. the downsides to learning a new language
   d. how Esperanto is being used in the modern day

Questions 145 - 152 refer to the passage below.

When the party entered the room, it consisted of only five: Mr. Bingley, his two sisters, the husband of the eldest, and another young man.

Mr. Bingley was good-looking and gentlemanlike; he had a pleasant countenance, and easy, unaffected manners. His sisters were fine women, with an air of decided fashion. His brother-in-law, Mr. Hurst, merely looked the gentleman; but his friend Mr. Darcy soon drew the attention of the room by his fine, tall person, handsome features, noble appearance, and the report of his having ten thousand a year. The gentlemen pronounced him to be a fine figure of a man, the ladies declared he was much handsomer than Mr. Bingley, and he was looked at with great admiration for about half the evening, till his manners gave a disgust which turned the tide of his popularity; for he was discovered to be proud, to be above his company, and above being pleased; and his large estate in Derbyshire could then not save him from having a most forbidding, disagreeable countenance, and being unworthy to be compared with his friend.

Mr. Bingley had soon made himself acquainted with all the principle people in the room; he was lively and unreserved, danced every dance, was angry that the ball closed so early, and talked of giving one himself at Netherfield. Such amiable qualities must speak for themselves. What a contrast between him and his friend!

145. What is the name of the other young man mentioned in the first line of the passage?

 a. Mr. Hurst
 b. Mr. Bingley
 c. Mr. Darcy
 d. Mr. Bennett

146. Which of the following best characterizes Mr. Bingley?

 a. He is charming and polite but reserved in his interactions with others.
 b. He is conceited and believes he's the most important guest.
 c. He is uncomfortable in large group settings.
 d. He has a friendly demeanor and enjoys being around other people.

147. What type of narration is used?

 a. first person
 b. second person
 c. third person
 d. both second and third person

148. The room's reaction to Mr. Darcy changed drastically from admiration at the start of the evening to passionate dislike by the end of the evening. This dramatic change in situation is best described as

 a. ironic
 b. metaphoric
 c. symbolic
 d. poetic

149. The setting of this story is likely

 a. an elegant room filled with wealthy people.
 b. a small apartment of close friends.
 c. an assembly room in a high school.
 d. an outdoor party with people from the local community.

150. Which of the following is likely to occur next?

 a. Mr. Darcy will dance with many women in the room.
 b. Mr. Bingley will organize a dance at his own estate.
 c. Mr. Darcy will be asked to leave the party.
 d. Mr. Bingley quarreled with the hosts of the party for ending it early.

151. Which of the following occurred when Mr. Darcy entered the room?

   a. Guests distrusted him.
   b. His appearance was preferred to Mr. Bingley's.
   c. The men were jealous of the attention he received.
   d. Guests believed he was conceited.

152. What does Mr. Darcy's "having ten thousand a year" indicate?

   a. He is impoverished and guests are sympathetic.
   b. He is struggling financially and deserves the guests' assistance.
   c. He is middle class and on equal terms with the guests.
   d. He is quite wealthy and thus admired.

Vocabulary

Instructions: Choose the word that means the same, or about the same, as the underlined word.

153. A genuine person

   a. kind
   b. authentic
   c. friendly
   d. realistic

154. To lack tact

   a. sensitivity
   b. worry
   c. aggressiveness
   d. friendliness

155. A corrupt politician

   a. candid
   b. unethical
   c. unhappy
   d. angry

156. An antique armoire

   a. pen
   b. necklace
   c. instrument
   d. wardrobe

157. The detrimental decision

   a. harmful
   b. unapologetic
   c. contentious
   d. uneasy

158. Optimum conditions

   a. good
   b. optional
   c. ideal
   d. poor

159. To condone behavior

   a. clarify
   b. condemn
   c. applaud
   d. excuse

160. To show poise

   a. happiness
   b. grace
   c. maturity
   d. emotion

161. The argumentative man

   a. sad
   b. combative
   c. insincere
   d. impoverished

162. To endorse a candidate

   a. defraud
   b. listen to
   c. dislike
   d. support

163. The biased article

   a. objective
   b. supportive
   c. partisan
   d. negative

164. The composed woman

   a. musical
   b. calm
   c. forthright
   d. anxious

165. To obstruct progress

   a. support
   b. slow
   c. block
   d. enable

166. The odious statement

   a. important
   b. unlikely
   c. tragic
   d. despicable

167. To bring <u>reproach</u>

a. unhappiness
b. encouragement
c. disagreement
d. dishonor

168. The <u>pensive</u> man

a. beautiful
b. temperamental
c. bashful
d. thoughtful

169. The <u>brusque</u> response

a. abrupt
b. mean
c. flowery
d. sanguine

170. To <u>blatantly</u> lie

a. sneakily
b. flagrantly
c. reluctantly
d. easily

171. The <u>eminent</u> scholar

a. distinguished
b. notorious
c. brilliant
d. interested

172. The <u>pungent</u> odor

a. disgusting
b. subtle
c. strong
d. sweet

173. To <u>shirk</u> responsibility

a. welcome
b. share
c. avoid
d. covet

174. The <u>astute</u> teacher

a. friendly
b. incredulous
c. perceptive
d. flustered

Math Section 3

64 Questions, 45 Minutes

Instructions: Select the best answer.

175. Which of the following are reciprocals?

   a. 1, 2
   b. $\frac{3}{4}, \frac{4}{3}$
   c. -4, 4
   d. $\frac{1}{2}, 1$

176. What is $\frac{1}{4}$ of 24 minus 10?

   a. 6
   b. -8
   c. -4
   d. 2

177. Which property states that a number plus zero equals itself?

   a. the associative property
   b. the identity property
   c. the distributive property
   d. the commutative property

178. What is the value of the number 8 in this number: 386,912?

   a. 8,000
   b. 800
   c. 800,000
   d. 80,000

179. The product of a number and its double is 72. What is the number?

   a. 3
   b. 4
   c. 6
   d. 7

180. A 45° angle is

   a. right
   b. acute
   c. obtuse
   d. straight

181. 412 × 36

   a. 14, 832
   b. 3,708
   c. 15, 732
   d. 37,080

182. Which of the following pairs of consecutive even integers adds up to 14?

   a. 7, 7
   b. 4, 6
   c. 6, 8
   d. 0, 14

183. 8 is 3 less than 20% of what number?

   a. 11
   b. 55
   c. 5
   d. 20

184. 4 meters and 34 centimeters
   - 2 meters and 39 centimeters

   a. 1 meter and 95 centimeters
   b. 2 meters and 5 centimeters
   c. 4 meters and 15 centimeters
   d. 6 meters and 73 centimeters

185. What is 4.37902 x 10^6 in standard notation?

   a. 4,379,020
   b. 437,902
   c. 43,792
   d. 43,790,200

186. What is the base of a triangle with area 24 and height 4?

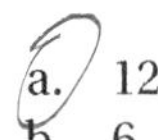
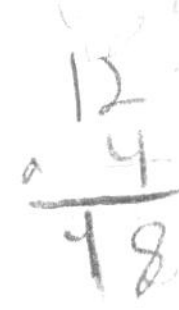

a. 12
b. 6
c. 48
d. 28

187. Solve: 14 + (-8) - 7 + (-9) + 6

a. 4
b. 12
c. -3
d. -4

188. The lines below are

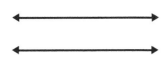

a. perpendicular
b. parallel
c. intersecting
d. line segments

189. Examine the two views of the solid shape shown below. What could the shape be?

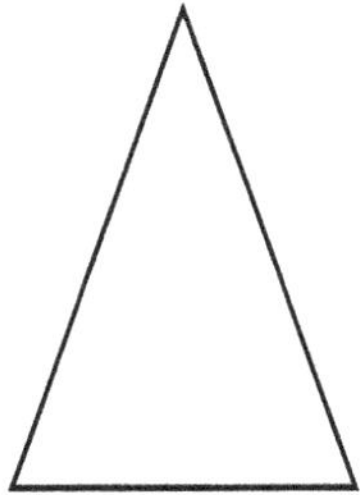

a. triangular pyramid
b. square pyramid
c. square prism
d. cone

190. Round .34567 to the thousandth place.

a. .3457
b. .345
c. .346
d. .3456

191. Convert .84 into a fraction.

a. $\frac{19}{20}$
b. $\frac{17}{20}$
c. $\frac{18}{25}$
d. $\frac{21}{25}$

192. A survey was taken at Middletown Elementary School to determine which musical instrument students were most interested in learning. If there are 200 students at the school, how many more students preferred piano over violin?

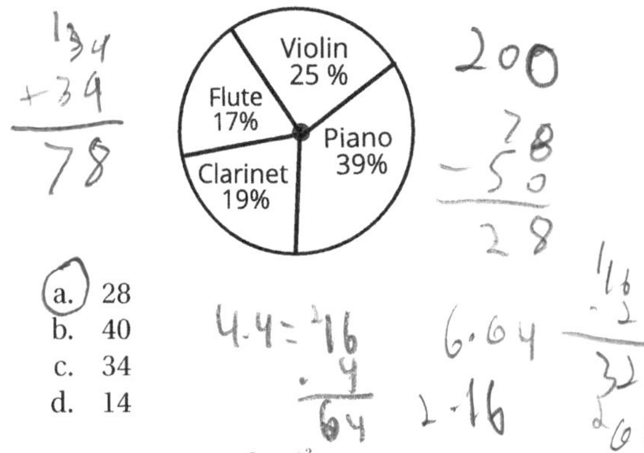

a. 28
b. 40
c. 34
d. 14

193. Find the value of: $\frac{6 \times 4^3}{2 \times 4^2}$

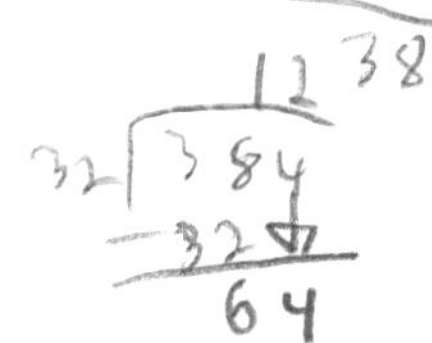

a. 24
b. 12
c. 6
d. 3

194. Dean practiced his free throws all weekend before the basketball team tryout. At the end of the weekend, Dean calculated that 89% of the free throws he shot were successful. If Dean successfully made 267 free throws, how many total free throws did he attempt?

a. 280
b. 300
c. 320
d. 330

195. Sean took his Algebra 1 final, which had a total of 175 questions on it. If Sean answered 27 questions incorrectly, what percentage of questions did he answer correctly? Round to the nearest tenth of a percent.

a. 15.4%
b. 72.4%
c. 84.5%
d. 84.6%

196. Solve for x: |-5 - 7| + x = 9

a. -3
b. 21
c. 11
d. -7

197. Solve: $\frac{5}{3} + \frac{5}{8}$

a. $\frac{10}{11}$
b. $\frac{55}{24}$
c. $\frac{5}{11}$
d. $\frac{25}{24}$

198. If $\frac{2}{3}x = 12$, what does x - 4 equal?

a. 14
b. 18
c. 8
d. 4

199. Savannah's car uses 13.6 gallons of gas for a 248 mile trip. To the nearest hundredth, how miles per gallon does Savannah's car use?

a. 19.00
b. 19.45
c. 18.37
d. 18.24

200. Solve: $\sqrt{81} - 5 \times 3 =$

a. 66
b. -6
c. -8
d. 24

201. Lyndsey is painting a wall in her bedroom. The width of the wall is 12 feet and the height of the wall is 9 feet. How many square feet will she be painting?

a. 96 sq. feet
b. 42 sq. feet
c. 48 sq. feet
d. 108 sq. feet

202. What is the perimeter of an equilateral triangle with a base of 8?

a. 64
b. 16
c. 24
d. 32

203. At a car dealership, three salesman each sold an average of 14 cars in one week. A fourth salesman sold 22 cars in one week. What is the average number of cars sold by all four salesmen in one week?

a. 14
b. 15
c. 20
d. 16

204. 3 gallons, 2 quarts, 3 pints
- 2 gallons, 3 quarts, 1 pint

a. 1 gallon, 3 quarts, 2 pints
b. 3 quarts, 2 pints
c. 1 gallon, 1 quart, 2 pints
d. 2 quarts, 2 pints

205. In two weeks, Lucy drove 1,568 miles. On average, how many miles did she drive each day?

a. 112
b. 115
c. 123
d. 142

206. Kelsey arrived at her dance competition at 8:35 AM. She stayed until the competition finished at 4:45 PM. How long was she at the competition?

a. 8 hours and 50 minutes
b. 9 hours and 10 minutes
c. 7 hours and 50 minutes
d. 8 hours and 10 minutes

207. In the parallelogram below, which lines are parallel?

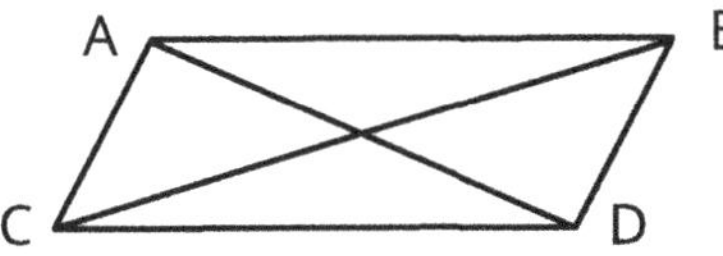

a. AC and BD
b. AB and AD
c. CB and AD
d. CD and BD

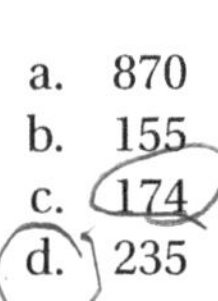

208. Everytown Elementary school made $2,145 from a bake sale. Each bakery item cost $3 for students and $5 for non-students. If 425 bakery items were sold to students, how many were sold to non-students?

a. 870
b. 155
c. 174
d. 235

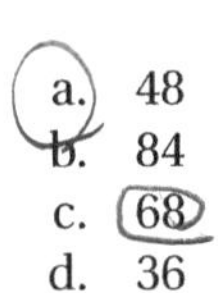

209. The ratio of adults to children that live in a neighborhood is 3:4. If there are 36 adults in the neighborhood, how many people live in the neighborhood total?

a. 48
b. 84
c. 68
d. 36

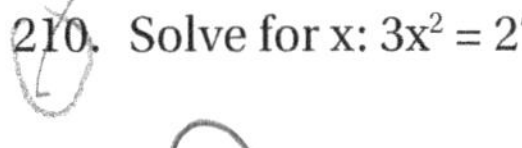

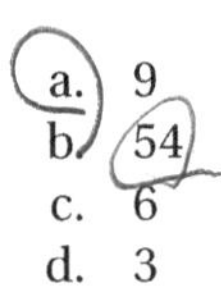

210. Solve for x: $3x^2 = 27$

a. 9
b. 54
c. 6
d. 3

211. Five basketball players score 5, 1, 8, 15, and 6 points in a game. What was the average number of points scored per player in the game?

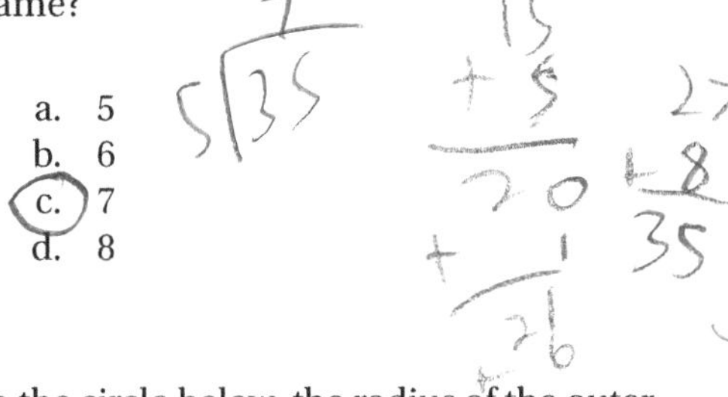

a. 5
b. 6
c. 7
d. 8

212. In the circle below, the radius of the outer circle is 8 and the radius of the inner circle is 5. What is the area of the shaded region in terms of π?

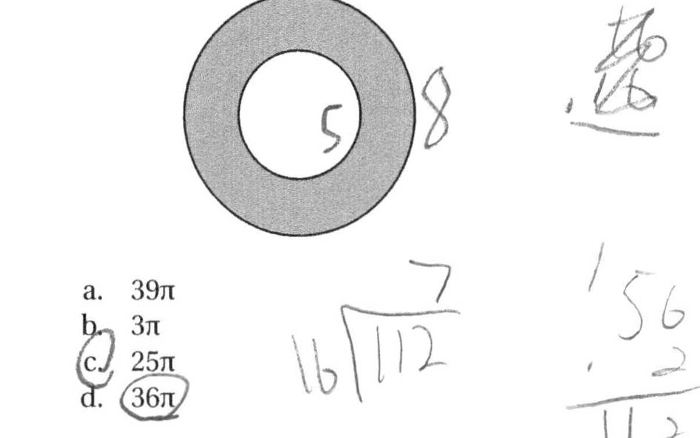

a. 39π
b. 3π
c. 25π
d. 36π

213. Carter is baking cupcakes for his brother's graduation party. He uses 2 cups of sugar for every 16 cupcakes. How much sugar does Carter need to bake 56 cupcakes?

a. 6.5
b. 8
c. 7.5
d. 7

214. Darius bought a $80 pair of shoes on sale for $52. What percent discount did he receive on the shoes?

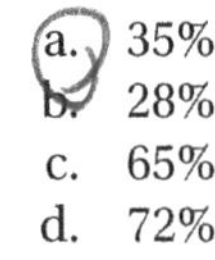

a. 35%
b. 28%
c. 65%
d. 72%

215. Rhiannon put her hand into a jar with 3 quarters, 4 dimes, and 2 nickels. If she pulled out one coin at random, what is the probability it would be a quarter?

a. 2/9
b. 1/3
c. 3/4
d. 1/2

216. Solve: $2x - 4 < 8$.

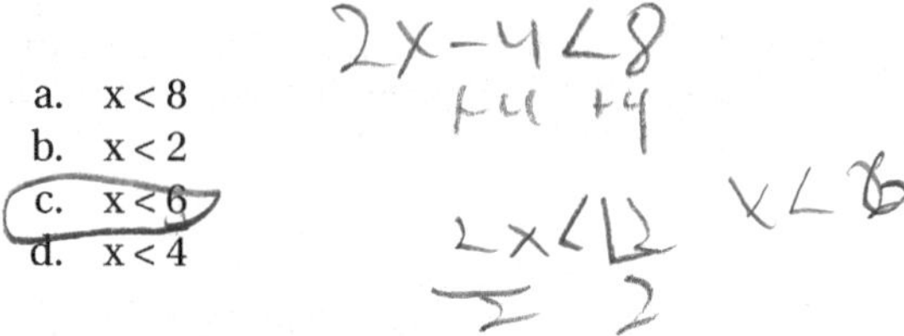

a. $x < 8$
b. $x < 2$
c. $x < 6$
d. $x < 4$

217. How many prime numbers are between 4 and 16?

a. 2
b. 3
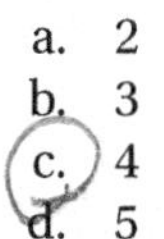
c. 4
d. 5

218. In the equation below, if $x = 3$ and $y = -1$, what is z?

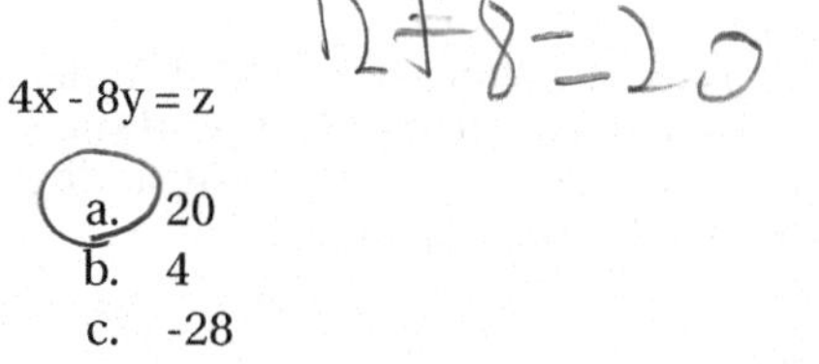

$4x - 8y = z$

a. 20
b. 4
c. -28
d. -4

219. If angle B is congruent to angle C, what is the measure of angle C?

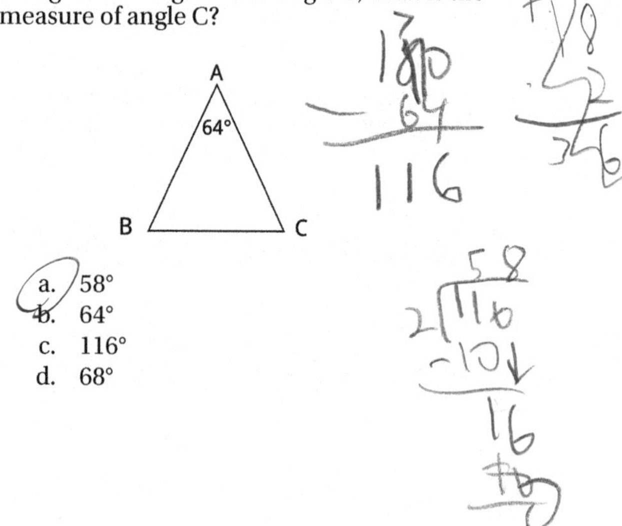

a. 58°
b. 64°
c. 116°
d. 68°

220. Taylor is painting the attic. Two of the walls each measure 117 square feet and the other two each measure 105 square feet. One gallon of paint will cover 400 square feet. How many gallons of paint does Taylor need to purchase to paint the attic?

a. 1 gallon
b. 2 gallons
c. 3 gallons
d. 4 gallons

221. Dan owns a large, rectangular painting that has a width of 35 inches and length of 74 inches. He has a smaller copy of it printed so that the width of the reduced portrait is 4.2 inches. What is the length of the reduced portrait? Round to the nearest tenth.

a. 8.3 inches
b. 8.8 inches
c. 8.9 inches
d. 17.6 inches

222. A piece of chocolate cake weighs 8.67 ounces. If 61% of the weight of the cake is due to flour, how many ounces of flour are in the piece of cake? Round to the nearest hundredth.

a. 4.89 ounces
b. 5.03 ounces
c. 5.28 ounces
d. 5.29 ounces

223. What is the measure of angle A?

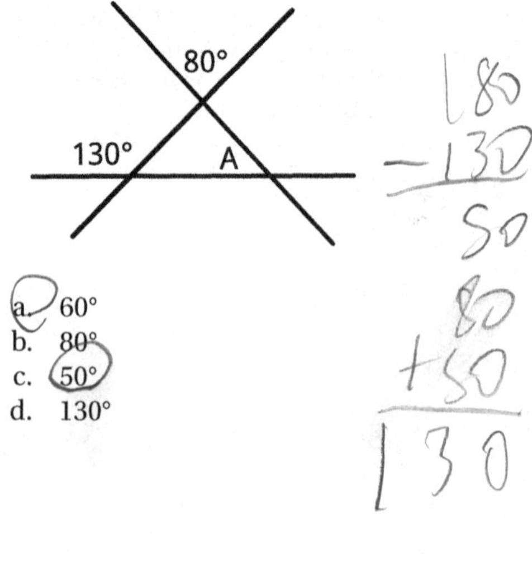

a. 60°
b. 80°
c. 50°
d. 130°

224. How old am I if 120 minus four times my age is 36?

a. 20
b. 21
c. 32
d. 34

225. What is the area of the figure below?

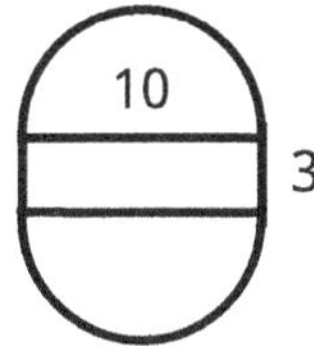

a. $30 + 100\pi$
b. $26 + 25\pi$
c. $26 + 10\pi$
d. $30 + 25\pi$

226. Examine the rectangle below. The rectangle is divided into

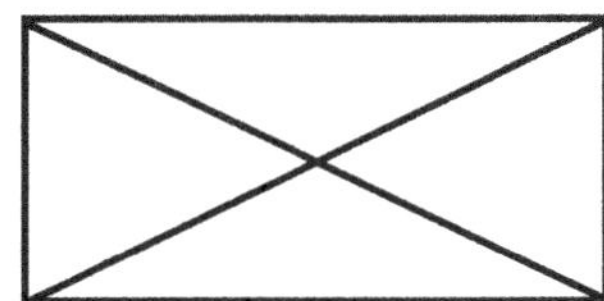

a. two acute triangles and two obtuse triangles.
b. two right triangles and two acute triangles.
c. two right triangles and two obtuse triangles.
d. four acute triangles.

227. How many inches are in 4.84 yards?

a. 36 in
b. 116.16 in
c. 145.2 in
d. 174.24 in

228. The table below shows how many pets were purchased at a pet store over the course of three months.

	April	**May**	**June**
Cats	16	25	19
Dogs	24	20	36
Rabbits	8	5	6
TOTAL	48	50	61

In May, what percent of the animals purchased were NOT dogs?

a. 30%
b. 40%
c. 50%
d. 60%

229. Solve for c: $4 - 2c = 10$

a. 3
b. 7
c. -2
d. -3

230. Which of the following values for x satisfies the following inequality: $2x - 7 < 9$

a. $x < 16$
b. $x < 1$
c. $x < 8$
d. $x > 2$

231. What is the volume of a rectangular prism with height 3 inches, width 7 inches, and depth 2 inches?

a. 21 in^3
b. 42 in^3
c. 12 in^3
d. 36 in^3

232. While on vacation in Australia, Alyssa noticed that one liter of gas cost $1.40 Australian dollars (AUD). How much would one gallon of gas cost in Australian dollars? Assume 1 gallon = 3.79 liters.

a. $5.31 AUD
b. $5.53 AUD
c. $0.35 AUD
d. $0.39 AUD

233. Southtown High School's average daily attendance for six years is tracked in the chart below.

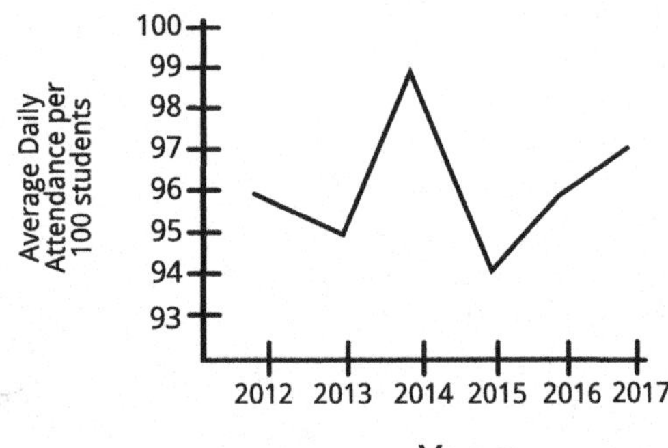

If there are 500 students in the school, on average, how many students attended class each day in 2013?

a. 94
b. 480
c. 95
d. 475

234. Alexi takes the bus from Townsville to Cityville. He leaves Townsville at 11:30 AM and arrives at Cityville at 2:00 PM. If the bus is traveling 54 mph for the entire trip, how far away are the cities from each other?

a. 108 miles
b. 124 miles
c. 135 miles
d. 189 miles

235. ABDC is a square with side 6. What is the area of triangle ACD?

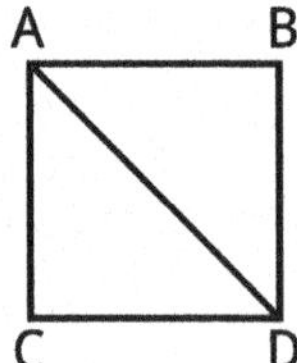

a. 6
b. 12
c. 18
d. 36

236. What is the median of the following group of numbers?

4, 2, 1, 6, 12, 10, 12, 8

a. 6
b. 7
c. 8
d. 12

237. Nell earned $670.56 at her summer job. She earned an additional $325 for watching her little brother. If she spent $156.75 on gas and travel expenses, how much money does Nell have at the end of the summer?

a. $837.71
b. $1,152.31
c. $838.81
d. $948.23

238. Solve for x: $\frac{4}{3}x = \frac{5}{8}$

a. $\frac{15}{32}$
b. $\frac{5}{6}$
c. $\frac{6}{5}$
d. $\frac{1}{2}$

Language Section 3

60 Questions, 25 Minutes

Usage and Mechanics

Instructions: For questions 239-278, check the sentences for errors of usage, capitalization, or punctuation. If there is no error, choose D.

239.

a. Daniel looked at the dreary sky through his office window.
b. Jacqueline was the faster runner of the four sisters.
c. John's mother allows him only one hour of screen time per day.
d. No mistakes.

240.

a. Corey can run a six-minute mile!
b. Marissa wants to by a new dress for the upcoming dance.
c. When all was said and done, Chris was just happy to be home.
d. No mistakes.

241.

a. You have the option of beef, chicken, or fish for dinner at the wedding reception.
b. Aunt Magda makes delicious soup whenever one of her family members isn't feeling well.
c. "Remember to bring your permission slip for the field trip back by Thursday!" Ms. Kim exclaimed.
d. No mistakes.

242.

a. Its expected to rain every day this week.
b. Amanda loves to play her saxophone with the jazz band.
c. Michael hosts a game night for his friends every Thursday.
d. No mistakes.

243.

a. Michelle loves to paint and sculpt in her free time.
b. The sidewalks were especially slick once the snow started to melt.
c. Christina carried less boxes into the garage than Anthony did.
d. No mistakes.

244.

a. Since Jude stays up until 1:00 am every night, it is no wonder that he can barely stay awake during first period math.
b. Madison and Samantha always choose each other as partners when our teacher assigns group projects.
c. All of my older siblings studied French in school, but I am more interested in learning German.
d. No mistakes.

245.

a. "I'm thinking of painting my room this weekend," Brian said.
b. "You just don't get it," Tia muttered sullenly.
c. The boys has taken out the trash.
d. No mistakes.

246.

a. Chris loves to ride the roller coasters with the highest drops.
b. Sandra loves to go to the zoo and see the red pandas.
c. Their isn't any milk left in the carton.
d. No mistakes.

247.

a. Mr. Harmon my biology teacher wrote a very nice letter of recommendation for my college applications.

b. I'm looking forward to some much needed rest and relaxation during my vacation next week.

c. Please lay the blanket over the bed.

d. No mistakes.

248.

a. The ripped-up swimmer's towel was left by the side of the pool.

b. You must proceed with caution when driving during a winter storm.

c. Travis volunteered at the local food bank every weekend.

d. No mistakes.

249.

a. Worst fear: a swarm of bees flying towards her.

b. Some cicada species only appear once every seventeen years!

c. Ilana loves when the monarch butterflies flutter through her garden every spring.

d. No mistakes.

250.

a. Maria is extremely excited to be starting high school next year.

b. "Please pick up some orange juice when you go to the grocery store, said Malcolm.

c. The Internal Revenue Service, or IRS, is responsible for collecting taxes.

d. No mistakes.

251.

a. My new shoes make me feel like I can run one hundred miles per hour!

b. On a day like today, all I want to do is sit on the couch with my dog and watch television.

c. After hours of painstaking work, Melia finally finished her science fair project.

d. No mistakes.

252.

a. It was so warm in the classroom that Mr. Jones had five fans blowing at once.

b. Katie didn't think she could do it, but she successfully ran a marathon this weekend.

c. May I please go to the concert with my friends Friday night.

d. No mistakes.

253.

a. That was the most exciting football game I have ever seen!

b. Mariel is a voracious reader who will sometimes read multiple novels in one weekend.

c. Him and my sister will be getting married on Saturday.

d. No mistakes.

254.

a. My brother shouted, "You better be in the car by 4:30 or I'm leaving without you"!

b. Janet loved to plan out elaborate group costumes for herself and her friends to wear on Halloween.

c. Andrew's iron unexpectedly broke, so he was forced to go to work wearing a very wrinkled shirt.

d. No mistakes.

255.

a. Morgan was dismayed to find that his laptop battery died just as his three-hour train ride began.

b. Spinning through the air and sticking the landing, the crowd gave the gymnast a standing ovation.

c. A rainbow appeared as the destructive storm dissipated.

d. No mistakes.

256.

a. Stephanie always double checks that she unplugged her hair straightener before she leaves the house.
b. Apples are a healthy and delicious snack.
c. I was suppose to turn in the assignment on Tuesday, but I forgot to do so.
d. No mistakes.

257.

a. Mike has a signature dance that he came up with all on his own.
b. Oliver was less than amused when his alarm clock went off at 4:30 am.
c. Coffee and tea are Pablo's favorite beverages.
d. No mistakes.

258.

a. I can't believe it's already March!
b. The weather, which jumped up forty degrees in one day, was very unpredictable.
c. Susans dog loves taking long walks around the neighborhood.
d. No mistakes.

259.

a. Carolyn loves gardening and has the largest garden in her neighborhood.
b. My favorite classes are history and english.
c. The speaker's microphone stopped working during the presentation.
d. No mistakes.

260.

a. The books' in the library were falling apart.
b. Can you tell me where LaGuardia International Airport is?
c. They're going to the Chicago Bulls basketball game on Saturday night.
d. No mistakes.

261.

a. My teacher shouted, "Don't run in the hallways!"
b. I've never seen no one go to the library during recess.
c. Who wants to go to George's party with me?
d. No mistakes.

262.

a. I try not to let my fear of spiders affect me.
b. It's easier to get everyone to study for a test if the teacher hands out a study guide.
c. Their always going to the beach on the weekends.
d. No mistakes.

263.

a. Even though everyone got his or her ticket for free, no one went to the movie.
b. My class goes on a field trip to Central Park every spring.
c. My mom was born in Denver Colorado.
d. No mistakes.

264.

a. Although Tiana was one of the youngest students, she was the fastest runner in the school.
b. "I wish summer break were longer," Heath sighing.
c. If I had studied more for the test, I could have gotten an A.
d. No mistakes.

265.

a. Even though they hated the cold, the boys dove into the freezing lake.
b. My cousins live South of us, and we take a road trip to visit them each year.
c. Mariska's dog happily ate its bone.
d. No mistakes.

266.

a. Ice skating is my favorite thing to watch in the Winter Olympics.

b. Reagan won the poetry competition because she was the most creative writer.

c. "There are several strains of the flu going around this year, " the scientist said.

d. No mistakes.

267.

a. EJ has the same amount of toys as Kumar.

b. To whom should I address this letter?

c. I want to visit three countries in Europe: Italy, France, and Spain.

d. No mistakes.

268.

a. Before my trip I still need to pack my clothes shoes, and games.

b. Every Fourth of July I go to see the fireworks with my friends.

c. Why don't you go to school early to ask Mr. Cruz for help?

d. No mistakes.

269.

a. Annie's preparing for her spring break trip to Kenya.

b. I was to scared to go into the haunted house.

c. The action movie's special effects were incredible.

d. No mistakes.

270.

a. Where do you go to high school, Landon?

b. Carmen, who was a bridesmaid in her sister's wedding, went to the store to buy a bridesmaid dress.

c. Chandra was the oldest of the three sisters'.

d. No mistakes.

271.

a. Among our group of friends, I'm the quietest.

b. Since I had only eight things in my cart, I was able to go to the check out line for shoppers with fewer than ten items..

c. "Ouch!" Emily exclaimed after she stubbed her toe.

d. No mistakes.

272.

a. "Maybe you can come to the library with me," I suggested "so we have a quiet place to study."

b. Have you ever seen the stars in the woods at night?

c. His favorite parts of summer camp were hiking, roasting marshmallows, and making new friends.

d. No mistakes.

273.

a. Please accept this gift as a token of my appreciation.

b. After making a touchdown in the last few seconds of the game, the crowd cheered for the football player.

c. The speeding police car turned on its siren.

d. No mistakes.

274.

a. Smiling, I handed the little girl an ice cream cone.

b. From a distance it looked like the silver skyscraper was the taller building in the city.

c. "Michael, eat your dinner," my mother prompted.

d. No mistakes.

275.

a. The Stegosaurus had plates on its back for protection.

b. Although I typically love Thai food, I'm not in the mood for it tonight.

c. Yellowstone national park is one of my favorite places.

d. No mistakes.

276.

a. For the first day of school, I need: books, pens, and pencils.

b. Barbara always wanted to be a flight attendant.

c. Although I'd prefer not to, the doctor told me I need to lie down and rest for the next few days.

d. No mistakes.

277.

a. After school we are going to go to the library to study for our English test.

b. My sister's cat is the sweetest animal I've ever known.

c. The principal gave Maya and I an award for our science fair project.

d. No mistakes.

278.

a. The winter thunderstorm was one of the strangest things I've ever saw.

b. Tobias asked, "Why don't you want to watch the movie?"

c. Unfortunately, it was too cold to go to the beach last Saturday.

d. No mistakes.

Spelling

Directions: For questions 279-288, look for errors in spelling. If there is no error, choose D.

279.

a. Can you sumit your application as soon as possible?

b. I sincerely hope you apologized.

c. I have not received any directions, yet.

d. No mistakes.

280.

a. Unfortunately, I have eaten enough dessert for all of us.

b. Alot of students are upset that Mr. Fair will retire this year.

c. Treason is a particularly grave crime with severe punishment.

d. No mistakes.

281.

a. On December 26th my family in England celebrates Boxing Day.

b. I definiately don't want to run out of gas on this dark, country road.

c. The cake tasted delicious and didn't have too many calories or saturated fats.

d. No mistakes.

282.

a. I wouldn't expect that Sharese would treat you differently after your vacation.

b. Missing the bus has put Kaylee in a bit of a dilemma.

c. The students quickly disappeared once the principal arrived at the restaurant.

d. No mistakes.

283.

a. My uncle is convinced of the existence of aliens.

b. Let's not get into an argument over foreign affairs again.

c. The transtion from middle school to high school can be difficult.

d. No mistakes.

284.

a. The actress on the awards show looked glamorous in her evening gown.

b. I will definitely phone the counselor once I arrive home.

c. Are you familar with this version of Shakespeare's Romeo?

d. No mistakes.

285.

a. I immediatly liked the new student with maroon hair.

b. Knowledge is the only attribute you can bring with you anywhere you go.

c. It's entirely unnecessary for you to call the chaperone; I'm sure they are okay.

d. No mistakes.

286.

a. What possessed you to ask for such an incredibly high raise?

b. Anytime one applies for a job he or she must give references.

c. My dog has a tendency to whine and whimper when he needs to go out.

d. No mistakes.

287.

a. It's challenging when both the president and vice-president are absent from the meeting.

b. I'll be contented whereever life takes me.

c. Cori treated her break-up with Craig as if it were a catastrophe.

d. No mistakes.

288.

a. The officer on patrol confisicated all the materials he found in the trunk.

b. The punishment delivered by Mrs. Butchko was a tad excessive.

c. Going to private school will provide the students with different advantages.

d. No mistakes.

Composition

Directions: For questions 289-298, read the question and select the best answer.

289. Choose the best word to join the thoughts together.

The storm was looming; _______________, we took shelter in our basement.

a. therefore

b. so

c. thus

d. again

290. Choose the best word to join the thoughts together.

Julien bit his lip; _______________, there was not much blood

a. so

b. because

c. as a result

d. however

291. Choose the group of words that best completes the sentence.

Playing outside, _______________________.

a. is hard to keep warm in the cold.

b. I find it difficult to stay warm in the cold.

c. can be hard to stay warm in the cold.

d. I find that I can not stay warm in the outside.

292. Which of these expresses the idea most clearly?

a. In order to perform well on the exam, the students made sure to attend all of the teacher's study sessions.

b. The students made sure, in order to perform well on the exam, to attend all of the teacher's study sessions.

c. The teacher had study sessions. In order to perform well, the students made sure to attend all of them for the exams

d. In order to perform well on the exam, the students made sure to attend all of his study sessions.

293. Which of these expresses the idea most clearly?

a. Playing with her puppy, she lost track of it.

b. Losing track of time Yesenia playing with her puppy.

c. She lost track of it playing with her puppy.

d. Playing with her puppy, Yesenia lost track of time.

294. Which of these expresses the idea most clearly?

   a. Missing lunch, the sandwich looked delicious.
   b. Because I missed lunch, the sandwich looked delicious.
   c. After missing lunch, the sandwich looked delicious.
   d. The sandwich looked delicious after missing lunch.

295. Which of these sentences fits best under the topic "Service Projects Benefit Everyone"?

   a. Students should complete a minimum of thirty service learning hours by the end of 8th grade.
   b. When I volunteered at the soup kitchen, it felt great knowing I was helping someone else.
   c. The high schools in the United States offer some of the best opportunities for service learning.
   d. My family and I have spent several spring breaks building housing in Uganda.

296. Which of the following topics is best for a one-page essay?

   a. Effective Study Habits for Final Exams
   b. The Great Lakes: Home to Diverse Wildlife
   c. How to Thread a Needle in 30 Seconds
   d. The Long and Short Term Causes of WWI

297. Where should the sentence "Dogs are pack animals and generally enjoy being around other dogs. " be placed in the following paragraph?

(1)A dog park is great place for your dog to exercise, especially if you do not have a large backyard. (2) They can run off leash without the danger of running into the street. (3) Furthermore, parks facilitate socialization of dogs. (4) Dog parks are even a great way for other dog owners to meet.

   a. Before sentence 1
   b. After sentence 1
   c. Between sentences 2 and 3
   d. Between sentence 3 and 4

298. Which sentence does NOT belong in the paragraph?

Veganism is a more extreme version of vegetarianism. (2) Vegans eat or use nothing that is an animal product, whereas a vegetarian will usually eat dairy or consume eggs. (3) Pescatarians are like vegetarians, but they will also eat fish. (4) People choose veganism for a variety of reasons. (5) Most commonly people report being vegan for health, animal welfare, and environmental motives.

   a. 2
   b. 3
   c. 4
   d. 5

Answer Key

Verbal

1. D
2. D
3. C
4. B
5. C
6. A
7. A
8. A
9. B
10. D
11. A
12. B
13. D
14. C
15. C
16. B
17. A
18. B
19. D
20. B
21. A
22. D
23. A
24. C
25. C
26. D
27. D
28. A
29. B
30. B
31. A
32. B
33. C
34. A
35. C
36. C
37. B
38. D
39. B
40. B
41. A
42. C
43. B
44. B
45. D
46. C
47. B
48. B
49. C
50. D
51. A
52. C
53. A
54. C
55. C
56. C
57. A
58. D
59. C
60. D

Quantitative

61. B
62. A
63. C
64. C
65. A
66. B
67. B
68. B
69. A
70. D
71. C
72. C
73. B
74. A
75. D
76. C
77. A
78. D
79. B
80. A
81. C
82. A
83. D
84. D
85. A
86. A
87. D
88. C
89. C
90. C
91. B
92. B
93. C
94. A
95. D
96. B
97. C
98. C
99. B
100. B
101. C
102. C
103. B
104. A
105. B
106. A
107. A
108. C
109. D
110. D
111. D
112. B

Reading

113. B
114. D
115. A
116. C
117. A
118. B
119. D
120. C
121. B
122. C
123. B
124. D
125. A
126. D
127. A
128. D
129. D
130. C
131. B
132. C
133. D
134. A
135. C
136. B
137. C
138. B
139. D
140. C
141. A
142. B
143. D
144. D
145. C
146. D
147. C
148. A
149. A
150. B
151. B
152. D
153. B
154. A
155. B
156. D
157. A
158. C
159. D
160. B
161. B
162. D
163. C
164. B
165. C
166. D
167. D
168. D
169. A
170. B
171. A
172. C
173. C
174. C

Math

175. B
176. C
177. B
178. D
179. C
180. B
181. A
182. C
183. B
184. A
185. A
186. A
187. D
188. B
189. B
190. C
191. D
192. A
193. B
194. B
195. D
196. A
197. B
198. A
199. D
200. B
201. D
202. C
203. D
204. B
205. A
206. D
207. A
208. C
209. B
210. D
211. C
212. A
213. D
214. A
215. B
216. C
217. C
218. A
219. A
220. B
221. C
222. D
223. C
224. B
225. D
226. A
227. D
228. D
229. D
230. C
231. B
232. A
233. D
234. C
235. C
236. B
237. C
238. A

Language

239. B
240. B
241. D
242. A
243. C
244. D
245. C
246. C
247. A
248. A
249. A
250. B
251. D
252. C
253. C
254. A
255. B
256. C
257. D
258. C
259. B
260. A
261. B
262. C
263. C
264. B
265. B
266. D
267. A
268. A
269. B
270. C
271. D
272. A
273. B
274. B
275. C
276. A
277. C
278. A
279. A
280. B
281. B
282. D
283. C
284. C
285. A
286. D
287. B
288. A
289. A
290. D
291. B
292. A
293. D
294. B
295. B
296. A
297. D
298. B

HSPT Test 4

Verbal Section 4

60 Questions, 16 Minutes

Instructions: Select the best answer.

1. Ink is to printer as lead is to

   a. pen
   b. steel
   c. pencil
   d. wood

2. Which word does *not* belong with the others?

   a. officer
   b. general
   c. military
   d. major

3. Kasper eats more vegetables than Marco. Marco eats more vegetables than Simone and Antonio. Simone eats more vegetables than Antonio. If the first two statements are true, the third statement is

   a. true
   b. false
   c. uncertain

4. Which word does *not* belong with the others?

   a. frog
   b. toad
   c. salamander
   d. trout

5. Which word does *not* belong with the others?

   a. go
   b. move
   c. slow down
   d. proceed

6. Counterfeit means the *opposite* of

   a. fake
   b. money
   c. illegal
   d. real

7. Lizzie lives directly south of Darla. Darla lives directly west of Joaquin and Edith. Joaquin lives south of Lizzie. If the first two statements are true, the third statement is

   a. true
   b. false
   c. uncertain

8. The math book is wider than the history book. The history book is narrower than the literature book. The history book is the narrowest book. If the first two statements are true, the third statement is

   a. true
   b. false
   c. uncertain

9. Acquire most nearly means

   a. ask
   b. obtain
   c. tell
   d. object

10. Superficial means the *opposite* of

    a. over
    b. deep
    c. smart
    d. fake

11. Which word does *not* belong with the others?

    a. ice cream
    b. rocky road
    c. vanilla
    d. neapolitan

12. Slide is to playground as rollercoaster is to

    a. water slide
    b. amusement park
    c. ferris wheel
    d. fast

13. Truncate most nearly means

    a. gather
    b. extend
    c. pack
    d. shorten

14. The French Club has fewer members than the Spanish Club and Math Club. The Math Club has more members than the German Club. The French Club has more members than the German Club. If the first two statements are true, the third statement is

    a. true
    b. false
    c. uncertain

15. Which word does *not* belong with the others?

    a. hear
    b. see
    c. whisper
    d. feel

16. Corpulent means the *opposite* of

    a. thin
    b. body
    c. short
    d. bulky

17. Bus is to transport as bucket is to

    a. water
    b. spill
    c. carry
    d. sponge

18. Which word does *not* belong with the others?

    a. valley
    b. mountain
    c. gorge
    d. canyon

19. Diego bowls more strikes than Ahmed. Ahmed bowls more strikes than Keaton. Keaton bowls the least number of strikes. If the first two statements are true, the third statement is

    a. true
    b. false
    c. uncertain

20. Cacophony means the *opposite* of

    a. telephone
    b. quiet
    c. din
    d. loud

21. German is to language as carpet is to

    a. flooring
    b. cloth
    c. ground
    d. soft

22. Cold is to frigid as hot is to

    a. challenging
    b. sweat
    c. sweltering
    d. humid

23. Wrought most nearly means

    a. hammer
    b. dance
    c. made
    d. play

24. Fatima has $0.79. George has $0.25 more than Fatima but $0.13 less than Pavol. Pavol has more money than Fatima. If the first two statements are true, the third statement is

    a. true
    b. false
    c. uncertain

25. Stethoscope is to doctor as whistle is to

    a. nurse
    b. coach
    c. game
    d. player

26. Which word does *not* belong with the others?

 a. horse
 b. donkey
 c. pony
 d. wolf

27. It's hotter in Bakerville than Cookeville. It's colder in Pastrytown than in Cookeville. It is coldest in Cookeville. If the first two statements are true, the third statement is

 a. true
 b. false
 c. uncertain

28. Mark's dog runs faster than Niki's dog. Niki's dog runs faster than Jenna's dog. Jenna's dog is the slowest. If the first two statements are true, the third statement is

 a. true
 b. false
 c. uncertain

29. Scrutinize means the *opposite* of

 a. explore
 b. probe
 c. examine
 d. ignore

30. Which word does *not* belong with the others?

 a. swing
 b. slide
 c. playground
 d. monkey bars

31. Stanza is to poetry as stem is to

 a. tree
 b. science
 c. piston
 d. plant

32. A precipitous fall is

 a. clumsy
 b. minor
 c. scary
 d. steep

33. Which word does *not* belong with the others?

 a. word
 b. verb
 c. noun
 d. adjective

34. Dissuade means the *opposite* of

 a. encourage
 b. deter
 c. misplace
 d. roam

35. The vindictive comment is

 a. vallant
 b. pleasant
 c. forgiving
 d. vengeful

36. Germs are to illness as distraction is to

 a. distraught
 b. accident
 c. calm
 d. cell phone

37. Anarchy most nearly means

 a. ruler
 b. haze
 c. government
 d. disorder

38. Which word does *not* belong with the others?

 a. dollars
 b. euros
 c. pounds
 d. currency

39. Sage most nearly means

 a. smart
 b. kind
 c. doctor
 d. dull

40. Turtle is to slow as church is to

   a. building
   b. Sunday
   c. sacred
   d. pews

41. Which word does *not* belong with the others?

   a. cookie
   b. cupcake
   c. ice cream
   d. cake

42. Which word does *not* belong with the others?

   a. cot
   b. bed
   c. futon
   d. chair

43. Sincere means the *opposite* of

   a. trustworthy
   b. deceptive
   c. calculated
   d. unworthy

44. Pancakes and waffles cook more slowly than eggs. Eggs cook more quickly than bacon, but more slowly than toast. Bacon cooks more quickly than pancakes. If the first two statements are true, the third statement is

   a. true
   b. false
   c. uncertain

45. Simultaneous means the *opposite* of

   a. concurrent
   b. asynchronous
   c. practiced
   d. cloned

46. Which word does *not* belong with the others?

   a. sick
   b. ill
   c. healthy
   d. unwell

47. Depict most nearly means

   a. toss
   b. operate
   c. characterize
   d. conceal

48. Abe grew more flowers than Julia. Julia grew fewer flowers than Amanda. Amanda grew more flowers than Abe. If the first two statements are true, the third statement is

   a. true
   b. false
   c. uncertain

49. Which word does *not* belong with the others?

   a. cashew
   b. almond
   c. pecan
   d. nut

50. Car is to drive as ship is to

   a. sail
   b. truck
   c. deliver
   d. swim

51. Which word does *not* belong with the others?

   a. beef
   b. meat
   c. pork
   d. venison

52. Reminisce most nearly means

   a. recall
   b. forget
   c. pursue
   d. shrink

53. A rational argument is

   a. quick
   b. stored
   c. thoughtless
   d. wise

54. Fido can run faster than Rover. Sparky can run faster than Fido. Of the three dogs, Sparky can run the fastest. If the first two statements are true, the third statement is

    a. true
    b. false
    c. uncertain

55. Ubiquitous means the *opposite* of

    a. omnipresent
    b. scarce
    c. quiet
    d. forfeited

56. Deficient most nearly means

    a. earnest
    b. hostile
    c. deadly
    d. inadequate

57. Which word does *not* belong with the others?

    a. solid
    b. liquid
    c. matter
    d. gas

58. Bob mowed fewer lawns than Eloise. Eloise mowed more lawns than Jack. Jack mowed the fewest lawns. If the first two statements are true, the third statement is

    a. true
    b. false
    c. uncertain

59. A whimsical idea is

    a. sensible
    b. fanciful
    c. quick
    d. deliberated

60. Which word does not belong with the others?

    a. tea
    b. soda
    c. apple
    d. juice

Quantitative Section 4

52 Questions, 30 Minutes

Instructions: Select the best answer.

61. The quotient of 16 and 2 is 5 more than what number?

    a. 8
    b. 37
    c. 13
    d. 3

62. Examine (A), (B), and (C) and find the best answer.

    (A) $.07 \times 10^{-3}$
    (B) 70×10^{-5}
    (C) 700×10^{-7}

    a. (A) is equal to (B) but less than (C)
    b. (A) is equal to (C)
    c. (B) is less than both (A) and (C)
    d. (B) is greater than (C)

63. The sum of 7 and 5 is what percent of 60?

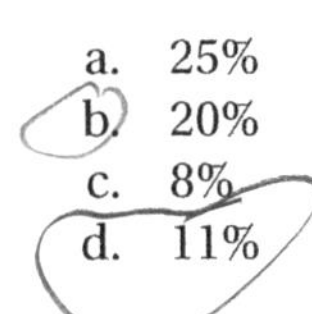

    a. 25%
    b. 20%
    c. 8%
    d. 11%

64. Examine the square and rectangles below and find the best answer.

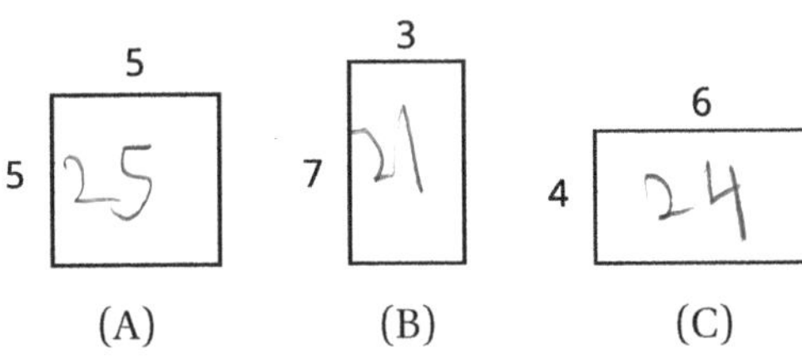

    a. The area of (A) is larger than the area of (B)
    b. The areas of (B) and (C) are equal
    c. The area of (C) is larger than the area of (A)
    d. The area of (C) is smaller than the area of (B)

65. What is the next number in the following series: 27, 9, 18, 6, 12, ____?

    a. 24
    b. 6
    c. 4
    d. 36

66. Review the series: A, 3, C, 7, E, 11, ___, ___. Find the missing letter and number.

    a. H, 14
    b. G, 14
    c. G, 15
    d. H, 15

67. Look at the series: 9, 4, 7, 12, 5, 36, ___. What is the next number?

    a. 72
    b. 3
    c. 2
    d. 18

68. Examine figure below and select the best answer.

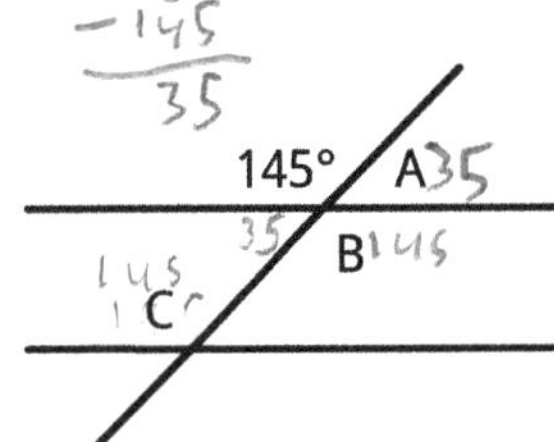

    a. A + B = C + 145
    b. A = C
    c. C + A = 145
    d. A + 145 = C + A

69. Review the series: 112, 56, 28, 14, 7, ___. What number should come next?

    a. 3.5
    b. 0
    c. 4.5
    d. 4

70. Look at the series: 1, 5, 10, 14, 28, ___. Find the next number.

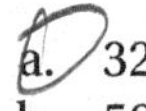

a. 32
b. 56
c. 33
d. 46

71. The average of 8, 10, and 15 is equal to 4 plus what number?

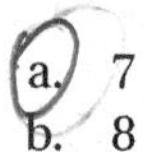

a. 7
b. 8
c. 9
d. 10

72. Examine (A), (B), and (C) and find the best answer.

(A) 5 quarters, 1 nickel, 3 pennies
(B) 2 quarters, 6 dimes, 2 nickels, 4 pennies
(C) 4 quarters, two dimes, 6 pennies

a. (A) is smaller than (C) but larger than (B)
b. (C) is larger than (B) but smaller than (A)
c. (A) and (B) are both smaller than (C)
d. (B) is smaller than (A) but larger than (C)

73. The product of $\frac{1}{4}$ and what number is the sum of 1, 5, and 6?

a. 12
b. 24
c. 48
d. 36

74. Examine (A), (B), and (C) and find the best answer.

(A) 4 feet
(B) 1 yard, 8 inches
(C) 50 inches

a. (B) is larger than (A) but smaller than (C)
b. (B) is larger than (A) and (B)
c. (A) is larger than (B) but smaller than (C)
d. (A) is smaller than (B) and (C)

75. Review the series: 13, 8, 16, 6, 19, ___. Find the missing number.

a. 4
b. 22
c. 3
d. 17

76. Examine the equilateral triangle below and find the best answer.

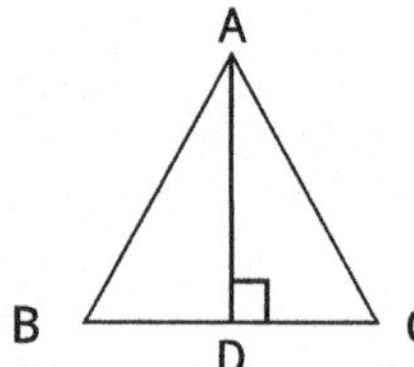

a. $\overline{AB}$ is equal to $\overline{AD}$ and $\overline{AC}$
b. $\overline{AB}$ and $\overline{AC}$ are equal and greater than $\overline{AD}$
c. $\overline{AD}$ is greater than $\overline{AC}$
d. $\overline{CD}$ is less than $\overline{AB}$ but greater than $\overline{AD}$

77. What roman numeral should come next in this series: XII, 2, X, 5, IIX, 8, ___?

a. VII
b. V
c. VI
d. IV

78. What is the next number in the following series: 15, 30, 20, 40, 30, ___?

a. 20
b. 50
c. 45
d. 60

79. $\frac{2}{3}$ of $\frac{1}{5}$ of 30 is what number?

a. 2
b. 4
c. 6
d. 8

80. Look at the series: 19 ,21, 7, ___ , 3, 5. Find the missing number.

a. 1
b. 9
c. 6
d. 4

81. Examine (A), (B), and (C) and find the best answer.

(A) 30% of 50
(B) 40% of 25
(C) 110% of 5

a. (A) is greater than (B) but less than (C)
b. (B) is greater than (A) and (C)
c. (C) is less than (A) and (B)
d. (A) is less than (B) but greater than (C)

82. Fifteen is thirty percent of what number?

a. 10
b. 20
c. 30
d. 50

83. What is the next number in the following series: 80, 75, 15, 10, 2, ____?

a. 0
b. -3
c. -2
d. -5

84. Review the series: 25, 9, 30, 7, 35, ___, 40. Find the missing number.

a. 25
b. 4
c. 5
d. 45

85. What number added to 20% of 60 equals 19?

a. 4
b. 5
c. 7
d. 9

86. Examine (A), (B), and (C) and find the best answer when x is equal to -1.

(A) $2(x + x)$
(B) $3(x)$
(C) $4x - x$

a. (A) is greater than (B) but less than (C)
b. (B) is less than than (A) and (C)
c. (C) is less than (B) and (A)
d. (B) and (C) are equal and greater than (A)

87. What is the missing number in the following series: 4, 4, 8, ____, 96, 480.

a. 8
b. 16
c. 24
d. 36

88. Examine (A), (B), and (C) and find the best answer when $x > 2$.

(A) x^2
(B) $(x)(x)$
(C) $2x$

a. (A), (B). and (C) are all equal
b. (B) and (C) are equal
c. (C) is greater than (B)
d. (A) and (B) are equal

89. What is the next number in the following series: 3, 3.02, 3.04, 3.06, 3.08, ____.

a. 3.010
b. 4
c. 4.1
d. 3.1

90. The circle below is drawn to scale. Examine the circle and choose the best answer.

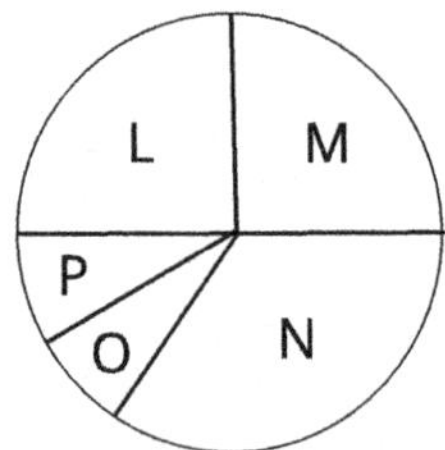

a. The sum of L and P are equal to M
b. N is larger than M
c. L and P are equal to one another
d. O is larger than the sum of N and M

91. Look at the series: 8, 16, ____, 24, 20, 40. What is the missing number?

a. 8
b. 18
c. 12
d. 36

92. A circle has a radius of 5. Choose the answer below that is true.

a. The radius is larger than the circumference.
b. The diameter is larger than the area.
c. The area is larger than the diameter.
d. The circumference is half the area.

93. Three less than six times the square root of nine is

a. 15
b. 0
c. 9
d. 51

94. What is the next number in the following series: 5, 13, 7, 7, ___, 1, 11?

a. 9
b. 7
c. 5
d. 0

95. What number divided by two is equal to nine more than seven times nine?

a. 200
b. 144
c. 35
d. 189

96. Review the following series: 1, 4, 16, ___, 256, 1024. What number is missing?

a. 20
b. 41
c. 64
d. 128

97. Examine (A), (B), and (C) and find the best answer.

(A) $(x + 4)(x + 4)$
(B) $(x + 4)^2$
(C) $x^2 + 8x + 16$

a. (A) equals (C), but (B) equals $x^2 + 16$
b. (A) equals (B) which equals (C)
c. (A) equals $2x + 8$, which is the same as (B)
d. (C) equals (B), but not (A)

98. 28 is $\frac{3}{5}$ of what number?

a. $16\frac{4}{5}$
b. $46\frac{2}{3}$
c. $52\frac{1}{4}$
d. 60

99. Examine (A), (B), and (C) and find the best answer.

(A) 18 - 2 × (3 + 4)
(B) 18 - 2 × 3 + 4
(C) (18 - 2) × 3 + 4

a. (B) > (C) < (A)
b. (C) > (B) < (A)
c. (A) < (B) < (C)
d. (A) = (B) = (C)

100. What is the next number in the following series: 52, 58, 66, 72, 80, ____

a. 82
b. 84
c. 86
d. 88

101. Examine (A), (B), and (C) and find the best answer.

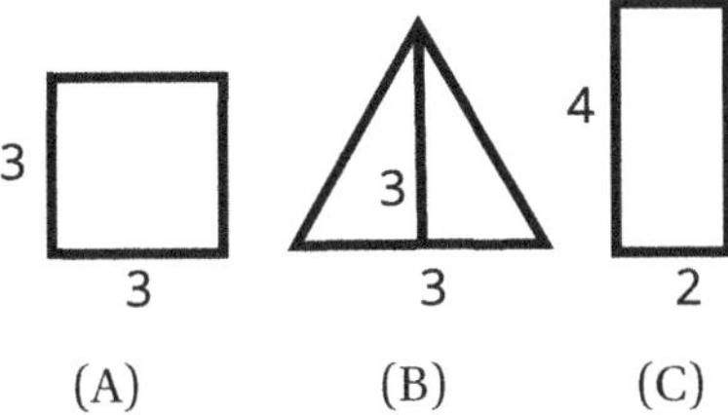

a. Area of (A) = Area of (B) > Area of (C)
b. Area of (A) > Area of (C) > Area of (B)
c. Area of (B) = Area of (A) < Area of (C)
d. Area of (A) = Area of (B) = Area of (C)

102. 4 cubed is 3 cubed less than what number?

a. 27
b. 37
c. 64
d. 91

103. Examine (A), (B), and (C) and find the best answer.

(A) 1 × 0.001
(B) 10 × 0.0001
(C) 10 × 0.00001

a. (A) = (B) < (C)
b. (B) = (C) > (A)
c. (A) = (B) > (C)
d. (A) = (B) = (C)

104. What is next in the following series: 1, E, 9, M, 17, ____

a. U
b. Q
c. 20
d. 21

105. Examine regular polygons (A), (B), and (C) and find the best answer.

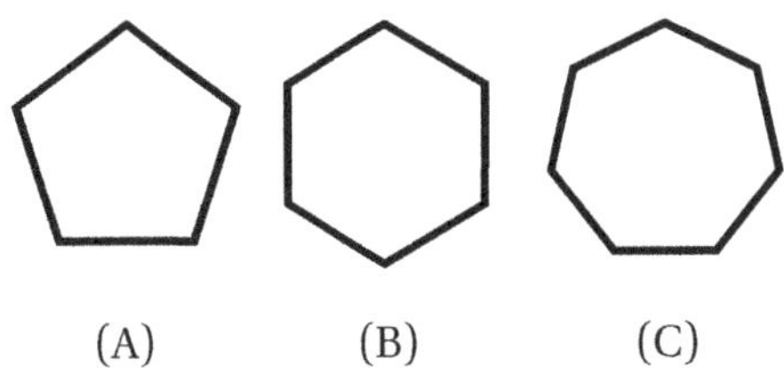

a. The sum of the interior angles of (C) is greater than the sum of (A) or (B)'s interior angles
b. The sum of the interior angles of each figure is 360°
c. (C) is a hexagon, (B) is a heptagon, and (A) is a pentagon
d. The perimeter of each figure must equal the perimeter of the other figures

106. What is the next number in the following series: 32, 16, 48, 24, 72, ____?

a. 26
b. 30
c. 36
d. 100

107. What is the next number in the following series: 5.125, $5\frac{1}{4}$, 5.375, $5\frac{1}{2}$, 5.625, ____?

(A) 5.75
(B) $5\frac{3}{4}$
(C) $5\frac{5}{8}$
(D) 6

108. What number is 3 less than $\frac{1}{2}$ of $\frac{1}{4}$ of 128?

a. 13
b. 16
c. 19
d. 32

109. What are the missing numbers in the following series: 9, X, 11, XII, ___, ____?

a. 13, XX
b. 12, XIIII
c. 13, XIV
d. XIII, 14

110. Consider the following figure. The unshaded region has a radius of 4, while the distance between the outer edge of the unshaded region and the outer edge of the shaded region is 3. Which of the following statements is true?

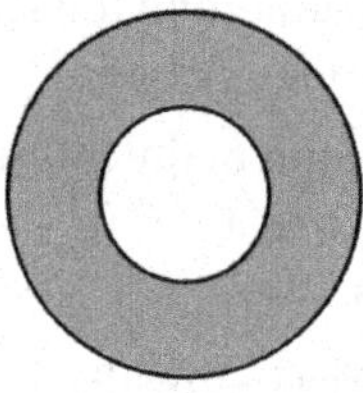

a. The area of the shaded region is 16π
b. The area of the entire figure is 14π
c. The area of the shaded region is 33π
d. The area of the unshaded region is 8π

111. What are the missing numbers in the following series: 52, 44, 37, ___, 26, ___?

a. 35, 20
b. 34, 24
c. 31, 21
d. 31, 22

112. 16 is 4 more than 20% of what number?

a. 8
b. 12
c. 60
d. 64

Reading Section 4

62 Questions, 25 Minutes

Reading Comprehension

Instructions: Read each passage carefully and mark one answer for each question.

Questions 113 - 122 refer to the passage below.

A high-pitched scream broke through Lyra's consciousness, crying "Get away, get away!"

Alarmed, Lyra leapt out of bed, ready to fight. She sprinted toward her window, certain that the sound was coming from outside. Her heart racing, she opened the window and peered down at the street below. She was surprised to find that the street had been transformed. It was no longer the lonely street of the night before, but rather, a bustling marketplace alive with movement and activity. Children were playing near their parents, giggling, screeching, and teasing each other. It wasn't until she shook off the last remnants of sleep that she realized that she had heard a child's delighted squeal, not a scream of distress.

As she watched the children play, Lyra was struck by how normal the scene outside was. People were safe here. How is it possible, Lyra wondered, for people to be so carefree and happy in one place and so frightened and sad in another?

There was a light tapping on the door, followed by the uncertain voice of her uncle. "Lyra, are you awake?" Her uncle cautiously entered the room, his lanky frame casting a long shadow on the polished wooden floorboards. His eyes brightened when he saw her standing by the window. "You should come downstairs and get something to eat...it's getting late, and your aunt is worried about you. There's a change of clothes for you on the chair." He gave her a quick smile and left, quietly shutting the heavy wooden door behind him.

Lyra reluctantly pulled herself away from the window, revelling in the feeling of safety that had overcome her. A wave of sadness and guilt passed over her as she thought of her sister and brother. Pushing the thought aside, she pulled on the shirt and pants that her uncle had set out for her.

Stepping out of her room, Lyra wearily made her way down to the kitchen from the attic bedroom. As she reached the second floor, she was startled to feel her feet sink into a soft, plush rug. She smiled. She had never set foot on a rug like this before; her family had always been poor and unable to afford such luxuries.

113. Why was Lyra alarmed when she woke up?

a. She was worried that her uncle would be mad at her if she overslept.
b. She was nervous about staying in a new place.
c. She woke up from a bad dream.
d. She thought someone was screaming and needed her help.

114. In the first paragraph, the author's description of the street as "lonely" is an example of which literary technique?

a. simile
b. symbolism
c. personification
d. metaphor

115. What is Lyra's opinion of her aunt and uncle?

a.
b. She likes them, but is really nervous about staying in their house.
c. She feels comfortable with them.
d. She is upset by how welcoming they are.
e. She is intimidated by their wealth and hospitality.

116. Lyra's uncle can be described as

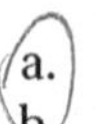

a. kind
b. extremely nervous
c. exasperated
d. ebullient

117. Based on the information in the passage, what was Lyra's old life like?

a. She was lonely, but wealthy.
b. She felt angry and restless.
c. She felt anxious and lonely.
d. She was scared and poor.

118. What surprised Lyra about her aunt and uncle's home?

a. the way it was organized
b. its beauty
c. its luxurious furnishings
d. the wooden floorboards

119. Throughout this passage, Lyra can be described as

a. on edge, but content
b. terrified, but excited
c. mindless and unquestioning
d. aggressive and ungrateful

120. One can infer that Lyra's siblings

a. are also at Lyra's aunt and uncle's house
b. are safe and staying with other relatives
c. are back at Lyra's home and unsafe
d. are playing outside on the street

121. The metaphor "wave of sadness" is used to indicate Lyra's

a. fluctuation between feeling sad and exhilarated
b. regret that she is not staying closer to the ocean
c. sudden, overwhelming sense of sadness
d. remorse that she did not bring her parents with her

122. What do you anticipate is going to happen after Lyra goes downstairs?

a. Her uncle will cautiously ask Lyra to leave their home and stay somewhere else.
b. Lyra will eat breakfast with her aunt and uncle.
c. Lyra's aunt will ask her to help get groceries from the market.
d. Her aunt and uncle will berate her for being late to breakfast.

Questions 123 - 132 refer to the passage below.

The guinea pig is a species of rodent that is native to South America. While no one seems to know for certain why they are called guinea pigs, their shape suggests a small pig, and the name guinea may be derived from the word Guiana, a region in South America. In size, shape, and fur texture, they resemble a squirrel or rabbit. They have large bodies, short legs, small feet, no tails, and come in a wide range of colors. A guinea pig attains its full-grown weight of two to three pounds at around eighteen months of age.

When Europeans first explored the Andean region of South America, they found domesticated guinea pigs in the homes of indigenous people, who raised them for food. In fact, Guinea pig meat (known as "cuy") is still a delicacy in South America. The animals were introduced into Europe as pets in the 16th century, and since that time they have spread all over the world.

Guinea pigs are vegetarians, and have a similar diet to that of rabbits. They are healthy, clean, quiet, and have no offensive odor. They are also very easily tamed; in fact, there is probably no animal in the world that is simpler to handle. The rodents readily adapt themselves to new conditions and seem to do equally well in city or country.

Guinea pigs are hearty creatures, largely immune to the disease epidemics that make raising poultry and rabbits so uncertain. Some guinea pigs die of sickness, of course, but typically just when they have been neglected or improperly fed. Contagious diseases that often wipe out whole flocks of poultry or pens of rabbits are unknown among guinea pigs.

All of these factors make raising guinea pigs a very pleasant occupation.

123. According to the passage, how are guinea pigs different from rabbits?

a. Their diet is different.
b. They typically don't get diseases.
c. They have more fur.
d. They are larger.

124. This passage is primarily about

a. the eating habits of guinea pigs
b. South American animals
c. the history and habits of guinea pigs
d. how to raise a guinea pig

125. When were guinea pigs introduced into Europe?

a. the 1600s
b. the 1700s
c. the 1400s
d. the 1500s

126. Based on its usage in the passage, indigenous most nearly means

a. native
b. American
c. impoverished
d. wealthy

127. What is NOT a benefit to owning a guinea pig?

a. They are clean.
b. They rarely get sick.
c. They are very loyal.
d. They are easily tamed.

128. Why does the author include the paragraph about the guinea pigs' resistance to disease?

a. to argue that guinea pigs should be eaten
b. to explain why the South American people kept guinea pigs in their home
c. to explain why guinea pigs can live in either the city or the country
d. to provide support for why guinea pigs are easy to raise

129. How would you describe the author's attitude about guinea pigs?

a. complimentary
b. antagonistic
c. fervent
d. indecisive

130. In South America, guinea pigs were primarily used as

    a. pets
    b. guard animals
    c. a food source
    d. entertainment

131. What do you think the author will write about in the next paragraph?

    a. other animals that are pleasant companions
    b. guidelines for raising guinea pigs
    c. an argument against domesticating guinea pigs
    d. an explanation of the different types of guinea pigs

132. This excerpt might be found in

    a. a travel brochure for South America
    b. a textbook
    c. a guide to raising guinea pigs
    d. a newspaper article

Questions 133 - 142 refer to the passage below.

It is commonly known that Japanese students spend more time in school than their American counterparts. In Japan, students attend approximately 240 days of school a year, while American students are typically in school for only 180 days. By the age of 18, Japanese students have attended more hours of school than American college graduates. Perhaps less known is the emphasis Japan places on community in their school system.

Kumi is an unique attribute of this system. Students in Japan do not move from class to class like students in the United States do. Instead, teachers change classes and students remain with their kumi, or homeroom, all day, all year, and often from one year to the next. Each kumi consists of 40 to 50 students who are expected to work together as a family or small community. In order to build unity within the kumi, students participate in a variety of activities together like athletics, musical events, and even overnight field trips. Students from one kumi often compete against students from another.

The kumi is truly a student's home away from home. Students are encouraged to bring items from home to make the room look nice and feel more welcoming—no custodians needed! Kumi students clean their classroom daily by sweeping the floors, straightening desks, and cleaning boards. In some schools, common areas like hallways and restrooms are also cleaned by students on a weekly basis.

While some middle and high schools in the United States have homerooms, they typically only meet briefly once a day. The students do not remain together for all classes, and class sizes in the United States rarely surpass 30 kids. In fact, many parents in the US would find a class size of 40 or 50 alarming. Likewise, American students rarely clean their own classrooms, except as a form of punishment. However, both Japanese schools and American schools emphasize school spirit and activities outside the class to help foster community.

133. Which of the following would be a good title for this passage?

   a. "Kumi: Better Than American Homerooms"
   b. "Kumi: The Japanese School System"
   c. "Kumi: A Japanese Classroom Community"
   d. "Kumi: A Select Group of Students"

134. According the passage students in the same kumi

   a. compete against one another
   b. are expected to cooperate
   c. will likely not be in the same kumi next year
   d. are not friends with students in other kumis

135. Based on its usage in the passage, attribute most nearly means

   a. acknowledgment
   b. reward
   c. virtue
   d. characteristic

136. What was the author's purpose or intent when writing this passage?

   a. to convince Americans to switch to a kumi style of homeroom
   b. to compare and contrast Japanese and American school systems
   c. to explain what kumis are
   d. to elaborate the problems kumis would have in the United States

137. Based on the passage, one might expect an American student to wash desks

   a. if it were required by the homeroom
   b. never, because American schools employ custodians
   c. if he or she was caught drawing on a desk
   d. as part of school spirit

138. One similarity that both American and Japanese school share is

   a. class size
   b. school spirit
   c. duration of homeroom
   d. length of school year

139. How many more days does an average Japanese student spend in class compared to an American?

    a. 100 days
    b. 180 days
    c. 60 days
    d. 240 days

140. All of the following activities might take place in a kumi EXCEPT

    a. choir practice
    b. a game of baseball
    c. plans for a weekend trip
    d. students leaving garbage on the floor

141. Based on its usage in the passage, <u>foster</u> most nearly means

    a. parent
    b. back
    c. take care of
    d. promote

142. Based on the passage, how might American homerooms and Japanese kumis be similar?

    a. Both might participate in school spirit activities
    b. Both might remain together throughout the day
    c. Both might contain about 40 students
    d. Both might be like a family

Questions 143 - 152 refer to the passage below.

In Tsarist Russia, life was difficult for women. Russia was a largely rural, patriarchal (male-dominated) society. Men controlled all aspects of life and held absolute power over their families. Divorce was virtually impossible. Education was poor for most people but especially bad for women, and illiteracy was commonplace. Women gave birth to nine children on average, in hopes that half would survive to adulthood.

The Communist Revolution of 1917 brought promises of great change for the common man and woman. At its core, Communism is a philosophy and governmental system that declares wealth should be shared equally by everyone in a society. Communist ideology states that women are equal to men, and should be liberated from the restrictive roles of homemaker and mother. Soviet leader Vladimir Lenin argued that housework wasted women's valuable labor potential by chaining them to the kitchen and nursery. The conflict between traditional Russian views on womanhood and the values being promoted by the revolution became known as the woman question, an issue the Soviet government never completely solved.

Soon after the October Revolution and the end of Russian involvement in World War I, the country descended into a terrible civil war. The demand for Russian manpower during both wars further damaged the patriarchal economy by pushing women into the workplace. To compensate for lost husbands and fathers, women assumed the role of ensuring the survival of their families. Post-revolution food shortages led to <u>rampant</u> starvation, so many women worked during the day and then searched for food and fuel at night. Epidemic diseases also killed millions; typhus alone was responsible for 1.5 million deaths between 1918-1919. Great numbers of Russian children were orphaned when their parents became casualties of war, starvation, or disease. Russian women blamed Communist leaders for these hardships, complaining, "You deceived us, you told us there would be plenty but the opposite is true. Life is more difficult." It was in this environment that the communists attempted to answer the woman question.

143. Based on its usage in the passage, <u>rampant</u> most nearly means

    a. abandoned
    b. moderate
    c. widespread
    d. sparse

144. According to the passage, what directly increased women's suffering after the Revolution of 1917

    a. the Communists
    b. Vladimir Lenin's philosophy
    c. the tsar
    d. the civil war

145. Which of the following would be a good title for this passage?

    a. "You Deceived Us"
    b. "Tsarist Oppression"
    c. "The Woman Question"
    d. "The 1917 Revolution"

146. What do you think the author will write about in the next paragraph?

    a. how the Communists changed life for women
    b. how the civil war impacted men
    c. the leaders of communism
    d. the difference between Tsarist Russia and Communist Russia

147. Which of the following was true for women living in Tsarist Russia?

    a. They could read.
    b. Many worked outside the home.
    c. Most lived in the rural countryside.
    d. Some were divorced.

148. According the the passage, if a Russian woman had 6 children how many would probably survive to adulthood?

    a. 1
    b. 2
    c. 3
    d. 4

149. What was the author's purpose in writing this passage?

a. to criticize communism
b. to advocate for women's rights
c. to explain how life for Russian women changed under communism
d. to praise the tsar

150. Based on the passage, predict one change communism may bring for women.

a. free daycare for children
b. financial benefits for having large families
c. incentives to stay home
d. laws making women the property of their husband

151. According to the passage, women were initially likely to

a. support the communists
b. support the tsar
c. be indifferent to politics
d. fight in the civil war

152. One can predict that eventually

a. communism answered the woman question
b. women overthrew the communists
c. Russian turned into a matriarchy
d. communism affected women in both positive and negative ways

Vocabulary

Instructions: Choose the word that means the same, or about the same, as the underlined word.

153. A passive person

a. difficult
b. sleepy
c. inactive
d. uncompromising

154. Abundant resources

a. incredible
b. plentiful
c. scarce
d. some

155. The man faltered

a. hesitated
b. fell
c. advanced
d. rushed

156. To enhance an experience

a. enjoy
b. create
c. improve
d. encapsulate

157. Inconstant support

a. steady
b. erratic
c. poor
d. hesitant

158. The despondent man

a. familiar
b. irate
c. tired
d. dejected

159. An implicit agreement

a. implied
b. tentative
c. short term
d. unanimous

160. The bellicose man

a. unhappy
b. antagonistic
c. stoic
d. calm

161. The diligent student

a. thoughtful
b. unmotivated
c. hardworking
d. meek

162. The unassailable evidence

a. unconvincing
b. interesting
c. indisputable
d. timely

163. A meticulous worker

a. conscientious
b. careless
c. motivated
d. curmudgeonly

164. An ingenious solution

a. foolish
b. uninspiring
c. interesting
d. brilliant

165. To abdicate the throne

a. seize
b. share
c. give up
d. covet

166. The esteemed professor

a. dedicated
b. beloved
c. easygoing
d. disliked

167. The <u>disparaging</u> remark

a. biased
b. derogatory
c. encouraging
d. critical

168. An <u>apathetic</u> citizen

a. indifferent
b. involved
c. opinionated
d. pitiful

169. To <u>rectify</u> the situation

a. repeat
b. improve
c. worsen
d. correct

170. A <u>diplomatic</u> solution

a. creative
b. civil
c. ineffective
d. cruel

171. A <u>lackluster</u> performance

a. compelling
b. terrible
c. dull
d. strong

172. To <u>stifle</u> creativity

a. constrain
b. question
c. encourage
d. dictate

173. A <u>voracious</u> reader

a. reluctant
b. conscientious
c. struggling
d. avid

174. The <u>ostentatious</u> jewelry

a. beautiful
b. extravagant
c. immaterial
d. unseemly

Math Section 4

64 Questions, 45 Minutes

Instructions: Select the best answer.

175. $\frac{(-3 - 4)}{(11 + 3)}$

(A) $\frac{1}{2}$
(B) $-\frac{1}{2}$
(C) $\frac{1}{14}$
(D) 14

176. $(-3)^3$

a. 9
b. -9
c. 27
d. -27

177. What is the smallest measurement?

a. 4 centimeters
b. 50 millimeters
c. $\frac{1}{2}$ meter
d. 1 kilometer

178. Which of the following is the LCM of 6 and 8?

a. 8
b. 12
c. 48
d. 24

179. What is the reciprocal of $-\frac{3}{4}$?

a. $\frac{3}{4}$
b. $-\frac{4}{3}$
c. $\frac{4}{3}$
d. 3

180. An equilateral triangle has perimeter 18. What is the length of one of its sides?

a. 9
b. 8
c. 6
d. 18

181. How do you write .00004756 in scientific notation?

a. 4.756×10^{-5}
b. $4,756 \times 10^{-8}$
c. $.4756 \times 10^{-4}$
d. 4.756×10^{-6}

182. What is the diameter of a circle with area 64π?

a. 32
b. 16
c. 8
d. 4

183. Given the two sets of numbers A = {2, 3, 4, 8} and B = {2, 3, 5, 7, 8}, what is $A \cap B$?

a. {4, 5 7}
b. {2, 3, 4, 5, 7, 8}
c. {2, 3, 8}
d. {2, 8}

184. The commutative property is demonstrated in which of the following problems:

a. $4 + (5 + 3) = (4 + 5) 3$
b. $3 + 6 = 6 + 3$
c. $2 + 0 = 2$
d. $4 (2 + 3) = (4 \times 2) + (4 \times 3)$

185. Order from least to greatest: $-\frac{11}{3}$, 4.4, $\frac{9}{2}$, -4.1.

a. $-\frac{11}{3}$, 4.4, -4.1, $\frac{9}{2}$
b. $-\frac{11}{3}$, -4.1, 4.4, $\frac{9}{2}$,
c. $\frac{9}{2}$, 4.4, $-\frac{11}{3}$, -4.1
d. -4.1, $-\frac{11}{3}$, 4.4, $\frac{9}{2}$

186. An obtuse angle is

a. greater than 90°
b. less than 90°
c. 90°
d. 180°

187. Which of the following might be a value for x:

5x - 7 > 8

a. 2
b. 3
c. 5
d. $\frac{1}{5}$

188. What is the base of a triangle with area 24 and height 8?

a. 2
b. 3
c. 6
d. 12

189. 8 is what percent of 50?

a. 15
b. 16
c. 17
d. 18

190. What is the volume of a cube with side y?

a. y
b. y^3
c. y^2
d. 3y

191. 7 + 4(5 - 3) - 2 =

a. 13
b. 15
c. 18
d. 19

192. $3.2 + \frac{8}{5} =$

a. 4.8
b. 11.2/5
c. 1.6
d. 4.6

193. $|4 - 7| - 3 =$

a. -5
b. -6
c. 6
d. 0

194. What is the measure of angle A?

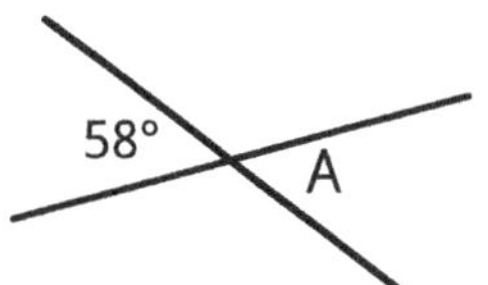

a. 58°
b. 122°
c. 150°
d. Not enough information to determine.

195. What is 20% of 30% of 110?

a. 6
b. 6.6
c. 33
d. 22

196. Angle A is congruent to angle B. Angle A is 38°. What is the measure of angle B?

a. 52°
b. 142°
c. 38°
d. 83°

197. What is the place value of the number 6 in the number .98642?

a. tenth
b. hundredth
c. thousandth
d. tens

198. Blueberries from the farm can be shipped in 15 pound crates. If the farmers picked 300 pounds of blueberry, how many crates do they need for shipping?

a. 10 crates
b. 12 crates
c. 15 crates
d. 20 crates

199. What is the square root of 81 plus the square root of 144?

a. 20
b. 21
c. 22
d. 23

200. What is shown below?

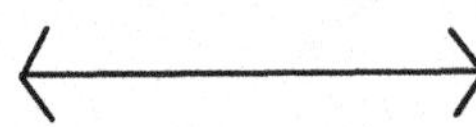

a. ray
b. line segment
c. angle
d. line

201. Solve for a: 5 = 3a - 7

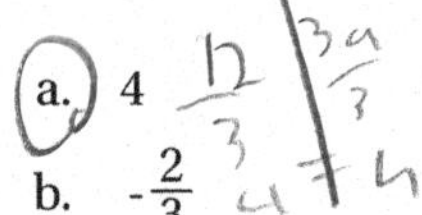

a. 4
b. $-\frac{2}{3}$
c. 3
d. 12

202. Rose spent a total of $637.45 on her lawn care from the months of June through October. How much did she spend on average per month?

a. $53.12
b. $91.06
c. $106.24
d. $127.49

203. Julia and Jenna both walk dogs. They earn $12 for each dog they walk. On average Julia walks 30 dogs a week and Jenna 40 dogs a week. If Julia sprains her ankle and Jenna has to walk all of the dogs. How much money will Jenna earn in one week?

a. $360
b. $460
c. $840
d. $970

204. What is the mode of the numbers below?

2, 7, 5, 12, 21, 5, 6

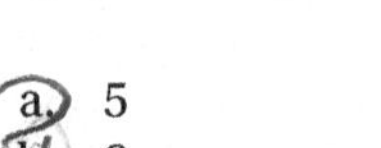

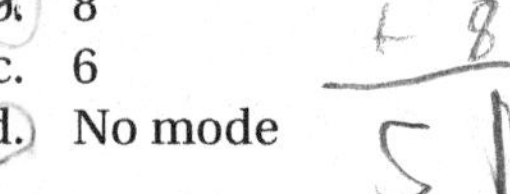

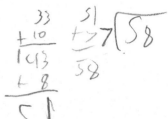

a. 5
b. 8
c. 6
d. No mode

205. Henry is working on putting together a scale model of a propeller plane in which every $\frac{1}{2}$ inch on the model represents 1 foot on the real plane. If scale model is 7.5 inches long, how long is the real plane?

a. 8.5 ft
b. 9 ft
c. 12 ft
d. 15 ft

206. On Monday night, Antonio did homework from 3:30 PM to 5:45 PM. He then took a break and finished the rest of his homework from 6:45 PM to 9:15 PM. How long did he spend on his homework total?

a. 2 hours and 15 minutes
b. 4 hours and 30 minutes
c. 2 hours and 30 minutes
d. 4 hours and 45 minutes

207. Which of the following choices will satisfy the inequality: $-\frac{7}{2} < x < 1.4$?

a. $\frac{7}{2}$
b. -4
c. $-\frac{5}{4}$
d. 2.7

208. A consulting firm randomly sent out a survey to an undisclosed number of email accounts. After waiting a week, the firm discovered that only 48% of the surveys that were sent out were actually answered. If 2880 surveys were answered, how many total surveys did the firm initially send?

a. 1382
b. 1498
c. 3120
d. 6000

209. Zack earned scores of 85%, 60%, and 75% on his last three tests. If he wants to maintain a 75% average, what must he score on his fourth test?

a. 75%
b. 80%
c. 85%
d. 90%

210. Identify one solution for x in the following problem: $x^2 - 24 = 12$

a. 6
b. 8
c. 12
d. 18

211. Solve for x: $5x - 7 = 2(x - 6)$

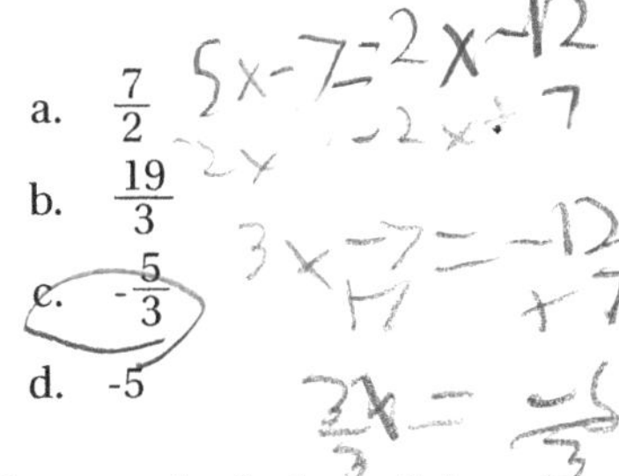

a. $\frac{7}{2}$
b. $\frac{19}{3}$
c. $-\frac{5}{3}$
d. -5

212. Adara received a box of chocolate candies for her birthday. The box contains 5 milk chocolates, 4 dark chocolates, and 3 white chocolates. If she pulls out a candy at random, what is the probability that it will not be a white chocolate?

a. $\frac{1}{3}$
b. $\frac{1}{4}$
c. $\frac{3}{4}$
d. $\frac{2}{3}$

213. A local farmer's market is selling strawberries at $2.75 per carton. If you have $15 to spend on strawberries, how many cartons can you buy?

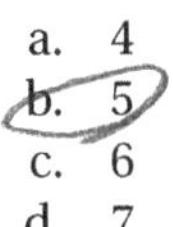

a. 4
b. 5
c. 6
d. 7

214. An entire kindergarten class of 30 students weighs 1,300 pounds. The classroom measures 60 feet by 30 feet. What is the average weight each square foot of the class is supporting? Round to the nearest 10th.

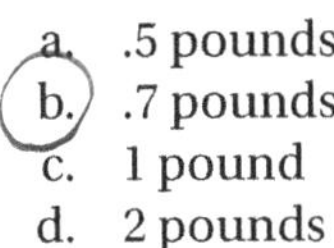

a. .5 pounds
b. .7 pounds
c. 1 pound
d. 2 pounds

215. Charlotte bought a paint set for 70% of the original price. If she paid $43.75, how much did the paint set originally cost? Round to the nearest cent.

a. $30.63
b. $56.88
c. $62.50
d. $74.38

216. The table below shows the number of books read by 20 students in a second grade class in a month.

Number of Books	Number of Students
1	4
2	7
3	4
4	5

What is the average number of books read?

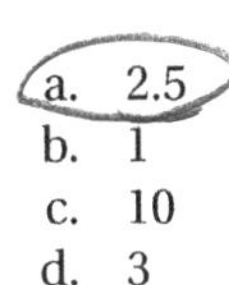

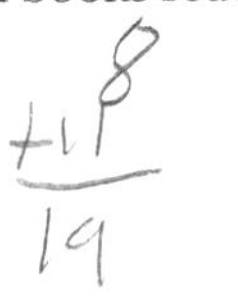

a. 2.5
b. 1
c. 10
d. 3

217. A carpenter needs to cut a board of wood into 3 pieces that are each 4 feet 2 inches long. If wood is only sold by the foot, how many feet must he buy?

a. 10 feet
b. 11 feet
c. 12 feet
d. 13 feet

218. ABCD is a rectangle. What is the area of triangle ACD?

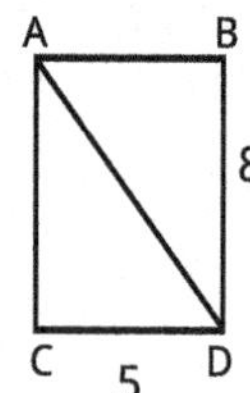

a. 20
b. 40
c. 30
d. 10

219. Which transformation makes the letter Z appear unchanged?

a. reflection across a horizontal line
b. reflection across a vertical line
c. rotation 90° clockwise
d. rotation 180°

220. Simplify: $\sqrt{80x^2y}$

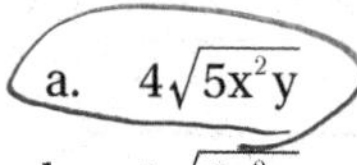

a. $4\sqrt{5x^2y}$
b. $2\sqrt{5x^2y}$
c. $2x\sqrt{5y}$
d. $4x\sqrt{5y}$

221. Raina needs several 7-inch long ribbons for a crafting project. The ribbon is sold in spools that are 3-feet long. If Raina needs 60 ribbons for her project, how many spools will she need to purchase?

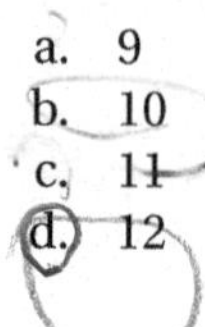

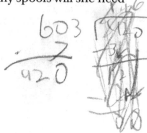

a. 9
b. 10
c. 11
d. 12

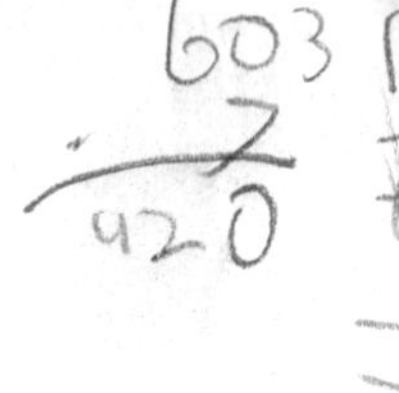

222. What is the width of a rectangular prism with height 5, length 4, and volume 60?

a. 12
b. 15
c. 4
d. 3

223. Syed and Martin are taking a 280 mile road trip. How many minutes will it take for them to arrive at their destination if they are driving 70 miles per hour for their entire trip?

a. 4
b. 6
c. 240
d. 260

224. Diedre is planting new grass on her entire lawn. If her yard measures 21 feet by 18 feet, how many square yards of grass does she need to plant?

a. 378 square yards
b. 42 square yards
c. 126 square yards
d. 63 square yards

225. Caidan has $5 less than three times the amount Mia has. If Caidan has $31, how much does Mia have?

a. $8.67
b. $12
c. $14
d. $108

226. A tree that is 10 ft tall casts a shadow that is 15 ft long. If another nearby tree casts a shadow that is 18 ft long, how tall is the tree?

a. 11 ft
b. 12 ft
c. 15 ft
d. 27 ft

227. David earns \$3000 a month. Each month, 25% of his pay is used for rent, 30% is used for food, 10% is used for entertainment, and the rest is put in savings. How much money does David use for savings and food each month?

a. \$900
b. \$1,050
c. \$1,950
d. \$2,250

228. On the number cube below the opposite sides add up to 8. Which choice below could be another view of the cube?

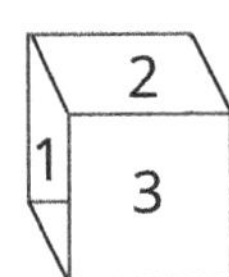

a. 5 3 7
b. 5 2 4
c. 7 5 8
d. 6 7 5

229. Solve for r: $\frac{8r}{7} = \frac{1}{7}$

a. $\frac{8}{7}$
b. $-\frac{3}{8}$
c. $\frac{4}{7}$
d. $\frac{1}{8}$

230. In the equation below, if x = -1 and y = -2, what is z?

$3y + 4x = z$

a. -10
b. -11
c. 10
d. 11

231. Anderson did a survey of his school to determine which season was each student's favorite. His results are outlined in the pie chart below:

If there are 300 students in his school, how many students listed summer or spring as their favorite season?

a. 138
b. 186
c. 194
d. 48

232. How many fluid ounces are in 4.5 cups?

a. 27 fl oz
b. 36 fl oz
c. 54 fl oz
d. 72 fl oz

233. How many feet are in 3.4 miles?

a. 14,212 ft
b. 14,552 ft
c. 17,612 ft
d. 17,952 ft

234. $4 \times 10^4 + 3 \times 10^2 + 2 \times 10$

a. 40,302
b. 4,320
c. 40,320
d. 43,020

235. On an airplane, the ratio of pilots to flight attendants to passengers is 1 : 2 : 27. If there are 135 passengers on an airplane, how many flight attendants are there?

a. 6
b. 8
c. 9
d. 10

236. High school students and their parents were surveyed to determine movie preferences. The survey participants were asked how many comedy, action, and drama movies they had watched in the past year. Each group's results were then averaged together and presented in the table below.

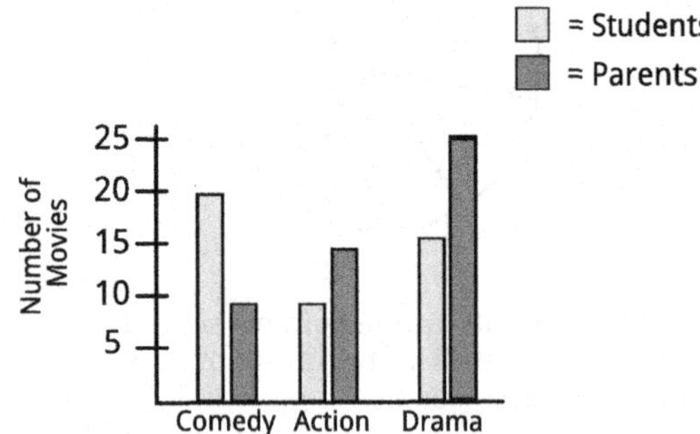

According to the data presented, on average, how did parents and students differ in their viewing of drama movies?

a. Students watched 5 more drama movies than parents.
b. Parents watched 10 more drama movies than students.
c. Students watched 15 more drama movies than parents.
d. Students watched 10 more drama movies than parents.

237. A sheet of paper was folded in half 3 times as shown below. What were the original dimensions of the paper?

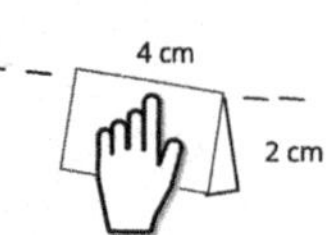

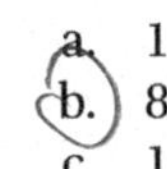

a. 16 cm × 8 cm
b. 8 cm × 8 cm
c. 16 cm × 16 cm
d. 32 cm × 8 cm

238. Julien, Noelle, and Mark share a pizza. If Julien ate $\frac{1}{3}$ of the pizza and Noelle ate $\frac{1}{5}$. How many pieces did Mark eat if the pizza had a total of 30 slices?

a. 11
b. 12
c. 13
d. 14

Language Section 4

60 Questions, 25 Minutes

Usage and Mechanics

Instructions: For questions 239-278, check the sentences for errors of usage, capitalization, or punctuation. If there is no error, choose D.

239.

a. The girls' had a pet dog, fish, and cat.
b. Mark has always dreamed of living in Phoenix, Arizona.
c. Siobhan won trophies for three sports: field hockey, volleyball, and lacrosse.
d. No mistakes.

240.

a. If you'd like, we still can go to the parade tomorrow.
b. Greg or his brothers needs to pick up Conor from school today.
c. Our basketball team won the state championship, even though our star player was injured.
d. No mistakes.

241.

a. Keisha quickly ran home after falling off her bike.
b. The history museum has a special exhibit I'd like to see.
c. "I'm not feeling too good," I moaned, "so I'm going to lie down."
d. No mistakes.

242.

a. Marielle's dance team won the competition, so they got ice cream to celebrate.
b. What's your sister's name Kevin?
c. The computer technician told me that she had never seen that type of error before.
d. No mistakes.

243.

a. My neighbor's lawn mower wakes me up every Sunday morning.
b. What grade did you get on your French test?
c. After I went to the store.
d. No mistakes.

244.

a. My Aunt Shanice tells the funniest stories.
b. Tim, Terra, and Brandi rode their bikes all summer.
c. The girls' parents told them that they could only go to the concert if they went together.
d. No mistakes.

245.

a. Everyone on the soccer team got his or her uniform last Tuesday.
b. Who's going to see the play this Saturday?
c. I don't know whether I should take French or Italian next year.
d. No mistakes.

246.

a. I took a flight from Chicago, Illinois to Fort Lauderdale, Florida.
b. When I snuck up behind my mom, she exclaimed, "You scared me!"
c. His sister registered for her college classes, toured the campus, and was searching for housing.
d. No mistakes.

247.

a. Since Saad gave the cake to Tegan and I, we assumed we were supposed to split it.
b. Scott was the tallest player on his school's basketball team.
c. My dad could watch birds for hours, but I think that it's boring.
d. No mistakes.

248.

a. The dove swooped down gracefully to eat its food.
b. There are fewer than five children left in Ms. Scarmani's class.
c. When I go to band practice, I carefully lay down my clarinet on my lap while waiting for my teacher.
d. No mistakes.

249.

a. Kathleen, who loved animals, begged her mom for a kitten when they passed by the pet store.
b. "Actually," my aunt said, "I'd love to watch your soccer game."
c. The post office was closed on Labor day, so Josiah was not able to mail the package.
d. No mistakes.

250.

a. The little boy played in the sandbox with his toys.
b. My mom and I love baking blueberry banana muffins together.
c. Who's coming?
d. No mistakes.

251.

a. LeShawn and Phillip had the highest grades in their class.
b. My backpack was really messy because I never cleans it out.
c. My school held a fundraiser so our band could play in Macy's Thanksgiving Day Parade.
d. No mistakes.

252.

a. I checked out five history books from the library.
b. Although many people think the capitol of Australia is Sydney, they are incorrect.
c. It's too warm outside to go ice skating at an outdoor rink.
d. No mistakes.

253.

a. My little brother, Antonio, was born on October 4, 2016.
b. Ronin asked me, "Why did you go to the movie without me"?
c. Are you buying yourself a new dress for the homecoming dance?
d. No mistakes.

254.

a. The largest of the two boxes was also the lightest.
b. My sister and I were invited to our neighbor's wedding, but we weren't able to attend.
c. I have less confidence in my public speaking ability than Omar.
d. No mistakes.

255.

a. My parents and I took a taxi to the airport when we went to Mexico last year.
b. I think we should drive Lexi to school tomorrow?
c. They're going to eat dinner at Centertown Diner tonight.
d. No mistakes.

256.

a. My aunt Julie will celebrate her 97th birthday on February 16.
b. Despite having a lot of energy during the day, Emily felt too tired to go out to dinner in the evening.
c. Kahil picked up the purple child's toy from the ground.
d. No mistakes.

257.

a. It had been over two hours, and no one in the waiting area had gotten to see their doctor.

b. Harper, Kimiko, and Penelope had a sleepover at Aliyah's house and stayed up all night.

c. She'd never seen so few people at the department store before.

d. No mistakes.

258.

a. After school, I'm going to take the express train to the art museum.

b. Saya didn't like mushrooms; consequently, she declined to try Martin's mushroom soup.

c. My younger brother is going to loose his first tooth soon.

d. No mistakes.

259.

a. The child played nice with the books in the library.

b. Niki and Mark make an excellent couple.

c. Sam and Ela ate pizza and played at the party.

d. No mistakes.

260.

a. Professor Calkins gave Marcus and his friends high scores.

b. Sandra, I'd like to introduce you to my boss.

c. I don't mind working late but I do mind getting up early.

d. No mistakes.

261.

a. He is best friends with both Sarah and I.

b. Either Julia or Jenna will grade the test.

c. My favorite book of all time is *Pride and Prejudice.*

d. No mistakes.

262.

a. Unfortunately, I cannot finish the laundry.

b. Because my mom overslept, I was late to school.

c. Stop running, or you will skin your knee!

d. No mistakes.

263.

a. Dr. Lyons exclaimed, "My how big you've gotten"!

b. My aunt is expecting a new baby any day now.

c. We all participated in the school concert.

d. No mistakes.

264.

a. My younger sister is usually in some kind of trouble.

b. I met my best friend in first grade.

c. I fell off my bike after the road had became wet.

d. No mistakes.

265.

a. Please don't tell on me.

b. Because I absolutely love any type of chocolate.

c. To whom should I give the package?

d. No mistakes.

266.

a. Oh my gosh I forgot to let the dog in!

b. It's never too late to say you are sorry.

c. Pera, where did you say your family emigrated from?

d. No mistakes.

267.

a. She slowly skipped to school, enjoying all the sounds of spring.

b. Ignore my brother; he's usually irritating.

c. Which of the triplets can run faster?

d. No mistakes.

268.

a. March came in like a lion and went out like one too!
b. Mila is always moving to the beat, dancing up a storm, or she's loud in general.
c. Can you take this message back to Uncle Brian?
d. No mistakes.

269.

a. I can't tell the twins apart from one another.
b. My son learned to ride on a balance bike.
c. She easily transitioned to a new school and new town.
d. No mistakes.

270.

a. I love all animals accept snakes.
b. After the snowstorm, the whole neighborhood was out of electricity.
c. I was invited to three different parties this weekend.
d. No mistakes.

271.

a. Josie or her friends will meet you at the restaurant.
b. Bodi, Luka, and me came in third place.
c. Peanut allergies can be deadly to many students.
d. No mistakes.

272.

a. When do you expect the race to end?
b. Fatima is horribly shy around strangers.
c. Trevor's favorite season is Autumn.
d. No mistakes.

273.

a. "Work hard and play hard" is a motto I live by.
b. Winston my new dog is still not potty trained.
c. The children looked out the window, anxiously awaiting the arrival of their cousins.
d. No mistakes.

274.

a. Her friends opinions were often hard to decipher.
b. Everyone has his or her own take on the food fight at lunch today.
c. If I could, I'd paint every room in my house red.
d. No mistakes.

275.

a. Seamus screamed, "Stop"! but it was too late.
b. Declan is one of the only boys in his Irish dance class.
c. The tractor still ran despite being over twenty years old.
d. No mistakes.

276.

a. In reality, very few people are geniuses.
b. I'm not sure whose turn it is I know that I already played twice.
c. If you need help in math, you should go to the math office during lunch.
d. No mistakes.

277.

a. My brother's band is playing at the Vic Theatre this weekend.
b. Bridgit can't eat much for breakfast, or she gets sick.
c. Phil is so nice without a bit of arrogance in his demeanor.
d. No mistakes.

278.

a. I collect sand from all the places I've travelled.
b. The church service was canceled due to an impending storm.
c. I love children, but hate babysitting.
d. No mistakes.

Spelling

Directions: For questions 279-288, look for errors in spelling. If there is no error, choose D.

279.

a. The magician made his assistant disappear.

b. Lois carefuly unwrapped the present from her brother.

c. The business closed early for Presidents' Day.

d. No mistakes.

280.

a. It's facsinating to learn about the newest technology.

b. After months of studying and hard work, she passed her final exam and received a diploma.

c. My cousins and I took an international flight last year.

d. No mistakes.

281.

a. Mateo was exceptionally respectful and kind.

b. The firefighter received an award for her couragous actions.

c. It's easy to assume that you won't make mistakes on something you have done many times.

d. No mistakes.

282.

a. The committee decided to build a park rather than a swimming pool.

b. Aidan was easily embarrassed.

c. Last year, I went to the theater with my class to see a performance of one of Shakespeare's plays.

d. No mistakes.

283.

a. Many of the zoo's exhibits were closed due to the frigid weather.

b. Hareem has played soccer with his dad every weekend since he was a kindergartener.

c. My mom's long explanation was unnecesary: I already knew what I had done wrong.

d. No mistakes.

284.

a. The minature chair was the perfect size for my little sister's dollhouse.

b. Hudson washed the cutlery in the dishwasher every evening.

c. It's so exhilarating to dive into a swimming pool!

d. No mistakes.

285.

a. Zoe was hopeful that she would receive an A on her final examination.

b. My nephews were so greatful that we took them to the museum over winter break.

c. Afraid that he would miss his flight, Farad woke up exceptionally early to head to the airport.

d. No mistakes.

286.

a. The brilliant scientist is going to announce his discovery tomorrow.

b. Hannah and Samara recommended that we go to the new movie theater near the museum.

c. He acheived his childhood dream of becoming a firefighter.

d. No mistakes.

287.

a. Zara specifically requested to try out for the varsity basketball team even though she was only a freshman.

b. The senery in the national park was beautiful and serene.

c. Next year, I'm going to play trombone in the high school's orchestra.

d. No mistakes.

288.

a. It takes years of practice and incredible discipline to become a professional athlete.

b. Millie often exagerated her professional accomplishments.

c. My older cousin is a sophomore at the college that I hope to attend.

d. No mistakes.

Composition

Directions: For questions 289-298, read the question and select the best answer.

289. Choose the best word to join the thoughts together.

Maria studied consistently and diligently for her chemistry class every night; ________ she earned an A+ on the final exam.

a. accordingly,

b. nonetheless,

c. immediately,

d. besides,

290. Choose the best word(s) to join the thoughts together.

Pasta is truly one of the world's favorite and most diverse foods, ________ the over 300 different pasta shapes available across the globe.

a. despite

b. evidenced by

c. in fact

d. notwithstanding

291. Choose the group of words that best completes the sentence.

Before engaging in any strenuous physical activity ________.

a. stretch because it is important

b. it is important to stretch because stretching helps to avoid injuries that can happen if you don't stretch

c. it is important to stretch thoroughly in order to avoid injury

d. stretching is good

292. Which of these sentences expresses the idea most clearly?

a. Colleen and Sarah wished to be included in the project.

b. They, meaning Sarah and Colleen, wished to be included in the project.

c. Wishing to be included in the project were Sarah and Colleen.

d. Sarah wished to be included in the project and Colleen did too.

293. Which of these sentences expresses the idea most clearly?

a. Favorite things to do on vacation for Mandy are hiking, skiing, and relaxing.

b. Skiing, hiking, and relaxing are Mandy's favorite on vacation things to do.

c. Mandy's favorite things to do on vacation are hiking, to ski, and relaxing.

d. Mandy's favorite things to do on vacation are hiking, skiing, and relaxing.

294. Which of these sentences expresses the idea the most clearly?

a. Marcus was terrified of heights but rode the ferris wheel with him because he wanted to ride it.
b. Marcus rode with him despite fear.
c. Although Marcus was terrified of heights, he faced his fear and rode the ferris wheel with Tony.
d. Tony rode the ferris wheel with Marcus even though Marcus was terrified of heights which made it tough for him to do.

295. Which of the following topics is best for a one-page essay?

a. The History of World War II
b. Modern Genetics and Its Applications in Medicine
c. A Brief Synopsis of the 2018 Winter Olympics
d. The Art of the Italian Renaissance

296. Which of these sentences fits best under the topic "How to Warm Up Before Singing"?

a. Warming up helps you sing better.
b. Singers who do not warm up do not sound as good as those who do.
c. Do a variety of warm ups that use different vowel and consonant sounds and hit the lower, middle, and upper parts of your vocal register.
d. Warming up before singing is fun!

297. Which sentence does NOT belong in the paragraph?

Mike had always wanted to visit Yellowstone National Park. (2) The National Park Service was created by Congress in 1916. (3) He finally was able to plan his trip to Yellowstone for the last week in May. (4) Once he arrived, he was awestruck by the natural beauty of the park.

a. 1
b. 2
c. 3
d. 4

298. Where should the sentence "In contrast, more modern musicals typically have scores that are influenced by modern pop and rock music" be placed in the following paragraph?

Not all musicals are alike and can vary greatly depending on when they were written. (2) For example, musicals of the early to mid-20th century relied heavily on the traditions of opera and vaudeville shows. (3) Regardless of which style you prefer, there is something for everyone to enjoy in the world of musical theater!

a. Before sentence 1
b. Between sentences 1 and 2
c. Between sentences 2 and 3
d. After sentence 3

Answer Key

Verbal

1. C
2. C
3. C
4. D
5. C
6. D
7. B
8. A
9. B
10. B
11. A
12. B
13. D
14. C
15. C
16. A
17. C
18. B
19. A
20. B
21. A
22. C
23. C
24. A
25. B
26. D
27. B
28. A
29. D
30. C
31. D
32. D
33. A
34. A
35. D
36. B
37. D
38. D
39. A
40. C
41. C
42. D
43. B
44. C
45. B
46. C
47. C
48. C
49. D
50. A
51. B
52. A
53. D
54. A
55. B
56. D
57. C
58. C
59. B
60. C

Quantitative

61. D
62. B
63. B
64. A
65. C
66. C
67. B
68. D
69. A
70. A
71. A
72. B
73. C
74. C
75. A
76. B
77. C
78. D
79. B
80. B
81. C
82. D
83. B
84. C
85. C
86. D
87. C
88. D
89. D
90. B
91. C
92. C
93. A
94. A
95. B
96. C
97. B
98. B
99. C
100. C
101. B
102. D
103. C
104. A
105. A
106. C
107. B
108. A
109. C
110. C
111. D
112. C

Reading

113. D
114. C
115. B
116. A
117. D
118. C
119. A
120. C
121. C
122. B
123. B
124. C
125. D
126. A
127. C
128. D
129. A
130. C
131. B
132. C
133. C
134. B
135. D
136. C
137. C
138. B
139. C
140. D
141. D
142. A
143. C
144. D
145. C
146. A
147. C
148. C
149. C
150. A
151. A
152. D
153. C
154. B
155. A
156. C
157. B
158. D
159. A
160. B
161. C
162. C
163. A
164. D
165. C
166. B
167. B
168. A
169. D
170. B
171. C
172. A
173. D
174. B

Math

175. B
176. D
177. A
178. D
179. B
180. C
181. A
182. B
183. C
184. B
185. D
186. A
187. C
188. C
189. B
190. B
191. A
192. A
193. D
194. A
195. B
196. C
197. C
198. D
199. B
200. D
201. A
202. D
203. C
204. A
205. D
206. D
207. C
208. D
209. B
210. A
211. C
212. C
213. B
214. B
215. C
216. A
217. D
218. A
219. D
220. D
221. D
222. D
223. C
224. B
225. B
226. B
227. C
228. D
229. D
230. A
231. B
232. B
233. D
234. C
235. D
236. B
237. B
238. D

Language

239. A
240. B
241. C
242. B
243. C
244. A
245. D
246. C
247. A
248. D
249. C
250. A
251. B
252. B
253. B
254. A
255. B
256. C
257. A
258. C
259. A
260. C
261. A
262. D
263. A
264. C
265. B
266. A
267. C
268. B
269. D
270. A
271. B
272. C
273. B
274. A
275. A
276. B
277. D
278. C
279. B
280. A
281. B
282. D
283. C
284. A
285. B
286. C
287. B
288. B
289. A
290. B
291. C
292. A
293. D
294. C
295. C
296. C
297. B
298. C

HSPT Test 5

Verbal Section 5

60 Questions, 16 Minutes

Instructions: Select the best answer.

1. Which word does *not* belong with the others?

   a. appetizer
   b. dessert
   c. meal
   d. main course

2. Tamara's ice cream melted more quickly than Henry's ice cream. Milo's ice cream melted more slowly than Tamara's ice cream. Milo's ice cream melted more quickly than Henry's ice cream. If the first two statements are true, the third statement is

   a. true
   b. false
   c. uncertain

3. Intermittent most nearly means

   a. sporadic
   b. steady
   c. interesting
   d. sudden

4. Explicit means the *opposite* of

   a. average
   b. ambiguous
   c. clear
   d. everlasting

5. There are no wimples on wocketts. Some wocketts are grompettes. Grompettes have no wimples. If the first two statements are true, the third statement is

   a. true
   b. false
   c. uncertain

6. Bird is to insect as shark is to

   a. bite
   b. snake
   c. fish
   d. seaweed

7. Which word does *not* belong with the others?

   a. author
   b. poet
   c. actor
   d. composer

8. Mesa means the *opposite* of

   a. west
   b. flat
   c. round
   d. gorge

9. Which word does *not* belong with the others?

   a. walk
   b. hike
   c. trail
   d. run

10. Mina read more books than Clark. Clark read more books than Samson and Grant. Mina read more books than Samson. If the first two statements are true, the third statement is

    a. true
    b. false
    c. uncertain

11. Which word does *not* belong with the others?

    a. washing machine
    b. dryer
    c. clothesline
    d. clothes

12. Saturate most nearly means

    a. wring
    b. fatten
    c. soak
    d. dehydrate

13. Bake is to cake as fry is to

    a. bacon
    b. french
    c. oil
    d. muffins

14. Which word does *not* belong with the others?

    a. pleasant
    b. disagreeable
    c. nice
    d. cordial

15. Pizza is less expensive than sushi. Salad is less expensive pizza. Sushi is less expensive than salad. If the first two statements are true, the third statement is

    a. true
    b. false
    c. uncertain

16. Erroneous most nearly means

    a. timid
    b. strict
    c. faulty
    d. smelly

17. Obsolete means the *opposite* of

    a. antiquated
    b. current
    c. oblique
    d. delete

18. Which word does *not* belong with the others?

    a. remove
    b. multiply
    c. reduce
    d. subtract

19. Oration most nearly means

    a. speech
    b. print
    c. literature
    d. less

20. Jorge has three nickels more than Jordan. Teresa has ten cents less than Jorge. Jordan has more money than Teresa. If the first two statements are true, the third statement is

    a. true
    b. false
    c. uncertain

21. Reclusive means the *opposite* of

    a. argumentative
    b. private
    c. withdrawn
    d. sociable

22. Barber is to hair as dermatologist is to

    a. head
    b. skin
    c. office
    d. trim

23. Which word does *not* belong with the others?

    a. drizzle
    b. thunderstorm
    c. monsoon
    d. downpour

24. Morose most nearly means

    a. excitable
    b. ambivalent
    c. dour
    d. angry

25. Shell is to oyster as helmet is to

    a. bicycle
    b. plastic
    c. protect
    d. head

26. Panacea most nearly means

    a. bread
    b. cooking vessel
    c. remedy
    d. continent

27. Janet collected more soda cans for recycling than Samantha. Cynthia collected fewer soda cans than Janet. Janet collected the most soda cans. If the first two statements are true, the third statement is

    a. true
    b. false
    c. uncertain

28. Which word does *not* belong with the others?

    a. Chicago
    b. Boston
    c. San Francisco
    d. London

29. The zenith of a mountain is _________ ?

    a. its steepest side
    b. its highest point
    c. its base
    d. where the most wildlife is

30. Cardigan is to sweater as recliner is to

    a. comfortable
    b. button
    c. chair
    d. warm

31. Affable means the *opposite* of

    a. sleepy
    b. rude
    c. friendly
    d. intelligent

32. Which word does *not* belong with the others?

    a. whole number
    b. letter
    c. fraction
    d. decimal

33. Oliver has more pets than Sandra. Melinda has more pets than Sandra. Oliver has more pets than Melinda. If the first two statements are true, the third statement is

    a. true
    b. false
    c. uncertain

34. Which word does *not* belong with the others?

    a. beard
    b. moustache
    c. goatee
    d. hair

35. Dog is to mammal as turtle is to

    a. legs
    b. ocean
    c. animal
    d. reptile

36. Belie means the *opposite* of

    a. affirm
    b. beguile
    c. stomach
    d. disprove

37. Acrimonious most nearly means

    a. peaceful
    b. caustic
    c. neutral
    d. friendly

38. Which word does *not* belong with the others?

    a. neon
    b. argon
    c. helium
    d. carbon dioxide

39. Dan is taller than Brian. Brian is taller than Jamie. Jamie is taller than Dan. If the first two statements are true, the third statement is

    a. true
    b. false
    c. uncertain

40. Walk is to stroll as leap is to

a. jump
b. crawl
c. spin
d. sit

41. Which word does *not* belong with the others?

a. sleeping
b. dozing
c. nap
d. snoozing

42. The state fair was more crowded than the county fair. The county fair was less crowded than the renaissance fair. The renaissance fair was the least crowded. If the first two statements are true, the third statement is

a. true
b. false
c. uncertain

43. Scarce most nearly means

a. scant
b. frightened
c. abundant
d. brave

44. Lucid means the *opposite* of

a. understandable
b. clear
c. incoherent
d. thick

45. Which word does *not* belong with the others?

a. piano
b. organ
c. harpsichord
d. guitar

46. Which word does *not* belong with the others?

a. asteroid
b. moon
c. meteor
d. comet

47. Singer is to voice as to painter is to

a. paint
b. hands
c. canvas
d. artist

48. Jamal's office is northwest of Esther's office. Esther's office is southeast of Pedro's office. Pedro's office is north of Jamal's office. If the first two statements are true, the third statement is

a. true
b. false
c. uncertain

49. Mutable most nearly means

a. silently
b. whisper
c. changeable
d. avoidable

50. Demolish most nearly means

a. construct
b. destroy
c. demo
d. polish

51. Which word does *not* belong with the others?

a. Australia
b. South America
c. Africa
d. continent

52. Board game is to board as tennis is to

a. game
b. court
c. player
d. ball

53. Lei enjoys camping more than Mona and Greg. Greg enjoys camping more than Paul. Mona enjoys camping more than Paul. If the first two statements are true, the third statement is

a. true
b. false
c. uncertain

54. Lax means the *opposite* of

    a. casual
    b. absence
    c. abundance
    d. strict

55. Philanthropist most nearly means

    a. benefactor
    b. philosopher
    c. volunteer
    d. businessperson

56. Boisterous means the *opposite* of

    a. solemn
    b. loud
    c. rambunctious
    d. angry

57. Which word does *not* belong with the others?

    a. restaurant
    b. cafe
    c. movie theatre
    d. banquet hall

58. Which word does *not* belong with the others?

    a. circle
    b. shape
    c. hexagon
    d. pentagon

59. Earth is to solar system as reef is to

    a. fish
    b. land
    c. ocean
    d. universe

60. Orange kerfuffles are heavier than green kerfuffles. Purple striped kerfuffles and brown spotted kerfuffles are not lighter than green kerfuffles. Green kerfuffles are the lightest. If the first two statements are true, the third statement is

    a. true
    b. false
    c. uncertain

Quantitative Section 5

52 Questions, 30 Minutes

Instructions: Select the best answer.

61. Examine the triangle and find the best answer.

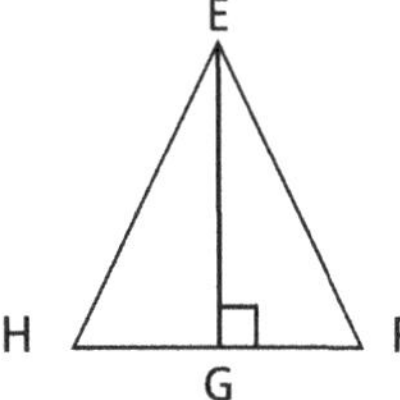

a. EF is equal to GF
b. EG is equal to GF
c. EG is greater than EF
d. GF is less than EF

62. What is two more than seven times twelve?

a. 80
b. 86
c. 73
d. 84

63. Examine (A), (B), and (C) and find the best answer.

(A) 10×10^0
(B) 20×10^1
(C) 1×10^2

a. $(A) > (B) > (C)$
b. $(C) > (A) < (B)$
c. $(A) = (C)$
d. $(C) < (A) > (B)$

64. Look at this series: 100, 50, ___ , 35, 55. What number should fill the blank?

a. 65
b. 70
c. 25
d. 10

65. What is 10 less than $\frac{2}{3}$ of 36?

a. 62
b. 44
c. 18
d. 14

66. 16 is what percent of 80?

a. 10%
b. 20%
c. 35%
d. 44%

67. Examine (A), (B), and (C) and find the best answer.

(A) 1% of 300
(B) 10% of 30
(C) 100% of 3

a. $(A) > (B) > (C)$
b. $(C) > (A) < (B)$
c. $(A) = (B) = (C)$
d. $(C) < (A) > (B)$

68. Review this series: 100, 150, ___ , 250, 300. What number should fill the blank?

a. 200
b. 300
c. 100
d. 175

69. What number is 15 percent of 36?

a. 4.5
b. 4
c. 5.4
d. 54

70. Examine (A), (B), and (C) and find the best answer.

(A) The volume of cube with a side of 3

(B) The volume of rectangular prism with a height of 6, width of 4, and length of 3

(C) The volume of a cube with a side of 5

a. (A) > (B) > (C)
b. (C) > (B) > (A)
c. (B) > (A) > (C)
d. (C) < (A) > (B)

71. What number is five less than the average of thirty, fifteen, and nine.

a. 11
b. 12
c. 13
d. 14

72. What is the missing number in the following series: 3, 3, 12, 9, 48, ___, 192?

a. 15
b. 45
c. 24
d. 27

73. What number is three more than the square root of 81?

a. 3
b. 6
c. 9
d. 12

74. Examine the following series: 23, 12, ___, 12, 17, 12, 14. What number is missing?

a. 15
b. 19
c. 20
d. 26

75. Examine the cube and find the best answer.

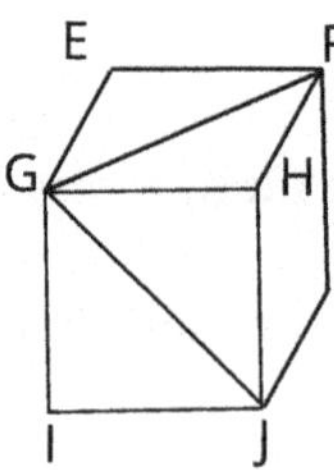

a. EF is longer than GH
b. GF is longer than GI
c. IJ is longer than GJ
d. GF is equal to EF

76. Review this series: 37, 39, ___, 15, 5. What is the missing number?

a. 29
b. 41
c. 13
d. 17

77. Examine the figure below. Select the largest answer.

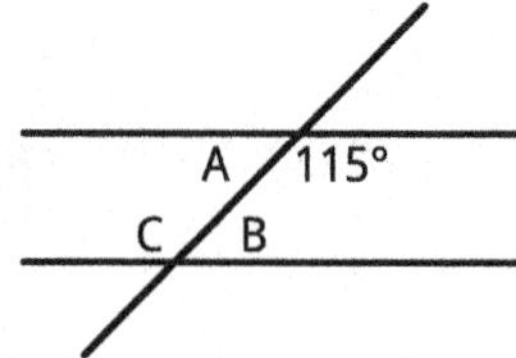

a. A + B
b. C - A
c. C + A
d. B - C

78. Review the series: 12, 24, A, 13, 26, B, ___. Find the next number.

a. 14
b. 28
c. C
d. 11

79. Look at the following series: VI, 4, IX, 6, XII, 8, ___. What number or roman numeral is missing?

a. XIV
b. XV
c. XVI
d. X

80. Examine the figure below and (A), (B), and (C) and find the best answer.

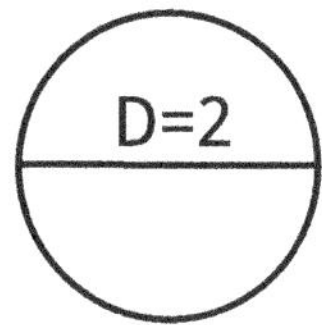

(A) The area of the circle
(B) The diameter of the circle
(C) The circumference of the circle

a. (A) is greater than both (B) and (C)
b. (C) is smaller than both (A) and (B)
c. (B) is greater than both (A) and (C)
d. (B) is smaller than both (A) and (C)

81. Review this series: 3, 4, 6, 9,____, ____, 24, 31. What numbers are missing?

a. 13, 17
b. 14, 19
c. 13, 18
d. 14, 20

82. Examine (A), (B), and (C) and find the best answer.

(A) $8 + 3 \times 2$
(B) $2 + 3 \times 8$
(C) $3 + 8 \times 2$

a. (A) is equal to (C) and more than (B)
b. (A) is more than both (B) and (C)
c. (B) is more than (C), but less than (A)
d. (A) is less than both (B) and (C)

83. What is the missing number in the following series: 4, 8, 16, ____, 64, 128?

a. 24
b. 32
c. 48
d. 36

84. Review the following series: 8, 32, 12, 48, 28, ____, ____. What numbers are missing?

a. 112, 92
b. 112, 72
c. 52, 92
d. 72, 122

85. What is 50% of 80% of 160?

a. 128
b. 64
c. 36
d. 76

86. Review the following series: 14, 12, 20, ____, ____, 24, 32. What numbers are missing?

a. 18, 26
b. 12, 14
c. 18, 28
d. 28, 26

87. Examine (A), (B), and (C) and find the best answer.

(A) .36
(B) $\frac{1}{3}$
(C) 35%

a. (A) > (B) > (C)
b. (B) > (A) > (C)
c. (A) > (C) > (B)
d. (C) < (A) < (B)

88. Review this series: 81, 64, ____, ____, 9, 68, 3. What numbers are missing?

a. 32, 68
b. 27, 67
c. 32, 67
d. 27, 66

89. What is 20 less than the quotient of 56 and 4?

a. 6
b. -6
c. 7
d. -7

90. In the problem below, a is an integer greater than 2. Examine (A), (B), and (C) and find the best answer.

(A) $a \times a$
(B) a^3
(C) $2a$

a. (A) is greater than (B), but smaller than (C)
b. (A) is greater than (C) but smaller than (B)
c. (A) is equal to (C), but smaller than (B)
d. (A), (B), and (C) are equal

91. What number is missing from the following series: -1, -3, 1, 3, 7, 21, ___?

a. 25
b. 26
c. 42
d. 14

92. Examine (A), (B), and (C) and select the largest answer.

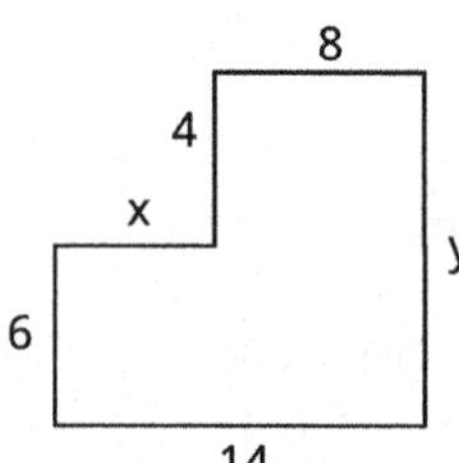

a. x - y
b. x
c. y
d. y - x

93. Examine the following series: $\frac{1}{4}$, $\frac{1}{2}$, 1, $\frac{5}{4}$, $\frac{7}{4}$, What number should come next?

a. $\frac{9}{4}$
b. 2
c. $\frac{3}{2}$
d. $\frac{5}{2}$

94. Examine (A), (B), and (C) and find the best answer.

(A) $(21 \div 7) \times 2$
(B) $(32 \div 8) \times 2$
(C) $(48 \div 12) \times 2$

a. (C) is equal to (A) but less than (B)
b. (B) is equal to (C) and greater than (A)
c. (A) is less than (B) and greater than (C)
d. (C) is greater than (B) but less than (A)

95. Examine this series: 53, 65, 56, 62, 59, 59, ___, ___.What numbers should come next?

a. 56, 62
b. 65, 56
c. 62, 56
d. 65, 59

96. $\frac{2}{5}$ of 20 is equal to the quotient of 16 and what number?

a. 2
b. 4
c. 8
d. 1

97. Review this series: 11, 18, 24, 29, 33, ___. What number should come next?

a. 38
b. 35
c. 37
d. 36

98. Examine (A), (B), and (C) and find the best answer.

(A) $8 + 3^2$
(B) 4^2
(C) $11 + 2^2$

a. (A) is greater than (C) but less than (B)
b. (B) is less than both (A) and (C)
c. (A) is greater than both (B) and (C)
d. (A) is equal to (B)

99. Examine (A), (B), and (C) and find the best answer.

(A) (B) (C)

a. (B) and (C) are equally shaded.
b. (A) is less shaded than (B) and equally shaded to (C)
c. (C) is more shaded than (B) but less shaded than (A)
d. (B) is less shaded than (C) but more shaded than (A)

100. Look at this series: 23, 18, 15, 10, 7, ___. What number should come next?

a. 4
b. 2
c. 6
d. 1

101. The quotient of 24 and 3 is equal to what percent of 40?

a. 20%
b. 5%
c. 25%
d. 50%

102. Review the following series: II, IV, VI, IIX, X, ___. What number should come next?

a. XI
b. XV
c. VIII
d. XII

103. The square root of 36 is equal to the quotient of 48 and what number?

a. 8
b. 12
c. 18
d. 22

104. Examine (A), (B), and (C) and find the best answer.

(A) $\frac{2}{5}$ of 30
(B) $\frac{3}{4}$ of 16
(C) $\frac{1}{4}$ of 48

a. (A) is equal to (C) but less than (B)
b. (A), (B), and (C) are all equal
c. (B) is equal to (C) but less than (A)
d. (A) is more than both (B) and (C)

105. What is the next number in the following series: 50, 25, 20, 10, 5, ___?

a. 0
b. 2
c. 2.5
d. 3

106. $\frac{1}{6}, \frac{1}{3}, \frac{1}{2}, \frac{2}{3}, \frac{5}{6},$ ___

a. 1
b. $\frac{7}{6}$
c. $\frac{4}{3}$
d. $\frac{3}{2}$

107. 30% of 60 is equal to the product of 2 and what number?

a. 18
b. 8
c. 20
d. 9

108. What is the next number in the following series: 47, 41, 35, 29, 23, ___?

a. 16
b. 15
c. 17
d. 20

109. What is $\frac{1}{5}$ of 60 divided by 2?

a. 12
b. 6
c. 3
d. 8

110. Examine (A), (B), and (C) and find the best answer.

(A) 1 quarter, 1 dime, 1 nickel, 1 penny
(B) 1 quarter, 2 dimes
(C) 3 dimes, 1 nickel, 4 pennies

a. (A) + (C) < (A) + (B)
b. (A) = (C)
c. (A) - (C) > (B) - (C)
d. (B) + (C) < (A)

111. Examine (A), (B), and (C) and find the best answer.

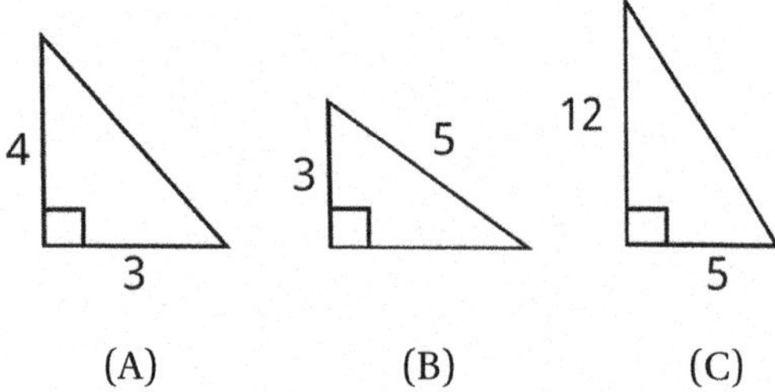

(A) The area of triangle A
(B) Three times the missing side of triangle B
(C) The hypotenuse of triangle C

a. (C) is greater than (B) which is greater than (A)
b. (A) is less than (B) but greater than (C)
c. (B) is greater than both (A) and (C)
d. (A) is equal to (B) but less than (C)

112. Look at this series: 90, 80, 92, 40, 94, 20, ____. What number should come next?

a. 10
b. 30
c. 92
d. 96

Reading Section 5

62 Questions, 25 Minutes

Reading Comprehension

Instructions: Read each passage carefully and mark one answer for each question.

Questions 113 - 120 refer to the passage below.

Steve Tolman had done a wrong thing and he knew it. While his parents and sister Doris had been absent in New York for a weekend visit, the boy had taken the six-cylinder car from the garage without permission and carried a crowd of his friends to Torrington to a football game. And that was not the worst of it, either. At the foot of the long hill leading into the village the mighty leviathan had come to a halt, refusing to move another inch, and Stephen now sat helplessly in it, awaiting the aid his comrades had promised to send back from the town.

Steve scowled with chagrin and disappointment. The catastrophe served him right. Unquestionably, he should not have taken the car without asking. He had never driven it all by himself before, although many times he had successfully driven it when his father had been at his elbow. What reason had he to suppose a mishap would befall him when they were not around? It was infernally hard luck!

Goodness only knew what was the matter with the car. Probably something was smashed, something that might require days or even weeks to repair, and would cost a lot of money. How angry his father would be!

His friends had not given him much sympathy, either. They had been ready enough to egg him on into wrong-doing and had made of the adventure the jolliest lark imaginable; but when the fun had been transformed into calamity they had deserted him with incredible speed. It was easy enough for them to wash their hands of the affair and leave him to the solitude of the roadside; the automobile was not theirs and when they got home they would not be confronted by irate parents.

113. Steve's attitude can best be described as

a. furious
b. regretful
c. jovial
d. sad

114. Why did Steve take the car out without his parents' permission?

a. He wanted to prove to himself that he could drive.
b. He had to take his sister to New York.
c. His friends pressured him into it.
d. He loved driving.

115. During this passage, where is Steve?

a. sitting in his car in a repair shop
b. standing on the road, waiting for help to come
c. sitting in his stalled car at the bottom of the hill
d. sitting in his car outside of the Torrington football game

116. When Steve describes his car as "the mighty leviathan," what literary device is he using?

a. simile
b. imagery
c. onomatopoeia
d. metaphor

117. What happened to Steve's car?

a. Steve drove off the hill.
b. Steve crashed it into another car.
c. His friends crashed it.
d. It broke down.

118. In the final paragraph, the author uses the metaphor "wash their hands of the affair" to

   a. show how easy it was for Steve's friends to abandon him when things went wrong
   b. suggest that Steve's friends got dirty trying to fix his car and had to wash up
   c. argue that Steve's friends should not be held responsible for Steve's problems
   d. suggest that Steve's friends were going to clean up and then get help

119. Prior to the day of the story, had Steve driven the car?

   a. Yes, he drove it with his sister, Doris.
   b. Yes, he drove it with his father.
   c. Yes, he drove his family to New York for a weekend trip.
   d. No, he'd never driven the car before.

120. What type of narration is used in the story?

   a. first person
   b. second person
   c. third person
   d. none of the above

Questions 121 - 128 refer to the passage below.

Many people falsely believe that the scientific term "theory" has the same meaning as the casual, everyday version of the word. In reality, they're very different concepts. This misconception leads to confusion and frustration for both scientists and the public.

In its everyday use, a theory is nothing more than an educated guess. Often, it describes something as basic as a hunch that is based on little to no evidence. For instance, a student might have a theory that their school cafeteria accidentally purchased a 100-year supply of pudding, built from the observation that pudding is served with almost every lunch. Although this is not an impossible explanation for why there is so much pudding available, it's not a very reasonable conclusion either. So, while the student could certainly call that idea a theory in the <u>vernacular</u> sense, it is really just a guess (or hypothesis) according to scientific standards.

A scientific theory, on the other hand, represents almost the exact opposite of a guess: it's considered scientific fact, alongside scientific law. On that note, it's important to remember that theories and laws are not the same thing. Laws are descriptions of scientific phenomena, while theories offer explanations for those events. Basically, laws describe how something happens in science, and theories explain why it happens. Although theories usually include laws, neither one is superior in terms of truthfulness.

In order for a prediction to become a scientific theory, almost all doubt about its accuracy has to be eliminated. This process typically takes many years of testing, in which every single experiment has to prove that the prediction of the theory is correct, time after time. If any evidence is found that disproves the theory, or if any alternative explanations are discovered, the theory is either adjusted or discarded. In this way, science has arrived at the theory of gravity, cell theory, and many other theories that help us understand the world we live in.

121. According to the passage, a scientific theory is

  a. a guess
  b. a scientific law
  c. a highly accurate and well tested prediction
  d. a hypothesis

122. Why does the author include the pudding example?

  a. to show that everyday theories can be very accurate
  b. to clarify how an everyday theory is different than a scientific law
  c. to describe how a scientist would define a theory
  d. to illustrate that an everyday theory is little more than a guess

123. As it is used in the passage, what does the word <u>vernacular</u> mean?

  a. scientific
  b. informal
  c. unreasonable
  d. adolescent

124. Which of the following would be an appropriate title for this passage?

  a. "Defining the Scientific Theory"
  b. "Theories versus Laws"
  c. "The Theory of Gravity"
  d. "Why Trust Scientific Laws?"

125. The author would likely describe which of the following as a scientific theory?

  a. The sky is blue.
  b. The earth rotates around the sun.
  c. My dogs hate taking baths, therefore, all dogs hate taking baths.
  d. Many diseases occur because microorganisms called germs invade the body.

126. According to the passage, which is the most accurate?

  a. educated guesses
  b. scientific laws
  c. scientific theories
  d. scientific theories and laws are equally accurate

127. In which type of text would you expect to find this passage?

    a. a science magazine for non-scientists
    b. a newspaper
    c. a memoir
    d. a college-level physics textbook

128. If a scientist finds evidence to disprove an aspect of a scientific theory, which of the following could happen next?

    a. The theory will be strengthened.
    b. The theory will be turned into a scientific law.
    c. The theory will be adjusted.
    d. Nothing will happen.

Questions 129 - 135 refer to the passage below.

Denim trousers had been a popular workwear option for labor-based industries in Europe and America for more than a century by the time Levi Strauss and Jacob Davis patented what they called "waist overalls" on May 20th, 1873. The pair intended to take advantage of the demand that had been created by the 1848 California Gold Rush, and their pants were designed specifically with prospectors, cowboys, and other hard laborers in mind. Accordingly, their indigo-dyed cotton trousers featured metal rivets that reinforced weak spots, to help the pants stand up to the wear and tear of life in the American West. These "waist overalls" are now thought of as the first modern blue jeans.

In the mid-20th century, blue jeans began to make the leap from a purely functional clothing item to a fashion statement. After the pants became a key aesthetic feature of hip young stars like James Dean and Elvis Presley, jeans were adopted by would-be rebels everywhere. Although men remained the primary market, jeans gained popularity among women after actress Marilyn Monroe sported a pair in movies like Some Like it Hot and The Misfits. At a time when most women were still expected to wear skirts, jeans represented a daring alternative.

Today, jeans are a <u>staple</u> item in most American wardrobes. Today, most jeans differ significantly from their predecessors. Traditional jeans are made from a thicker, stiffer fabric that often requires significant breaking-in. The use of thinner, mixed fabrics and artificial dyes of newer jean options prevent dramatic shrinkage in the wash and help keep color from leaking onto skin and clothing. While the old-fashioned options are less trendy, their durable fabric remains a steadfast choice for rough and practical wear.

129. In which century did jeans first become fashionable?

   a. 1700s
   b. 1800s
   c. 1900s
   d. 2000s

130. According to the passage, which of the following is true about Levi Strauss and Jacob Davis?

   a. They invented denim trousers.
   b. They invented modern American blue jeans.
   c. They made blue jeans fashionable among the general public.
   d. They encouraged women to wear their blue jeans.

131. As it is used in the passage, what does the word <u>staple</u> mean?

   a. unusual
   b. attach
   c. unique
   d. standard

132. In which way are traditional jeans different than modern jeans?

   a. Traditional jeans are made of a thinner material.
   b. Traditional jeans do not shrink in the wash.
   c. Traditional jeans are made of a stiffer material.
   d. Traditional jeans are made with artificial dyes.

133. In the 1800s, what type of person would most likely wear blue jeans?

   a. housewives
   b. factory workers
   c. businessmen
   d. celebrities

134. When jeans became a fashion statement, what did they symbolize?

   a. beauty
   b. tradition
   c. youth
   d. rebellion

135. Based on the information in the last paragraph, in which scenario would the traditional, old fashioned jeans be superior to the more modern jeans?

   a. Setting up a tent while camping.
   b. Playing board games with friends.
   c. Going to a party.
   d. Relaxing around the house.

136. This passage is primarily about

   a. the history of blue jeans
   b. Levi Strauss and Jacob Davis
   c. waist trousers
   d. celebrities' influence on the popularity of blue jeans

Questions 137 - 144 refer to the passage below.

No one knows exactly when or where yoga was first practiced, but most historians agree that yoga originated somewhere in India at least 2,500 years ago. The first written mentions of yoga are found in the ancient Sanskrit texts that comprise the earliest Hindu scriptures, the Vedas. During the Vedic Period (1500-500 BCE), yoga was a religious ritual practiced by those seeking enlightenment. While ancient yoga most likely bore little resemblance to the modern activity, the underlying spiritual goals of self-improvement and harmony remain.

The development of Hatha yoga in the 8th century arguably marks the beginnings of what we now think of as yoga. Hatha-style yoga introduced the use of physical poses as a way to influence the mental state, and includes most other forms of yoga such as Vinyasa, Ashtanga, and Yin yoga.

A Hindu monk named Swami Vivekananda brought yoga to the West in the late 1800s, where it initially gained traction among transcendentalist philosophers and artists. Vivekananda's speech at the 1893 World's Fair in Chicago earned a standing ovation, and he became a respected speaker across the United States and Europe. He promoted yoga as a way to strengthen and unify the mind and body, and he is often seen as the father of modern yoga. However, yoga did not really enter mainstream western society until the second half of the 20th century, when newly developed styles such as Bikram began to popularize yoga as a physical fitness option.

Yoga has become increasingly trendy in the last few decades, and many studies have been done on the effects of regular practice. The extent of yoga's impact remains controversial, but alleged benefits include improved balance, flexibility, cardiovascular function, mood, and focus.

137. How does modern yoga differ from yoga that was practiced prior to the 8th century?

a. Yoga was more popular before the 8th century.
b. Ancient yoga was not a religious activity, unlike modern yoga.
c. Modern yoga focuses on goals like self-improvement and harmony, whereas ancient yoga did not.
d. Ancient yoga was not as physical as modern yoga.

138. If Swami Vivekananda had never traveled to the West, it is likely that

a. the transcendentalist movement would have suffered
b. fewer Americans would practice yoga today
c. he would not have discovered the yoga styles of Hatha and Vinyasa
d. more people in the US and Europe would benefit from yoga

139. As it is used in the passage, the word comprise most nearly means

a. form
b. contrast
c. separate
d. settle

140. Based on the information from the passage, American philosophers were most likely interested in yoga because it

a. was a religious ritual
b. represented another culture
c. provided increased flexibility
d. unified the mind and body

141. The author most likely defines Hatha yoga in order to

a. show how it marked a turning point in the development of modern yoga
b. give context for Swami Vivekananda's speech at the Chicago World's Fair
c. explain yoga in the Vedic Period
d. imply suspicion about its alleged benefits

142. The information given in the passage implies that Bikram yoga

   a. is the same thing as Vinyasa yoga
   b. involves less stretching than other styles of yoga
   c. focuses on physical challenge more than other yoga styles
   d. was started by the same monks that created Ashtanga yoga

143. Which of these options would most likely follow the last paragraph?

   a. an analysis of the therapeutic effects of yoga
   b. descriptions of current influential yoga teachers
   c. a critical comparison between yoga and other exercises, such as swimming
   d. an in-depth discussion on the differences between modern and ancient yoga

144. What are the Vedas?

   a. a series of beliefs held by Sanskrit people
   b. the first yoga instruction books
   c. Hindu religious texts
   d. the historical record of post-Vedic Period India

Questions 145 - 152 refer to the passage below.

Polygraphs are often presented as high-tech, foolproof tools of justice when they are depicted in fiction and pop culture. In reality, polygraph technology is outdated, prone to errors, and easy to manipulate. The machines are based on the premise that many people become nervous when they lie, and that physical displays of anxiety (such as sweating and increased heart rate) will betray someone who is pretending to tell the truth. Contrary to popular belief, the device is not able to tell the difference between guilt and innocence whatsoever. All the polygraph can do is take note of a person's physical state during questioning; everything else is up for human interpretation.

The mechanics of lie-detection have advanced shockingly little since polygraphs were first designed roughly a century ago. Basically, the machine works by recording a few key bodily signs, such as heart rate, blood pressure, breathing, and sweating. During a polygraph test, a subject is connected to the instrument's sensors and then asked a series of questions. After the interrogation is complete, the subject's physical and verbal responses are compared and analyzed for inconsistencies.

Unfortunately, many people are immediately made uncomfortable by the test itself, which means they display physical signs of lying no matter what and risk failing as a result. This dangerous pattern has led to an unknown number of wrongful convictions. In the last few decades alone, modern DNA evidence has exonerated over a thousand individuals who had previously been found guilty of crimes they did not commit. On the other hand, savvy liars can pass a polygraph by using breathing and meditation techniques, clenching specific muscle groups, and employing various other tactics so that the machine is unable to correctly match their verbal answers with their physical signs.

145. During a polygraph test, which of the following is measured?

    a. DNA
    b. breathing
    c. intelligence
    d. body temperature

146. This passage is primarily about

    a. the criminal justice system
    b. how to pass a polygraph test
    c. the invention of the lie-detector
    d. the flaws of polygraph machines

147. As it is used in the passage, the word exonerated most nearly means

    a. imprisoned
    b. convinced
    c. exiled
    d. absolved

148. According to the passage, one reason that polygraphs are unreliable is

    a. the machinery is old-fashioned
    b. most criminals know how to meditate
    c. lie-detection technology is too sophisticated to interpret
    d. most people don't sweat when they are nervous

149. If it were not for DNA testing, it is likely that

    a. polygraph testing would be more effective
    b. fewer innocent people would be imprisoned
    c. more people would work as detectives
    d. more innocent people would be imprisoned

150. Why do many people believe that polygraphs are trustworthy?

    a. because science proves that lie-detection works
    b. because of the way polygraphs are presented in media
    c. because the devices were effective when first invented
    d. because of the way police detectives talk about them

151. An innocent person will most likely still fail a polygraph test if

    a. they clench specific muscles
    b. they remain calm
    c. they fidget
    d. their heart rate increases

152. The author most likely includes information about how long ago polygraph machines were invented

    a. to reinforce the idea that the technology is outdated
    b. to illustrate the point that polygraphs have a long and illustrious history
    c. to remind the reader that time passes quickly
    d. to highlight how much has changed in the last 100 years

Vocabulary

Instructions: Choose the word that means the same, or about the same, as the underlined word.

153. To feel <u>confined</u>

a. calm
b. locked
c. open
d. restricted

154. A <u>diversity</u> of viewpoints

a. variety
b. collection
c. uniformity
d. disagreement

155. The family's <u>discord</u>

a. happiness
b. conflict
c. harmony
d. frustration

156. A significant <u>obstacle</u>

a. dissatisfaction
b. advantage
c. impediment
d. decline

157. A <u>commendable</u> action

a. unworthy
b. kind
c. admirable
d. unlikely

158. A <u>furtive</u> glance

a. arrogant
b. hostile
c. humorous
d. secretive

159. The <u>verbose</u> speech

a. wordy
b. articulate
c. important
d. scholarly

160. To <u>impair</u> judgement

a. improve
b. diminish
c. solidify
d. clarify

161. The <u>abridged</u> novel

a. revised
b. best-selling
c. copyrighted
d. shortened

162. The <u>innocuous</u> question

a. tough
b. embarrassing
c. fascinating
d. harmless

163. A <u>spiteful</u> response

a. malicious
b. challenging
c. truncated
d. exhaustive

164. A <u>methodical</u> approach

a. tedious
b. disciplined
c. slow
d. insightful

165. A <u>cordial</u> greeting

a. quick
b. enthusiastic
c. amicable
d. insincere

166. The <u>haughty</u> woman

a. pushy
b. tempestuous
c. beautiful
d. snobbish

167. The <u>antiquated</u> viewpoint

a. thoughtful
b. anachronistic
c. tainted
d. fascinating

168. A <u>candid</u> remark

a. forthright
b. clear
c. dishonest
d. important

169. To <u>impose</u> restrictions

a. lift
b. halt
c. enforce
d. discuss

170. A <u>fortuitous</u> meeting

a. intentional
b. humbling
c. apathetic
d. lucky

171. A <u>unanimous</u> decision

a. contentious
b. practical
c. uncontested
d. unwise

172. An <u>ulterior</u> motive

a. alternative
b. questionable
c. concealed
d. obvious

173. A <u>facetious</u> comment

a. flippant
b. strong
c. cruel
d. easygoing

174. The <u>thrifty</u> man

a. insincere
b. frugal
c. careless
d. wealthy

Math Section 5

64 Questions, 45 Minutes

Instructions: Select the best answer.

175. What number divides evenly into 243?

   a. 6
   b. 4
   c. 3
   d. 8

176. 14 is what percent of 80? Round to the nearest tenth.

   a. 1.8%
   b. 17.0%
   c. 1.7%
   d. 17.5%

177. What is the remainder when 19 is divided by 4?

   a. 1
   b. 2
   c. 3
   d. 4

178. How many unique prime factors does 60 have?

   a. 1
   b. 2
   c. 3
   d. 4

179. What is 45.1 times 7.3?

   a. 329.23
   b. 3292.3
   c. 3.293
   d. 32.93

180. What symbol should go in the circle:

   $\frac{15}{7}$ ○ 1.9?

   a. $>$
   b. $<$
   c. $\geq$
   d. $\leq$

181. What is the place value of the number 2 in the following number: 24.569?

   a. hundreds
   b. ones
   c. tenths
   d. tens

182. What is shown below?

   a. line
   b. ray
   c. line segment
   d. angle

183. What is the area of a triangle with base x and height 2y?

   a. xy
   b. 2xy
   c. $\frac{1}{2}$ xy
   d. x + 2y

184. $\frac{2}{5}$ of what number is the product of 8 and 2?

   a. 40
   b. 16
   c. 20
   d. 64

185. Write .000762 in scientific notation

a. 7.62×10^{-3}
b. 7.62×10^{-4}
c. $.762 \times 10^{4}$
d. $.762 \times 10^{6}$

186. In a social science course, a student scored 75% on one test, 88% on another test, and 90% on each of the other tests. If the student's average for the course is exactly 85.75%, what is the total number of tests that the student has taken in the course?

a. 1
b. 2
c. 3
d. 4

187. The square root of 45 is between which two numbers

a. 4 and 5
b. 5 and 6
c. 6 and 7
d. 7 and 8

188. What number is 8 less than 3 times 9?

a. 27
b. 19
c. 1
d. -19

189. Which of the following numbers is NOT a multiple of 7?

a. 54
b. 84
c. 56
d. 49

190. Three consecutive even integers, *a*, *b*, and *c*, add up to 30. What is the value of *b*?

a. 8
b. 10
c. 12
d. 14

191. Solve: $\frac{\frac{9}{7}}{\frac{3}{5}}$

a. $\frac{27}{35}$
b. $\frac{9}{17}$
c. $\frac{15}{7}$
d. $\frac{40}{21}$

192. If the length of a square's side is doubled, what happens to the square's area?

a. It stays the same.
b. It is doubled.
c. It is quadrupled.
d. It is cut in half.

193. The sum of a number and the square of itself is 42. What is the number?

a. 6
b. 4
c. 3
d. 8

194. Bianca ran a mile every day over her spring break.. On Monday she ran the mile in 8 minutes. On Tuesday and Wednesday, she ran it in 7.5 minutes. On Thursday she wasn't feeling well and ran it in 9 minutes. By Friday, she could run the mile in exactly 7 minutes. What was the range of Bianca's mile times?

a. 2 minutes
b. 7.5 minutes
c. 2.5 minutes
d. 9 minutes

195. Given the two sets of numbers A = {2, 3, 7, 9} and B = {1, 2, 4, 7}, what is A ∪ B?

a. {2, 7}
b. {1, 3, 4, 9}
c. {5, 8}
d. {1, 2, 3, 4, 7, 9}

196. The lines below are

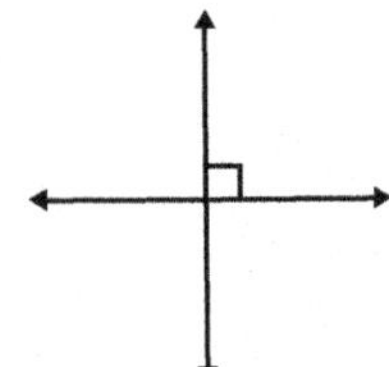

a. parallel
b. congruent
c. perpendicular
d. acute

197. A rectangle has an area of 42. Which of the following are possible side lengths for the rectangle?

a. 9 and 12
b. 3 and 14
c. 4 and 12
d. 3 and 18

198. Which of the following is equal to 7,098?

a. $7 \times 10^3 + 9 \times 10^1 + 8$
b. $7 \times 10^3 + 9 \times 10^1 + 8 \times 10$
c. $7 \times 10^4 + 9 \times 10^2 + 8 \times 10^0$
d. $7 \times 10^4 + 9 \times 10^2 + 8$

199. Amanda has a large jug that is completely filled with water in her apartment. She pours out 9 cups of it to use for boiling pasta. If the 9 cups of water was 30% of the water in the jug, how much water did the jug contain when it was full?

a. 20 cups
b. 23 cups
c. 30 cups
d. 33 cups

200. If 12 pounds of apples cost $63, how much would 17 pounds of apples cost?

a. $26.25
b. $72.50
c. $85.00
d. $89.25

201. The park district is having a sale on group fitness classes for new members. The first 3 classes cost just $10 each. Each additional class costs just $3. What would the total cost be for a member who took 12 group fitness classes?

a. $25
b. $36
c. $57
d. $120

202. What is the name of the figure below?

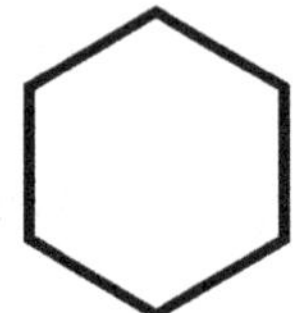

a. pentagon
b. hexagon
c. heptagon
d. octagon

203. Lyndsey is hosting a barbeque at her house for 38 people and needs a chair for each person. She has 12 folding chairs. She can borrow 7 additional chairs from her neighbor and 15 chairs from her sister. How many additional chairs does she need?

a. 4
b. 22
c. 34
d. 5

204. Anytown Elementary School took a class trip to a museum which was 60 miles away. If the bus left at 9 AM and was traveling 40 miles per hour, at what time did the bus arrive?

a. 9:30 AM
b. 10:30 AM
c. 7:30 AM
d. 10:00 AM

205. LMON is a square with side 8. What is the area of triangle LMO?

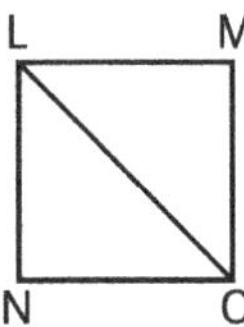

a. 16
b. 64
c. 36
d. 32

206. Solve for x: $x^2 + 3 = 19$

a. 4
b. 6
c. 8
d. 16

207. The table below shows which types of movie tickets were purchased at a movie theatre over the course of three days.

	Friday	Saturday	Sunday	TOTAL
Adult	45	56	50	151
Senior	15	18	25	58
Child	12	30	34	76
TOTAL	72	98	105	285

Approximately what percent of tickets purchased by seniors were purchased on Saturday?

a. 43%
b. 31%
c. 35%
d. 26%

208. Solve for n: $2n - 5 = 6n - 7$

a. $\frac{1}{2}$
b. -3
c. 3
d. $-\frac{1}{2}$

209. The speed limit on a road in Canada is 70 kilometers per hour. How many miles per hour is this if there are 0.62 miles in 1 kilometer? Round your answer to the nearest tenth.

a. 43.4 mph
b. 112.7 mph
c. 47.9 mph
d. 115.8 mph

210. A group of 4 friends bought an extra large pizza for $24.95 and a 2 liter bottle of soda for $3.25. If they split the cost of the pizza and soda equally, how much would each of them spend?

a. $7.00
b. $6.20
c. $7.05
d. $6.25

211. If $b \geq 4$, which of the following must be true?

a. $b^2 < 64$
b. $b^2 - 2 \geq 14$
c. $b^2 + 2 \leq 20$
d. $b^2 \geq 60$

212. What is the value of x in the triangle below?

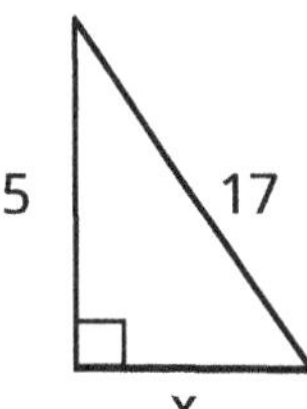

a. 12
b. 9
c. 13
d. 8

213. Abby has a collection of red and blue marbles. She has 49 blue marbles which make up 35% of her total number of marbles. How many red marbles does she have?

a. 17
b. 91
c. 112
d. 140

214. Carter is baking two different types of cookies. One type calls for two tablespoons of baking powder. The other calls for two teaspoons of baking powder. How many teaspoons of baking powder will Carter use total?

a. 4
b. 6
c. 8
d. 10

215. A parallelogram has how many pairs of parallel lines?

a. 0
b. 1
c. 2
d. 4

216. A candy company created a new type of candy bar. The chart below represents the sales of the candy bar over the course of five years.

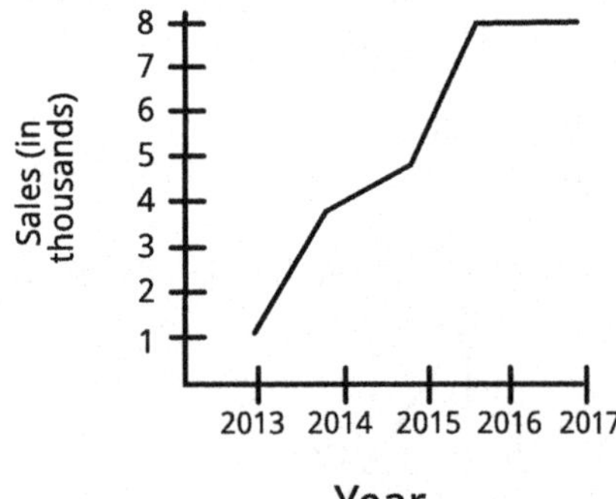

Approximately how many more bars were sold in 2017 than in 2013?

a. 1,000
b. 6,000
c. 7,000
d. 8,000

217. 4 gallons, 1 quarts, 3 pints
<u>-2 gallons, 3 quarts, 2 pints</u>

a. 2 gallons, 1 quart, 1 pint
b. 1 gallon, 2 quarts, 1 pint
c. 2 gallons, 1 quart, 1 pint
d. 1 gallon, 3 quarts, 1 pint

218. Caleb purchased a motorcycle with a loan that had a 6% interest rate. In the end, he paid $540 in interest payments. What was the original cost of the motorcycle?

a. $8,000
b. $9,000
c. $80,000
d. $90,000

219. Solve for x: $x - \sqrt{49} = 6$

a. -1
b. 8
c. 7
d. 13

220. Emmi bought 4 pounds of carrots at the farmer's market for $7. The next week, she purchased 6 pounds of carrots from the same farmer's market. What did the 6 pounds of carrots cost her?

a. $10
b. $11
c. $10.50
d. $9.50

221. In the isosceles triangle below with base $\overline{BC}$, what is the measure of angle C?

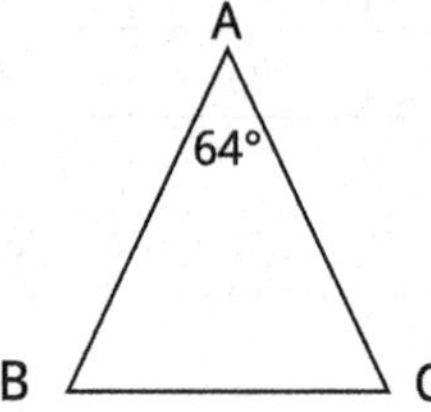

a. 58°
b. 64°
c. 62°
d. 54°

222. Emily cut a piece of fabric that was 2 yards, 2 feet wide into 4 inch strips. How many strips of fabric was she able to cut?

a. 16
b. 20
c. 28
d. 24

223. A cookie jar contains 3 chocolate chip cookies, 4 oatmeal cookies, and 2 sugar cookies. If I were to put my hand in the jar and pull out a cookie at random, what is the probability that I'd get a chocolate chip cookie?

a. $\frac{1}{2}$
b. $\frac{1}{3}$
c. $\frac{3}{4}$
d. $\frac{2}{3}$

224. Solve for x: 3x - 8 = 31

a. 7
b. 12
c. 13
d. 17

225. What is the mean of the following numbers:

36, 12, 35, 45, 12

a. 12
b. 35
c. 23
d. 28

226. A toy manufacturer ships 420 dolls to ABC's Toy Store in boxes. Each box can hold up to 32 dolls. What are the minimum number of boxes that the manufacturer can use to ship the dolls?

a. 13
b. 14
c. 15
d. 16

227. A three-dimensional version of a circle is called a

a. cylinder
b. cube
c. sphere
d. prism

228. A circle has a diameter of 6. What is the area of the circle? Assume π = 3.14 and round to the nearest hundredth.

a. 113.04
b. 28.26
c. 18.84
d. 9.42

229. Which of the following could be the coordinates of point A?

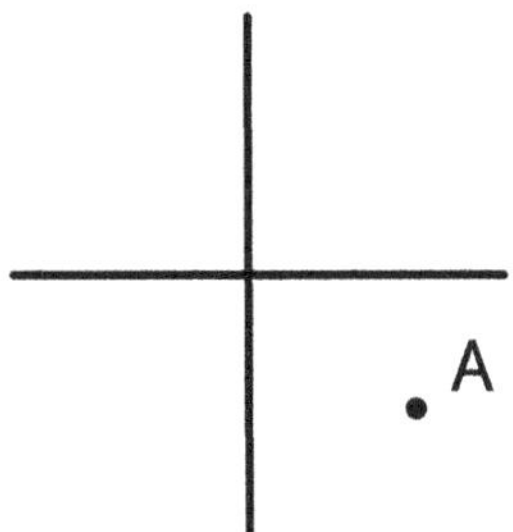

a. (-3, 4)
b. (4, 3)
c. (-3, -4)
d. (4, -3)

230. Diego and Callum arrive at the park at 10:40 AM. Their parents are picking them up at 3:30 PM. How long will they be at the park?

a. 4 hours, 10 minutes
b. 5 hours, 50 minutes
c. 4 hours, 50 minutes
d. 5 hours, 10 minutes

231. What is the area of the figure below?

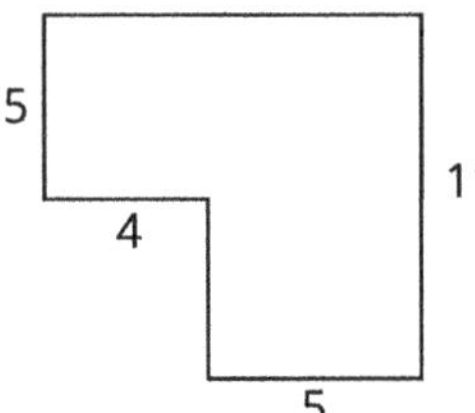

a. 75
b. 99
c. 55
d. 40

232. Grace is half as old as Ahmed, who is three times as old as Peggy. If Peggy is 24 years old, how old is Grace?

a. 34
b. 36
c. 27
d. 72

233. Erin is making pancakes for a fundraiser for her softball team. She uses 3 cups of flour for every 8 pancakes. If she is making 36 pancakes, how many cups of flour does she need?

a. 13
b. 13.5
c. 15
d. 14.5

234. A car dealership sells cars, SUVs, minivans. The pie chart below shows the percentage of each type of vehicle that the dealership sold last year. If the dealership sold 600 vehicles last year, how many were minivans?

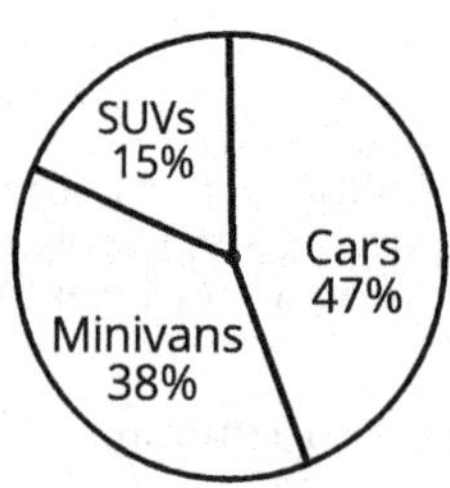

a. 228
b. 376
c. 98
d. 279

235. Solve for c: 4c - 5 = 23

a. 14
b. 8
c. 3
d. 7

236. Over the past few months, Charlotte has saved $47.41 of her allowance. This week, she saved an additional $6.70. If she uses her allowance to purchase a shirt that costs $32.50, how much money will she have left?

a. $54.11
b. $21.61
c. $22.65
d. $53.61

237. Three positive integers have a ratio of 1 : 2 : 3. If the largest integer is 18, what is the mean of the three integers?

a. 13
b. 12
c. 10
d. 8

238. What is the volume of a cube whose side length is 4?

a. 16
b. 12
c. 48
d. 64

Language Section 5

60 Questions, 25 Minutes

Usage and Mechanics

Instructions: For questions 239-278, check the sentences for errors of usage, capitalization, or punctuation. If there is no error, choose D.

239.

a. I could of told you that lying was not going to help your situation.
b. Remember me when you are away for summer vacation.
c. Time goes so quickly.
d. No mistakes.

240.

a. A massive wave almost knocked over my baby sister.
b. The ravages of civil war can still be felt all over Mozambique.
c. Leo shouted, "Give that to I!"
d. No mistakes.

241.

a. Running is a sport that is hard on your joints.
b. Using an assignment planner, helps the students know what they have for homework.
c. On vacation I love sleeping, fishing, and swimming.
d. No mistakes.

242.

a. I like all ice cream flavors, but chocolate is my favorite.
b. Juan transferred to our school from Jefferson Middle School.
c. Please lay the book on the table nearest the window.
d. No mistakes.

243.

a. Even though it would be terrifying, skydiving could be a lot of fun.
b. My dog is afraid of thunder and has to wear a special jacket.
c. If we don't hurry, we'll be late to History.
d. No mistakes.

244.

a. We drove through the tunnel on our way to New York City.
b. They're is nothing wrong with staying in on the weekends.
c. Stuart is looking forward to volunteering over his spring break.
d. No mistakes.

245.

a. When I got home from school, I put down my backpack, took out my textbook, and place it on the table.
b. When I visited San Francisco, I took a picture of the Golden Gate Bridge.
c. Tyrone's favorite meal is spaghetti carbonara.
d. No mistakes.

246.

a. Georgann locked up her familys horse stable before heading home.
b. I've always been fascinated by ancient history.
c. I'm not feeling well so I think I'm going to lie down.
d. No mistakes.

247.

a. My little sister exclaimed, “It stopped raining!”

b. There are a large number of textbooks in the classroom closet.

c. I learned to scuba dive when I lived in Sydney Australia.

d. No mistakes.

248.

a. I think that it’s too warm outside to wear a coat.

b. The larger room in the house was the master bedroom.

c. Camila and Jeffery performed a scene in front of their theater class.

d. No mistakes.

249.

a. It takes a lot of energy to babysit my neighbor’s three sons for an afternoon.

b. Even though he felt anxious, Calvin was able to calm down before his math final.

c. Me and my sister go camping at Lake Driftwood every summer.

d. No mistakes.

250.

a. “This is her.” my mother spoke into the phone.

b. My grandmother’s funeral was well attended.

c. The school principal was over fifteen minutes late to the school board meeting.

d. No mistakes.

251.

a. The monster being alone preyed on hapless individuals that he found in the park without protection.

b. I watched at least four movies on my sixteen hour flight to Africa.

c. The neighbors were concerned that no one had seen Mary-Ellen walking her dog yesterday.

d. No mistakes.

252.

a. Neither Jorge nor Bella can make it to the practice session.

b. They weren’t the only one who missed school today.

c. I can’t wait to help my little brother make his lemonade stand.

d. No mistakes.

253.

a. Tye arrived at rehearsal on time, but Lemont was late.

b. Illinois borders Wisconsin, Missouri, Indiana, Iowa, Tennessee, and Kentucky.

c. Boris went to the mall, and that he was alone.

d. No mistakes.

254.

a. The boys looked very similar.

b. “If at first you don’t succeed, try, try again”, is a quote my mother loves.

c. Donating blood is an easy way to help the Red Cross.

d. No mistakes.

255.

a. Traveling alone is my favorite way to travel.

b. It’s going to be a hot one today!

c. Wheres the restroom located?

d. No mistakes.

256.

a. In the past, I never cared about getting good grades.

b. I’ve been sick for almost half of spring break.

c. I should have left the stray dog alone.

d. No mistakes.

257.

a. The best way to stay healthy is to wash your hands frequently.

b. We ran out of soda halfway through the party.

c. Although I lost the game, I felt good knowing I played my best.

d. No mistakes.

258.

a. On Saturdays, I like to take a nap.
b. The two cats fought over the last bite of food in their dish.
c. Camelot is where King Arthur held court.
d. No mistakes.

259.

a. My dog Rocco loves to run around the yard.
b. It's going to be a beautiful day!
c. Of the five siblings, Maria was the better baker.
d. No mistakes.

260.

a. I'm going to go lie down because I have a headache.
b. Cassie was supposed to do the dishes but she chose to go out with her friends instead.
c. It still feels like the middle of winter even though it's April.
d. No mistakes.

261.

a. My favorite activities include running, cycling, and skating.
b. When Dan won tickets to the hockey game, he gave them to his best friend Evan as an early birthday gift.
c. Stephanie was devastated to learn that tickets to the concert were sold out.
d. No mistakes.

262.

a. The collection of scary stories are best read at night.
b. Can you believe how much they are charging for soda at this game?
c. Despite how hard he tried, Sam was unable to fall asleep.
d. No mistakes.

263.

a. Drink plenty of water on summer days to avoid dehydration.
b. The car was totalled, so it had to be toad away.
c. Rob is one of the funniest people in the world!
d. No mistakes.

264.

a. The smell of fresh herbs filled the kitchen as Armand cooked.
b. My cat enjoys knocking water glasses off of tables when she is bored.
c. Mark is excited to visit glacier national park in Montana with his family this summer.
d. No mistakes.

265.

a. Its going to rain all day so make sure to bring an umbrella!
b. Jeremy loves to learn about ancient civilizations.
c. Joey was practically glued to his cell phone the entire night.
d. No mistakes.

266.

a. It's important not to overmix when preparing cookie dough.
b. "Good morning and please turn to page 54 in your textbook, Ms. Sullivan said"
c. Mary was so tired after the marathon that she felt like she could sleep forever.
d. No mistakes.

267.

a. The project was progressing slower than the manager would have liked.
b. Did you know that groundhogs and woodchucks are the same animal?
c. The group of kids at the zoo are so excited to see the baby giraffe!
d. No mistakes.

268.

a. Nicole bought lemons limes and oranges for her famous punch.
b. Summer cannot arrive soon enough!
c. Karen was saddened and dismayed to find out that her favorite show had been cancelled.
d. No mistakes.

269.

a. The dog loved to play with its tennis ball.
b. "How often should I water this plant?" Martin asked.
c. Can you believe that the Colosseum is over 1,000 years old?
d. No mistakes.

270.

a. Jamie has been fighting a dreadful cold all weekend long.
b. Matilda went to the library and checked out a bunch of books which she proceeded to read all weekend and discovered that she preferred to read historical fiction most of all.
c. Brian loved to surprise his family with gifts all year round.
d. No mistakes.

271.

a. Does anyone have any questions about the assignment!
b. Tabitha attends the University of Chicago.
c. Sadly, the milk was all gone before Laura had a chance to pour some over her cereal.
d. No mistakes.

272.

a. Sandy's cousins class schedule was so much more arduous than mine.
b. Angie was headed to a well deserved vacation in Rome.
c. Snow in the middle of April is unusual and definitely unwanted.
d. No mistakes.

273.

a. The delicious soup came with the added benefit of keeping everyone warm on a chilly night.
b. When comparing Kevin and Nour, Kevin is the best swimmer.
c. Learning to play an instrument can be an exciting hobby!
d. No mistakes.

274.

a. My best friend's family has a cabin in the Appalachian mountains.
b. "It's time to go," Hannah sighed.
c. Although it's fun to perform in a play, I don't want to pursue acting as a career.
d. No mistakes.

275.

a. The women's volleyball team is having tryouts on Thursday, January 15.
b. I can ride my bike faster than my older brother.
c. Before we head to the airport, we need to pack: clothes, toiletries, and shoes.
d. No mistakes.

276.

a. Tomorrow, they're going to tell me if I got the job.
b. When we visited Australia, my mom and I went scuba diving at the Great Barrier Reef.
c. Marjorie went to the store to by eggs, bread, and bananas.
d. No mistakes.

277.

a. The River Thames is the longest river in England.
b. Lawrence pleaded with his mom "Please let me stay up late tonight."
c. After the baseball game, we are going to take a walk, go to dinner, and see a movie.
d. No mistakes.

278.

a. Calvin and Teresa work in the same office building and usually drive to work together.

b. I couldn't hardly hear the fire alarm because the movie was so loud.

c. The Secretary of State often meets with foreign leaders.

d. No mistakes.

Spelling

Directions: For questions 279-288, look for errors in spelling. If there is no error, choose D.

279.

a. Mirabella preformed in three musicals last year.

b. The long explanation was tiring and unnecessary.

c. Don't broadcast the fact that you've never played lacrosse before.

d. No mistakes.

280.

a. I can't beleive that it's already August.

b. Make sure that you save your restaurant receipt so that you get paid back.

c. The boulevard in my neighborhood is really beautiful in autumn.

d. No mistakes.

281.

a. The banquet hall was long and cavernous.

b. Do you want to go shopping next Wednesday evening?

c. I love the commerrcial with the dog and horses.

d. No mistakes.

282.

a. Leanne's writing was quite poetic but lacked brevity.

b. If you want to become a profesional hockey player, you need to practice every day.

c. The seafood restaurant's lobster bisque was legendary.

d. No mistakes.

283.

a. Persistance is the key to successful sales.

b. Jamal was an accomplished musician and composer.

c. Consuming honey puts babies at risk for contracting botulism.

d. No mistakes.

284.

a. Be aware of your surroundings, especailly when traveling to a new country.

b. My physician told me that she didn't believe that I had strep throat.

c. Ophelia loves to read eighteenth-century literature.

d. No mistakes.

285.

a. My nature magazine subscription just ended, and I'm not sure if I'm going to renew it.

b. Matt's numerous trophies were stacked against a wall in his bedroom.

c. The ubiquitous expression had lost meaning over the years.

d. No mistakes.

286.

a. My grandpa's chocolate-colored fedora was weathered from years of use.

b. The bizzare rock sculpture drew an incredible number of visitors.

c. The devoted dog folowed the little girl everywhere.

d. No mistakes.

287.

a. The govenor gave a speech at the opening of the new elementary school.

b. Despite my best efforts, I've never been good at geography.

c. Each autumn, I go apple picking at an orchard that is seventy miles away.

d. No mistakes.

288.

a. The company president left the meeting in a celebratory mood.

b. Marko invited his freind Jason over for dinner.

c. Even though my dog has a thundering bark, he is not at all aggressive.

d. No mistakes.

Composition

Directions: For questions 289-298, read the question and select the best answer.

289. Choose the best word to join the thoughts together.

I wish I started violin lessons when I was younger __________ I think I would have learned how to play more quickly.

a. although
b. because
c. thus
d. None of these

290. Choose the best word to join the thoughts together.

Madison has visited many cities in Canada, __________ Montreal, Toronto, and Vancouver.

a. certainly
b. similarly
c. frequently
d. including

291. Choose the best word to join the thoughts together.

The cyclone ruined the town's beaches, __________ causing a drop-off in tourism.

a. thus
b. so
c. nonetheless
d. surprisingly

292. Choose the group of words that best completes the sentence.

When she has free time, __________.

a. my mom worked on her garden, read a book, or watches a movie.

b. my mom is working on her garden, reading a book, or is watching a movie.

c. my mom works on her garden, reads a book, or watches a movie.

d. my mom work on her garden, read a book, or watch a movie.

293. Which of these expresses the idea most clearly?

a. When she took my friends and I to the beach, my mom insisted that we wear sunscreen, stay near the lifeguard, and go swimming in pairs.

b. When my mom took me and my friends to the beach, she insisted that we wear sunscreen, stay near the lifeguard, and go swimming in pairs.

c. Taking my friends and me to the beach, my mom insisted that we were wearing sunscreen, stay near the lifeguard, and always going swimming in pairs.

d. When taking my friends and I to the beach, my mom insisted that we wear sunscreen, stay near the lifeguard, and go swimming in pairs.

294. Which of these expresses the idea most clearly?

a. On my first airplane trip, my dad let me sit near the window, eat lots of sugary snacks, and bring my iPad and I had fun

b. Having fun on my first airplane trip, my dad let me sit near the window, use my iPad, and eat a lot of sugary snacks.

c. I had fun on my first airplane trip because my dad let me sit near the window, use my iPad, and eat a lot of sugary snacks.

d. To let me have fun on my first airplane trip, my dad had me sit near the window, using my iPad, and eating a lot of sugary snacks.

295. Which of the following topics is best for a one-page essay?

a. The Best Way to Shoot a Free Throw
b. An Analysis of the Training Routines of Professional Athletes
c. The Impact of Sports on Children
d. The Development of American Professional Sports

296. Which of these sentences fits best under the topic "Mathematics in Everyday Life"?

a. Math is a subject that a lot of people struggle to understand.
b. Most high school math students take Geometry after Algebra 1.
c. Many people find they use writing skills in everyday life.
d. You can use your math skills, specifically your knowledge of percents, to calculate a 20% tip for your waiter at a restaurant.

297. Which sentence does NOT belong in the paragraph?

When Lincoln's laptop broke, he went to the store to buy a new one. (2) He spent hours in the store because he had a hard time deciding which laptop he liked best. (3) A salesperson eventually helped him choose the best one and rang up his purchase. (4) It was a nice day outside and Lincoln walked home.

a. 1
b. 2
c. 3
d. 4

298. Where should the sentence "Many people confuse the grizzly bear and the black bear, but they are easy to tell apart. " be placed in the following paragraph?

Grizzly bears are significantly larger than black bears. (2) Grizzlies also have a distinctive hump on their shoulders. (3) Finally, if you look closely, you'll notice that the black bear has tall ears, whereas grizzlies have short, rounded ears.

a. Before sentence 1
b. After sentence 1
c. Between sentences 2 and 3
d. After sentence 3

Answer Key

Verbal

1. C
2. C
3. A
4. B
5. C
6. C
7. C
8. D
9. C
10. A
11. D
12. C
13. A
14. B
15. B
16. C
17. B
18. B
19. A
20. B
21. D
22. B
23. A
24. C
25. D
26. C
27. A
28. D
29. B
30. C
31. B
32. B
33. C
34. D
35. D
36. A
37. B
38. D
39. B
40. A
41. C
42. B
43. A
44. C
45. D
46. B
47. B
48. C
49. C
50. B
51. D
52. B
53. C
54. D
55. A
56. A
57. C
58. B
59. C
60. A

Quantitative

61. D
62. B
63. B
64. B
65. D
66. B
67. C
68. A
69. C
70. B
71. C
72. D
73. D
74. C
75. B
76. C
77. C
78. A
79. B
80. D
81. C
82. D
83. B
84. A
85. B
86. A
87. C
88. D
89. B
90. B
91. A
92. C
93. B
94. B
95. C
96. A
97. D
98. C
99. D
100. B
101. A
102. D
103. A
104. B
105. C
106. A
107. D
108. C
109. B
110. A
111. A
112. D

Reading

113. B
114. C
115. C
116. D
117. D
118. A
119. B
120. C
121. C
122. D
123. B
124. A
125. D
126. D
127. A
128. C
129. C
130. B
131. D
132. C
133. B
134. D
135. A
136. A
137. D
138. B
139. A
140. D
141. A
142. C
143. A
144. C
145. B
146. D
147. D
148. A
149. D
150. B
151. D
152. A
153. D
154. A
155. B
156. C
157. C
158. D
159. A
160. B
161. D
162. D
163. A
164. B
165. C
166. D
167. B
168. A
169. C
170. D
171. C
172. C
173. A
174. B

Math

175. C
176. D
177. C
178. C
179. A
180. A
181. D
182. B
183. A
184. A
185. B
186. D
187. C
188. B
189. A
190. B
191. C
192. C
193. A
194. A
195. D
196. C
197. B
198. A
199. C
200. D
201. C
202. B
203. A
204. B
205. D
206. A
207. B
208. A
209. A
210. C
211. B
212. D
213. B
214. C
215. C
216. C
217. B
218. B
219. D
220. C
221. A
222. D
223. B
224. C
225. D
226. B
227. C
228. B
229. D
230. C
231. A
232. B
233. B
234. A
235. D
236. B
237. B
238. D

Language

239. A
240. C
241. B
242. D
243. C
244. B
245. A
246. A
247. C
248. B
249. C
250. A
251. A
252. B
253. C
254. B
255. C
256. A
257. D
258. D
259. C
260. B
261. D
262. A
263. B
264. C
265. A
266. B
267. C
268. A
269. D
270. B
271. A
272. A
273. B
274. A
275. C
276. C
277. B
278. B
279. A
280. A
281. C
282. B
283. A
284. A
285. D
286. C
287. A
288. B
289. B
290. D
291. A
292. C
293. B
294. C
295. A
296. D
297. D
298. A

HSPT Test 6

Verbal Section 6

60 Questions, 16 Minutes

Instructions: Select the best answer.

1. Isla sold more cookies than Sienna and Sadie. Aaliyah sold more cookies than Daisy and Sadie. Sadie sold the fewest cookies. If the first two statements are true, the third statement is

   a. true
   b. false
   c. uncertain

2. Reckless means the *opposite* of

   a. cautious
   b. strict
   c. audacious
   d. callous

3. Comrade most nearly means

   a. foe
   b. soldier
   c. caretaker
   d. companion

4. Which word does *not* belong with the others?

   a. television show
   b. comedy
   c. movie
   d. play

5. Bellicose most nearly means

   a. beautiful
   b. hostile
   c. agreeable
   d. sleepy

6. The northern zoo has more red pandas than the southern zoo. The western zoo has fewer red pandas than the northern zoo. The southern zoo has the fewest number of red pandas. If the first two statements are true, the third statement is

   a. true
   b. false
   c. uncertain

7. Which word does *not* belong with the others?

   a. cherries
   b. raspberries
   c. strawberries
   d. oranges

8. Candid means the *opposite* of

   a. deceitful
   b. blunt
   c. photogenic
   d. active

9. Ocean is to water as prairie is to

   a. fire
   b. large
   c. grassland
   d. west

10. Blithe most nearly means

    a. old
    b. depressed
    c. bright
    d. jolly

11. The Springfield Bridge is longer than the Old Town Bridge. The Pawnee Bridge is shorter than the Springfield Bridge. The Springfield Bridge is the longest bridge of the three. If the first two statements are true, the third statement is

    a. true
    b. false
    c. uncertain

12. Dexterous most nearly means

    a. lazy
    b. smart
    c. clumsy
    d. agile

13. Which word does *not* belong with the others?

    a. salad
    b. soup
    c. pancakes
    d. sandwich

14. Dormant means the *opposite* of

    a. passive
    b. open
    c. active
    d. spacious

15. Which word does *not* belong with the others?

    a. motorcycle
    b. sled
    c. car
    d. scooter

16. Slow is to rapid as gloomy is to

    a. fast
    b. forlorn
    c. melancholy
    d. joyful

17. Rock sample A is heavier than rock sample C. Rock sample B is lighter than rock sample A. Rock sample A is the lightest of the three rock samples. If the first two statements are true, the third statement is

    a. true
    b. false
    c. uncertain

18. Frugal most nearly means

    a. not wasteful
    b. royal
    c. hilarious
    d. lavish

19. Which word does *not* belong with the others?

    a. swimming
    b. running
    c. waterskiing
    d. sailing

20. Haughty means the *opposite* of

    a. happy
    b. misbehaved
    c. conceited
    d. humble

21. Jaylen scores more touchdowns than Paxton, but fewer than Carson. Carson scores fewer touchdowns than Matteo. Matteo scores the most touchdowns. If the first two statements are true, the third statement is

    a. true
    b. false
    c. uncertain

22. Fig has a louder bark than Peanut and Hans. Hans has a softer bark than Buster. Buster has a louder bark than Peanut. If the first two statements are true, the third statement is

    a. true
    b. false
    c. uncertain

23. Which word does *not* belong with the others?

    a. France
    b. Sweden
    c. Spain
    d. Russia

24. Industrious most nearly means

    a. businesslike
    b. hardworking
    c. technical
    d. industrial

25. Ice hockey is to puck as lacrosse is to

    a. stick
    b. net
    c. goalie
    d. ball

26. Which word does *not* belong with the others?

    a. aluminum
    b. plastic
    c. copper
    d. iron

27. Inferior means the *opposite* of

    a. importance
    b. mediocre
    c. superior
    d. modest

28. Ignorant most nearly means

    a. unknowledgeable
    b. enlightened
    c. unnoticed
    d. innocent

29. All students at Northtown School live in the south or west. All students at Southtown School live in the east. Rosalie lives in the north so she attends Northtown School. If the first two statements are true, the third statement is

    a. true
    b. false
    c. uncertain

30. London is to England as Paris is to

    a. French
    b. Europe
    c. France
    d. Parisian

31. Grapes is to vine as apples is to

    a. bush
    b. vine
    c. tree
    d. stalk

32. Eccentric means the *opposite* of

    a. conventional
    b. concentric
    c. peculiar
    d. interesting

33. Perceptible most nearly means

    a. personal
    b. adaptable
    c. reachable
    d. noticeable

34. Which word does *not* belong with the others?

    a. pond
    b. stream
    c. ocean
    d. river

35. Which word does *not* belong with the others?

    a. geometry
    b. biology
    c. calculus
    d. algebra

36. It is warmer in Fairview than in Madison. It is colder in Madison than in Franklin and Bristol. It is warmest in Fairview. If the first two statements are true, the third statement is

    a. true
    b. false
    c. uncertain

37. Cut is to bandage as drain is to

    a. liquid
    b. plug
    c. sink
    d. bathtub

38. Allege most nearly means

    a. question
    b. state
    c. accuse
    d. aggrieve

39. Pacifist means the *opposite* of

    a. activist
    b. warmonger
    c. peacemaker
    d. protester

40. Which word does *not* belong with the others?

    a. flute
    b. clarinet
    c. violin
    d. tuba

41. The freeway has more lanes than the highway. The street has fewer lanes than the highway. The street has fewer lanes than the freeway. If the first two statements are true, the third statement is

    a. true
    b. false
    c. uncertain

42. Reclusive most nearly means

    a. gregarious
    b. solitary
    c. passive
    d. insect

43. Which word does *not* belong with the others?

    a. time zone
    b. pacific time
    c. central time
    d. mountain time

44. Reminisce most nearly means

    a. recollect
    b. foretell
    c. replenish
    d. placate

45. Synonym is to antonym as deep is to

    a. little
    b. expansive
    c. high
    d. shallow

46. The library is north of my house, which is located directly in between the post office and movie theatre. The hospital is south of the movie theatre. My house is south of the hospital. If the first two statements are true, the third statement is

    a. true
    b. false
    c. uncertain

47. 10 is to 15 as 20 is to

    a. 10
    b. 15
    c. 25
    d. 30

48. Which word does *not* belong with the others?

    a. house
    b. dwelling
    c. apartment
    d. townhouse

49. Which word does *not* belong with the others?

    a. ice
    b. snow
    c. liquid
    d. water

50. Flower is to tulip as tree is to

    a. forest
    b. leaf
    c. green
    d. birch

51. Which word does *not* belong with the others?

a. paint brush
b. pencil
c. marker
d. scissors

52. Leaves are to autumn as blossoms are to

a. flowers
b. spring
c. summer
d. warm

53. Brevity most nearly means

a. permanence
b. shortness
c. beauty
d. breathability

54. Which word does *not* belong with the others?

a. emotional
b. calm
c. serene
d. composed

55. Which word does not belong with the others?

a. carrots
b. turnips
c. potatoes
d. beans

56. Ideal means the *opposite* of

a. acute
b. mediocre
c. perfect
d. bad

57. Ivan studies more than Mira. Mira studies less than Luka. Luka studies more than Ivan. If the first two statements are true, the third statement is

a. true
b. false
c. uncertain

58. Which word does *not* belong with the others?

a. skiing
b. sledding
c. canoeing
d. ice skating

59. Ambiguous means the *opposite* of

a. uncertain
b. captivating
c. boring
d. clear

60. Becky has won more dance contests than Quinlan. Quinlan has lost fewer dance contests than Julia. Becky has won more dance contests than Julia. If the first two statements are true, the third statement is

a. true
b. false
c. uncertain

Quantitative Section 6

52 Questions, 30 Minutes

Instructions: Select the best answer.

61. Review this series: 2, 6, 18, ___,162, 486 What number is missing?

    a. 36
    b. 54
    c. 72
    d. 81

62. Examine (A), (B), and (C) and find the best answer.

    (A) $(24 \div 6) \times 3$
    (B) $(36 \div 6) \times 2$
    (C) $(48 \div 6) \times 1$

    a. (C) is equal to (A) but less than (B)
    b. (B) is greater than both (A) and (C)
    c. (C) is greater than (B) but less than (A)
    d. (A) is equal to (B) and greater than (C)

63. 26 is what percent of 130?

    a. 15
    b. 20
    c. 25
    d. 30

64. Examine (A), (B), and (C) and find the best answer.

    (A) $(-3) \times (-4) \times (-2)$
    (B) $(-3) + (-4) \times (-2)$
    (C) $(-3) \times (-4) + (-2)$

    a. $(A) < (C) > (B)$
    b. $(C) < (B) < (A)$
    c. $(A) > (B) > (C)$
    d. $(B) < (C) < (A)$

65. Examine the circles and (A), (B), and (C) and find the best answer. Assume $\pi = 3.14$.

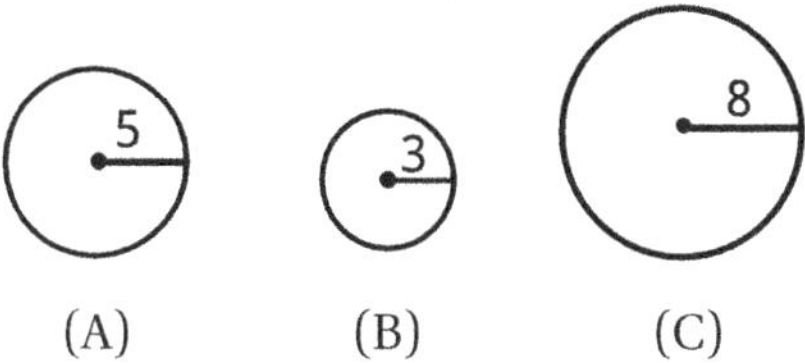

    (A) The diameter of circle A
    (B) The circumference of circle B
    (C) The radius of circle C

    a. (A) is greater than (B) and (C)
    b. (B) is greater than (C), but less than (A)
    c. (C) is greater than (A), but less than (B)
    d. (A) is greater than (C), but less than (B)

66. What number is missing from the following series: 7, 14, 12, 19, 17, ___ ?

    a. 24
    b. 26
    c. 15
    d. 28

67. Review at the following series: 6.5, 3.2 ,7.1, 4.0, 7.7, 4.8, ___. What numbers are missing?

    a. 8.4
    b. 5.6
    c. 8.3
    d. 5.7

68. Examine (A), (B), and (C) and find the best answer.

(A) The remainder of $\frac{12}{5}$

(B) The remainder of $\frac{18}{5}$

(C) The remainder of $\frac{21}{5}$

a. (A) - (B) = (C)
b. (A) + (C) = (B)
c. (A) + (B) = (C)
d. (C) - (B) = (A)

69. What numbers are missing from the following series: 23, 4, 19, ___, ___, 64, 11?

a. 16, 15
b. 12, 16
c. 12, 15
d. 16, 16

70. What numbers and/or roman numerals are missing from the following series: VIII, 13, X, 19, ___, ___, XIV, 31?

a. XI, 25
b. XII, 25
c. XII, 24
d. XI, 24

71. Based on the information in the figure below, select the best answer.

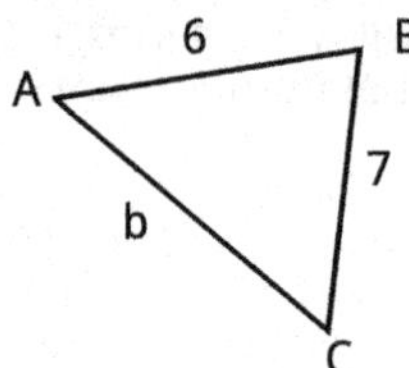

a. b < 13
b. b = 6.5
c. b = 13
d. b > 13

72. Examine this series: 78, 72, 66, 60, 54, ___.What number should come next?

a. 46
b. 50
c. 44
d. 48

73. What is 10% of 40% of 400?

a. 120
b. 40
c. 16
d. 32

74. Look at this series: O, 9, P, 13,___, ___, R, 21. What number and letter are missing?

a. Q, 16
b. Q, 17
c. T, 17
d. T, 16

75. Examine (A), (B), and (C) and find the best answer.

(A) $\frac{3}{4}$ of 16

(B) $\frac{2}{5}$ of 25

(C) $\frac{2}{3}$ of 12

a. (A) is greater than (B) but less than (C)
b. (B) is less than (C) and (A)
c. (C) is greater than (B) but less than (A)
d. (A) is greater than both (B) and (C)

76. What is the product of four and the square root of thirty six?

a. 24
b. 12
c. 72
d. 6

77. Examine the cube and (A), (B), and (C). Select the best answer.

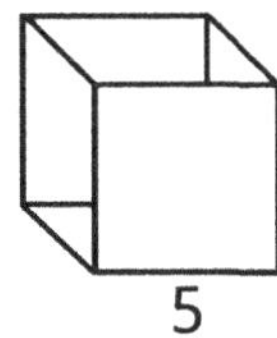

(A) The volume of the cube
(B) 100
(C) The area of one side of the cube

a. (A) is greater than (C) but less than (B)
b. (B) and (C) are both less than (A)
c. (B) is less than (C) but greater than (A)
d. (B) is less than both (A) and (C)

78. The quotient of $\frac{3}{2}$ and $\frac{1}{2}$ is two more than what number?

a. 1
b. -2
c. 2
d. 5

79. Look at this series: 9, 7, 6, 15, 3, 23, ____. What number should come next?

a. 30
b. 0
c. 1.5
d. 20

80. Review this series: A, E, I, M, Q, ___What letter should come next?

a. U
b. T
c. V
d. Z

81. 5 times what number is equal to 4 less than 19?

a. 15
b. 23
c. 3
d. 4

82. 5 more than what number is equal to the average of 11, 15, and 19?

a. 15
b. 9
c. 5
d. 10

83. Examine (A), (B), and (C) and select the best answer.

(A) (B) (C)

a. A < B < C
b. B = C
c. B > C > A
d. A = C

84. What numbers should come next in the following series: 2, 6, 4, 12, 10, ___, ___?

a. 30, 32
b. 30, 28
c. 20, 22
d. 20, 40

85. Examine (A), (B), and (C) and find the best answer.

(A) 30% of 90
(B) 45% of 80
(C) 60% of 60

a. (B) is equal to (C) and greater than (A)
b. (C) is greater than both (A) and (B)
c. (A) is equal to both (B) and (C)
d. (B) is less than both (A) and (C)

86. Examine (A), (B), and (C) and find the best answer.

(A) 5×10^5
(B) $.05 \times 10^6$
(C) 50×10^2

a. (A) + (C) < (B)
b. (B) + (C) > (A)
c. (A) - (B) > (C)
d. (A) + (B) = (C)

87. Look at this series: 80, 60, 20, 30, 5, ___. What number should come next?

a. 40
b. 50
c. 25
d. 15

88. Examine the rectangle below. Which of the following must be true?

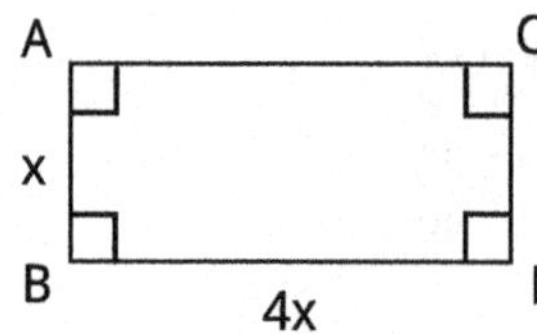

a. $\overline{AB} + \overline{AC} < \overline{CD} + \overline{BD}$
b. $\overline{AB} \times \overline{CD} = \overline{BD}$
c. $\overline{AB} \times \overline{BD} = CD \times \overline{BD}$
d. $\overline{AB} + \overline{CD} > \overline{BD}$

89. Examine (A), (B), and (C) and find the best answer. Assume y is a positive number smaller than 5.

(A) 3y + 2y
(B) 6y - y × 2
(C) y + 2(y + y)

a. (A) is equal to (B) is equal to (C)
b. (A) is equal to (C)
c. (B) is greater than both (A) and (C)
d. (C) is less than (B)

90. The quotient of 5 and $\frac{1}{5}$ is equal to the sum of 12 and what number?

a. -11
b. 13
c. 11
d. 37

91. What number should come next in the following series: 48, 47, 45, 42, 38, ___?

a. 32
b. 33
c. 34
d. 35

92. Review this series: 3, 12, 21, 30, 39, ___. What number should come next?

a. 47
b. 48
c. 49
d. 50

93. Examine the figure below and select the best answer

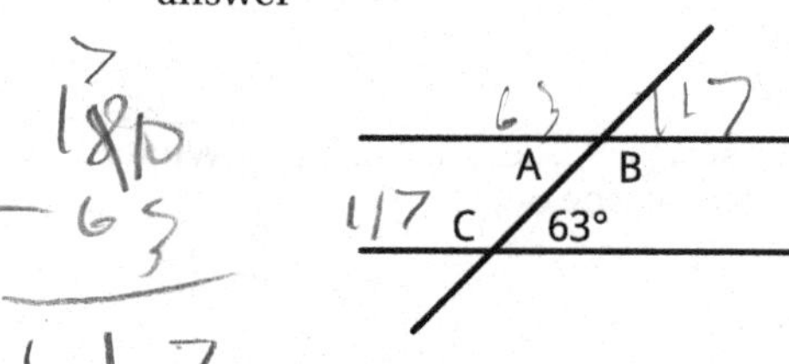

a. A + 63° = B
b. 180° - A = 63°
c. 63° + B = 90°
d. C - 63° = B - 63°

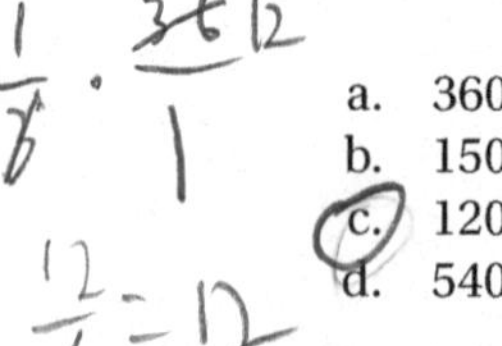

94. $\frac{1}{3}$ of 36 is equal to 10% of what number?

a. 360
b. 150
c. 120
d. 540

95. Review this series: 17, 14, 15, 12, 13, ___. What number should come next?

a. 12
b. 14
c. 10
d. 9

96. What number is missing in the following series: 92, 15, ____, 10, 98, 5, 101?

a. 95
b. 5
c. 90
d. 20

97. What number is twenty-three more than the product of eighteen and ten?

a. 194
b. 203
c. 150
d. 157

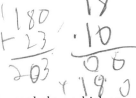

98. Examine the three figures below, which are drawn to scale Find the best answer.

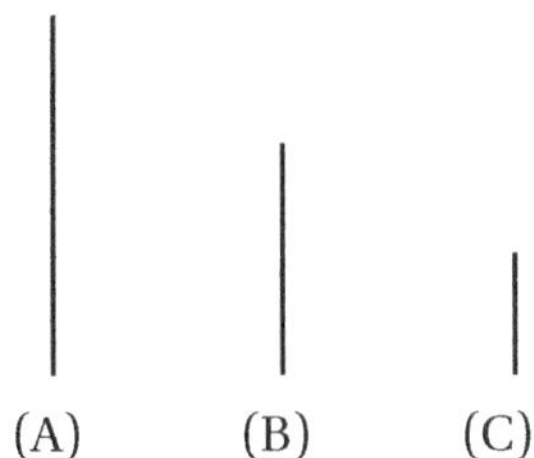

a. A > B < C
b. C > A > B
c. C < B < A
d. B < C > A

99. What number multiplied by 6 is $\frac{1}{5}$ of 300?

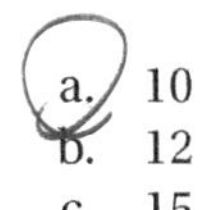

a. 10
b. 12
c. 15
d. 20

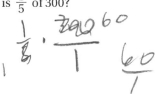

100. Look at this series: 48, 8, ____, 4, 12, 2. What number is missing?

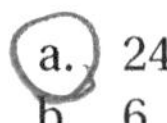

a. 24
b. 6
c. 26
d. 12

101. Examine (A), (B), and (C) and find the best answer.

(A) The number of prime numbers 1-5
(B) The number of even numbers 1-5
(C) The number of odd numbers 1-5

a. A is greater than B and C.
b. B is less than A but greater than C.
c. A and C are equal.
d. C is equal to B but less than A.

102. Review the series: 340, 68, 65, ____, 10, 2. What number is missing?

a. 15
b. 20
c. 13
d. 62

103. Examine the circle within the square below and select the best answer. Use 3.14 to represent pie.

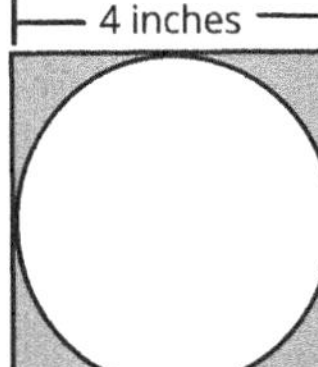

a. The area of the circle is approximately half the area of the square.
b. The areas of the square is approximately 3.44 inches larger than the circle.
c. The shaded area is approximately 10 inches smaller than the area of the square.
d. The area of the square and circle are equal.

104. What number is missing in the following series: $\frac{2}{9}$, $\frac{2}{3}$, 2, ____, 18, 54

a. 9
b. $2\frac{1}{3}$
c. $\frac{19}{3}$
d. 6

105. Examine (A), (B), and (C) and find the best answer.

(A) $\sqrt{5} + \sqrt{5}$
(B) $\sqrt{5} \times \sqrt{5}$
(C) $\sqrt{5} \div \sqrt{5}$

a. C < B > A
b. A < C < B
c. A > B = C
d. B = C > A

106. What number is missing in the following series: 7, 4, 32, _____, 232?

a. 256
b. 29
c. 3
d. 7

107. Eight times what number is the sum of seven squared and fifteen.

a. 3
b. 4
c. 8
d. 12

108. Look at this series: 3, 6, 12, ___, 33, 48. What number is missing?

a. 10
b. 22
c. 21
d. 20

109. What is the next number in the following series: V, X, XV, XX,___.

a. XXV
b. CV
c. VXX
d. 25

110. The sum of $\frac{1}{3}$ of 12 and 18 equals what number?

a. 14
b. 22
c. 10
d. 54

111. What is 15 percent of 80 divided by 4?

a. 2
b. 3
c. 4
d. 5

112. Review this series: 30, 300, 60, 600, _____, 1,200 What number is missing?

a. 1,200
b. 80
c. 200
d. 120

Reading Section 6

62 Questions, 25 Minutes

Reading Comprehension

Instructions: Read each passage carefully and mark one answer for each question.

Questions 113 - 122 refer to the passage below.

When John and Abigail Adams first took up residence in the newly constructed White House, their two dogs (comically named Juno and Satan) moved in with them. Since then, the president's house has been home to dozens of dogs and cats, as well as many less traditional pets.

In fact, many presidents kept undomesticated animals as pets. Adams' immediate successor, Thomas Jefferson, kept a pair of grizzly bear cubs on the White House lawn! He received the bears as a gift from explorer Zebulon Pike, who bought them during his expedition into the new western territories. A few years later, another predator was gifted into the presidential household when the famed Revolutionary War general, the Marquis de Lafayette, gave John Quincy Adams an alligator. The gator was kept in a White House bathroom, where it was allegedly used to prank the sixth US president's visitors. Similarly, Martin Van Buren was briefly the proud owner of two tiger cubs, which were sent to him by the Sultan of Oman. Although Van Buren intended to keep the cats in the White House, Congress quickly confiscated them and sent them to a local zoo instead.

Presidents Theodore Roosevelt and Calvin Coolidge undoubtedly take the cake for having the weirdest—and most numerous—pets during their terms in office. Roosevelt and his family were great animal lovers, despite the fact that Roosevelt was also an enthusiastic hunter. Due to his well-known interest in wildlife, many politicians sent him exotic animals to show their goodwill. While Roosevelt immediately sent some animals he received off to the zoo (including lions, a zebra, and a hyena), many others became beloved members of the family. Along with his numerous horses, dogs, and cats, some of Roosevelt's companions included: a black bear cub named Bill, a snake named Emily Spinach, a macaw named Eli Yale, and a badger named Josiah. Although many of them were <u>notorious</u> for biting and other forms of bad behavior, Roosevelt loyally defended them by claiming that they only bit people with lousy political beliefs.

113. Which two presidents mentioned in the passage had dogs as pets?

   a. Theodore Roosevelt and Calvin Coolidge
   b. John Adams and Theodore Roosevelt
   c. Thomas Jefferson and John Quincy Adams
   d. John Adams and Calvin Coolidge

114. According to the information provided in the passage, who was the sixth US president?

   a. Martin Van Buren
   b. Thomas Jefferson
   c. Marquis de Lafayette
   d. John Quincy Adams

115. How were John Adams' pets different than pets of the other presidents mentioned in this passage?

   a. John Adams had more pets than any other president.
   b. John Adams had an alligator, whereas the other presidents had more traditional pets.
   c. John Adams had traditional domesticated pets, whereas the other presidents had more exotic animals.
   d. John Adams did not have any pets, whereas the other presidents did.

116. Which of the following would be the most appropriate title for the passage?

   a. "Animals of the United States"
   b. "A History of the White House"
   c. "A Guide to Exotic Animals"
   d. "Pets of the White House"

117. Based on the information provided in the passage, what animal is Calvin Coolidge most likely to have as a pet?

a. a dog
b. fish
c. a lion
d. a cat

118. Why do you think the author included the detail about Roosevelt being a hunter?

a. because it demonstrated a contradiction with Roosevelt's apparent love of animals
b. because it showed why Roosevelt liked exotic pets more than domesticated pets
c. because it clarified why Roosevelt hunted his own pets
d. because the author did not approve of Roosevelt's interest in hunting

119. As it is used in the passage, what does the word <u>notorious</u> mean?

a. unusual
b. punished
c. praised
d. well-known

120. Who gave President Martin Van Buren two tiger cubs?

a. the Marquis de Lafayette
b. the Sultan of Oman
c. Zebulon Pike
d. John Quincy Adams

121. Why did the author write this passage?

a. to persuade the reader to purchase exotic pets
b. to critique the presidents' choice of pets
c. to inform the reader about the variety of pets presidents have owned
d. to encourage the reader to stand up for animal rights

122. What do you think the author will discuss in the next paragraph?

a. Calvin Coolidge's unusual pets
b. details about Theodore Roosevelt's wife and children
c. an explanation of what happened to Van Buren's tiger cubs
d. a discussion of the pets of United States citizens

Questions 123 - 132 refer to the passage below.

As I was coming home one day, I crossed paths with a small boy eating a banana. There was nothing remarkable in that, but as I neared McGinnis Court I saw another small boy, also eating a banana. A third small boy, engaged in the same activity, convinced me that coincidence was an unlikely cause. I trust that you, dear reader, will understand the relationship between these events and the sickening sense of loss that I felt upon witnessing them. Sure enough, when I reached my room the bananas were gone.

There was but one that knew of their existence, but one who frequented my window, but one who was capable of the gymnastics needed to climb up the wall and into my room in order to grab them-- and that was Melons. Melons the predator, Melons the fugitive, Melons, who was no doubt hiding out on some neighborhood rooftop at this very moment, celebrating his success.

I lit a cigar, and, drawing my chair to the window, began to wait. In a few moments, someone scurried passed my window. There was no mistaking that disreputable head... it was Melons, that crafty, juvenile villain.

He was clearly unable to resist the urge to revisit the scene of the crime. I smoked calmly, and gazed at him without speaking. He marched several times back and forth in front of my window with a half-friendly, half-belligerent expression, intended to represent the carelessness of innocence. At last he met my eye and announced gravely, "I know who took 'em. It was Carrots. Carrots is a bad boy."

I felt that this must end here. I rose sternly and addressed Melons.

"Melons, I know that you took those bananas. Your accusation regarding Carrots is ridiculous. You took those bananas, a felony offense under the Statutes of California. How far Carrots may have been accessory to the deed is not my intention to discuss. The act is complete. Your present conduct does nothing but prove my suspicion."

By the time I had finisned this exordium, Melons had disappeared, as I fully expected. I have not seen him since.

123. Given the information in the passage, McGinnis Court is most likely

   a. a famous tennis stadium
   b. the street the narrator lives on
   c. a dangerous area
   d. the nickname of a local judge

124. The literary technique best illustrated by the phrase "convinced me that coincidence was an unlikely cause" is

   a. analogy
   b. assonance
   c. allusion
   d. alliteration

125. From the description given in the passage, one can assume that Melons is

   a. younger than the narrator
   b. a ruthless criminal
   c. the narrator's friend
   d. clever but weak

126. Why does the narrator believe that Melons stole his bananas?

   a. Because Melons cannot resist fruit.
   b. Because Melons was the only one who was capable of stealing them.
   c. Because the other boys told the narrator that Melons had stolen the bananas.
   d. Because Melons regularly stole the narrator's belongings.

127. After arriving home, the narrator

   a. Makes dinner, then sits down on the couch to wait for Melons
   b. Waits for Melons while smoking a pipe
   c. Designs a trap to catch Melons
   d. Lights a cigar and sits by the window

128. How does the narrator feel towards Melons?

   a. irritated but loving
   b. sympathetic and worried
   c. exasperated and mistrustful
   d. furious but confused

129. When Melons returns to the narrator's home, he

   a. feigns innocence
   b. argues with the narrator
   c. apologizes
   d. explains himself

130. Where does this story take place?

   a. England
   b. Outside Melons' house
   c. A small town
   d. California

131. What does the narrator see that first arouses his suspicion?

   a. Melons, hiding on a neighbor's rooftop
   b. Several children eating bananas
   c. Melons and his friend Carrots, looking sneaky
   d. A pile of bananas outside his window

132. Which of the following best demonstrates the use of irony in the passage?

   a. The way Melons revisits the scene of his crime
   b. The fact that Melons is athletic enough to climb up the wall and into the narrator's window
   c. The serious way such a silly crime is described
   d. Melons' reaction to being accused by the narrator

Questions 133 - 142 refer to the passage below.

Stede Bonnet was a well-educated English gentleman, a wealthy landowner, and a famously <u>inept</u> pirate. At the age of 29, he made the bizarre decision to abandon his comfortable lifestyle and begin a new career as a criminal on Caribbean seas. He joined the profession in 1717, when legendary individuals like Edward Teach (AKA "Blackbeard") struck fear into the hearts of sailors everywhere in what is now referred to as "The Golden Age of Piracy."

Unlike Blackbeard and most of his contemporaries, however, Bonnet did not have any clear motivation to become a pirate. Buccaneers were often rebels from the lower classes, lured by the promise of freedom and riches beyond what they could ever achieve as law-abiding citizens. Most were bachelors and uneducated sailors, with little to lose and much to gain. Bonnet, on the other hand, owned a profitable 400-acre sugar plantation, had a wife and children, and (perhaps most importantly) had zero sailing experience.

Some historians believe that Bonnet was secretly going bankrupt, and turned pirate in the hope of acquiring some easy cash. Others suspect that Bonnet was deeply unhappy with his marriage, and saw seafaring as a way to escape his wife. It's even possible that Bonnet experienced some sort of mental breakdown, or that his wildly irresponsible decision to become a swashbuckling bandit was the result of a midlife crisis.

Whatever his motive, Bonnet's approach to captaining was as quaintly respectable as his background. Instead of stealing a ship or working his way up the ranks with an existing crew, Bonnet legally purchased a boat (which he named The Revenge) and hired sailors to man it. Soon after they set sail, Bonnet and his crew ran into Blackbeard, who was apparently amused by Bonnet's prim and proper <u>naiveté</u>. Blackbeard took Bonnet under his wing as a "guest," thus adding The Revenge to his own experienced fleet. Bonnet seemed resigned to the arrangement. He supposedly spent much of his time pouting in Blackbeard's library, or wandering around in his dressing gown. Eventually, Blackbeard got sick of babysitting, and left Bonnet, his crew, and The Revenge marooned on an island near North Carolina. Less than a year later, Bonnet was captured and arrested.

133. In which century did Bonnet become a pirate?

   a. 16th century
   b. 17th century
   c. 18th century
   d. 19th century

134. How was Bonnet different than most pirates?

   a. He was not married.
   b. He did not have a ship.
   c. He was wealthy.
   d. He was never caught.

135. As it is used in the passage, what is the best definition of the word <u>inept</u>?

   a. effective
   b. delusional
   c. aggressive
   d. incompetent

136. What is the most appropriate title for this passage?

   a. "Blackbeard: The Cruelest Pirate"
   b. "The Golden Age of Piracy"
   c. "1717: An Important Year"
   d. "Stede Bonnet: A Bumbling Pirate"

137. Based on the information provided in the passage, which of the following is NOT a possible reason that Bonnet became a pirate?

   a. He had an unhappy marriage.
   b. He wanted to escape the pressures of raising his children.
   c. He was going bankrupt.
   d. He had a mental breakdown.

138. Bonnet stayed on Blackbeard's ship because he

   a. was invited to
   b. wanted to learn how to become a better pirate
   c. was forced to by Blackbeard
   d. wanted to steal Blackbeard's ship

139. Why did the author include the sentence "Bonnet, on the other hand, owned a profitable 400-acre sugar plantation, had a wife and children, and (perhaps most importantly) had zero sailing experience"?

a. to compare Bonnet to modern day sailors
b. to demonstrate how unusual it was that Bonnet became a pirate
c. to explain why Blackbeard let Bonnet on his ship
d. to argue why Bonnet should not have been arrested

140. As it is used in the passage, what is the best definition of the word <u>naiveté</u>?

a. innocence
b. arrogance
c. callousness
d. friendliness

141. Which of the following would most likely publish this reading passage?

a. the editorial page of the newspaper
b. a history website
c. an academic journal
d. a geography textbook

142. What do you think the author will write about in the next paragraph?

a. an explanation of happened to Bonnet after his arrest
b. description of other famous pirates
c. an outline of Blackbeard's biggest successes as a pirate
d. a description of Bonnet's plantation

Questions 143 - 152 refer to the passage below.

The common American opossum is far from popular among most United States citizens. On the contrary, possums (as they're often called) are thought of as pesky, rat-like vermin that damage property and spread disease. However, these negative stereotypes are almost entirely false!

Many people assume that possums are closely related to rats due to their physical similarities, especially their long, hairless tails. In reality, possums are not related to rodents at all; they are the continent's only marsupials, and are therefore related to kangaroos and wallabies! Like their cousins from Down Under, female opossums give birth to young (called joeys), which they carry in special pouches.

Although possums have been known to get into trash cans in search of food, for the most part their scavenging habits are very beneficial. They primarily eat insects, small rodents, snakes, and carrion (dead animals). Far from being pests themselves, possums are nature's pest-control and sanitation workers. They are also solitary wanderers, and go from place to place every few days. So, there's no need to worry about groups of possums taking up residence in your backyard, even if one does stop by for a visit.

Opossums can look intimidating, but they are actually quite harmless to humans. When frightened, a possum's first instinct is to stand very still, display all 50 of its teeth, and drool. If that fails, it will pretend to be dead, a tactic called "playing possum." While these behaviors may be <u>unnerving</u>, they are really just the possum's attempts to avoid conflict. Since possums are not very big, fierce, or strong, they are generally poor fighters. They are also rather clumsy and slow, which means they cannot rely on their ability to escape by running away. Their best hope is to appear scary and ill so that potential predators will avoid them.

Perhaps the most undeserved stereotype about possums is that they spread disease, particularly rabies. In fact, possums are almost immune to rabies, because they have an unusually low body-temperature that makes it difficult for the virus to take hold.

143. Based on the information in this passage, one can infer that possums drool when threatened because

    a. they are preparing to bite
    b. drooling is one way they "play possum"
    c. the shine created by their saliva makes their teeth look sharper
    d. drooling makes them look ill, which can deter predators

144. Which of the following animals are most closely related to opossums?

    a. skunks
    b. wallabees
    c. racoons
    d. rats

145. The author of the passage would most likely agree that

    a. negative beliefs about possums are mostly incorrect
    b. possums are dangerous but useful
    c. possums are not as unpopular as they should be
    d. people should leave food outside to attract possums to their yards

146. Without possums, it is likely that

    a. neighborhoods would be cleaner
    b. coyote populations would decline
    c. diseases would spread more easily among other wildlife
    d. rodent populations would increase

147. All of the following statements are false, EXCEPT

    a. possums will disrupt trash cans
    b. possums are naturally aggressive towards humans
    c. possums often damage people's property by building large group nests
    d. possums frequently carry diseases

148. Based on its use in the passage, unnerving most nearly means

a. fearless
b. whimsical
c. spooky
d. understandable

149. According to the information given in the passage, which of the following options would most likely change popular assumptions about the relationship between possums and rats?

a. if possums had short, fluffy tails
b. if the sounds made by possums and rats were less similar
c. if more people knew that possums eat snakes
d. if possums were larger

150. This passage is primarily about

a. why wildlife is important to local ecosystems
b. how to keep possums away from your property
c. the defensive behaviors of the American opossum
d. how possums are misunderstood

151. Which of the following makes possums unique in North America?

a. They are marsupials.
b. They are disliked by most people.
c. They eat carrion.
d. They tend to wander from place to place.

152. According to the information given in the passage, possums are different from pests because

a. possums prefer to stay in one place and eat other pests
b. possums are nocturnal and often shy
c. possums are clumsy, slow, and bad at fighting
d. possums are harmless, helpful scavengers

Vocabulary

Instructions: Choose the word that means the same, or about the same, as the underlined word.

153. A blatant lie

a. subtle
b. white
c. significant
d. obvious

154. A synopsis of the play

a. reading
b. summary
c. performance
d. revision

155. A petty argument

a. serious
b. thoughtful
c. insignificant
d. sporadic

156. The chaotic scene

a. disorderly
b. beautiful
c. organized
d. shocking

157. A forged signature

a. elaborate
b. faked
c. messy
d. simple

158. The congenial host

a. easygoing
b. standoffish
c. organized
d. friendly

159. The idle employees

a. hardworking
b. innovative
c. inactive
d. angry

160. The precise instructions

a. detailed
b. clear
c. vague
d. technical

161. To rescind an order

a. defy
b. revoke
c. adjust
d. follow

162. A diplomatic response

a. governmental
b. weak
c. tactful
d. unexpected

163. The grandiose gesture

a. friendly
b. subtle
c. arrogant
d. extravagant

164. Infinite possibilities

a. incredible
b. endless
c. limited
d. possible

165. To hinder progress

a. impede
b. encourage
c. avoid
d. inspire

166. A derogatory comment

a. encouraging
b. brusque
c. demeaning
d. honest

167. The companies amalgamated

a. split apart
b. argued
c. agreed
d. combined

168. The exalted leader

a. unpopular
b. eminent
c. effective
d. uncompromising

169. A veneer of confidence

a. facade
b. plethora
c. degree
d. lack

170. An aptitude for math

a. talent
b. dislike
c. eagerness
d. difficulty

171. Malicious gossip

a. fascinating
b. shocking
c. spiteful
d. harmless

172. To contemplate a problem

a. solve
b. avoid
c. exacerbate
d. ponder

173. An amiable greeting

a. cautious
b. friendly
c. lighthearted
d. sudden

174. An inopportune moment

a. perfect
b. belated
c. fleeting
d. inconvenient

Math Section 6

64 Questions, 45 Minutes

Instructions: Select the best answer.

175. The product of two consecutive numbers is 12. What are the numbers?

a. 2, 6
b. 5, 7
c. 2, 12
d. 3, 4

176. What is the least common multiple of 6 and 14?

a. 14
b. 28
c. 42
d. 84

177. Solve: $4 + 2(1 + 4)^2 - \frac{8}{2}$

a. 50
b. 100
c. 34
d. 10

178. Convert $\frac{4}{7}$ into a percent. Round to the nearest tenth.

a. 60.2%
b. 57.1%
c. 42.9%
d. 52.6%

179. Solve: 27.96 - 9.58

a. 19.34
b. 17.89
c. 16.44
d. 18.38

180. Write out eight hundred twenty six thousand nine hundred two in numerals.

a. 826, 920
b. 82,692
c. 826,902
d. 820,692

181. Solve for d: 5d - 11 = 14

a. $\frac{3}{5}$
b. 5
c. 3
d. 2

182. What is the value of the number 3 in this number: 453,792?

a. 30,000
b. 3,000
c. 300
d. 300,000

183. Which point is on a line segment?

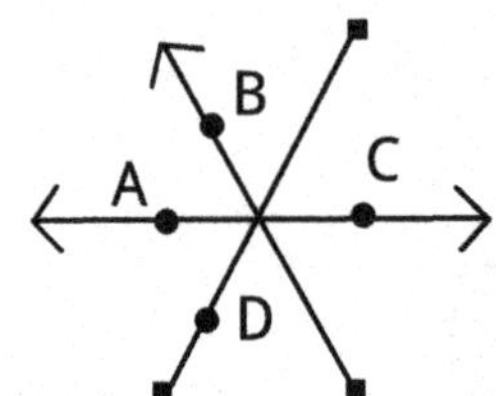

a. A
b. B
c. C
d. D

184. Given the two sets of numbers A = {2, 3, 5, 8} and B = {1, 2, 5, 7}, what is $A \cap B$?

a. {2, 5}
b. {1, 2, 3, 5, 7, 8}
c. {1, 3, 7}
d. {2, 3, 5, 8}

185. The base of a triangle is x and the area is 12. What is the triangle's height?

a. 12x
b. $\frac{24}{x}$
c. $\frac{12}{x}$
d. 24x

186. A number added to 25% of itself equals 60. What is the number?

a. 12
b. 36
c. 48
d. 50

187. The rectangle below has perimeter 40. What is the value of x?

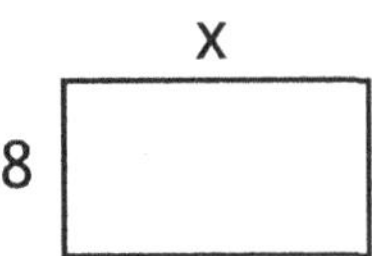

b. 8
c. 10
d. 12

188. Angle A is 27° and complementary to angle B. What is the measure of angle B?

a. 63°
b. 27°
c. 153°
d. 163°

189. What is 15 less than the square root of 144?

a. 3
b. 57
c. -3
d. 129

190. The quotient of 27 and what number is $\frac{3}{4}$ of 12?

a. 2
b. 3
c. 6
d. 9

191. Which example illustrates the commutative property?

a. $(4 \times 2)\,3 = 4\,(2 \times 3)$
b. $6\,(4 + 8) = 24 + 48$
c. $4 \times 6 = 6 \times 4$
d. $4 \times 1 = 4$

192. What is 7.12×10^{-4} in standard notation?

a. .000712
b. .00712
c. 71,200
d. 7,120

193. What is the reciprocal of $\frac{2}{3}$?

a. 2
b. $-\frac{2}{3}$
c. $-\frac{3}{2}$
d. $\frac{3}{2}$

194. How many cups are in a gallon?

a. 8
b. 24
c. 12
d. 16

195. The volume of a cube is 27. What is the cube's side length?

a. 13.5
b. 9
c. 3
d. 81

196. Solve: $(-5)^3$

a. 125
b. -125
c. 25
d. -25

197. Last year, Tara was paid $12.72 an hour by her employer. This year, she is being paid $13.04 an hour by her employer. How much more is she earning this year for a 7 hour shift?

a. $2.24
b. $3.76
c. $2.76
d. $2.34

198. A group of middle school students acted in their annual spring play. The number of actors from each grade is shown in the graph below. What was the difference between the grade with the highest number of actors and the grade with the lowest number of actors?

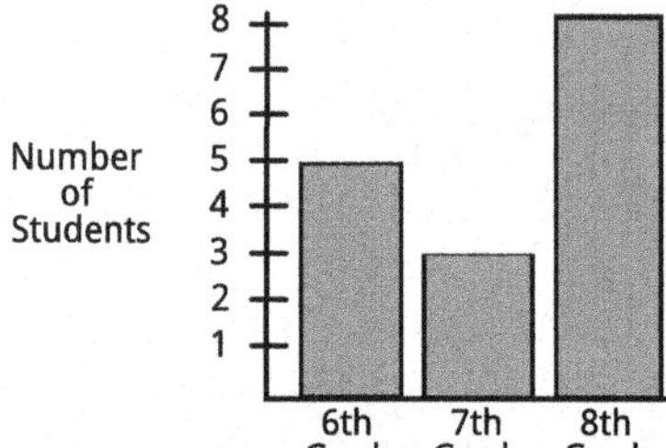

a. 2
b. 3
c. 5
d. 6

199. Casey bought a $40 shirt on sale for $34. What percent discount did she get on the shirt?

a. 12%
b. 15%
c. 75%
d. 77%

200. If 6x = 24, what is 2x + 5?

a. 4
b. 3
c. 13
d. 12

201. On her first three math tests, Daphne scored 84%, 92%, and 76%. What score would she need on her fourth test to raise her average to 87%?

a. 91%
b. 88%
c. 96%
d. 98%

202. What is the area of the shaded region in the rectangle below?

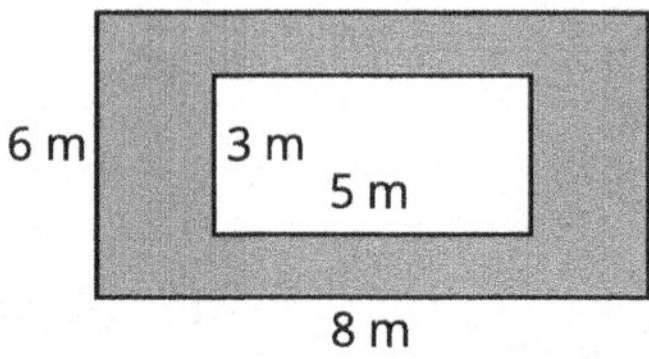

a. 15 m^2
b. 36 m^2
c. 48 m^2
d. 33 m^2

203. On the blueprint for Claire's house, 1 inch represents 4 feet. Her rectangular living room is 3 inches by 5 inches on the blueprint. In feet, what is the area of Claire's living room?

a. 240 sq. feet
b. 220 sq. feet
c. 210 sq. feet
d. 260 sq. feet

204. An art room has 3 green paints, 4 purple paints, 2 red paints, and 3 blue paints. If I were to choose a paint at random, what is the probability I'd choose a red paint?

a. $\frac{1}{4}$
b. $\frac{2}{13}$
c. $\frac{2}{5}$
d. $\frac{1}{6}$

205. Owen sold two-thirds of his movies and then bought 15 more. If he currently owns 27 movies, how many did he have originally?

a. 33
b. 36
c. 27
d. 24

206. A flight from Montreal to Mexico City leaves at 7:25 AM and arrives at 1:35 PM. How long is the flight?

a. 6 hours, 10 minutes
b. 6 hours, 50 minutes
c. 7 hours, 10 minutes
d. 5 hours, 50 minutes

207. A library contains 2,000 books. The ratio of fiction to non-fiction books in the library is 3:2. How many non-fiction books does the library contain?

a. 1,200
b. 600
c. 1,400
d. 800

208. Last week, Keisha rode her bicycle 126 miles. On average, how many miles did she ride each day?

a. 8
b. 16
c. 18
d. 22

209. Mark buys a $60 video game and pays 8% tax on the game. What is the total amount he pays for the game, including tax?

a. $60.00
b. $64.80
c. $66.00
d. $4.80

210. What could be the name of the figure below?

a. trapezoid
b. cube
c. prism
d. parallelogram

211. Solve: $-3x < 6$

a. $x < -2$
b. $x > -2$
c. $x < 2$
d. $x > 2$

212. If the volume of the rectangular prism below is 24 cm^3, what is x?

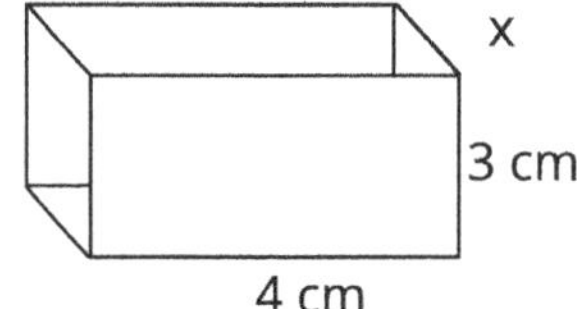

a. 2 cm
b. 4 cm
c. 3 cm
d. 6 cm

213. If $12x - 6y = 12$ and $x = 5$, what is y?

a. -2
b. 8
c. 15
d. 2

214. In a right triangle, two of the angles of MUST be

a. right
b. obtuse
c. acute
d. isosceles

215. Solve: $3^2 + 6^2 =$

a. 81
b. 36
c. 18
d. 45

216. Cate has a 5 gallon bucket filled with water. She uses 2 gallons and 3 quarts to water her vegetable garden. How much water is left in the bucket?

a. 2 gallons and 2 quarts
b. 3 gallons and 1 quart
c. 2 gallons and 1 quart
d. 3 gallons and 2 quarts

217. Find side c.

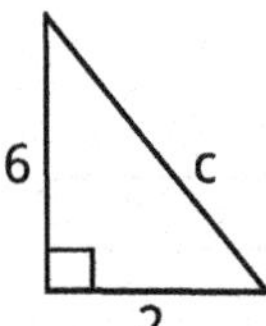

a. $2\sqrt{10}$
b. $4\sqrt{10}$
c. $4\sqrt{5}$
d. 5

218. Milo and his three friends went out to dinner and evenly split their bill. If each of them paid $13.34, what was the total bill?

a. $40.02
b. $26.68
c. $53.36
d. $49.34

219. Winston scored a 90%, 80%, 75%, and and an 85% on his math quizzes. If his teacher drops his lowest quiz grade, what is his average quiz score for the class?

a. 61%
b. 82%
c. 85%
d. 90%

220. Simplify: $\sqrt{140x^3y^4}$

a. $2xy^2\sqrt{35x}$
b. $4xy^2\sqrt{35x}$
c. $140xy^2$
d. $2\sqrt{35x^3y^4}$

221. In the inequality $3x - 2 < 7$, x must be less than what number:

a. 2
b. 3
c. 7
d. 9

222. It took Carmondy 45 minutes to drive home from work. If she was driving 30 miles per hour for her entire trip, what distance did she drive?

a. 1350 miles
b. 13.5 miles
c. 25 miles
d. 22.5 miles

223. Lucy opened up a savings account which earns 7.25% interest annually. Lucy put $625 in the account and then left it alone for a year. How much money would be in the account after the year had elapsed? Round answer to the nearest cent.

a. $45.31
b. $1,078.13
c. $624.83
d. $670.31

224. Amy earned the following quiz scores 10, 9, 8, 8, 7, 8, 7, 6 and 10. What was the mode of her scores?

a. 7
b. 8
c. 9
d. 10

225. Mable bought 1 gallon containers of fruit punch for her birthday party. How many eight ounce glasses can she get from a 1 gallon container of punch?

a. 2
b. 8
c. 10
d. 16

226. Which letter below contains a horizontal line of symmetry?

a. A
b. E
c. N
d. L

227. The table below shows the number of trees planted in a city's park in May.

Number of Trees	Number of Parks
0	3
1	2
2	1
3	4
4	2

What is the average number of trees planted per park during May?

a. 1.5
b. 2
c. 2.7
d. 3

228. Rodrigo is having new carpet installed in his living room. If his living room measures 12 feet by 19 feet, and carpet costs $4.00 a square foot, how much will it cost to purchase carpet for the entire room?

a. $1044
b. $912
c. $228
d. $684

229. In the equation below, if a = -3 and b = 6, what is c?

$4b - 2a = c$

a. 30
b. -24
c. 0
d. 12

230. Lauren opened a lemonade stand. On the first day, she sold 5 glasses of lemonade and 10 glasses of pink lemonade for a total of $6.25. On the second day, she sold 5 glasses of lemonade and 15 glasses of pink lemonade for a total of $8.75. What is the cost of one glass of pink lemonade?

a. $0.25
b. $0.50
c. $0.75
d. $1.00

231. 3 yards, 1 feet, 8 inches
-2 yards, 2 feet, 2 inches

a. 1 foot, 6 inches
b. 1 yard, 1 foot, 6 inches
c. 2 feet, 6 inches
d. 1 yard, 2 feet, 6 inches

232. When folded, which shape best describes the figure below?

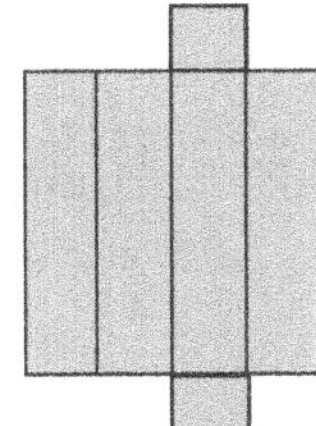

a. cube
b. rectangular prism
c. sphere
d. triangular prism

233. What is the area of a circle with circumference 14π? Assume $\pi = 3.14$.

a. 43.96
b. 153.86
c. 49
d. 615.44

234. Nicole is making pancakes for her her daughter's track team pancake fundraiser. Her recipe calls for 3.5 teaspoons of baking powder. She needs to make 6 batches of the recipe to make enough pancakes. How much baking powder, in tablespoons, does she need?

a. 21 tablespoons
b. 14 tablespoons
c. 7 tablespoons
d. 3.5 tablespoons

235. John earns $42,300 a year, of which 24% goes to taxes. How much does John earn after taxes?

a. $10,152
b. $10,575
c. $31,725
d. $32,148

236. The table below shows the year of publication of five novels.

Novel	Year of Publication
Pride and Prejudice	1813
Frankenstein	1818
Jane Eyre	1847
Great Expectations	1860
Middlemarch	1871

How many years after Frankenstein's publication was Middlemarch published?

a. 63
b. 57
c. 53
d. 67

237. Emily's car can travel 443 miles on 22 gallons of gasoline. How many miles can she travel on 33 gallons? Round your answer to the nearest tenth.

a. 656.8 miles
b. 660 miles
c. 664.5 miles
d. 667 miles

238. Solve for x: $x^2 - 9 = 55$

a. 8
b. 9
c. 32
d. 16

Language Section 6

60 Questions, 25 Minutes

Usage and Mechanics

Instructions: For questions 239-278, check the sentences for errors of usage, capitalization, or punctuation. If there is no error, choose D.

239.

a. Michelle could not wait to go horseback riding this summer.
b. Matt and Mindy left there car at home.
c. Rose was reprimanded for being rude to her classmates.
d. No mistakes.

240.

a. Mary and Sean are both good swimmers, but Mary is the fastest of the two.
b. Bob and Linda tended a small vegetable patch at the community garden together.
c. Mowing the grass is Dan's least favorite chore.
d. No mistakes.

241.

a. Although there are many great museums in Chicago, The Field Museum is Kyle's favorite.
b. When comparing a book to its film adaptation, the book is usually better.
c. *Of mice and men* by John Steinbeck is one of Mariel's favorite books.
d. No mistakes.

242.

a. Mrs. Wilcott, Jessica's math teacher assigned her some extra credit to make up for her poor test score last week.
b. Jackie injured herself on the job and was confined to bed rest for a week.
c. Lauren prefers sweet over savory breakfast.
d. No mistakes.

243.

a. Its difficult to learn a new language, but it can also be very rewarding!
b. Jodi remembers a time when you could watch cartoons only on Saturday mornings.
c. Laura loves collecting fan art of her favorite comic book characters.
d. No mistakes.

244.

a. Aunt Erin knitted scarves for all of us for Christmas.
b. Josie loves to jump in puddles during a summer rainstorm.
c. Were you able to hear the instructions clearly.
d. No mistakes.

245.

a. Colleen likes to drink hot tea with honey and lemon when she is feeling under the weather.
b. This batch of cookies are especially delicious!
c. Aaron's family moved here from South Carolina.
d. No mistakes.

246.

a. Cameron jauntily skipped through the meadow on the lovely spring morning.
b. Miguel prefers to drink milk with his breakfast instead of juice.
c. Will's favorite herbs to cook with include basil, thyme, and rosemary.
d. No mistakes.

247.

a. Who would like to present their project first, Ms. Wilson asked the class.

b. Apples are a nutritious snack that can satisfy any sweet tooth.

c. Dan opened up all the windows in his apartment so that he could get some fresh air.

d. No mistakes.

248.

a. Peter worked very diligently on his science project.

b. Dennis sold the baseball bat to his friend made of aluminum.

c. Gwen was excited to head north for the weekend.

d. No mistakes.

249.

a. Marty was looking forward to auditioning for the spring musical.

b. Rosie fights hard for the things she believes in.

c. Cassandra forgot to complete her math homework before the weekend.

d. No mistakes.

250.

a. Rachel was scared of performing the monologue in front of the whole class.

b. Gordy is on the fast track towards earning a football scholarship.

c. Me and my brother went to the carnival this weekend.

d. No mistakes.

251.

a. Please pick up eggs bread, and juice at the store this afternoon.

b. Barney did not wish to go to the networking event this evening.

c. Jason needed some rest after not sleeping well over the last few nights.

d. No mistakes.

252.

a. Samuel worked part-time at the diner after school.

b. Anton was the better student of the entire class.

c. The cactus plant required infrequent watering.

d. No mistakes.

253.

a. Claude could not wait to visit the lake this weekend where he was excited to relax, swim, and catch up on some reading while he was on vacation which he had not done in a while.

b. Lizzie has a vast collection of coins that she inherited from her parents.

c. Ginger was a finalist in the school's spelling bee.

d. No mistakes.

254.

a. Brian who is my cousin always comes with me when I go to summer camp.

b. Tracy is very excited for her dance recital on October 15.

c. Jake was dreading working on the book report he put off until the last minute.

d. No mistakes.

255.

a. The weather was unusually overcast and gloomy for a summer day.

b. Marys cat Whiskers loves to play with string.

c. Construction made Sarah's commute immensely tedious.

d. No mistakes.

256.

a. Amy loves to have mint chocolate chip ice cream on a hot day.

b. Jason's apartment was a bit of a mess.

c. The recipe calls for one cup of sugar and two cups of flower.

d. No mistakes.

257.

a. Tiffany was ravenous at dinner because she hadn't had time to eat lunch.

b. Although it was a long trip, it was nice to spend time with my family.

c. Howard is going to Atlanta last summer.

d. No mistakes.

258.

a. The storm brought a much needed cold front to the town after a long heat wave.

b. Nate suspected that his roommate took the last granola bar.

c. The library held an interesting workshop on organization last month.

d. No mistakes.

259.

a. Every year my parents and I travel east to New York.

b. One day, I'd love to go to the Super bowl.

c. Whose red leather jacket is this?

d. No mistakes.

260.

a. The boys' coach told him that he needed to practice at least 90 minutes a day.

b. I love eating vegetables such as cauliflower, broccoli, and carrots.

c. LaToya found her kitten's toy under the living room sofa.

d. No mistakes.

261.

a. It's easy to run a 5k if you train every day.

b. That's incredible!

c. Stephen didn't know weather he should walk to school or take the bus.

d. No mistakes.

262.

a. "I'm really sorry," I told Ms. Jackson, "but I wasn't able to finish my homework last night."

b. This winter we should go sledding at North Bay Park .

c. My birthday is September, 29.

d. No mistakes.

263.

a. Samara loved books; therefore, she spent hours browsing through the shelves of the new bookstore.

b. The caramel candy was the sweetest of the two candies in the jar.

c. They're going to their aunt Maria's house for dinner.

d. No mistakes.

264.

a. "Karolina," my sister shouted, "we're going to be late!"

b. Falling quickly and silently, the snow covered the streets in a blanket of white.

c. The water's temperature affected the outcome of my science experiment.

d. No mistakes.

265.

a. Sadly, I've never had a chance to travel outside of the United States.

b. Although he was new to the school, Principal Calkins was able to quickly make a lot of positive changes.

c. After school, I eat a snack, complete my homework, and watch television.

d. No mistakes.

266.

a. I love going peach picking in Georgia every summer.

b. "Fantastic!" my mom exclaimed.

c. Abdul's Uncle ate all the ice cream from the freezer.

d. No mistakes.

267.

a. The principal reason I'm quitting the team is that I keep getting injured.

b. Hasan has more baseball cards then I do.

c. The children took their bicycles inside when it started to rain.

d. No mistakes.

268.

a. "I'm going to apply for the summer camp counselor job" I told my mom.

b. Since it was too cold to run outside, Christine jogged on her treadmill.

c. The table at the elegant restaurant was covered in a linen tablecloth, decorated with fresh flowers, and set with fine china.

d. No mistakes.

269.

a. It's easier to study a little bit each day than to cram the night before a test.

b. Marshall had fewer than three days to practice for his big game.

c. If we want to get ice cream later this afternoon, everyone has to do their chores.

d. No mistakes.

270.

a. Proudly, Josh told me that he ran his first marathon last year.

b. Myla gave my sister and me a piece of her birthday cake.

c. It's freezing outside, put on some gloves.

d. No mistakes.

271.

a. The red sports car sped through the intersection.

b. The team won the state's championship trophy.

c. The little boy walk all the way to the park by himself.

d. No mistakes.

272.

a. After I fell asleep last night, I'm having bad dreams.

b. The girl's car skidded to a halt on the dark, icy road.

c. Samir spent his summer watching movies, going to the beach, and playing sports.

d. No mistakes.

273.

a. My brother and I play video games together every Saturday morning.

b. Each November, my school raises money for two different charities.

c. Have you considered learning how to speak Spanish.

d. No mistakes.

274.

a. I earned less money this summer than my sister.

b. Raul and Kevin let his dog out in the yard.

c. The plumber was able to fix the sink's leaky faucet that day.

d. No mistakes.

275.

a. After it got dark outside we looked at the stars.

b. Can you lay down one test on each student's desk?

c. Who's going to watch the fireworks with me on the Fourth of July?

d. No mistakes.

276.

a. The larger of the two pillows got stained when Bryan spilled his drink.

b. "So, Mahreen sighed, "I guess this means we won't be going to the concert tonight."

c. The professional photographer, who was a family friend, gave us a discount on our photos.

d. No mistakes.

277.

a. To whom should I address the letter?

b. Pavel got elected to the city council even though there were several other candidates.

c. Despite its widespread support, the new law had no affect.

d. No mistakes.

278.

a. Kayla has the cleanest locker I've ever seen!

b. The childrens' garden was bursting with blues, reds, and purples.

c. After the opera, we ate dinner at an Italian restaurant.

d. No mistakes.

Spelling

Directions: For questions 279-288, look for errors in spelling. If there is no error, choose D.

279.

a. Tanya and her friends go to the playground every Saturday morning.

b. It looks like it is going to rain, so I'm going to bring my umbrella to school.

c. Milo agreed to go to the confrence with me after I told him it would be in Hawaii.

d. No mistakes.

280.

a. Raven, my best friend from kindergarden, moved to Pennsylvania before we started first grade.

b. My sister-in-law decided to become a truck driver, so she got her commercial driver's license.

c. A disease ravaged the orchard and by autumn no fruit was left on the trees.

d. No mistakes.

281.

a. I was really disappointed that I couldn't go to the movies with my friends.

b. Every year my family takes a vacation to a different national park.

c. Sean announced he was quitting his job, but he gave no further explenation.

d. No mistakes.

282.

a. Kara wants to become an enviornmental scientist when she grows up.

b. We went to a fancy restaurant for my grandmother's eightieth birthday.

c. The computer technician accidentally deleted my history paper.

d. No mistakes.

283.

a. The moving company broke my favorite coffee table.

b. I occasionaly walk to school with Karin and Isabella.

c. My favorite animals at the zoo are the elephants, giraffes, and cougars.

d. No mistakes.

284.

a. I can vaccum the carpet if you don't mind unloading the dishwasher.

b. The attorney thought the judge's verdict was unfair.

c. We're so grateful for the unexpected present!

d. No mistakes.

285.

a. Julianne is interested in learning more about astronomy and the solar system.

b. The computer technician told me that I would have to purchase a new laptop.

c. The equipment that you need to play ice hockey is quite expensive.

d. No mistakes.

286.

a. My sister and I share a bedroom but have seperate closets and dressers.

b. The car dealership had a special discount for military veterans.

c. The company president is retiring at the end of this year.

d. No mistakes.

287.

a. Avery and Michael auditioned for the school's musical even though neither of them had performed before.

b. I forgot to sign up for the field trip and am unsure of how to procceed.

c. The outdoor concert ended earlier than anticipated due to an incoming thunderstorm.

d. No mistakes.

288.

a. Olivia had a unique perspective that I hadn't considered before.

b. The sun peeked out from behind the rainclouds, giving me hope that my field hockey game wouldn't be cancelled.

c. Last summer, I threw a suprise party for my best friend.

d. No mistakes.

Composition

Directions: For questions 289-298, read the question and select the best answer.

289. Choose the word that best joins the sentences.

It looked as though Selma had lost her chance to make the drill team. ___________, at the last minute, the coach decided to add one more spot to his roster.

a. Thus

b. Consequently

c. Fortunately

d. Although

290. Choose the word that best joins the thoughts together.

Ideally, you should not save all of your studying until the night before ___________ it will be hard to retain the information.

a. because

b. while

c. and

d. however

291. Choose the group of words that best completes this sentence.

Running to catch the bus,

a. Roland slipped on the wet concrete and skinned his knee on the wet concrete.

b. the wet concrete causing Roland to slip resulted in a skinned knee.

c. he, Roland, skinned his knee and slipped on the wet concrete.

d. Roland slipped and skinned his knee on the wet concrete.

292. Which of these expresses the idea most clearly?

a. When looking to adopt a dog, it's better to adopt a dog from a shelter rather than a pet store because at pet stores they might come from a puppy mill.

b. It's better to adopt a dog from a shelter than to purchase one at a pet store because dogs at pet stores often come from puppy mills.

c. Purchasing a dog at a shelter is best because dogs at pet stores often come from puppy mills.

d. Pet store dogs often come from puppy mills; shelter dogs are better and should be adopted.

293. Which of these expresses the idea most clearly?

a. At Kruger National Park, rangers guard the animals twenty-four hours a day to prevent the poaching of rhinos for their horns.
b. Poaching is a serious problem at Kruger National Park; rangers are on guard twenty-four hours but many rhinos are still killed for their horns which is a problem.
c. Because poaching is so problematic at Kruger National Park, rangers guard the animals twenty-four hours a day and many rhinos are killed in order to get their horns.
d. Rhinos are killed for their horns at Kruger National Park; rangers try and protect them but many are still killed for their horns.

294. Which of these expresses the idea most clearly?

a. When she ran away from home, she packed only what was absolutely necessary.
b. In order to run away from home she packed only what was needed.
c. She packed only what she needed when she decided to run away from home.
d. Running away from home, she packed only what she absolutely needed.

295. Which of the following topics is best for a one-page essay?

a. The Many Uses of the Wheel
b. The History of the Automobile Around the World
c. Henry Ford's Idea for the Model-T
d. Daily Schedule of Boxcar Races at Field Elementary School

296. Which of these best fits under the topic "Civil War Destroys Most of Mozambique's Infrastructure"?

a. The United Nations does not typically get involved in the civil affairs of a nation.
b. Civil war has devastating consequences on any nation but particularly impacts developing countries.
c. Remnants of the decade long civil war, such as empty schools and hospitals, can be found throughout Mozambique.
d. The Portuguese ruled Mozambique for close to five hundred years.

297. Which sentence does not belong in the paragraph?

Noe knew she wanted to be a dancer but wasn't sure how. 2) She was already thirteen, and most of the girls in her ballet class had been dancing since they were toddlers. 3) Ballet's origins can be traced back to the Italian Renaissance. 4) That summer Noe took private lessons from her teacher and attended a special dance camp. 5) Today, Noe is proud to announce that she has the lead in this year's production of *The Nutcracker*.

a. sentence 1
b. sentence 2
c. sentence 3
d. sentence 5

298. Where should the sentence "Interestingly, there are some breeds of penguins that live outside the Antarctic in places like Madagascar and the Galapagos Islands." be placed?

Despite popular belief, penguins and polar bears do not live in the same location. 2) Polar bears are found only at the North Pole and penguins at the South Pole. 3) Polar bears reside in the Arctic and penguins the Antarctic. 4) It's probably a good thing that these two species are destined never to meet. 5) Penguins would no doubt become part of a polar bear's diet!

a. after sentence 1
b. before sentence 4
c. after sentence 2
d. before sentence 5

Answer Key

Verbal

1. C
2. A
3. D
4. B
5. B
6. C
7. D
8. A
9. C
10. D
11. A
12. D
13. C
14. C
15. B
16. D
17. B
18. A
19. B
20. D
21. A
22. C
23. D
24. B
25. D
26. B
27. C
28. A
29. B
30. C
31. C
32. A
33. D
34. C
35. B
36. C
37. B
38. C
39. B
40. C
41. a
42. B
43. A
44. A
45. D
46. B
47. C
48. B
49. C
50. D
51. D
52. B
53. B
54. A
55. D
56. D
57. C
58. C
59. D
60. C

Quantitative

61. B
62. D
63. B
64. A
65. D
66. A
67. C
68. B
69. A
70. B
71. A
72. D
73. C
74. B
75. D
76. A
77. B
78. A
79. B
80. A
81. C
82. D
83. C
84. B
85. A
86. C
87. D
88. C
89. B
90. B
91. B
92. B
93. D
94. C
95. C
96. A
97. B
98. C
99. A
100.A
101. C
102. C
103. B
104. D
105. A
106. B
107. C
108. C
109. A
110. B
111. B
112. D

Reading

113. B
114. D
115. C
116. D
117. C
118. A
119. D
120. B
121. C
122. A
123. B
124. D
125. A
126. B
127. D
128. C
129. A
130. D
131. B
132. C
133. C
134. C
135. D
136. D
137. B
138. C
139. B
140. A
141. B
142. A
143. D
144. B
145. A
146. D
147. A
148. C
149. A
150. D
151. A
152. D
153. D
154. B
155. C
156. A
157. B
158. D
159. C
160. A
161. B
162. C
163. D
164. B
165. A
166. C
167. D
168. B
169. A
170. A
171. C
172. D
173. B
174. D

Math

175. D
176. C
177. A
178. B
179. D
180. C
181. B
182. B
183. D
184. A
185. B
186. C
187. D
188. A
189. C
190. B
191. C
192. A
193. B
194. D
195. C
196. B
197. A
198. C
199. B
200. C
201. C
202. D
203. A
204. D
205. B
206. A
207. D
208. C
209. B
210. D
211. B
212. A
213. B
214. C
215. D
216. C
217. A
218. A
219. C
220. A
221. B
222. D
223. D
224. B
225. D
226. B
227. B
228. B
229. A
230. B
231. C
232. B
233. B
234. C
235. D
236. C
237. C
238. A

Language

239. B
240. A
241. C
242. A
243. A
244. C
245. B
246. D
247. A
248. B
249. D
250. C
251. A
252. B
253. A
254. A
255. B
256. C
257. C
258. D
259. B
260. A
261. C
262. C
263. B
264. D
265. D
266. C
267. B
268. A
269. C
270. C
271. C
272. A
273. C
274. B
275. A
276. B
277. C
278. B
279. C
280. A
281. C
282. A
283. B
284. A
285. D
286. A
287. B
288. C
289. C
290. A
291. D
292. C
293. A
294. A
295. C
296. C
297. C
298. B

HSPT Test 7

Verbal Section 7

60 Questions, 16 Minutes

Instructions: Select the best answer.

1. Renowned most nearly means

   a. disliked
   b. unknown
   c. famous
   d. intelligent

2. Uniformity means the *opposite* of

   a. variety
   b. colorful
   c. clarity
   d. constancy

3. Chloe plays outside longer than Maggie and Lei. Lei plays outside longer than Martin. Martin does not play outside as long as Chloe. If the first two statements are true, the third statement is

   a. true
   b. false
   c. uncertain

4. Corrode most nearly means

   a. smash
   b. strengthen
   c. bring together
   d. wear away

5. Which word does *not* belong with the others?

   a. fur
   b. feathers
   c. bone
   d. scales

6. Which word does *not* belong with the others?

   a. tiny
   b. average
   c. miniscule
   d. puny

7. Second is to minute as hour is to

   a. century
   b. minute
   c. month
   d. day

8. Valentina is taller than Juan and Micah. Juan and Savannah are taller than Bob. Savannah is taller than Micah. If the first two statements are true, the third statement is

   a. true
   b. false
   c. uncertain

9. Musician is to pianist as scientist is to

   a. nurse
   b. chemist
   c. biology
   d. subject

10. Which word does *not* belong with the others?

    a. pen
    b. quill
    c. paper
    d. pencil

11. Towel is to dry as broom is to

    a. mop
    b. push
    c. floor
    d. sweep

12. Pacify most nearly means

    a. intensify
    b. appease
    c. give
    d. encourage

13. Anytown Store is having a better sale than Everytown Store. Valleytown Store is having a better sale than Everytown Store, but a worse sale than Hilltown Store. Everytown Store is having the worst sale. If the first two statements are true, the third statement is

    a. true
    b. false
    c. uncertain

14. Which word does *not* belong with the others?

    a. pants
    b. capris
    c. shorts
    d. shirt

15. Which word does *not* belong with the others?

    a. toast
    b. cereal
    c. chili
    d. soup

16. Rigorous means the *opposite* of

    a. careless
    b. difficult
    c. austere
    d. smooth

17. Covert means the *opposite* of

    a. hidden
    b. convert
    c. open
    d. easy

18. Which word does *not* belong with the others?

    a. SUV
    b. motorcycle
    c. minivan
    d. car

19. All purple haired trolls have pointy noses and rounded ears. All blue haired trolls have pointy ears. If a troll has blue hair, it must have a pointy nose. If the first two statements are true, the third statement is

    a. true
    b. false
    c. uncertain

20. Hamper means the *opposite* of

    a. delay
    b. catch
    c. impede
    d. allow

21. Enumerate most nearly means

    a. guess
    b. conceal
    c. calculate
    d. endorse

22. Refrain means the *opposite* of

    a. abstain
    b. indulge
    c. shun
    d. play

23. Patrick's scores more baskets than Henry. Aga scores more baskets than Patrick. Aga scores fewer baskets than Henry. If the first two statements are true, the third statement is

    a. true
    b. false
    c. uncertain

24. Which word does *not* belong with the others?

    a. orange
    b. carrot
    c. apple
    d. kiwi

25. Domain most nearly means

    a. territory
    b. sky
    c. range
    d. surrender

26. Turnip is to root as stool is to

   a. lab
   b. office
   c. seat
   d. floor

27. Which word does *not* belong with the others?

   a. teaspoon
   b. tablespoon
   c. cup
   d. spatula

28. Jon lives directly north of Allison and northeast of Rachel. Allison lives directly east of Omar. Omar lives southeast of Jon. If the first two statements are true, the third statement is

   a. true
   b. false
   c. uncertain

29. Chastise most nearly means

   a. support
   b. hurt
   c. scold
   d. purify

30. Which word does *not* belong with the others?

   a. subway
   b. bus
   c. public transportation
   d. train

31. Malicious means the *opposite* of

   a. excitable
   b. benevolent
   c. malleable
   d. spiteful

32. Sleeve is to coat as sill is to

   a. window
   b. fabric
   c. close
   d. dark

33. Ocean A is deeper than Ocean B. Ocean C is more shallow than Ocean A. Ocean B is deeper than Ocean C. If the first two statements are true, the third statement is

   a. true
   b. false
   c. uncertain

34. Newspapers are to stands as prescriptions are to

   a. pills
   b. illness
   c. pharmacies
   d. doctor

35. Lemons are more bitter than limes. Oranges are sweeter than lemons. Limes are more bitter than oranges. If the first two statements are true, the third statement is

   a. true
   b. false
   c. uncertain

36. Liberate means the *opposite* of

   a. imprison
   b. free
   c. steal
   d. war

37. Which word does *not* belong with the others?

   a. zoo
   b. lion
   c. elephant
   d. bear

38. Devious most nearly means

   a. confident
   b. direct
   c. trustworthy
   d. calculating

39. Which word does *not* belong with the others?

   a. giraffe
   b. opossums
   c. kangaroos
   d. koalas

40. Snails are slower than sloths. Sloths are faster than turtles. Snails are faster than turtles. If the first two statements are true, the third statement is

a. true
b. false
c. uncertain

41. Barbaric most nearly means

a. groomed
b. kind
c. savage
d. depressed

42. Janine has a larger baseball card collection than Greg. Stephen has a larger baseball card collection than Janine. Greg has a smaller card collection than Stephen. If the first two statements are true, the third statement is

a. true
b. false
c. uncertain

43. Which word does *not* belong with the others?

a. iguana
b. snake
c. chameleon
d. monkey

44. Beef is to hamburger as flour is to

a. grain
b. bread
c. cheese
d. food

45. Catastrophic most nearly means

a. disastrous
b. warm
c. dull
d. successful

46. Which word does *not* belong with the others?

a. throw
b. catch
c. toss
d. hurl

47. Which word does *not* belong with the others?

a. carpet
b. hardwood
c. tile
d. floor

48. Track is to run as pool is to

a. swim
b. water
c. swimmers
d. diving board

49. Colossal means the *opposite* of

a. tiny
b. immense
c. statuesque
d. negative

50. Tyler ran farther than Bruce. Bruce did not run as far as Jaren. Jaren ran farther than Tyler. If the first two statements are true, the third statement is

a. true
b. false
c. uncertain

51. Which word does *not* belong with the others?

a. elm
b. oak
c. tree
d. fir

52. Big is to gargantuan as small is to

a. forgetful
b. looming
c. microscopic
d. large

53. Pinnacle most nearly means

a. base
b. hill
c. height
d. valley

54. Eroded most nearly means

    a. crumbled
    b. persevered
    c. strengthened
    d. moved

55. Jim has taken more science classes than Johnny. Johnny has taken fewer science classes than Mayim. Of the three, Johnny has taken the fewest science classes. If the first two statements are true, the third statement is

    a. true
    b. false
    c. uncertain

56. Famine means the *opposite* of

    a. abundance
    b. fashion
    c. ownership
    d. poverty

57. Which word does *not* belong with the others?

    a. block
    b. street
    c. road
    d. avenue

58. Tundra is to frigid as ocean is to

    a. arid
    b. tall
    c. dry
    d. aqueous

59. Pulverized most nearly means

    a. thrown
    b. eaten
    c. baked
    d. crushed

60. Which word does *not* belong with the others?

    a. chilled
    b. polar
    c. tropical
    d. frozen

Quantitative Section 7

52 Questions, 30 Minutes

Instructions: Select the best answer.

61. $\frac{1}{6}$ of 48 is equal to the sum of 3 and what number?

    a. 11
    b. 6
    c. 5
    d. 12

62. If the triangle below is an isosceles triangle with base $\overline{BC}$, which of the following must be true?

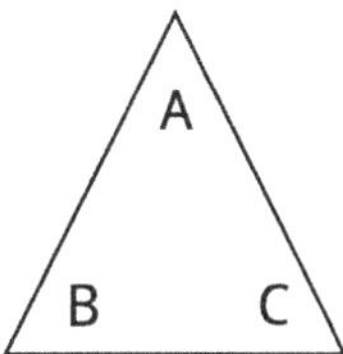

    a. $\angle A < \angle B$
    b. $\angle B = \angle C$
    c. $\angle C = \angle A$
    d. $\angle B < \angle C$

63. Look at the series: 50, 25, 45, 20, 40, 15, ___. What is the next number?

    a. 35
    b. 10
    c. 20
    d. 25

64. 35% of 60 is equal to the product of 3 and what number?

    a. 63
    b. 8
    c. 21
    d. 7

65. Review the series: 44, 42, 14, 12, 4, ___. Find the next number.

    a. 3
    b. 2
    c. 8
    d. 1

66. The sum of 18 and 11 is 7 less than what number?

    a. 22
    b. 29
    c. 36
    d. 35

67. Examine the figure below and select the best answer.

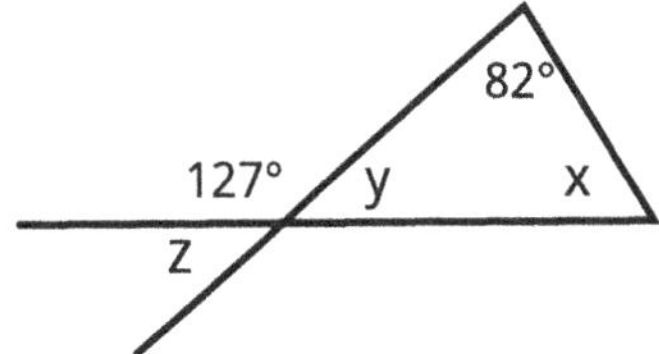

    a. $z < y$
    b. $x > y$
    c. $x < y$
    d. $z < x$

68. Examine (A), (B), and (C) and find the best answer.

    (A) 2 dimes, 6 nickels, 5 pennies
    (B) 2 quarters, 4 pennies
    (C) 9 nickels, 11 pennies

    a. (A) - (B) = (C) - (A)
    b. (B) + (C) < (A) + (B)
    c. (C) < (A)
    d. (C) - (A) > (A) - (B)

69. Look at this series: X, 9, IIX, 7, VI, ___. Find the next number or roman numeral.

    a. 6
    b. 5
    c. V
    d. 4

70. Examine (A), (B), and (C) and find the best answer.

(A) $2(5 - 1) + 5$
(B) $(6 - 2)^2$
(C) $3^2 - 6$

a. (B) - (C) < (A)
b. (A) - (C) > (B)
c. (A) + (C) = (B)
d. (A) + (C) < (B)

71. The sum of the cube of 2 and what number is equal to 15?

a. 8
b. 9
c. 11
d. 7

72. What is the next number in the following series: 2, 4, 6, 12, 10, 36, ___?

a. 12
b. 14
c. 38
d. 16

73. Examine the series: 23, 10, 20, 10, 17, 10, ___. What number should come next?

a. 14
b. 15
c. 13
d. 10

74. What is $\frac{1}{3}$ of $\frac{3}{5}$ of 30?

a. 3
b. 2
c. 9
d. 6

75. Examine (A), (B), and (C) and find the best answer.

(A) $\frac{4}{5}$ of 60
(B) $\frac{3}{5}$ of 70
(C) $\frac{6}{5}$ of 40

a. (C) is greater than both (A) and (B)
b. (A) is equal to (C) and greater than (B)
c. (B) is less than (C) but greater than (A)
d. (A) is equal to (B) but less than (C)

76. What is 50% of 40% of 80?

a. 16
b. 20
c. 40
d. 32

77. Review the series: 4, 8, 7, 11, 10, ___. What number should come next?

a. 13
b. 12
c. 9
d. 14

78. Examine the square and rectangles below and find the best answer.

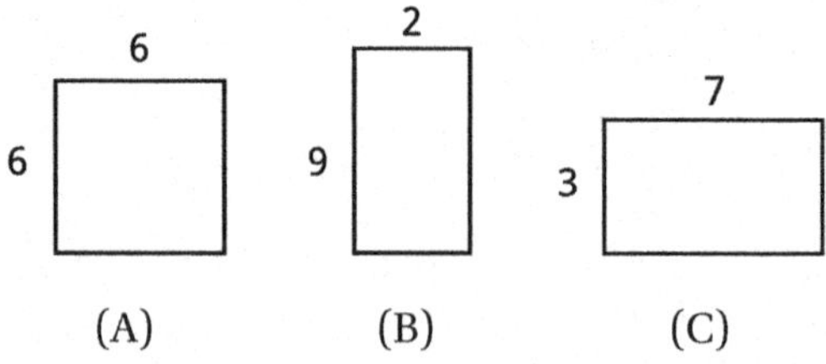

a. The perimeter (B) and (C) are equal
b. The perimeter of (C) is larger than the perimeter of (A)
c. The perimeter of (B) is smaller than the perimeter of (A)
d. The perimeter of (C) is larger than the perimeter of (B)

79. Twelve less than two fifths of twenty-five is

a. -2
b. -1
c. 7
d. 8

80. What number subtracted from 19 leaves 3 more than 12?

a. 23
b. 18
c. 3
d. 4

81. What is the missing number in the following series: 48, 2, ___, 7, 36, 12, 30

a. 5
b. 30
c. 42
d. 10

82. What is the missing number in the following series: 5, 15, 19, 5, 23,_____, 5

a. 27
b. 19
c. 4
d. 10

83. Solve (A), (B), and (C) and then compare to find the best answer.

(A) -2×-2
(B) $(-2)^2$
(C) The reciprocal of $\frac{1}{4}$

a. (B) is greater than (A) and (C)
b. (C) is greater than (A) and (B)
c. (A) is greater than B but less than (C)
d. (A) and (B) and (C) are equal

84. Review the series: $\frac{1}{3}, \frac{2}{3},$ ___, $\frac{4}{3}, \frac{5}{3}, 2$

a. 1
b. $\frac{3}{4}$
c. 2
d. $\frac{3}{6}$

85. Examine (A), (B), and (C) and find the best answer.

(A) -3 + 2 - 5
(B) -4 - 3 - 1
(C) -7- 6 - 4

a. (B) is greater than (A) and (C)
b. (C) is less than (A) and (B)
c. (A) is greater than (B) but less than (C)
d. (A), (B), and (C) are all equal.

86. What number is $\frac{1}{5}$ the average of 4, 5, 6, 12, 15, and 18?

a. 2
b. 5
c. 6
d. 8

87. Examine the rectangle and triangle below to choose the best answer.

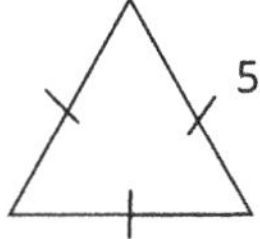

a. The perimeter of both shapes is equal
b. The perimeter of the rectangle is three times the perimeter of the triangle
c. The perimeter of the triangle is $\frac{1}{4}$ the perimeter of the rectangle.
d. The perimeter of the rectangle is larger than the perimeter of the triangle

88. What number is missing from the series: 13, 19, 16, 22, ____, 25?

a. 28
b. 19
c. 18
d. 21

89. Examine (A), (B), and (C) and find the best answer.

(A) 33%
(B) $\frac{1}{4}$
(C) .65

a. (A) is greater than (B) and (C)
b. (C) is greater than (A) or (B)
c. (A), (B), and (C) are equal
d. (B) is less than (A) but greater than (C)

90. Review the series: 12, 14, 18, 24, 32, ____. Find the next number.

a. 36
b. 40
c. 42
d. 34

91. Examine (A), (B), and (C) and find the best answer.

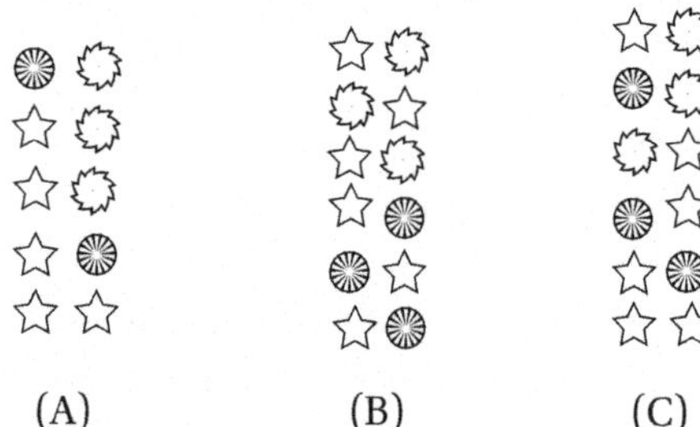

(A) (B) (C)

a. (A), (B), and (C) contain an equal number of
b. (A) has more than (B)
c. (C) has the fewest
d. (B) has fewer than (C) but more than (A)

92. What number is eight more than fifteen percent of eighty?

a. 10
b. 18
c. 20
d. 24

93. Look at this series: 300, ____, 48, 8, 6, 1. What number is missing?

a. 50
b. 96
c. 64
d. 288

94. Use the image below to select the best answer.

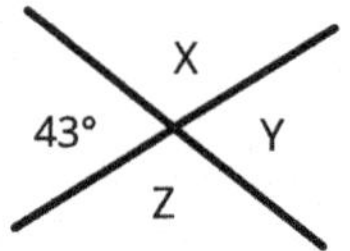

a. Angle X and Angle Y are equal
b. Angle Z and Angle X are equal
c. Angle Y is greater than Angle X
d. Angle Y and Angle Z are equal

95. What number is missing from the following series: 6, 30, ____, 125, 120, 600?

a. 100
b. 65
c. 150
d. 25

96. Examine (A), (B), and (C) and find the best answer if a=2.

(A) $3a^2 + 3a^2$
(B) $2a^2 \times 2a$
(C) 20a

a. (A) is larger than (C) and smaller than (B)
b. (B) is larger than both (A) and (C)
c. (A) is smaller than (C) but larger than (B)
d. (B) is larger than a (A) but smaller than (C)

97. Examine this series: II, 6, IV, ___, ___, 14, VIII. What roman numeral and number are missing?

a. 10, VI
b. 8, VI
c. 10, V
d. 8, V

98. What is 45% of 80?

a. 32
b. 40
c. 36
d. 42

99. Review the series below: 272, 136, ___, 34, 17. What number is missing?

a. 78
b. 74
c. 63
d. 68

100. Examine the squares below and (A), (B), and (C). Select the best answer.

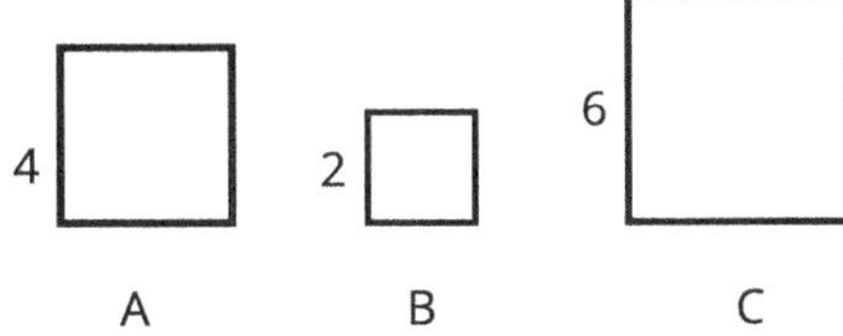

(A) the perimeter of A
(B) the area of B
(C) one side of C

a. (A) < (B) < (C)
b. (B) < (C) < (A)
c. (A) < (C) < (B)
d. (C) < (A) < (B)

101. Six is two plus one-fourth of what number?

a. 16
b. 4
c. 12
d. 8

102. What are the missing numbers from the series below: -8, -2, -4, 2, ___, 6?

a. 8
b. 4
c. 0
d. -2

103. Examine the following series: 31, 25, 19, 13, 7, ___. What number is missing?

a. 1
b. 2
c. 3
d. 4

104. Examine the figures below and (A), (B), and (C). Select the best answer.

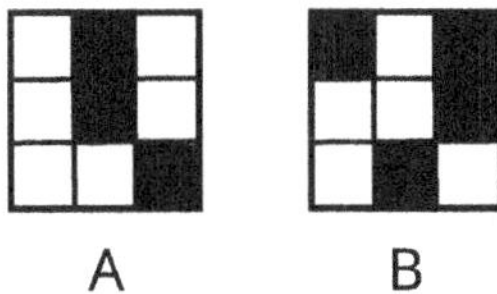

(A) The number of white squares in A
(B) The number of black squares total
(C) The number of white squares in B

a. (A) is equal to (C) and less than (B)
b. (A) is less than both (B) and (C)
c. (C) is greater than (A) and less than (B)
d. (B) is greater than both (A) and (C)

105. Review the following series and find the missing numbers: 2.5, $\frac{6}{2}$, 4.0, ___, ___, $\frac{12}{2}$, 7.0, $\frac{15}{2}$

a. $\frac{8}{2}$, 4.5
b. $\frac{10}{2}$, 5.5
c. $\frac{9}{2}$, 5.5
d. $\frac{9}{2}$, 6.5

106. Examine (A), (B), and (C) and find the best answer.

(A) $3 \times 2 - 8$
(B) $3(2 - 8)$
(C) $8 - 3 \times 2$

a. $(C) < (A) > (B)$
b. $(C) < (A) < (B)$
c. $(C) > (A) > (B)$
d. $(C) > (A) < (B)$

107. Look at this series: 56, 80, 60, 72, 64, 64, ____, ____. What numbers are missing?

a. 66, 60
b. 68, 60
c. 68, 56
d. 66, 56

108. Consider the following series: 7, 14, 17, ____, 37, 74. What number is missing?

a. 24
b. 27
c. 34
d. 21

109. Examine (A), (B), and (C) and find the best answer.

(A) 3.5×10^3
(B) $350,000 \times 10^{-2}$
(C) 35,000

a. (A) is equal to (B) and less than (C)
b. (A) is equal to (C) and more than (B)
c. (C) is equal to (B) and more than (A)
d. (C) is equal to (B) and less than (A)

110. Review the following series: 168, 163, 157, 150, 142, What number should come next?

a. 132
b. 134
c. 131
d. 133

111. What is 15 less than the square root of 64?

a. -7
b. 49
c. 17
d. -8

112. What number is missing from this series: 90, 30, 27, 9, 6, ___?

a. 2
b. 3
c. -2
d. 4

Reading Section 7

62 Questions, 25 Minutes

Reading Comprehension

Instructions: Read each passage carefully and mark one answer for each question.

Questions 113 - 122 refer to the passage below.

From AD 1206-1227, Genghis Khan and his Mongol armies rode across Asia with terrifying speed and ferocity, conquering everything in their path. In that 21-year span, the Mongol Empire expanded to roughly 10 million square miles, more than twice the size that the Ancient Roman Empire reached after centuries of conquest. In fact, the Mongol Empire remains the second largest empire (and the largest contiguous land empire) in history, surpassed only by the Great British Empire of the 19th and 20th centuries.

Today, Genghis Khan is largely remembered as a brutal warrior—a reputation that is well deserved. On more than one occasion, he destroyed entire towns when the inhabitants refused to surrender to him. However, he was also a brilliant politician and a strong believer in the power of diversity. As a result, the Mongol Empire was a shockingly progressive, well-organized society in many ways.

Since the empire stretched from the Pacific Ocean to Central Europe (covering modern-day China, the Middle East, and Russia), its people had a wide range of religions, languages, and customs. Instead of trying to force conquered citizens to adhere to a common Mongol culture, Genghis Khan put a system of laws in place to ensure racial and religious tolerance. He outlawed the previously common practice of abducting women for marriage, and enforced strict punishments for the crimes of stealing, torturing, and kidnapping. He also promoted education, lowered taxes, and re-established the Silk Road, an enormous system of protected trade and communication routes that allowed goods and ideologies to be exchanged across the empire.

Ironically, this system of unity and prosperity may have ultimately caused the empire's downfall. Roughly 100 years after Genghis Khan died, the bubonic plague spread along the Silk Road routes and killed an estimated 50% of the population. Between the disease and the weakening leadership of Genghis Khan's successors, the Mongol Empire had disintegrated by the mid-14th century.

113. The Mongol Empire and the Great British Empire differed in all of the following ways EXCEPT

a. the Mongol Empire was smaller
b. the Great British Empire was not a contiguous land empire
c. the Mongol Empire came before the Great British Empire
d. the Great British Empire was less advanced

114. How long was Genghis Khan in power?

a. 100 years
b. 21 years
c. 12 years
d. 10 years

115. What was ironic about the success of the Silk Road?

a. Travelers on the Silk Road carried the plague throughout the empire.
b. The Silk Road gave bandits easy access to travelers.
c. The Great British Empire invaded in order to capture the Silk Road.
d. The Silk Road ruined the diversity of the empire.

116. Which of the following would be a good title for this passage?

a. "Genghis Khan: Man, Myth, Legend"
b. "Comparing Empires: Ancient Rome vs the Mongol Empire"
c. "War and Politics"
d. "Brutal Progress: a Brief Examination of the Mongol Empire"

117. Select the option which correctly displays the empires from smallest to largest

    a. Great British Empire < Ancient Roman Empire < Mongol Empire
    b. Ancient Roman Empire < Mongol Empire < Great British Empire
    c. Mongol Empire < Great British Empire < Ancient Roman Empire
    d. Mongol Empire < Ancient Roman Empire < Great British Empire

118. Based on its use in the passage, <u>contiguous</u> most nearly means

    a. connected
    b. confusing
    c. remaining
    d. vague

119. The progressive laws of the Mongol Empire were especially surprising given

    a. how old-fashioned Genghis Khan was as a ruler
    b. the diversity and size of the empire
    c. the ruthless reputation of Genghis Khan and his military policies
    d. the way the Silk Road encouraged communication and trade

120. The Ancient Roman Empire

    a. stretched from the Pacific Ocean to Central Europe
    b. was also ruled by Genghis Khan at one point
    c. was less than half the size of the Mongol Empire
    d. was one reason the Mongol Empire fell

121. The author most likely includes examples of Mongol law and political policy to

    a. convince the reader that the Mongol Empire was a great place to live
    b. emphasize that Genghis Khan destroyed towns that did not surrender
    c. illustrate the advanced aspects of the Mongol civilization
    d. prove that strict laws are the only way to enforce good behavior

122. Which of the following would most likely follow the last paragraph?

    a. a description of Genghis Khan's childhood
    b. an analysis of the empire's decline
    c. an in-depth history of the Silk Road
    d. a scientific debate about the bubonic plague

Questions 123 - 132 refer to the passage below.

For centuries, doctors have knowingly prescribed fake medicines to their patients. Interestingly, some patients seem to get real benefits from these pretend remedies, even when there is no medical reason for that to happen. This controversial phenomenon —known as the placebo effect—demonstrates the incredible power that the brain has over the rest of the human body. Essentially, the placebo effect indicates that if patients believe that a medicine will help them, their minds will send signals to their bodies to begin healing processes.

The term "placebo" comes from a Latin phrase meaning, "I shall please." This idea can be traced back to 1,000 years ago, when people would show up at funerals and sweet-talk the mourners by pretending to know the dead person. If they successfully flattered the grieving family, they would often be invited to stay for dinner and even spend the night. In this way, these fakers were able to "please" the relatives of the deceased, and score free meals and lodging!

While modern placebos are intended to help patients, not to take advantage of mourners, there is still an element of deception involved in their use. After all, if a doctor informs a patient that (s)he is being prescribed a fake medicine, the placebo is unlikely to work. Instead, the person must believe that the treatment is genuine, which puts doctors in the tricky position of needing to deceive patients in order to help cure them.

One way the medical community is attempting to address this issue is through treatment studies, in which all patients are informed that they will receive either a placebo or a real drug. In this way, doctors can measure and compare the results of both treatments, since the people being given fake medications are technically aware of that possibility. However, some scientists have argued that although such studies may be useful in determining how effective the real drugs are, they may not be effective demonstrations of the potential power of placebos. Since patients in the study might doubt whether they are taking a real medication, their brains potentially lack the necessary conviction to heal their bodies.

123. As used in the passage, the word conviction most nearly means

   a. accusation
   b. judgment
   c. faith
   d. pressure

124. The earliest concept of a "placebo" can be traced back to

   a. medical treatment studies
   b. early Latin textbooks
   c. lying doctors
   d. fake mourners

125. In which of the following ways does the placebo effect demonstrate the power of the human brain?

   a. the brain's beliefs can cause the body to heal itself
   b. the body, brain, and medicine work together to fight illness
   c. the brain intuitively knows when medicines are fake
   d. the real medicines are usually less effective than placebos

126. Given the information in the passage, one can infer that because of placebos

   a. doctors are more trustworthy than they would be otherwise
   b. scientists have developed a complete understanding of the human brain
   c. some patients have experienced benefits that real drugs could not provide
   d. no one understands how medications affect the body

127. What is the "tricky position" doctors are put in?

a. they want to use real medications and are forced to use placebos
b. they must tell the truth but would prefer to lie to their patients
c. they believe real drugs are inferior to placebos but have to prescribe them anyway
d. they want their patients to improve but do not want to lie to them

128. Some scientists believe that treatment studies are not an effective way to judge the power of placebos because

a. doctors must inform patients that they are not taking a real medicine
b. when patients think there is a chance that they're taking a placebo, their minds are less likely to convince their bodies to heal
c. such studies are inherently immoral
d. real medications are always more effective

129. The author most likely includes the history of the word "placebo" in order to

a. entertain the reader
b. explain the way placebos work on patients
c. provide the reader with some basic knowledge of Latin
d. emphasize the moral conflict associated with placebos

130. This passage would most likely be found in

a. an online encyclopedia
b. a neighborhood newspaper
c. a literary essay
d. an 18th century book about medicine

131. Based on the information in the passage, which of the following is most likely?

a. placebos will eventually be made illegal
b. scientists will discover that the placebo effect is almost entirely imaginary
c. doctors will become more comfortable deceiving patients
d. research on placebos will further our understanding on medicine and the brain

132. Which of the following best characterizes the main idea of this passage?

a. The medical community has a moral responsibility to be honest with patients.
b. Placebos have a long and complex history.
c. Without the placebo effect, no one would ever recover from illness.
d. More patients should consider signing up for treatment studies.

Questions 133 - 142 refer to the passage below.

Black Beauty, the classic 1877 novel by Anna Sewell, was published at a time when horses were viewed and treated more like tools than living creatures. However, the book's popularity (combined with its groundbreaking first-person portrayal of the title character's life as a horse in Victorian England) had an intense emotional impact on readers that ultimately changed society's stance on animals.

As his name would suggest, Black Beauty was depicted as a stunning ebony-colored horse, initially prized by his owners for his good looks, size, and strength. However, when Beauty was injured by and then scarred from a fall they no longer considered him worth keeping. The gentle and hardworking gelding was then sold off to a series of increasingly cruel owners, who made Beauty work to the point of exhaustion in the dirty, unsafe conditions of downtown London.

Sewell's heart-rending description of Beauty's hardships was most likely informed by empathy as well as sympathy; at the age of 14, she suffered a fall that severely injured both of her ankles. Unlike the protagonist of her novel, Sewell never recovered. She was an invalid for the remaining 44 years of her life.

Due to the nature of her injury, she was unable to walk but still capable of riding a horse. So, in an age when everything from transportation to manufacturing to warfare relied on equine labor, horses may have nevertheless represented something uniquely significant for Sewell: freedom.

Her love and appreciation is palpable in Black Beauty, and early readers found themselves relating to animals in a new way. The book became a centerpiece of the anti-cruelty movement, and animal rights activists distributed copies on the street. As public opinion towards horses became more compassionate, public policy changed too. Soon, many of the harsh and inhumane treatments described in Black Beauty were outlawed.

133. What is the main idea of this passage?

a. Black Beauty is a fascinating book that everyone should read.
b. Anna Sewell's injury as a teenager was life-changing.
c. Novels can change society at a fundamental level.
d. Black Beauty prompted readers to treat animals with more humanity and compassion.

134. As it is used in the passage, what does the word equine mean?

a. human
b. mechanical
c. horse
d. intense

135. One can infer that Black Beauty was mistreated by his owners in London because

a. he was difficult to train and surly
b. his owners viewed him as a pet rather than as a workhorse
c. his owners thought of him as a means to get work completed, rather than as a living being
d. he was scarred from his fall and unsightly

136. How were Anna Sewell and Black Beauty alike?

a. They were both injured.
b. They were both mistreated.
c. They both preferred the countryside to London.
d. They both recovered from serious injuries.

137. Who was the narrator of Black Beauty?

a. Anna Sewell
b. Black Beauty
c. Black Beauty's owners
d. The narrator is unknown

138. How old was Anna Sewell when she died?

a. 44
b. 68
c. 14
d. 58

139. Which of the following is the author likely to discuss next?

   a. other novels written by Anna Sewell
   b. a full plot summary of Black Beauty
   c. specific details about what types of cruel treatments were outlawed
   d. an influential animal rights activist

140. As it is used in the passage, what does the word palpable mean?

   a. lacking
   b. noticeable
   c. surprising
   d. unlikely

141. In the second paragraph, why did the author include the "gentle and hardworking" description of Black Beauty?

   a. to indicate that Black Beauty did not do anything to cause his mistreatment
   b. to persuade the reader that Black Beauty was a beautiful horse
   c. to show why Black Beauty was mistreated
   d. to combat the widespread perception that Black Beauty was lazy

142. Based on the information in the passage, it is likely that Black Beauty

   a. was only read by a small group of animal rights activists
   b. was largely unpopular until modern times
   c. was widely read soon after it was published
   d. was only popular among the upper class

Questions 143 - 152 refer to the passage below.

Once on a dark winter's day, when the yellow fog hung so thick and heavy in the streets of London that the lamps were lighted and the shop windows blazed with gas as they do at night, an odd-looking little girl sat in a cab with her father.

"Here we are, Sara," said Captain Crewe, making his voice sound cheerful. Then he lifted Sara out of the carriage and they mounted the steps to the house. As they walked inside, Sara observed that although the house was respectable and well furnished, everything in it was ugly and severe. Even the armchairs in the sitting room had hard bones in them.

"I don't like it, Papa," she said. "But then I dare say soldiers—even brave ones—don't really LIKE going into battle."

Captain Crewe laughed outright at this. "Oh, little Sara," he said. "What shall I do when I have no one to say solemn things to me?"

"But why do solemn things make you laugh so?" inquired Sara.

"Because you are such fun when you say them," he answered, laughing still more. And then suddenly he stopped laughing all at once and looked as if tears had come into his eyes.

It was just then that Miss Minchin entered the room. She was very like her house, Sara felt: tall and dull, and respectable and ugly. She had large, cold, fishy eyes, and a large, cold, fishy smile. It spread itself into a very large smile when she saw Sara and Captain Crewe. She had heard that he was rich and willing to spend a great deal of money on his daughter.

"It will be a great privilege to have charge of such a beautiful and promising child, Captain Crewe," she said, taking Sara's hand and stroking it.

Sara stood quietly, with her eyes fixed upon Miss Minchin's face. "Why does she say I am a beautiful child?" she was thinking. "I am not beautiful at all. I have short black hair and green eyes; besides which, I am a thin child and not fair in the least. She is beginning by telling a story."

She was mistaken, however, in thinking she was an ugly child. She was a slim creature and had an intense, attractive face. Her eyes were greenish gray, it is true, but they were big, wonderful eyes with long, black lashes. Still she was very firm in her belief that she was an ugly little girl, and she was not at all elated by Miss Minchin's flattery.

After Sara had known Miss Minchin longer she learned why she had said it: she said the same thing to each papa and mamma who brought a child to live at her school.

143. Which literary technique does the author use in the phrase "Even the armchairs in the sitting room had hard bones in them?"

a. simile
b. symbolism
c. irony
d. metaphor

144. Sara can be described as

a. silly and playful
b. serious and thoughtful
c. eager and happy
d. rude and childish

145. Sara and Captain Crewe are visiting Miss Minchin because

a. she is an old friend of Captain Crewe's
b. she might adopt Sara
c. Sara may attend Miss Minchin's boarding school
d. Captain Crewe hopes to marry her one day

146. In the second paragraph, Sara compares herself to a soldier going into battle. What does this image symbolize?

   a. Sara's aggressive nature
   b. Sara's feelings about being at Miss Minchin's house
   c. Sara's frustration about being told that she is beautiful
   d. Sara's sadness about her difficult trip to Miss Minchin's house

147. Why does Sara think she is unattractive?

   a. because Miss Minchin told her she was not beautiful
   b. because she had blonde hair
   c. because she had never been told she was beautiful
   d. because she did not consider her physical qualities to be beautiful

148. Miss Minchin's house might be described as

   a. well kept but unattractive
   b. tiny and ugly
   c. sophisticated and interesting
   d. grand but somewhat shabby

149. When Sara describes Miss Minchin as "beginning by telling a story," she means that Miss Minchin is

   a. an excellent storyteller
   b. overpromising what she can offer Sara
   c. beginning her relationship with Sara by lying to her
   d. an unkind person

150. Based on the information in the passage, during which time of day does the passage take place?

   a. at night
   b. at sunset
   c. during the day
   d. at dawn

151. Sara views Miss Minchin with

   a. admiration
   b. hatred
   c. suspicion
   d. disinterest

152. During which time period does this story take place?

   a. the future
   b. the past
   c. the present
   d. unknown

Vocabulary

Instructions: Choose the word that means the same, or about the same, as the underlined word.

153. A <u>bold</u> action

a. brave
b. thoughtful
c. hesitant
d. interesting

154. The <u>secluded</u> house

a. gloomy
b. busy
c. isolated
d. unique

155. An <u>exhaustive</u> search

a. quick
b. cursory
c. circuitous
d. comprehensive

156. A <u>notable</u> achievement

a. infamous
b. insignificant
c. extraordinary
d. secret

157. A <u>mediocre</u> dinner

a. delicious
b. average
c. exotic
d. terrible

158. To <u>enlist</u> her help

a. secure
b. reject
c. downplay
d. plead

159. To <u>replenish</u> the supplies

a. use
b. deplete
c. pack
d. refill

160. To <u>devise</u> a plan

a. dismiss
b. conceive
c. support
d. berate

161. The <u>scowling</u> man

a. disinterested
b. excited
c. grimacing
d. sad

162. The <u>tedious</u> speech

a. condescending
b. interesting
c. scholarly
d. dull

163. A <u>singular</u> experience

a. unique
b. personal
c. positive
d. interesting

164. The difference was <u>immaterial</u>

a. significant
b. fascinating
c. partial
d. irrelevant

165. To <u>sever</u> communications

a. worsen
b. continue
c. terminate
d. improve

166. To <u>interrogate</u> a suspect

a. listen to
b. question
c. intimidate
d. compliment

167. To <u>depress</u> the switch

a. pull
b. push down
c. stop
d. break

168. Adequate <u>remuneration</u>

a. rations
b. numeration
c. energy
d. compensation

169. A <u>bellicose</u> attitude

a. combative
b. dour
c. inconsistent
d. fatigued

170. The <u>reticent</u> student

a. angry
b. intelligent
c. reserved
d. motivated

171. An <u>intangible</u> reward

a. good
b. impalpable
c. unlikely
d. impressive

172. A <u>conceited</u> person

a. wealthy
b. rude
c. fashionable
d. arrogant

173. An <u>underhanded</u> comment

a. deceitful
b. subtle
c. helpful
d. furious

174. An <u>expansive</u> search

a. costly
b. extensive
c. limited
d. cursory

Math Section 7

64 Questions, 45 Minutes

Instructions: Select the best answer.

175. 14 is what percent of 70?

a. 12%
b. 15%
c. 18%
d. 20%

176. What is the perimeter of a rectangle with an area of 30 mm^2 and a side of 5 mm?

a. 60 mm
b. 22 mm
c. 130 mm
d. 24 mm

177. Solve: $\frac{3(9-5)}{2(6-8)}$

a. -3
b. 3
c. 6
d. -6

178. Which property is illustrated by the following:

2 + 0 = 2

a. distributive property
b. commutative property
c. associative property
d. identity property

179. Solve: $-2(-4)^2$

a. 36
b. -36
c. 32
d. -32

180. Given the two sets of numbers A = {3, 4, 8, 9} and B = {1, 2, 3, 4}, what is A ∩ B?

a. {1, 2, 8, 9}
b. {3, 4, 8, 9}
c. {3, 4}
d. {1, 2, 3, 4, 8, 9}

181. Solve: $\frac{\frac{8}{3}}{\frac{1}{6}}$

a. $\frac{4}{9}$
b. 14
c. 2
d. 16

182. An acute angle is

a. less than 90°
b. greater than 90°
c. 180°
d. 90°

183. Which of the following is less than 7 quarts?

a. 2 gallons
b. 20 cups
c. 16 pints
d. 3 gallons

184. If x = 5, what symbol should go in the circle:

2x - 3 O 9?

a. >
b. <
c. ≥
d. =

185. What is the reciprocal of $-\frac{4}{5}$?

a. $-\frac{5}{4}$
b. $\frac{4}{5}$
c. $\frac{5}{4}$
d. 4

186. Solve: -5 + 7 - 14 + 8

a. -4
b. 6
c. -5
d. 10

187. What is the area of the circle below?

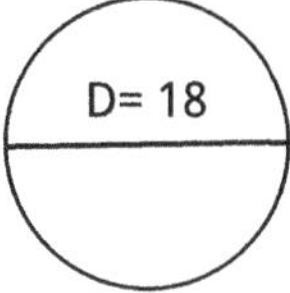

a. 18π
b. 81
c. 81π
d. 9π

188. What is the least common multiple of 12 and 9?

a. 72
b. 48
c. 24
d. 36

189. A square has an area of 36 inches. What is its perimeter?

a. 36 in
b. 24 in
c. 18 in
d. 12 in

190. The sum of three consecutive integers is 12. What is the largest integer?

a. 3
b. 4
c. 5
d. 6

191. 87.5% is equal to

a. $\frac{5}{6}$
b. $\frac{7}{8}$
c. $\frac{8}{9}$
d. $7\frac{1}{2}$

192. Solve: 42.32 - 7.145

a. 34.17
b. -29.13
c. 31.15
d. 35.175

193. Which of the following is a perfect square?

a. 121
b. 90
c. 50
d. 120

194. In the following number, which place value does 4 occupy?

37.154

a. hundreths
b. hundreds
c. thousands
d. thousandths

195. 2 yards, 1 foot, 9 inches
-1 yard, 2 feet, 4 inches

a. 2 feet, 5 inches
b. 1 yard, 5 inches
c. 1 yard, 1 foot, 5 inches
d. 3 feet, 1 foot, 3 inches

196. What is the name of the following figure?

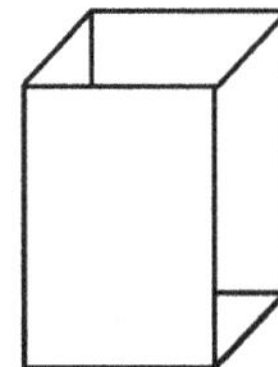

a. triangular prism
b. cone
c. rectangular prism
d. cylinder

197. A family went to the movie theatre and bought five tickets. Two adult tickets were priced at \$9.75 each and three student tickets were priced at \$6.25 each. They then ordered 1 large popcorn for \$5.25 and 5 small sodas at \$3.25 each. How much in total did the family spend at the theatre?

a. \$60.25
b. \$59.75
c. \$57.50
d. \$54.75

198. The lines below are

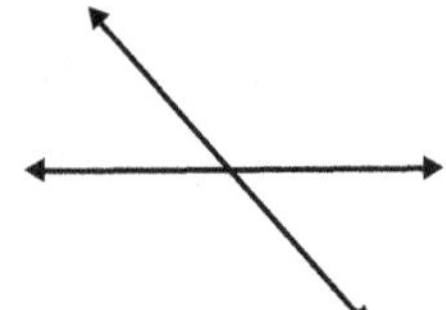

a. parallel
b. line segments
c. perpendicular
d. intersecting

199. Which of the following is equal to 5,803?

a. $5 \times 10^3 + 8 \times 10^1 + 3$
b. $5 \times 10^3 + 8 \times 10^2 + 3$
c. $5 \times 10^4 + 8 \times 10^2 + 3 \times 10$
d. $5 \times 10^4 + 8 \times 10^2 + 3$

200. Which of the following might be a value for x in this inequality: $4x - 2 < 6$

a. 3
b. 2
c. 6
d. -2

201. Renee is planning a trip to Peru, so she stopped by the bank to exchange some dollars for soles. If the exchange rate is 3.3 soles per dollar, how many soles will Renee get for \$122 dollars? Round to the nearest hundredth.

a. 36.97 soles
b. 402.60 soles
c. 37.00 soles
d. 403.40 soles

202. Jessica is training for a marathon. In the past two weeks she's run a total of 112 miles. On average, how many miles is Jessica running a day?

a. 5
b. 6
c. 7
d. 8

203. Solve for x: $5 - 2x = 0$

a. 0
b. $\frac{5}{2}$
c. -2
d. 5

204. Mary is painting a wall that is 8 feet high and has an area of 96 square feet. How wide is the wall?

a. 10 feet
b. 11 feet
c. 12 feet
d. 9 feet

205. The table below shows the number of books checked out from the library by each library visitor throughout a day.

Number of Books	Number of Visitors
0	5
1	4
2	4
3	4
4	3

What is the average number of books checked out of the library by each visitor?

a. 1.5
b. 2.4
c. 1.8
d. 3

206. On spelling tests, a student scored 70% on one test, 80% on another test, and 85% on each of the remaining tests. The student's average for the spelling tests was exactly 81%. What is the total number of spelling tests that the student has taken in the course?

a. 2
b. 3
c. 4
d. 5

207. Charlotte buys a new pair of jeans that are on sale for 40% off of the original price. All items sold at the store are also charged a 5% sales tax after all discounts have been applied. If the jeans originally cost $85, how much will Charlotte pay? Round to the nearest cent.

a. $48.45
b. $51.00
c. $53.55
d. $55.35

208. There are 96 people total in a department store. If the ratio of managers to cashiers to customers is 1 : 2 : 9, how many cashiers are there?

a. 16
b. 20
c. 8
d. 72

209. Simplify: $\sqrt{92x^2y}$

a. $2xy\sqrt{23y}$
b. $4x^2\sqrt{23y}$
c. $2x\sqrt{23y}$
d. $4x\sqrt{23y}$

210. Aneesh has to complete 30 math problems for homework. It takes him between 1 and 2 minutes to complete each problem. Which choice below is the best approximation of how long it will take Aneesh to complete all of his math problems?

a. 10 minutes
b. 20 minutes
c. 30 minutes
d. 45 minutes

211. A triangle has a height of 7 and base of 12. What is its area?

a. 42
b. 21
c. 84
d. 72

212. What is the median of the following group of numbers 2, 5, 4, 18, 23, 4, and 8.

a. 4
b. 5
c. 8
d. 21

213. Solve for d: $4(2d + 3) = -12$

a. -2
b. -3
c. 3
d. 0

214. Amanda took a flight from Chicago to Shanghai, a distance of 7000 miles. The plane was flying at an average speed of 560 mph. How long was Amanda's flight?

a. 12.5 hours
b. 11.8 hours
c. 12.0 hours
d. 12.9 hours

215. Candy at the amusement park is sold by the ounce. 1 ounce of candy costs $0.30. If Penelope buys a total of 1 pound 5 ounces of candy, how much will she be charged?

a. $0.45
b. $7.20
c. $6.30
d. $4.50

216. Anytown Middle School's 7th and 8th grade classes went to the county fair. The amount of time, on average, that each class of students spent on various activities is outlined in the graph below.

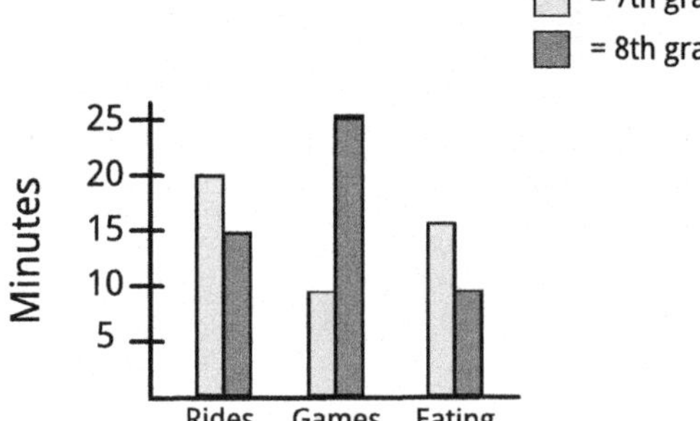

Approximately many more minutes did the 7th graders spend on rides than the 8th graders spent eating?

a. 5
b. 10
c. 15
d. 20

217. What is the measure of angle A?

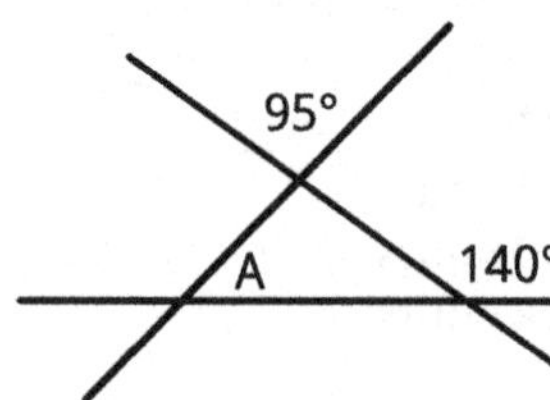

a. 45°
b. 50°
c. 30°
d. 35°

218. Monica ran 4 miles in 35 minutes. If she keeps up this pace, how long would it take her to run 9 miles?

a. 1 hour, 7 minutes, 30 seconds
b. 1 hour, 18 minutes, 45 seconds
c. 1 hour, 30 minutes
d. 1 hour, 41 minutes, 15 seconds

219. Solve: $x^2 - 5 = 76$

a. 7
b. 8
c. 9
d. 9.5

220. In a survey of student's favorite fruit, 35% of students said strawberries, 45% said apples, and 20% said bananas. If 400 students responded to the survey, how many students said that either bananas or apples were their favorite fruit?

a. 80
b. 140
c. 180
d. 260

221. Joanna participated in a 30 mile triathlon, which involves running, bike riding, and swimming. If she ran for the first ten miles and rode her bike for the next fifteen miles, how long did she swim for?

a. 3 miles
b. 4 miles
c. 5 miles
d. 10 miles

222. What is the area of the figure below?

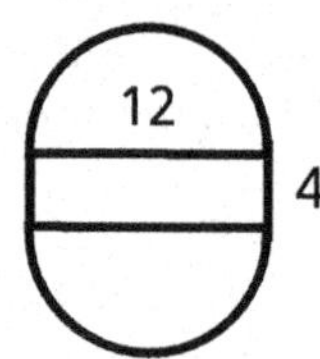

a. $48 + 144\pi$
b. $48 + 36\pi$
c. $32 + 36\pi$
d. $32 + 144\pi$

223. Carolyn is baking three different types of muffins. One type calls for one tablespoon of baking powder, the second calls for one teaspoon of baking powder, and the third calls for three teaspoons of baking powder. How many teaspoons of baking powder will Carolyn use total?

a. 5
b. 7
c. 8
d. 13

224. In the triangle below, if ∠B is congruent to ∠C, what is the measure of ∠A?

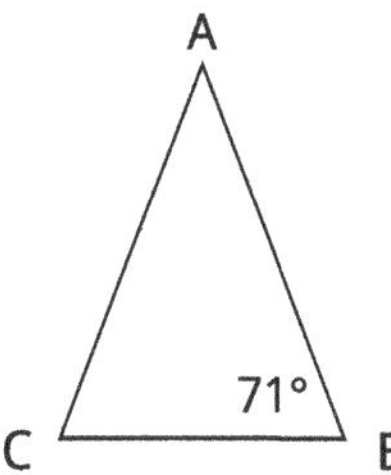

a. 28°
b. 109°
c. 71°
d. 38°

225. Deon has a stack of cards numbered from 1 - 15. If he pulls out a card at random, what is the probability that it will be even?

a. $\frac{1}{15}$
b. $\frac{7}{15}$
c. $\frac{1}{3}$
d. $\frac{8}{15}$

226. Christine performed in the show choir competition on Saturday from 10:15 to 1:30 PM and on Sunday from 2:30 PM to 4:15 PM. How much time did she spend performing over the entire weekend?

a. 4 hours and 30 minutes
b. 1 hour and 45 minutes
c. 5 hours
d. 3 hours and 15 minutes

227. An average adult male is made up of between 57% and 60% water by weight. If Cameron, an average adult male, weighs 175 pounds, which of the following could represent the weight of the water in his body?

a. 97 lbs
b. 102 lbs
c. 106 lbs
d. 110 lbs

228. How many edges does a triangular prism have?

a. 8
b. 9
c. 10
d. 12

229. The square of a positive number minus itself is 20. What is the number?

a. 5
b. 10
c. 8
d. 4

230. Solve for y: $\frac{1}{2}y = 8$

a. 4
b. 8
c. 16
d. 24

231. In the coordinate plane below, in which quadrant would you find (-3, 6)?

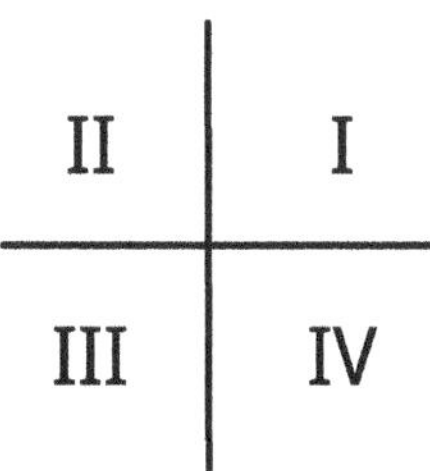

a. I
b. II
c. III
d. IV

232. Alyssa is making a costume for her son. She purchased 2 yards of fabric which she must cut into 4 inch strips. How many strips of fabric can she cut from the fabric she purchased?

a. 18 strips
b. 8 strips
c. 21 strips
d. 9 strips

233. What is the height of a rectangular prism with width 5, length 3, and volume 75?

a. 10
b. 5
c. 15
d. 6

234. A railway company is tracking the percentage of trains that arrive at their destination on time. The data they collected can be found in the table below.

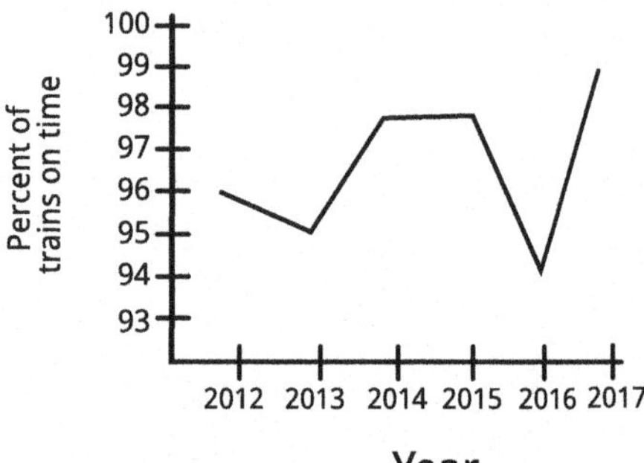

Between which two years did the train's on time performance improve most dramatically?

a. 2013 to 2014
b. 2014 to 2015
c. 2015 to 2016
d. 2016 to 2017

235. What three-dimensional figure can be made by folding this paper pattern:

a. cone
b. triangular prism
c. pyramid
d. rectangular prism

236. How many 4 inch by $3\frac{3}{4}$ inch patches can be cut from fabric that is 4 inches by 10 inches?

a. 1
b. 2
c. 3
d. 4

237. Allen eats a cheeseburger at a local restaurant, which is listed as containing 750 calories. If Allen consumes 2500 calories in a day, what percent of his daily caloric intake is this cheeseburger?

a. 30%
b. 33%
c. 37%
d. 40%

238. Terrence borrowed 18 books from the library. This is five more than half the number of books than Sanali borrowed. How many books did Sanali borrow?

a. 26 books
b. 46 books
c. 7 books
d. 9 books

Language Section 7

60 Questions, 25 Minutes

Usage and Mechanics

Instructions: For questions 239-278, check the sentences for errors of usage, capitalization, or punctuation. If there is no error, choose D.

239.

a. I ate my ice cream quick so it wouldn't melt.
b. My school's principal greeted us on the first day of school.
c. The toy car had a visible scratch on its trunk.
d. No mistakes.

240.

a. Labor Day is always celebrated on the first Monday of September.
b. The smaller of the two houses was painted blue, white, and beige.
c. Last Sunday night, my mom and I baked her famous chocolate chip cookies.
d. No mistakes.

241.

a. It's too early to tell whether we'll have a snow day tomorrow.
b. Alvin decided that he wanted to visit his sister over spring break.
c. When Casey was in College, she moved to Australia for a semester.
d. No mistakes.

242.

a. The international soccer game was attended by thousands of fans.
b. Luis valued the council of his favorite teacher, Mr. Bechtel.
c. "Girls, don't forget," my coach announced, "everyone needs to pick up her uniform before going home."
d. No mistakes.

243.

a. Emilia is the nicest person I've ever met.
b. When I invited my sister to come to the concert, she exclaimed, "I'd love to go with you"!
c. It was so dark outside that I easily could have gotten lost.
d. No mistakes.

244.

a. The car broke down on the side of the road because its engine gave out.
b. Tomorrow, I went to the grocery store with my mom.
c. Ms. Maklin gives less homework than any other teacher I've had.
d. No mistakes.

245.

a. I'm so excited that Deshaun was accepted into his top choice university!
b. Jackie took dance lessons when she was in elementary school.
c. Cornelius was the funnier boy in his whole school.
d. No mistakes.

246.

a. He handed the toy to his brother which was broken.
b. During the basketball game, Reis shouted, "Throw me the ball!"
c. Isla has less experience babysitting than I do.
d. No mistakes.

247.

a. I try to buy gifts that are unique, practical, and unexpected.
b. They're going to the state fair later this afternoon.
c. Isabellas' piano teacher is retiring next year.
d. No mistakes.

248.

a. Next summer, Zane and I will try to get jobs at the waterpark.
b. Strangely, the metal fence had less rust on it than it did last year.
c. "I'd like to try cooking dinner for Mom tonight," my sister offered.
d. No mistakes.

249.

a. The club posted its attendance list for the year.
b. Their are always two sides to a story.
c. Although Rahim loved the book, it took him over two months to finish it.
d. No mistakes.

250.

a. It's fascinating to think about how people's lives were affected by the invention of the internet.
b. To whom should I give the gift?
c. Last year, congressman Alvarez visited our school.
d. No mistakes.

251.

a. My cousin's kitchen renovations took way too long.
b. I bought all of my art supplies, including: paint, brushes, and a canvas.
c. Before we go, we should check the weather forecast.
d. No mistakes.

252.

a. James gave she and her sister a bouquet of flowers after their performance.
b. Whose house are we going to after school tomorrow?
c. The girls' laughter echoed through the school's hallways.
d. No mistakes.

253.

a. The Indian restaurant, which opened on Main St. last year, has excellent naan.
b. Christines family goes camping in Michigan each year.
c. The groundhogs dug into the house's foundation.
d. No mistakes.

254.

a. The company lost a large amount of money when the stock market crashed.
b. Even though it rained every day I loved visiting my aunt in California.
c. I'm so sorry I bumped into you; please accept my apologies.
d. No mistakes.

255.

a. I'm going to lie down on the couch, but I promise I won't fall asleep.
b. I learned to scuba dive when I visited the Great Barrier Reef.
c. Deborah shouted "snowball fight!"
d. No mistakes.

256.

a. Does anyone want to take their cupcakes home?
b. Please sit down!
c. I don't often eat cake, but I wanted to give myself a treat today.
d. No mistakes.

257.

a. The store which had been open for over 20 years, permanently closed yesterday.
b. Cindee drove from Chicago, Illinois to Delray Beach, Florida.
c. Every summer my family takes a cruise on the Mississippi River.
d. No mistakes.

258.

a. After we go to the pumpkin farm, we'll stop for hot apple cider.
b. Even though Kay and I see each other every day at school, we talk every night on the phone.
c. Arjun slipped on the spilled drink and almost falled.
d. No mistakes.

259.

a. Please water the plants while I'm away on vacation.
b. I've studied german for over ten years, but I don't think I'll ever be fluent.
c. Time will tell if Sam can get his grades turned around.
d. No mistakes.

260.

a. Today is my grandma's birthday.
b. There are two answers to the question.
c. You're lunch is ready.
d. No mistakes.

261.

a. California is the most populous state.
b. The roof on my house is tile.
c. When should we expect Noemi?
d. No mistakes.

262.

a. "Close the door before you let all the cool air out!" exclaimed Bodi.
b. People don't use dictionaries no more.
c. Today was pirate day in physical education class.
d. No mistakes.

263.

a. Luka is going to the library, and Justine is going to the bookstore.
b. The secretary needed my name and social security number.
c. Trevor Noah, a famous comedian, wrote a memoir about life in South Africa.
d. No mistakes.

264.

a. Maddie wants to study studio arts in college.
b. I don't like the humidity in Florida.
c. Tiffany my sister lives across the street from the local high school.
d. No mistakes.

265.

a. The mayor is up for re-election.
b. Does Professor, Smith, live on campus?
c. The prison population has exploded in the last decade.
d. No mistakes.

266.

a. Tammy Duckworth is the first senator to have a baby while in office.
b. Eleanor of Aquitaine was a powerful monarch in the Middle Ages.
c. Will Mom be late for the ballet recital?
d. No mistakes.

267.

a. I hope Ritu will bring me back a sari from India.
b. Ronnie is studying to be a doctor.
c. Give the tickets to Mary and she.
d. No mistakes.

268.

a. Fools Rush In is my favorite Elvis Presley song.
b. This has been the coldest April in almost 100 years.
c. I wish middle school had nap time.
d. No mistakes.

269.

a. Malaria is a deadly disease passed to humans from mosquitos.
b. For camping you need a tent, a sleeping bag, and a sense of adventure.
c. The dog chased after the mail truck and misses his afternoon walk.
d. No mistakes.

270.

a. The laptop was too expensive.
b. All of the technicians had technical training.
c. I'm sorry that you and her are no longer friends.
d. No mistakes.

271.

a. The heat rose; and the snow melted.
b. It's impossible to make an appointment with an infectious disease doctor.
c. Unfortunately, we have to move at the end of the school year.
d. No mistakes.

272.

a. Charles or his sisters wants to stop by after practice.
b. My family is trying to go meatless on Mondays.
c. Buddy and Cassie moved overseas last year.
d. No mistakes.

273.

a. I love Mexican culture and food.
b. The students in the classroom, including those that played sports.
c. Oliver prefers dinosaurs to snakes.
d. No mistakes.

274.

a. They rode their bikes north and hiked the rest of the way up the mountain.
b. Tom plays the lottery every week, even though he knows he won't win.
c. I have a large seashell collection from all my travels.
d. No mistakes.

275.

a. In Charleston, South Carolina, you can see Fort Sumter.
b. My Girl Scout troop sold less cookies this year than last.
c. My grandma likes to say, "You catch more bees with honey."
d. No mistakes.

276.

a. If I am chosen as class president, I will ensure that all students have access to the vending machines.
b. Learning a new skill takes patience.
c. I need: toothpaste, a blow dryer, and new shoes for my trip.
d. No mistakes.

277.

a. "Missing the bus," our principal said, "is no longer an excuse for being late to school."
b. I feel bad that he was grounded.
c. There going to meet us at the carnival before dinner.
d. No mistakes.

278.

a. The secretary congratulated the students for their handling of a food fight warmly.
b. All complaints and compliments should be filed at the main office.
c. Most of my friends are gluten-free, but I love bread.
d. No mistakes.

Spelling

Directions: For questions 279-288, look for errors in spelling. If there is no error, choose D.

279.

a. I definitely want to travel to Europe and Australia when I get older.
b. The salesman guaranteed that the warranty would cover accidental damage.
c. Malia is fascinated by ancient Rome and wants to become a historian.
d. No mistakes.

280.

a. The michievous toddler climbed up on the family's kitchen table.

b. I carefully unwrapped the antique vase so that it wouldn't break.

c. Shoranda verified that she was with her cousins all weekend.

d. No mistakes.

281.

a. The collectible comic book was worth over ten thousand dollars.

b. Professor Khan aquired a rare manuscript on his trip to Egypt.

c. My schedule often changes, so don't hesitate to call me before you come over.

d. No mistakes.

282.

a. My mom's accounting business hired five new employees.

b. The homeowners purchased a new refridgerator for their kitchen.

c. Although Jaxon occasionally walks to school, he typically takes the bus.

d. No mistakes.

283.

a. Regular oil changes are an important part of car maitenance.

b. The painter created a beautiful portrait of my grandmother for her birthday.

c. Are you familiar with the new Indian restaurant near the expressway?

d. No mistakes.

284.

a. Muriel submitted an application for a retail position and got an interview.

b. I recommend that you ask an expert for advice on how to fix your furnace.

c. The university provided relevent information about the new policy.

d. No mistakes.

285.

a. My neice absolutely loved going to the amusement park with me last week.

b. I thought that the orangutans were the highlight of the zoo.

c. The teacher wrote that evening's homework on the classroom's whiteboard.

d. No mistakes.

286.

a. Christian went whitewater rafting last week and had an incredible time.

b. My mom made my favorite desert, chocolate cake, for my graduation party.

c. My next-door neighbor, who is a renowned scientist, is the smartest person I've ever met.

d. No mistakes.

287.

a. The couple hired a professional photographer for their upcoming wedding.

b. Mowing the lawn and trimming the bushes took Craig most of Saturday afternoon.

c. My family got into an arguement over where we should go on vacation.

d. No mistakes.

288.

a. The couple bought a new couch, armchair, and coffee table at the furniture store.

b. On our last day at the cabin, we went hiking in the forest and canoeing in the lake.

c. It takes a lot of dicsipline to become fluent in a second language.

d. No mistakes.

Composition

Directions: For questions 289-298, read the question and select the best answer.

289. Choose the best word to join the thoughts together.

Morgan had three cups of coffee this morning; ____________he was very alert and a bit jittery during the meeting.

a. consequently,
b. however,
c. besides,
d. also,

290. Choose the best word(s) to join the thoughts together.

The speed of light is truly mind-boggling! _____________ it takes only about eight minutes for light from the sun to reach Earth, even though it is over 92 million miles away!

a. First,
b. For example,
c. Subsequently,
d. Truly,

291. Choose the group of words that best completes the sentence.

While watching a movie at a theater, ____________________.

a. you should silence and put it away.
b. it is polite to silence and put away your cell phone because a phone ringing or a bright screen can ruin the movie experience for others so really it's best just to put it away.
c. it is polite, courteous, and thoughtful to silence and put away your cell phone.
d. it is polite to silence and put away your cell phone.

292. Which of these sentences expresses the idea most clearly?

a. Dan and Nicole could not get the drawing software to function properly.
b. The drawing software, used by Dan and also by Nicole, could not be made to function properly.
c. Function properly is what Dan and Nicole could not get the drawing software to do.
d. Dan and Nicole, the users of the non-functioning drawing software, could not get it to work.

293. Which of these sentences expresses the idea most clearly?

a. Of the three brothers, he is taller than one and also the other one.
b. He is the tallest.
c. James is the tallest of the three Nicholson brothers.
d. James is taller than his younger brother and taller than his other younger brother.

294. Which of these sentences expresses the idea most clearly?

a. Marco, can you help him with the homework?
b. Homework help your brother needs from you Marco.
c. Can you go do that with him?
d. Marco, can you go help your brother with his homework?

295. Which of the following topics is best for a one-page essay?

a. A History of Ballet
b. Plants and Photosynthesis
c. A Brief Review of the Local Production of *The Sound of Music*
d. The Major Battles of the War of 1812

296. Which of these sentences fits best under the topic "How to Properly Prepare Scrambled Eggs"?

a. Eggs are an excellent source of protein.
b. Make sure to keep the heat low; if the pan is too hot the eggs will overcook and dry out.
c. Chicken eggs are the most typical egg eaten in America, but there are many other kinds that are available.
d. Eggs provide structure and rise to baked goods.

297. Which sentence does NOT belong in the paragraph?

Water is unusual in many ways. (2) For example, unlike most substances, water expands instead of contracts when it freezes. (3) Ice cold water is especially good on a hot summer day. (4) Also, individual water molecules stick to one another more so than the molecules of other substances do, which creates surface tension.

a. 1
b. 2
c. 3
d. 4

298. Where should the sentence "Furthermore, algebra helps improve overall logic and analytical thinking skills that are used outside of math class." be placed in the following paragraph?

Many students think that learning algebra is pointless, but it actually does a lot of good! (2) For example, algebra often forces the student to break a complicated problem down into smaller steps, which is a valuable skill to have in the real world. (3) Even if it doesn't feel like it now, skills picked up in algebra will be useful for years to come!

a. Before sentence 1
b. Between sentences 1 and 2
c. Between sentences 2 and 3
d. After sentence 3

Answer Key

Verbal

1. C
2. A
3. A
4. D
5. C
6. B
7. D
8. C
9. B
10. C
11. D
12. B
13. A
14. D
15. A
16. A
17. C
18. B
19. C
20. D
21. C
22. B
23. B
24. B
25. A
26. C
27. D
28. B
29. C
30. C
31. B
32. A
33. C
34. c
35. C
36. A
37. A
38. D
39. A
40. C
41. C
42. A
43. D
44. B
45. A
46. B
47. D
48. A
49. A
50. C
51. C
52. C
53. C
54. A
55. A
56. A
57. A
58. D
59. D
60. C

Quantitative

61. C
62. B
63. A
64. D
65. B
66. C
67. C
68. A
69. B
70. C
71. D
72. B
73. A
74. D
75. B
76. A
77. D
78. C
79. A
80. D
81. C
82. A
83. D
84. A
85. B
86. A
87. D
88. B
89. B
90. C
91. a
92. C
93. A
94. B
95. D
96. D
97. A
98. C
99. D
100. B
101. A
102. C
103. A
104. D
105. C
106. C
107. C
108. C
109. A
110. D
111. A
112. A

Reading

113. D
114. B
115. A
116. D
117. B
118. A
119. C
120. C
121. C
122. B
123. C
124. D
125. A
126. C
127. D
128. B
129. D
130. A
131. D
132. B
133. D
134. C
135. C
136. A
137. B
138. D
139. C
140. B
141. A
142. C
143. D
144. B
145. C
146. B
147. D
148. A
149. C
150. C
151. C
152. B
153. A
154. C
155. D
156. C
157. B
158. A
159. D
160. B
161. C
162. D
163. A
164. D
165. C
166. B
167. B
168. D
169. A
170. C
171. B
172. D
173. A
174. B

Math

175. D
176. B
177. A
178. D
179. D
180. C
181. D
182. A
183. B
184. B
185. A
186. A
187. C
188. D
189. B
190. C
191. B
192. D
193. A
194. D
195. A
196. C
197. B
198. D
199. B
200. D
201. B
202. D
203. B
204. C
205. C
206. D
207. C
208. A
209. C
210. D
211. A
212. B
213. B
214. A
215. C
216. B
217. A
218. B
219. C
220. D
221. C
222. B
223. B
224. D
225. B
226. C
227. B
228. B
229. A
230. C
231. B
232. A
233. B
234. D
235. C
236. B
237. A
238. A

Language

239. A
240. D
241. C
242. B
243. B
244. B
245. C
246. A
247. C
248. D
249. B
250. C
251. B
252. A
253. B
254. B
255. C
256. A
257. A
258. C
259. b
260. C
261. D
262. B
263. D
264. C
265. B
266. D
267. C
268. A
269. C
270. C
271. A
272. A
273. B
274. B
275. B
276. C
277. C
278. A
279. D
280. A
281. B
282. B
283. A
284. C
285. A
286. B
287. C
288. C
289. A
290. B
291. D
292. A
293. C
294. D
295. C
296. B
297. C
298. C

HSPT Test 8

Verbal Section 8

60 Questions, 16 Minutes

Instructions: Select the best answer.

1. Which word does *not* belong with the others?

   a. praise
   b. commend
   c. applaud
   d. heckle

2. Fortitude most nearly means

   a. castle
   b. endurance
   c. sickly
   d. food

3. Thursday was cooler than Friday. Wednesday was warmer than Friday and Monday. Thursday is warmer than Monday. If the first two statements are true, the third statement is

   a. true
   b. false
   c. uncertain

4. Impede means the *opposite* of

   a. hobble
   b. touch
   c. hinder
   d. facilitate

5. Edible most nearly means

   a. palatable
   b. uneatable
   c. fixable
   d. tiresome

6. Aptitude most nearly means

   a. proficiency
   b. difficulty
   c. sympathy
   d. attitude

7. Coat is to warm as refrigerator is to

   a. freezer
   b. cool
   c. milk
   d. kitchen

8. Which word does *not* belong with the others?

   a. petal
   b. root
   c. flower
   d. stem

9. Rabbits have more babies than squirrels but fewer babies than mice. Squirrels have more babies than robins. Rabbits have more babies than robins. If the first two statements are true, the third statement is

   a. true
   b. false
   c. uncertain

10. Radical means the *opposite* of

    a. progressive
    b. minor
    c. profound
    d. repetitive

11. Players are to game as runners are to

    a. walkers
    b. speed
    c. race
    d. fast

12. Transient most nearly means

    a. scientific
    b. transit
    c. permanent
    d. passing

13. Atlanta is further than Tallahassee. Tallahassee is closer than Sacramento. Sacramento is closer than Atlanta. If the first two statements are true, the third statement is

    a. true
    b. false
    c. uncertain

14. Which word does *not* belong with the others?

    a. tulip
    b. fern
    c. rose
    d. daffodil

15. Console most nearly means

    a. judge
    b. comfort
    c. middle
    d. upset

16. Which word does *not* belong with the others?

    a. doctor
    b. hospital
    c. physician's assistant
    d. nurse

17. Bianca picked more apples than Shanda. Shanda picked more apples than Susan and Cheryl. Bianca picked more apples than Susan. If the first two statements are true, the third statement is

    a. true
    b. false
    c. uncertain

18. Petty means the *opposite* of

    a. weak
    b. important
    c. fun
    d. trivial

19. Robust most nearly means

    a. weak
    b. red
    c. strong
    d. metallic

20. Which word does *not* belong with the others?

    a. verify
    b. conceal
    c. substantiate
    d. confirm

21. Tangible means the *opposite* of

    a. concrete
    b. solid
    c. abstract
    d. sour

22. Cartographer is to map as sculptor is to

    a. paint
    b. statue
    c. ancient
    d. job

23. Bob's dairy farm produced more cheese this year than Gwen's. Gwen's dairy farm produced less cheese this year than Miriam's. Miriam's dairy farm produced the most cheese this year. If the first two statements are true, the third statement is

    a. true
    b. false
    c. uncertain

24. Wave is to tsunami as pebble is to

    a. landslide
    b. boulder
    c. ocean
    d. weather

25. Disperse most nearly means

    a. draw
    b. collate
    c. distribute
    d. disuse

26. Which word does *not* belong with the others?

    a. child
    b. human
    c. adult
    d. teen

27. All blue-eared woogies have purple hair. The mynar is a type of blue-eared woogie. The mynar has blue hair. If the first two statements are true, the third statement is

    a. true
    b. false
    c. uncertain

28. Which word does *not* belong with the others?

    a. rock
    b. marble
    c. granite
    d. limestone

29. Resolute most nearly means

    a. awful
    b. boring
    c. cautious
    d. determined

30. Which word does *not* belong with the others?

    a. car
    b. speedboat
    c. airplane
    d. kayak

31. Elegant is to plain as obsolete is to

    a. modern
    b. old
    c. dangerous
    d. beautiful

32. Calvin is older than Hannah. Jeremiah is younger than Calvin. Hannah is younger than Jeremiah. If the first two statements are true, the third statement is

    a. true
    b. false
    c. uncertain

33. Which word does *not* belong with the others?

    a. diamond
    b. gem
    c. ruby
    d. emerald

34. Detain means the opposite of

    a. constrain
    b. hide
    c. consider
    d. liberate

35. Ankle is to foot as wrist is to

    a. arm
    b. fingers
    c. hand
    d. fist

36. Which word does *not* belong with the others?

    a. enraged
    b. ecstatic
    c. infuriated
    d. livid

37. Barry has written more songs than Adam. Erica has written more songs than Barry. Adam has written the fewest songs. If the first two statements are true, the third statement is

    a. true
    b. false
    c. uncertain

38. Which word does *not* belong with the others?

    a. movie
    b. comedy
    c. drama
    d. action

39. Sleepy is to lethargic as tasty is to

    a. scrumptious
    b. disgusting
    c. healthy
    d. nutritious

40. Which word does *not* belong with the others?

    a. trout
    b. fish
    c. tuna
    d. cod

41. Wolf is to pack as fish is to

    a. water
    b. pond
    c. school
    d. trout

42. Deceit most nearly means

    a. candor
    b. immodesty
    c. difficulty
    d. dishonesty

43. Caleigh takes more classes than Keaton. Keaton takes fewer classes than Jackson and Claire. Claire takes fewer classes than Caleigh. If the first two statements are true, the third statement is
    a.
    b. true
    c. false
    d. uncertain

44. Contempt means the *opposite* of
    a. disdain
    b. respect
    c. together
    d. temperate

45. Jonquin lives north of Mikayla. Mikayla lives directly west of Laila and north west of Benjamin. Benjamin lives north of Jonquin. If the first two statements are true, the third statement is
    a. true
    b. false
    c. uncertain

46. Which word does *not* belong with the others?
    a. China
    b. Japan
    c. India
    d. Asia

47. Wide is to narrow as deep is to
    a. long
    b. cavernous
    c. tall
    d. shallow

48. Elated most nearly means
    a. delighted
    b. tardy
    c. encouraged
    d. elevated

49. Which word does *not* belong with the others?
    a. tranquil
    b. anxious
    c. worried
    d. nervous

50. Cheetah is to run as kangaroo is to
    a.
    b. walk
    c. hop
    d. Australia
    e. slow

51. Which word does *not* belong with the others?
    a. bottle
    b. drink
    c. mug
    d. cup

52. Naive means the *opposite* of
    a. ignorant
    b. discerning
    c. affluent
    d. experienced

53. Joey runs more than Henry. Joey runs less than Janice. Janice runs the most. If the first two statements are true, the third statement is
    a. true
    b. false
    c. uncertain

54. Alice's cakes are more elaborate than June and Ari's cakes. Ari's cakes are more elaborate than Malia's cakes, but less elaborate than John's cakes. John has the most elaborate cakes. If the first two statements are true, the third statement is
    a. true
    b. false
    c. uncertain

55. Mandate most nearly means
    a. manipulate
    b. convince
    c. order
    d. allow

56. Which word does *not* belong with the others?
    a. photographer
    b. artwork
    c. sculptor
    d. painter

57. Malignant means the *opposite* of

    a. benign
    b. poor
    c. deadly
    d. wealthy

58. Proponent means the *opposite* of

    a. objective
    b. opponent
    c. careless
    d. advocate

59. Which word does *not* belong with the others?

    a. mouse
    b. squirrel
    c. rodent
    d. guinea pig

60. Coddle most nearly means

    a. swaddle
    b. ignore
    c. praise
    d. pamper

Quantitative Section 8

52 Questions, 30 Minutes

Instructions: Select the best answer.

61. What number subtracted from eighty-six is three more than the product of four and five?

    a. 26
    b. 63
    c. 70
    d. 74

62. Look at the series: 3, 6, 36, ____, 234, 237. What is the missing number?

    a. 30
    b. 66
    c. 39
    d. 200

63. Examine (A), (B), and (C) and find the best answer.

    (A) 5^2
    (B) 4^1
    (C) 3^3

    a. A > B
    b. B > C
    c. A > C
    d. C < B

64. What is the next number in the following series: 37, 41, 46, 52, 59, ____.

    a. 66
    b. 67
    c. 61
    d. 70

65. In the figure below if C>B>A which of the following is true?

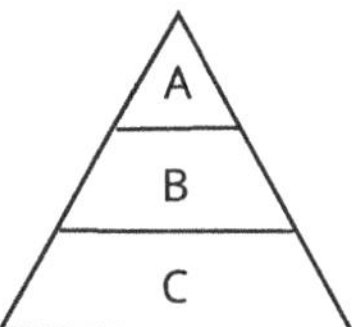

    a. B + A = C
    b. B > C
    c. A < C
    d. C - B = A

66. Examine the series: 6, 25, 13, 5, 20, 1, ___. What number should come next?

    a. 27
    b. 23
    c. 7
    d. 12

67. A and A' are drawn to scale and are the centers of their respective circles.

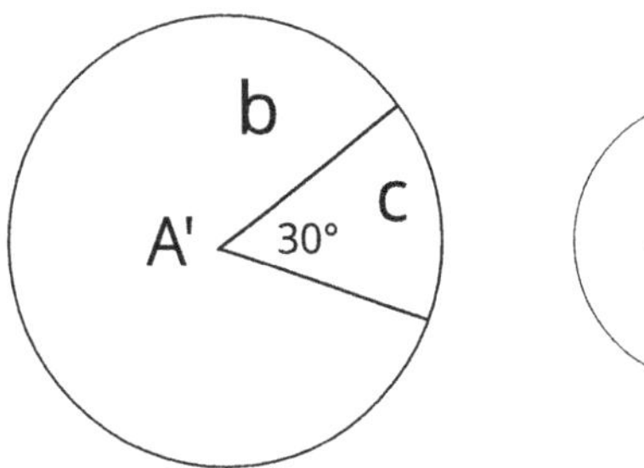

Choose the the best answer

    a. area e = area c
    b. area b > area d
    c. area b - area d = area e
    d. area c + area e = area d

68. $\frac{3}{4}$ of a number is 12 less than 15. What is the number?

a. 4
b. 12
c. 24
d. 36

69. What is 30% of 140 divided by 7?

a. 2
b. 4
c. 6
d. 8

70. What is the missing number in the following series: 9, 27, 21, ____, 57, 171?

a. 28
b. 33
c. 14
d. 63

71. Examine the coins below and choose the correct answer.

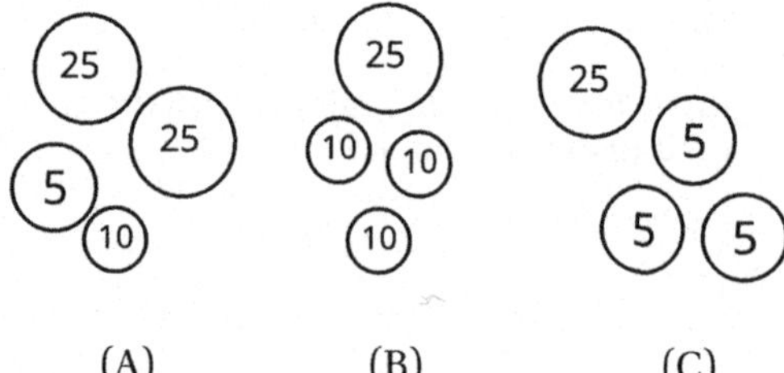

a. (A) > (C) > (B)
b. (B) + (C) > (A)
c. (A) - (C) > (B)
d. (B) + (C) < (A)

72. What is the missing number in the following series: 25, L, ____, C, 125, CL

a. XV
b. D
c. 75
d. 50

73. Examine (A), (B), and (C) and find the best answer.

(A) $\frac{1}{3}$ of 27
(B) $\frac{1}{4}$ of 24
(C) $\frac{1}{5}$ of 25

a. A - B > C
b. C > B < A
c. B + C = A
d. A > B > C

74. The cube of four divided by 8 is ____.

a. 2
b. 4
c. 6
d. 8

75. Review the series: 9, 18, 6, 12, 4, ____. Find the next number.

a. 6
b. 3
c. -2
d. 8

76. What number divided by 4 is $\frac{2}{5}$ of 60?

a. 6
b. 12
c. 24
d. 96

77. Based on the information presented below, choose the best answer.

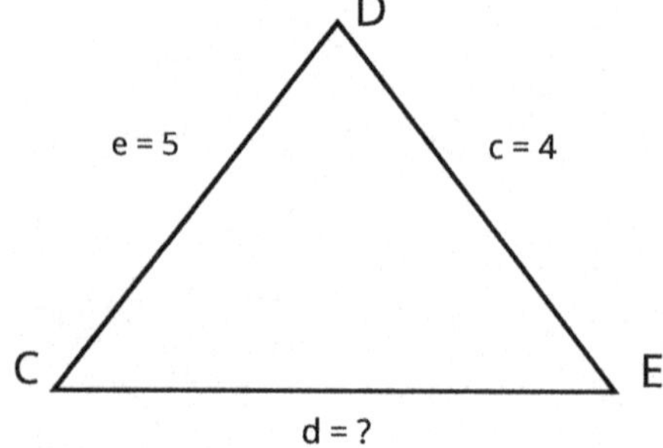

a. d > 12
b. d < 9
c. d = 9
d. d = 12

78. Examine the series: 45, 96, _____, 101, 35, 107. Find the missing number.

a. 103
b. 50
c. 98
d. 40

79. 16 is eight less than the product of 2 and what number?

a. 6
b. 24
c. 12
d. 18

80. Examine the series: 7, 10, 13, 16, 19, ____. What number should come next?

a. 21
b. 22
c. 23
d. 24

81. Examine (A), (B), and (C) and find the best answer.

(A) $\frac{5}{4} - \frac{3}{4}$
(B) $\frac{10}{8} - \frac{3}{4}$
(C) $\frac{3}{4} - \frac{5}{4}$

a. (A) = (B) = (C)
b. (A) - (B) > (C)
c. (A) + (C) > (B)
d. (B) - (C) = (A)

82. Review the following series: $\frac{1}{3}$, $\frac{5}{6}$, $\frac{4}{3}$, $\frac{11}{6}$, ____, $\frac{17}{6}$. Select the missing number.

a. $\frac{7}{3}$
b. $\frac{13}{6}$
c. $\frac{15}{6}$
d. $\frac{8}{3}$

83. Compare the number of flowers in (A), (B), and (C) and find the best answer.

(A)
❋ ❋
❋ ❋
❋ ❋
❋ ❋
❋ ❋
❋ ❋

(B)
❋ ❋ ❋
❋ ❋ ❋
❋ ❋
❋ ❋
❋

(C)
❋ ❋ ❋ ❋
❋ ❋ ❋
❋ ❋ ❋
❋ ❋

a. (A) is equal to (C) and greater than (B)
b. (A), (B), and (C) are equal
c. (A) is greater than (C), but less than (B)
d. (C) is equal to (B), but less than (A)

84. Review this series: Z, X, V, T, R, ___. What letter should come next?

a. Y
b. S
c. F
d. P

85. 12 is what percent of 60?

a. 15%
b. 20%
c. 25%
d. 30%

86. What numbers are missing from the following series: 47, 17, 37, 12, 27, ___, ___?

a. 7, 17
b. 8, 17
c. 7, 37
d. 6, 7

87. The quotient of what number and 28 is equal to $\frac{1}{7}$?

a. 2
b. 3
c. 4
d. 6

88. Review the series: 56, 28, ___, 7, 3.5. What number is missing?

a. 18
b. 16
c. 21
d. 14

89. Examine the figure below and (A), (B), and (C). Select the best answer.

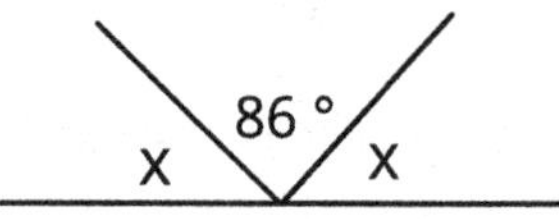

(A) 2x
(B) 86° - x
(C) x

a. (A) > (B) > (C)
b. (A) > (C) > (B)
c. (C) > (B) > (A)
d. (B) > (C) < (A)

90. Examine (A), (B), and (C) and find the best answer.

(A) $4 + 2 \times 9$
(B) $4 \times 2 + 9$
(C) $(4 + 2) \times 9$

a. (A) is larger than (B) but smaller than (C)
b. (A), (B), and (C) are equal
c. (A) is equal to (C) and larger than (B)
d. (C) is larger than (B) but smaller than (A)

91. Look at the following series: 10, 3, 13, 3, 16, ___, ___. What numbers are missing?

a. 3, 20
b. 13, 3
c. 3, 19
d. 10, 3

92. Examine (A), (B), and (C) and find the best answer.

(A) $\sqrt{4} + 8$
(B) $\sqrt{16} + 6$
(C) $\sqrt{25} + 5$

a. (B) + (C) > (A)
b. (B) > (C) > (A)
c. (C) - (B) > (A)
d. (B) + (A) = (C)

93. Thirteen plus the square root of 49 is what number?

a. 15
b. 17
c. 20
d. 23

94. Look at the series: 3, 4, 8, 9, 18, ___, ___. What are the next numbers?

a. 10, 20
b. 19, 20
c. 10, 38
d. 19, 38

95. Examine the cube below and (A), (B), and (C). Select the best answer.

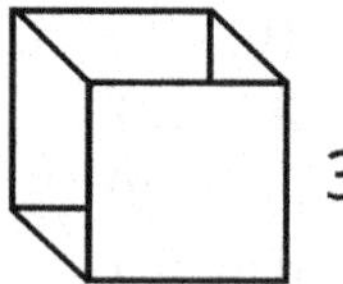

(A) the volume of the cube
(B) the area of one side of the cube
(C) 12

a. (A) < (B) < (C)
b. (A) > (B) > (C)
c. (B) < (C) < (A)
d. (C) < (A) < (B)

96. Look at the series: 21, 18, 9, 6, 3, ___. What is the next number?

a. 0
b. 1.5
c. 3
d. 6

97. The product of 3 and what number is equal to $\frac{1}{4}$ of 24?

a. 18
b. 2
c. 8
d. 6

98. 18 less than 44 is equal to 65% of what number?

a. 40
b. 26
c. 30
d. 36

99. Examine (A), (B), and (C) and find the best answer.

(A) 15% of 120
(B) 30% of 70
(C) 60% of 30

a. (A) is less than (B) but greater than (C)
b. (A) is equal to (B) but less than (C)
c. (A) is greater than (C) but less than (B)
d. (A) is equal to (C) but less than (B)

100. If, in the isosceles triangle below, $\overline{CA} = \overline{AB}$, which of the following must be true?

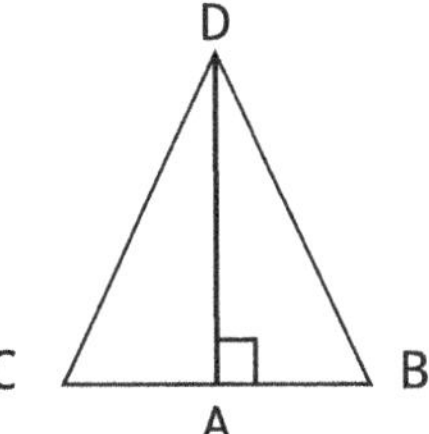

a. $\overline{CD}$ is equal to $\overline{CB}$ and $\overline{DB}$
b. $\overline{AB}$ is less than DB but greater than $\overline{DA}$
c. DB is greater than $\overline{DA}$ which is greater than $\overline{CA}$
d. CB is less than DB but greater than $\overline{DA}$

101. Look at the series: 0, 3, 6, 9, 18, ___. Find the next number.

a. 22
b. 15
c. 36
d. 21

102. What number or letter should come next in the series: D, 5, F, 7, H, 9, ___?

a. I
b. 10
c. J
d. K

103. Examine (A), (B), and (C) and find the best answer.

a. $.0083 \times 10^3$
b. 830×10^{-3}
c. $.83 \times 10^2$

d. (A) + (B) >(C)
e. (C) - (A) > (B)
f. (B) + (C) = (A)
g. (A) + (C) < (B)

104. The average of 4, 8, and 9 is equal to the sum of 1 and what number?

a. 7
b. 5
c. 9
d. 6

105. Review the series: 19, 12, 15, 14, 11, ___, ___. What numbers should come next?

a. 16, 7
b. 17, 7
c. 6, 16
d. 17, 6

106. Examine (A), (B), and (C) and find the best answer.

(A) 1.3
(B) $\frac{5}{4}$
(C) $\frac{4}{3}$

a. (B) is less than (A) but greater than (C)
b. (C) is greater than (A) but less than (B)
c. (A) is greater than (B) but less than (C)
d. (A) is equal to (C) and greater than (B)

107. 40% of 15 is equal to the quotient of 30 and what number?

a. 5
b. 6
c. 7
d. 8

108. What is the next number in the following series: 1, 4, 16, 64, ___?

a. 128
b. 256
c. 138
d. 254

109. Look at the series: .4, .8, 1, 2, 2.2, 4.4, ___. Find the next number.

a. 8.8
b. 4.6
c. 4.8
d. 5

110. Examine the circle below.

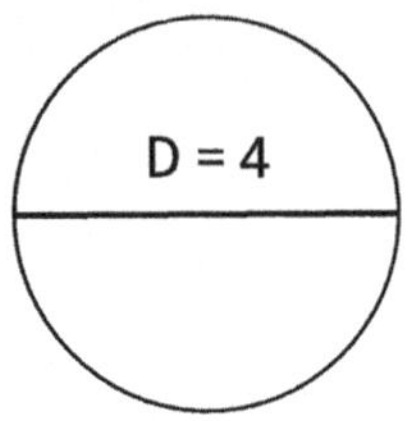

(A) The circle's circumference
(B) The circle's radius
(C) The circle's area

a. (B) is larger than (A) but smaller than (C)
b. (C) is equal to (B) and larger than (A)
c. (B) is larger than (C) but smaller than (A)
d. (A) is equal to (C) and larger than (B)

111. What is the next number in the following series; 14, 12, 16, 14, 18, ___

a. 15
b. 16
c. 14
d. 22

112. Look at the series: 25, 20, 16, 13, 11, ___. Find the next number.

a. 9
b. 7
c. 10
d. 8

Reading Section 8

62 Questions, 25 Minutes

Reading Comprehension

Instructions: Read each passage carefully and mark one answer for each question.

Questions 113 - 120 refer to the following passage.

Though various others were written beforehand, Samuel Johnson's A Dictionary of the English Language (1755) is often considered the first modern English dictionary. Compared with previous versions, it is incredibly thorough and informative. Johnson spent seven years defining the dictionary's 45,000 words, which range from basic vocabulary to bizarrely specific expressions. In contrast, most earlier dictionaries were far less comprehensive, partially because the original purpose of dictionaries was to explain particularly difficult words, not to record the entire language. The organization, spelling, and definitions of Johnson's dictionary also match today's dictionaries much more closely than previous versions.

Nevertheless, A Dictionary of the English Language shares one important flaw with the older ones: definitions are often vague or confusing, and show the limited knowledge and personal opinions of the writer. For example, if you use Edward Phillips' 1658 dictionary The New World of English Words to try and look up what a dog is, the only description you'll find is "A well known creature." Johnson's definition for cat, "A domestick animal that catches mice, commonly reckoned by naturalists the lowest order of the leonine species," is slightly more detailed than Phillips' dog definition, but both explanations are fairly useless unless the reader is already familiar with the animals.

To be fair, the same issue occurs in many later dictionaries as well. For instance, Noah Webster's An American Dictionary of the English Language includes an even more suspicious definition for "cat" than Johnson's version, despite being published in 1828 ("...The domestic cat needs no description. It is a deceitful animal, and when enraged, extremely spiteful."). Accordingly, some people argue that the first complete and accurate English dictionary did not exist until the Oxford English Dictionary (OED) was finished in 1928. It took 70 years to create the OED, but thanks to the persistence of editor James Murray, his team, and thousands of volunteers, its well-researched 414,800 definitions set a new standard for what an English dictionary should be.

113. As it is used in the passage, the word comprehensive most nearly means

 a. believable
 b. thorough
 c. amazing
 d. understandable

114. Compared to Samuel Johnson's dictionary, the Oxford English Dictionary

 a. took longer to complete
 b. defines fewer words
 c. includes more biased definitions
 d. is the first modern English dictionary

115. The author most likely includes definitions of the words "cat" and "dog" to

 a. explain to the reader what cats and dogs are
 b. show how expectations of spelling have changed over the years
 c. illustrate a common issue of early dictionaries
 d. include some humorous examples of historical stupidity

116. According to the passage, English dictionaries were originally intended to

 a. provide assistance with both grammar and spelling
 b. teach French and German immigrants how to speak English
 c. record the entire language
 d. define particularly difficult or unusual words

117. Which of the following best summarizes this passage?

   a. Accurate definitions are essential to language.
   b. Samuel Johnson wrote an impressive but flawed dictionary.
   c. English dictionaries have vastly improved over the past few hundred years.
   d. It is important to include as much detail as possible in definitions.

118. From the information given in the passage, you can infer that Noah Webster

   a. was a very patient and thorough editor
   b. was Samuel Johnson's bitter rival
   c. did not keep cats as pets
   d. lived in England

119. If Samuel Johnson's dictionary still set the standard for what an English dictionary should be, what would be the most likely result?

   a. Dictionaries would be less trustworthy.
   b. More people would use dictionaries on a daily basis.
   c. Public literacy rates would increase.
   d. The English language would include more words.

120. In what year did Edward Phillips publish his dictionary?

   a. 1928
   b. 1755
   c. 1658
   d. 1858

Questions 121 - 128 refer to the following passage.

For an extreme sport, skydiving is a surprisingly safe and popular activity. One reason for this is the accessibility of tandem jump options, which allow novice skydivers to experience the thrill of skydiving while strapped to a professional skydiver. Although tandem dives can be pricey, many people find the relative safety and minimal training commitment well worth the cost. For avid skydivers, tandem-style skydiving is a profitable business opportunity as well as a way to keep inexperienced would-be jumpers under supervision, which helps ensure everyone's safety.

While the training for tandem students is often as minimal as viewing a safety video, tandem instructors are held to rigorous standards. The World Air Sports Federation and its national representative organizations (such as the United States Parachuting Association and the British Parachuting Association) regulate participants using a licensing system. After a skydiver completes 25 jumps and passes written and oral tests, he/she can apply for a class A license. In most countries, skydivers must achieve a class D license before they can become certified tandem instructors. To get a class D license, skydivers must complete at least 500 jumps and another test, as well as demonstrate their <u>proficiency</u> with nighttime skydives, water landings, and other special circumstances.

Most skydivers take safety precautions very seriously, and the majority of injuries consist of minor foot and ankle injuries due to improper landings. Equipment is checked before each jump, and each set of gear includes two parachutes: a main parachute and a backup parachute. In case of emergency, skydivers detach their main parachute and use their backup (called a "reserve") instead. Still, it is impossible to avoid danger completely, and about 21 people die in skydiving incidents each year.

121. Tandem instructors and tandem students are different in that tandem students

  a. learn how to skydive independently
  b. earn a class A licence
  c. are rigorously trained on how to skydive
  d. are attached to an experienced skydiver

122. A skydiver who has completed 26 dives may

  a. have a class D license
  b. have a class A license
  c. be leading tandem skydives
  d. is considered a professional skydiver

123. The author most likely includes the information about the licensing system to

  a. persuade the reader to learn to skydive
  b. show that some skydivers can do water landings
  c. demonstrate how thoroughly tandem instructors are trained
  d. explain how skydiving safety equipment works

124. As it is used in the passage, <u>proficiency</u> most nearly means

  a. professionalism
  b. skill
  c. eagerness
  d. ignorance

125. Based on the information in the passage, which of the following is a possible downside to tandem skydiving?

  a. the extensive training required
  b. the serious safety concerns
  c. the licensing requirements
  d. the cost

126. Which of the following would be a possible title for this passage?

  a. "The Safety of Skydiving"
  b. "Tandem Jump Training"
  c. "Skydiving is Fun!"
  d. "Skydiving Equipment"

127. In what type of publication would you find this passage?

a. a novel
b. an academic journal
c. a sports magazine
d. an encyclopedia

128. A skydiver is injured. What is their most likely injury?

a. a sprained ankle
b. a fractured wrist
c. a concussion
d. a broken back

Questions 129 - 136 refer to the following passage.

During the Korean War, a Canadian navy destroyer named HMCS Cayuga was just about to begin its second tour of duty when Dr. Joseph C. Cyr was assigned as the ship's doctor. His skills were soon tested when the Cayuga rescued several dangerously wounded South Korean soldiers. Dr. Cyr performed surgery at sea (including removing a bullet from one man's chest and amputating another soldier's foot) and the soldiers survived in spite of their initially grave injuries.

Back in Canada, Dr. Joseph C. Cyr's mother was far from proud when she read about his successful heroism in the newspaper. In fact, she was confused and frightened. When she called her son, he confirmed that he had never joined the war effort and was still working as a doctor in New Brunswick. It became apparent that the man who had recently operated on the injured soldiers wasn't really named Joseph Cyr after all. Furthermore, he wasn't Canadian, he wasn't in the military, and he wasn't even a doctor. He was an American identity thief named Frank Demara, AKA "The Great Imposter."

Due to his impressive intelligence, photographic memory, and mind-boggling <u>audacity</u>, Demara convincingly held careers as a monk, a civil engineer, a cancer research scientist, a lawyer, and even a high-ranking prison administrator at various points in his life. He was a fast reader, and could often memorize what he needed to convincingly play his part by flipping through a book or two. Consequently, he could actually do the jobs — and do them well — even though he faked everything else about himself. He really did serve as the Cayuga's military doctor while he was on board, and performed the famous surgeries himself (after disappearing with a medical textbook for a while). So, even when a military investigation confirmed the Canadian Dr. Cyr's accusations, Demara was just sent home to America rather than charged for his crime.

129. Why wasn't Dr. Joseph Cyr's mother happy when she read the newspaper article about her son?

    a. Because she didn't approve of his involvement in the war.
    b. Because she was worried that he was not being careful.
    c. Because she didn't think that he was fighting in the war.
    d. Because she knew he had lied to her.

130. Which of the following was NOT one of Demara's occupations?

    a. soldier
    b. engineer
    c. doctor
    d. monk

131. If the famous operation had been a failure, it is possible that

    a. the Canadians would have lost the war
    b. Dr. Cyr would have been fired
    c. the South Korean soldier would have lost both of his legs
    d. Frank Demara would have been sent directly to prison

132. According to its use in the passage, <u>audacity</u> most nearly means

    a. insanity
    b. volume
    c. valor
    d. boldness

133. Why did Demara disappear with a medical textbook before performing surgery?

    a. He liked to refresh his medical knowledge on challenging procedures.
    b. He needed to rest and relax before the stressful operation.
    c. He valued privacy and did not want to be bothered.
    d. He had to read and memorize what he was supposed to do.

134. Unlike Frank Demara, Dr. Joseph Cyr

    a. was a coward
    b. did not join the navy during the Korean War
    c. was able to successfully perform difficult operations
    d. was American

135. This passage is mainly about

   a. the impressive feats of a famous liar
   b. how to be an imposter
   c. the life of Dr. Cyr
   d. the HMCS Cayuga

136. According to the passage, Demara was able to play so many different roles because

   a. he had an extensive educational background
   b. it was much easier to assume different identities in the past
   c. he was smart, with an excellent memory
   d. his confidence allowed him to easily manipulate those around him

Questions 137- 144 refer to the following passage.

Over the course of his six-decade career, legendary filmmaker Sir Alfred Hitchcock created more than 50 movies, many of which are considered groundbreaking classics. Hitchcock's distinctive style and plot choices earned him the title "The Master of Suspense" and brought international acclaim to his movies. In fact, films like Psycho, The Birds, North by Northwest, and other Hitchcock favorites remain popular to this day.

Hitchcock was born in London in the final year of the 19th century, and worked on silent films in Britain for over a decade before the first "talkie" was produced in 1927. By the time he moved to Hollywood in 1939, Hitchcock had already established himself as a force to be reckoned with. The smashing success of his first American film, Rebecca (1940), solidified his standing in the film industry, and won two Academy Awards— including Best Picture. Rebecca is a psychological thriller about a young woman whose marriage is haunted by the mysterious circumstances of her new husband's first wife's death and is often considered the first example of "film noir" style (which is now a standard category for dramatic crime movies).

Many critics argue that Rebecca marks the launching point for Hitchcock's Hollywood career as well as his <u>iconic</u> directing choices. Among other trademark techniques, Hitchcock is known for skillfully manipulating the audience through point-of-view camera perspectives, sudden plot twists, and screeching music. By combining these effects with ordinary, innocent characters, Hitchcock brought a new level of suspense to the scary movie genre.

137. Approximately how many years did Alfred Hitchcock work in the film industry?

 a. 6
 b. 50
 c. 60
 d. 10

138. As it is used in the passage, <u>iconic</u> most nearly means

 a. ordinary
 b. disliked
 c. risky
 d. widely recognized

139. Hitchcock's films can best be described as

 a. romantic
 b. thrilling
 c. depressing
 d. hopeful

140. The author included the detail "Rebecca is a psychological thriller about a young woman whose marriage is haunted by the mysterious circumstances of her new husband's first wife's death," to show

 a. how Hitchcock manipulated the audience
 b. what a silent film was like
 c. why people disliked Hitchcock
 d. an example of the film noir style

141. According to the passage, which of the following is an example of a technique Hitchcock used

 a. extreme close up camera shots
 b. long periods of silence
 c. piercing music
 d. predictable plot elements

142. In what year was Alfred Hitchcock born?

 a. 1899
 b. 1999
 c. 1927
 d. 1901

143. Which of the following is a possible title for this passage:

    a. "The Life and Death of Alfred Hitchcock"
    b. "Rebecca: A Modern Classic"
    c. "Alfred Hitchcock: The Master of Suspense"
    d. "A History of Modern Film "

144. What is the author likely to discuss in the next paragraph?

    a. another well-known Hitchcock film
    b. a new, up-and-coming film director
    c. this year's Academy Awards
    d. the history of silent films

Questions 145-152 refer to the following passage.

Most people look back at senior year of high school and remember experiences like prom and applying to colleges. For me, though, that time will always be the year my father brought Morton into our lives. I don't think I'll ever forgive him for that.

Father's unwavering love for Morton was perplexing to my brother and me, and it eventually infuriated Mother. At first, she limited herself to good-natured exasperation. She insisted that she was glad Father had found a hobby in retirement, even if it meant putting up with the smell, the scratches on the hardwood floors, and the cartons of bugs in the refrigerator. But the incident with the handyman was the last straw.

Morton had a low tolerance for strange guests in the house, which is to say that he almost always tried to bite them. Father liked to claim that Morton was just being protective of us, but that never made a lot of sense — he bit us only slightly less often than he bit strangers. In reality, Morton was an opportunist, and newcomers tended to make easier targets. While Charlie and I knew better than to casually stroll past any of Morton's hiding spots, the man who came to fix our refrigerator did not. In a naïve attempt to be polite, he even took his shoes off at the door. Morton had been lurking in the cabinet under the kitchen sink (his second-favorite ambush position), and I can imagine the joy he must have felt when he heard the handyman's sock-footed gait padding towards him. On the other hand, I can't begin to imagine what the poor man thought when my father's badger came launching out at him.

145. What type of animal is Morton?

   a. a lizard
   b. a cat
   c. a pig
   d. a badger

146. When this passage took place, the narrator was

   a. a young child
   b. an adult
   c. a teenager
   d. there is no indication of the narrator's age

147. How did the narrator's mother feel about Morton?

   a. She didn't like Morton at first, but she warmed up to him.
   b. She hated Morton from the moment he was brought into the house.
   c. At first she patiently tolerated Morton, but she eventually disliked him.
   d. She loved Morton.

148. What type of negative characteristic did Morton NOT exhibit?

   a. He bit people.

   b. He screeched loudly.
   c. He scratched the floors.
   d. He smelled.

149. What type of narration is used in this passage?

   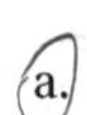
   a. first person
   b. second person
   c. third person
   d. omniscient

150. The sentence, "Father liked to claim that Morton was just being protective of us, but that never made a lot of sense — he bit us only slightly less often than he bit strangers" suggests that the narrator's father

   a. clearly understood Morton's flaws, but loved him anyway
   b. took care to keep Morton away from his family so that they stayed safe
   c. made excuses for Morton and did not always recognize his flaws
   d. encouraged Morton to bite people

151. What literary technique does the author use in the phrase “the handyman’s sock-footed gait padding towards him” ?

a. metaphor
b. imagery
c. personification
d. symbolism

152. Based on the information in the passage, what might happen next in the story?

a. Morton bites the handyman’s feet.
b. Morton growls at the handyman.
c. Morton bites the narrator.
d. Morton runs away from the handyman.

Vocabulary

Instructions: Choose the word that means the same, or about the same, as the underlined word.

153. The <u>pessimistic</u> man

a. optimistic
b. despondent
c. careful
d. angry

154. A successful <u>rebellion</u>

a. treaty
b. war
c. capture
d. revolt

155. To live in <u>harmony</u>

a. music
b. beauty
c. peace
d. proximity

156. To <u>permit</u> discussion

a. encourage
b. allow
c. force
d. stop

157. To react with <u>dismay</u>

a. alarm
b. disgust
c. concern
d. composure

158. A harsh <u>lecture</u>

a. question
b. discouragement
c. reprimand
d. conversation

159. To <u>forego</u> dinner

a. eat
b. enjoy
c. dislike
d. abstain from

160. To <u>amplify</u> the sound

a. distort
b. increase
c. sharpen
d. soften

161. A minor <u>skirmish</u>

a. accident
b. fall
c. fight
d. cut

162. The <u>taciturn</u> man

a. untalkative
b. angry
c. unkempt
d. tactful

163. To <u>expedite</u> the process

a. slow
b. alter
c. ignore
d. accelerate

164. She <u>recuperated</u> quickly

a. learned
b. recovered
c. sickened
d. ate

165. A unique <u>perspective</u>

a. viewpoint
b. interest
c. occupation
d. action

166. A <u>belligerent</u> man

a. lonely
b. exhausted
c. persistent
d. aggressive

167. An <u>enlightened</u> leader

a. charismatic
b. candid
c. informed
d. ignorant

168. To <u>expend</u> resources

a. supply
b. consume
c. donate
d. keep

169. A <u>replica</u> of the artwork

a. photograph
b. destruction
c. restoration
d. copy

170. A <u>tacit</u> agreement

a. unspoken
b. weak
c. careful
d. strong

171. To <u>ventilate</u> air

a. heat
b. scent
c. circulate
d. cool

172. An <u>indigent</u> person

a. angry
b. poor
c. sad
d. arrogant

173. A <u>lithe</u> ballerina

a. beautiful
b. coordinated
c. flexible
d. amateur

174. To <u>placate</u> a child

a. soothe
b. lecture
c. play with
d. punish

Math Section 8

64 Questions, 45 Minutes

Instructions: Select the best answer.

175. Solve: 512×28

a. 5120
b. 14, 336
c. 5010
d. 15, 236

176. What is the reciprocal of 6?

a. $-\frac{1}{6}$
b. $\frac{1}{6}$
c. -6
d. 36

177. If x = 2, what symbol should go in the circle:

4x - 2 O -6?

a. >
b. <
c. ≤
d. =

178. How many unique prime factors does 45 have?

a. 1
b. 2
c. 3
d. 4

179. 5 is 4 less than the quotient of 36 and what number?

a. -9
b. 31
c. 9
d. 4

180. Convert $\frac{5}{6}$ into a decimal. Round to the hundredths place.

a. .83
b. 1.20
c. .74
d. .91

181. Solve: 71.55 - 43.67

a. 28.65
b. 27.12
c. 28.92
d. 27.88

182. Given the two sets of numbers A = {1, 2, 3, 8} and B = {1, 8, 9}, what is $A \cup B$?

a. {1, 8}
b. {4, 5, 6, 7}
c. {1, 2, 3, 8, 9}
d. {2, 3}

183. What percent of 45 is 27?

a. 50%
b. 55%
c. 60%
d. 65%

184. It costs $54.00 to purchase 9 tickets to the school dance. How much does it cost to purchase 3 tickets?

a. $6
b. $9
c. $18
d. $24

185. What is the place value of the number 7 in the number .76239?

a. tenth
b. hundredth
c. ones
d. tens

186. What is the square root of 121?

a. 11.5
b. 11
c. 10.5
d. 12

187. A cube has side 2x. What is its volume?

a. 8x
b. $2x^3$
c. $4x^2$
d. $8x^3$

188. $\frac{3}{5}$ of 65 is 5 plus what number?

a. 31
b. 34
c. 39
d. 44

189. What is shown below?

a. line segment
b. ray
c. line
d. angle

190. In celebration of Arbor Day, the local elementary school planted 5 trees. The two middle schools planted 3 trees each, and the high school planted 5 trees. What was the average number of trees planted by the schools?

a. 2 trees
b. 3 trees
c. 4 trees
d. 5 trees

191. 8 tablespoons is equal to how many teaspoons?

a. 8 teaspoons
b. 24 teaspoons
c. 16 teaspoons
d. 32 teaspoons

192. What is the sum of $5 \times 10^4 + 3 \times 10^3 + 6 \times 10$?

a. 50,360
b. 53,006
c. 5,306
d. 53,060

193. On her first three poetry projects, Annette scored 82%, 90%, and 78%. What score would she need on her fourth project to raise her average to 85%?

a. 80%
b. 85%
c. 90%
d. 95%

194. When 29 is divided by 5, what is the remainder?

a. 2
b. 3
c. 4
d. 5

195. What is the least common multiple of 14 and 16?

a. 66
b. 126
c. 48
d. 112

196. Maria is laying down new sod in her backyard, which measures 15 ft by 30 feet. Sod comes in strips of 2 feet by 5 feet. How many strips of sod must she purchase?

a. 37.5
b. 40
c. 45
d. 52

197. Angle A measures 130°. What kind of angle is angle A?

a. acute
b. straight
c. obtuse
d. right

198. Solve: 2×-7^2

a. 98
b. -98
c. 49
d. -49

199. An equilateral triangle has a perimeter of 48. What is one side length of the triangle?

a. 12
b. 16
c. 24
d. 8

200. The table below shows which types of books were purchased at a bookstore over the course of three months.

	March	April	May	TOTAL
Fiction	54	42	60	156
Non-Fiction	37	41	39	117
Children's	42	44	45	131
TOTAL	133	127	144	404

Approximately what percent of the total number of children's books were purchased in April? Round to the nearest whole number.

a. 34%
b. 30%
c. 38%
d. 29%

201. Jill's company creates stuffed animal versions of family pets that are a perfect $\frac{1}{8}$ scale of the real animal. If Jill is creating a stuffed animal version of a dog that is 3 feet, 4 inches long from nose to tail, how long will the stuffed animal version be from nose to tail?

a. 4.75 inches
b. 5 inches
c. 5.25 inches
d. 5.5 inches

202. Which figure can have fewer than two sets of parallel lines?

a. parallelogram
b. trapezoid
c. square
d. rectangle

203. Jessa is on a flight from London to Paris. The pilot announced that the flight distance was 350 kilometers. How many miles will the flight travel? Assume 1 km = .62 miles.

a. 200 miles
b. 217 miles
c. 234 miles
d. 251 miles

204. In geometry, a cone has what shape as its base?

a. oval
b. square
c. triangle
d. circle

205. Marcella takes the bus from her house to her sister's house. The bus drives an average of 40 mph for the entire ride. If Marcella leaves her house at 5:30 PM and her sister lives 140 miles away, what time will he reach her sister's house?

a. 8:00 PM
b. 8:30 PM
c. 9:00 PM
d. 9:30 PM

206. In the triangle below, if ∠A is congruent to ∠C, what is the measure of ∠B?

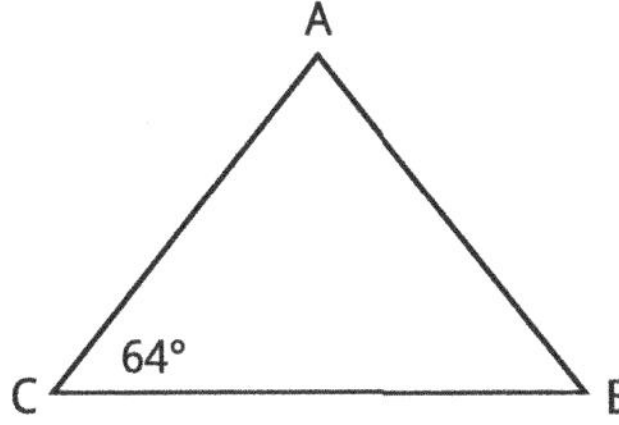

a. 64°
b. 48°
c. 128°
d. 52°

207. Brent and his mom are building a birdhouse. To do so, they have to cut 8 inch strips of wood. If they have 1 yard, 1 foot of wood, how many strips can they cut?

a. 3
b. 6
c. 8
d. 4

208. The square root of 100 multiplied by the square of 10 is what number?

a. 100
b. 1,000
c. 10,000
d. 100,000

209. A city is constructing an asphalt basketball court. The court will measure 94 feet by 50 feet. If asphalt costs $3.00 a square foot, how much will all of the asphalt for the quart cost?

a. $14,100
b. $864
c. $13,800
d. $1,500

210. At the local math and science academy, all students must sign up for one extracurricular activity. They can choose from The Rocketeers or The Mathletes. This year, 72 students, which is 45% of the total student body, chose The Mathletes. How many students attend the academy?

a. 104
b. 128
c. 160
d. 180

211. The sum of the interior angles of a regular pentagon is 540°. What is the measure of one interior angle?

a. 108°
b. 180°
c. 72°
d. 30°

212. An electronics store is selling three new models of televisions. The average daily sales of each model are represented in the chart below.

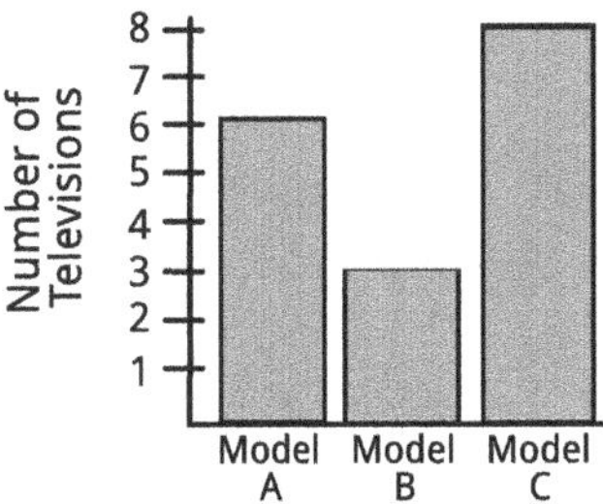

Based on the information in the chart, how many model B televisions will the store sell during a one-week period?

a. 15
b. 3
c. 7
d. 21

213. A 50 ft tall wind turbine casts a 125 ft shadow. How tall would a wind turbine that casts a 180 ft shadow be?

a. 68 ft
b. 72 ft
c. 79 ft
d. 82 ft

214. Solve: $(4 - 9)^2$

a. 65
b. 25
c. -65
d. -25

215. Sarah worked five more than twice as many hours as Nicole did. What is the maximum number of hours Nicole worked if together they worked 50 hours at most?

a. 10 hours
b. 15 hours
c. 20 hours
d. 25 hours

216. RSUT is a rectangle. What is the area of triangle RSU?

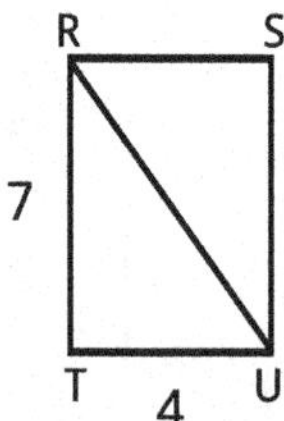

a. 21
b. 28
c. 16
d. 14

217. Solve for b: 4b - 8 = 2b + 12

a. 2
b. 10
c. 4
d. 12

218. Harper's truck car uses 11.4 gallons of gas for a 218 mile trip. To the nearest hundredth, how miles per gallon does Harper's truck use?

a. 18.21
b. 19.73
c. 19.12
d. 18.34

219. Which of the following could be the coordinates of point A?

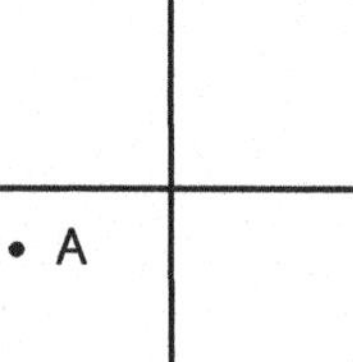

a. (-2, 5)
b. (-5, -2)
c. (-2, -5)
d. (5, -2)

220. How old am I if 10 plus three times my age is 58?

a. 16
b. 12
c. 9
d. 14

221. Eddie's playroom has 3 balls, 4 trucks, 5 dinosaurs, and 3 stuffed animals. If Eddie selected one toy at random, what is the probability that it would be a dinosaur?

a. $\frac{1}{5}$
b. $\frac{5}{14}$
c. $\frac{5}{12}$
d. $\frac{1}{3}$

222. Solve for x: 7x - 11 = 45

a. 8
b. 4
c. 5
d. 9

223. Daniel began babysitting his little sister at 10:45 AM and finished at 6:30 PM. How long did he babysit?

a. 7 hours, 45 minutes
b. 8 hours, 15 minutes
c. 7 hours, 15 minutes
d. 6 hours, 45 minutes

224. What is the area of the shaded region in the square below?

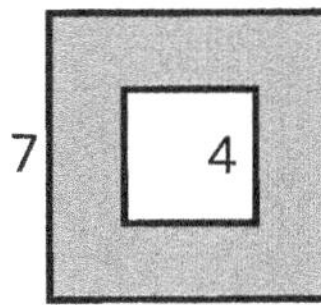

a. 16
b. 33
c. 49
d. 24

225. A clothing store has 24 t-shirts in stock. If the ratio of t-shirts to jeans in the store is 4 : 3, how many jeans does the store have in stock?

a. 24
b. 22
c. 18
d. 16

226. Which of the following choices will satisfy the inequality: -2.1 < x < .4?

a. 3.4
b. .5
c. -.4
d. -2.1

227. A mattress store sells three sizes of mattress: twin, queen, and king. The pie chart below outlines the percentage of each type of mattress the store sold last year. If the store sold 40 twin mattresses last year, how many mattresses did they sell total?

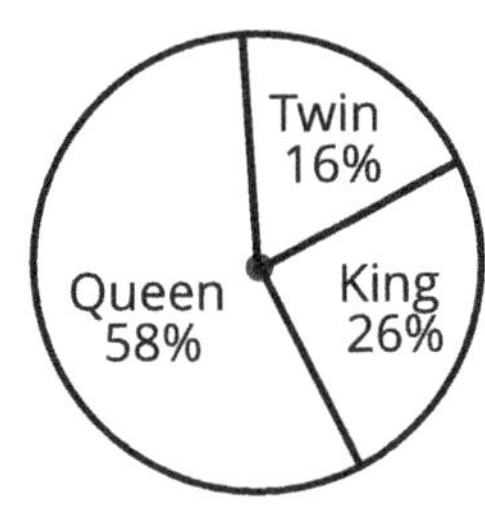

a. 280
b. 300
c. 230
d. 250

228. Toby poured 2.5 quarts of milk into a 1 gallon milk jug. In pints, how much room was left in the milk jug?

a. 3 pints
b. 8 pints
c. 6 pints
d. 2 pints

229. What is the perimeter of the figure below?

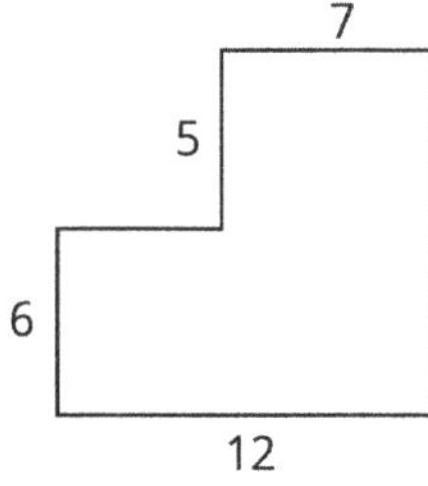

a. 107
b. 51
c. 123
d. 46

230. What is the value of x in this equation:

$4x - 3 = 17$

a. 1
b. 5
c. 3
d. 4

231. Alex purchased a car with a loan that had a 4% interest rate. In the end, he paid $560 in interest payments. What was the original cost of the car?

a. $13,000
b. $13,500
c. $14,000
d. $14,500

232. Three students in a class score 79%, 71%, and 98% on a test, respectively. What would a fourth student need to score for the students' average to be 83%?

a. 78%
b. 91%
c. 87%
d. 84%

233. Over the past few weeks, Malcolm has saved \$47.41 of his paycheck. This week, he saved an additional \$18.50. If Malcolm uses his savings to purchase a backpack that costs \$39.70, how much money will he have left?

a. \$26.21
b. \$25.79
c. \$27.19
d. \$65.91

234. Simplify: $\sqrt{84x^3y^2}$

a. $6x\sqrt{7xy}$
b. $2xy\sqrt{21x}$
c. $2\sqrt{21x^3y^2}$
d. $2xy\sqrt{21}$

235. A circle has an area of 121π. What is its diameter?

a. 22
b. 11
c. 121
d. 61

236. A 12 ounce bottle of hand soap costs \$2.60. How much should a 42 ounce bottle of the same hand soap cost?

a. \$10.40
b. \$9.80
c. \$9.10
d. \$8.60

237. What is the measure of x?

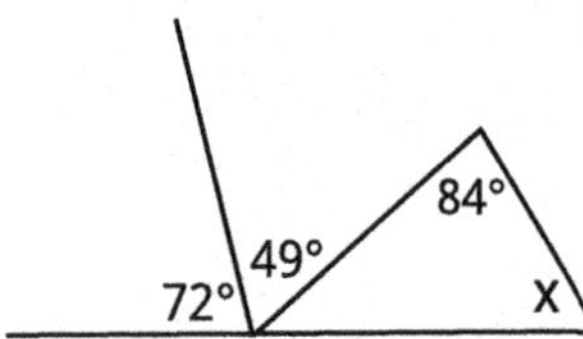

a. 49°
b. 59°
c. 43°
d. 37°

238. Kevin takes a taxi to the airport. The taxi fare cost \$18 and he gave the driver a 20% tip. How much did he spend on his entire taxi ride, including tip?

a. \$21.60
b. \$15.40
c. \$23.40
d. \$25.20

Language Section 8

60 Questions, 25 Minutes

Usage and Mechanics

Instructions: For questions 239-278, check the sentences for errors of usage, capitalization, or punctuation. If there is no error, choose D.

239.

a. Jeanne and Grace rented a canoe and paddled to the south side of the lake.

b. My neighbor, whose always been interested in politics, is running for a seat on city council.

c. My brother begged, "Can you please come with me to buy a suit for Cal's wedding?"

d. No mistakes.

240.

a. I love going to musicals but think that they are too expensive to see more than a few times a year.

b. Before school starts, I need to buy new clothes, get a haircut, and finish my summer reading.

c. Its difficult to get selected for the summer internship, but I decided to apply anyway.

d. No mistakes.

241.

a. My desk was covered in stacks of papers completely.

b. The largest of the three cities was also the farthest away.

c. Each member of the orchestra has to get his or her permission slip signed to go on the field trip.

d. No mistakes.

242.

a. Madeline has never been to a European Country, so she was excited to go to Spain next September.

b. "This is a challenging class so be prepared to work hard and ask for help if you need it," my teacher explained.

c. The city council decided to put a stop sign at the intersection of Main Street and Fifth Avenue.

d. No mistakes.

243.

a. A record number of people attended the summer festival.

b. The library had less books on World War II than I expected.

c. Although I disagreed with him, Will had a valid and interesting argument.

d. No mistakes.

244.

a. Due to the expected school closures, classes at my school will likely be more crowded.

b. The dog was lost after it was found walking without a leash.

c. Please talk among yourselves while I see to the door.

d. No mistakes.

245.

a. The baseball game was interrupted when a cat ran onto the field.

b. Items needed to bake cookies include flour, butter, eggs, and sugar; optional ingredients include chocolate, nuts, and other candies.

c. My sister's excuse for ruining my sweater is unacceptable, I can't believe it.

d. No mistakes.

246.

a. We lost the game but still won the tournament.

b. "How long until Christmas?" the excited child asked.

c. The last day of school is the day after Memorial day.

d. No mistakes.

247.

a. We still had snow on Monday April 16.
b. Zach is having a Lego themed birthday party.
c. Cici's grandmother dropped us off at the game.
d. No mistakes.

248.

a. My flight was delayed out of O'Hare international airport.
b. The sixth graders enjoy reading to the kindergarten class.
c. Daniel's favorite place to vacation is Italy.
d. No mistakes.

249.

a. When the weather warmed up, we put up the screens on our windows.
b. Los Angeles is the more populated city in California.
c. The window on the front of the house was broken.
d. No mistakes.

250.

a. The gift a doll bed was wrapped in floral paper.
b. Could you ask Gertie to step into my office?
c. At the amusement park, we lost track of time.
d. No mistakes.

251.

a. It's always difficult to get toddlers to eat their vegetables.
b. April is the rainiest month.
c. The local newspaper sent a prize to my friend and I.
d. No mistakes.

252.

a. I'm finally able to play tennis despite my knee injury.
b. I fell and stub my toe.
c. "When does the game start?" Arumi inquired.
d. No mistakes.

253.

a. My new friends and I are going out for pizza after school.
b. The mall is my least favorite place to shop.
c. My friends has a new puppy named Willie.
d. No mistakes.

254.

a. We were locked out of the house so we waited on the front porch.
b. We looked for the small, black dog.
c. I've told Amir that if he doesn't come in for help he will fail the class.
d. No mistakes.

255.

a. Marianna hurt her back she went to the doctor.
b. Teachers in Arizona are about to strike for better pay and retirement benefits.
c. At camp, the mosquitos are the size of small birds!
d. No mistakes.

256.

a. It's almost time for the party to start.
b. "Where do you think you're going?" the mother asked her child.
c. The effects of a good night sleep are innumerable.
d. No mistakes.

257.

a. I prefer the original film of The Great Gatsby to the newer version.
b. The bird flew swiftly overhead.
c. Please hand me the remote so that I can turn the game off.
d. No mistakes.

258.

a. The event is scheduled to start at 10 a.m. sharp.

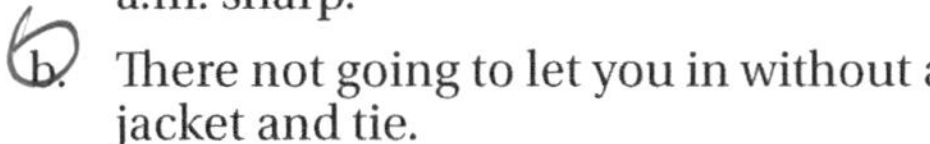

b. There not going to let you in without a jacket and tie.

c. I still need to raise over one hundred dollars for the walk-a-thon.

d. No mistakes.

259.

a. That's the largest cake I've ever seen!

b. Robbie's parents gave him a tie for his first job interview.

c. The childrens' clothing store is having a sale next weekend.

d. No mistakes.

260.

a. Carter and Tyler went scuba diving at the Great Barrier Reef.

b. Although it's unusual, hurricanes do sometimes occur as early as May.

c. I'm not sure whether I should accept the new position.

d. No mistakes.

261.

a. The student accidentally grabbed their classmate's notebook.

b. My uncle Michael travels throughout the United States, Canada, and Europe for his job.

c. Juliette graduated from college on May 19, 2004.

d. No mistakes.

262.

a. My dad can fall asleep anywhere; he fell asleep at the dinner table last night!

b. Talia and Alphonse are taking a coding class at the local community college.

c. Hiding in the corner of his crate, the veterinarian gently lifted the puppy onto the examination table.

d. No mistakes.

263.

a. "Its not my fault!" my little cousin exclaimed.

b. I love eating ice cream on a hot summer day.

c. As a surprise for her tenth birthday, Lia's dad built her a treehouse.

d. No mistakes.

264.

a. "Let's buy Tara's birthday present today," Hasan suggested.

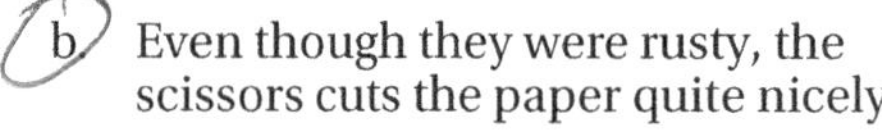

b. Even though they were rusty, the scissors cuts the paper quite nicely.

c. My school's marching band was chosen to play in our town's yearly parade.

d. No mistakes.

265.

a. Luca speaks five different languages: English, French, Spanish, Italian, and Mandarin.

b. "Run faster!" my coach yelled.

c. It's always been Ellie's dream to visit Vietnam one day.

d. No mistakes.

266.

a. Spot, the slowest of my two dogs, lagged behind as we walked to the park.

b. I missed fewer days of school than anyone else in my class.

c. My sister or her friends walk me home from school each day.

d. No mistakes.

267.

a. Every spring me and my mom go to the local forest preserve to look at the wildflowers.

b. My chemistry teacher accidentally set off the fire alarm during our class experiment.

c. There are a number of reasons that I decided not to play volleyball next fall.

d. No mistakes.

268.

a. January is my least favorite month of the year.

b. Can you believe that my English teacher gave me a C on my paper?

c. Kara volunteers' at the animal shelter every other Saturday.

d. No mistakes.

269.

a. Last winter, my grandmother taught me how to knit a scarf.

b. After I get back from my vacation I'm going to get all my photos printed; so I can show my friends what I did.

c. "I think I need to lie down," I sighed.

d. No mistakes.

270.

a. We have a swimming pool in my neighborhood, but I never have time to go swimming.

b. Traffic was really congested so we took side streets instead of the tollway.

c. It's faster to walk home than it is to take the bus.

d. No mistakes.

271.

a. I played basketball with Matt, Simone, and Joaquin.

b. Maya carefully moved the glass figurines from the shelf to the box.

c. "Can you do dishes after dinner"? my mom asked.

d. No mistakes.

272.

a. Melanie had a larger amount of dolls than her sister.

b. Even though it left on time, the train arrived at the station 14 minutes late.

c. Charlie and Annie went ice skating at the outdoor rink.

d. No mistakes.

273.

a. The race car swerved on the road and overtook its nearest opponent.

b. I'd love to visit Antarctica one day, but it's to difficult to get there.

c. Saad and his brother went to the candy store to buy some chocolate for their mother.

d. No mistakes.

274.

a. Even though his team lost, Ethan had a great time playing in the championship game.

b. "After I go home, I'm going to take a nap," Keira announced.

c. The classroom in the old, rundown building is going to be renovated in the winter.

d. No mistakes.

275.

a. Every student in the class is going to have their picture taken on Thursday.

b. I hope to one day become a vegetarian, so I'm slowly reducing the amount of meat I eat.

c. Neither Tom nor Edward wants to clean the garage this weekend.

d. No mistakes.

276.

a. Have you been to the new Mexican restaurant?

b. Javaris has the highest grade in our chemistry class and often helps other students study.

c. Our neighbors are excited when we talked to them about the volunteering opportunity.

d. No mistakes.

277.

a. Our principal has made some great improvements to our school.

b. Before heading to the beach, Risha bought all the essential items: a towel, a swimsuit, and a hat.

c. I was happy, and proud when my sister got into medical school.

d. No mistakes.

278.

a. My grandmother was a seamstress and made me a lot of dresses when I was young.

b. I told Kevin, "You should try out for the soccer team"

c. If you want to get a puppy, you must have the time to take care of it.

d. No mistakes.

Spelling

Directions: For questions 279-288, look for errors in spelling. If there is no error, choose D.

279.

a. The university admissions process can be quite stressful.

b. Martin was hopping that he would feel well enough to go to school tomorrow.

c. I took a self-defense class several weeks ago at the local community college.

d. No mistakes.

280.

a. The interior of the house was covered in cobwebs after years of neglect.

b. I can try to describe what it's like to go skydiving, but you really have to experience it for yourself.

c. My favorite part of history class was learning about the American goverment.

d. No mistakes.

281.

a. Initially, I thought I wanted to be a scientist, but I eventually decided I'd rather be an archeologist.

b. Verne walked solemnly to the cafeteria for detention.

c. After she won the competition, Terra's painting was displayed in the prestigious gallery.

d. No mistakes.

282.

a. It's incredible that it occasionally gets cold enough in Florida to snow!

b. Although my poodle is sweet, she isn't a very good gaurd dog.

c. Tourism is a huge industry in many Caribbean islands.

d. No mistakes.

283.

a. Winning my first marathon was an exhilarating experience!

b. The picture's dimensions were so unusual that I had to custom order a frame.

c. My grandma and grandpa were married fourty years ago today.

d. No mistakes.

284.

a. The view from the top of the mountain was breathtaking.

b. Kelsey and I had fascinating discussions about astronomy.

c. I was really embarrased that I forgot my professor's name when I ran into him outside of class.

d. No mistakes.

285.

a. The coldest day ever recorded was -135.8 degrees farenheit.

b. The deserted auditorium felt strange and surreal.

c. My economics teacher has taught at the high school for fewer than five years.

d. No mistakes.

286.

a. I borrowed a shirt from my sister and accidentally tore a hole in its sleeve.

b. The new teacher thought his jokes were really humourous.

c. Aubrey had always wondered what it would be like to be a politician.

d. No mistakes.

287.

a. Unfortunately, I forgot about my language arts test and didn't study.
b. Knowlege is just as important as wisdom.
c. The students complained that recess was too short considering how long they were in school each day.
d. No mistakes.

288.

a. The magician made the rabbit dissapear into the hat.
b. The graduation ceremony took place on a cold and blustery day.
c. Harper's gymnastics team is having a fundraiser next week.
d. No mistakes.

Composition

Directions: For questions 289-298, read the question and select the best answer.

289. Choose the best word to join the thoughts together.

Last year I wanted to take horseback riding lessons, __________ my mom wouldn't let me.

a. so
b. thus
c. in fact
d. None of these

290. Choose the best word to join the thoughts together.

The school's roof was leaking; __________ school was canceled for the day.

a. while,
b. consequently,
c. for example,
d. nevertheless,

291. Choose the group of words that best completes the sentence.

In the middle of hockey practice, Brayden __________.

a. slipping and falling on the ice.
b. slipped and falling on the ice.
c. was slipping on the ice and falling.
d. slipped and fell on the ice.

292. Which of these expresses the idea most clearly?

a. My sister and I took a special trip downtown for my birthday, drinking hot chocolate, going shopping, and having dinner.
b. For my birthday, my sister and I took a special trip downtown to drink hot chocolate, go shopping, and have dinner.
c. For my birthday, my sister and me took a special trip downtown - we were drinking hot chocolate, going to go shopping, and having dinner.
d. On our special downtown trip, my sister and I drank hot chocolate, were going shopping, and ate dinner for my birthday.

293. Which of these expresses the idea most clearly?

a. When Addison lost her dog, we put up posters, called the pound, searched the neighborhood, and we found her.
b. Putting up posters, calling the pound, and searching the neighborhood were the things we did to find Addison's dog who was lost.
c. We found Addison's lost dog by putting up posters, calling the pound, and searching the neighborhood.
d. Losing her dog, we helped Allison find him by putting up posters, calling the pound, and searching the neighborhood.

294. Which of the following topics is best for a one page essay?

   a. Conflicting Theories of Child Development
   b. Child Development: From Birth to Adolescence
   c. Child Rearing in Twentieth Century America
   d. None of the above

295. Which of these sentences fits best under the topic "The Founding of America"?

   a. George Washington, Thomas Jefferson, and Alexander Hamilton were instrumental in setting up the American system of government.
   b. The American Civil War was fought between the north and south.
   c. At one time, Britain had colonies in places such as America, India, and South Africa.
   d. The America of today is very different than it was 200 years ago.

296. Which of the following sentences offers the *least* support to the topic "The Positive Impact of Preschool."

   a. Studies have shown that students who attend preschool achieve higher standardized test scores in elementary and middle school.
   b. Preschool has an especially positive effect on low-income students.
   c. Some preschools are better than others.
   d. Some studies have indicated that students who attend preschool have higher incomes as adults.

297. Where should the sentence "This is especially important for people who cannot afford to purchase these items on their own" be placed in the paragraph below?

   Some may claim that libraries are less relevant today than in the past, but I would argue that they still fulfill an important role in our communities. (2) Libraries give every citizen free access to an incredible number of books, newspapers, and magazines. (3) In addition, technology such as ebooks, the internet, and even 3D printers are available for use. (4) Many libraries host classes, storytimes, and presentations that bring the community together.

   a. Before sentence 1
   b. After sentence 1
   c. Before sentence 3
   d. After sentence 4

298. Which sentence does NOT belong in the paragraph?

   The ice cream shop had been open for over a decade. (2) It was a beautiful day outside, so Noah and Mia decided to walk to the ice cream shop. (3) They each purchased a cone with two scoops of ice cream. (4) They ate their ice cream cones outside on a park bench.

   a. 1
   b. 2
   c. 3
   d. 4

Answer Key

Verbal

1. D
2. B
3. C
4. D
5. A
6. A
7. B
8. C
9. A
10. B
11. C
12. D
13. C
14. B
15. B
16. B
17. A
18. B
19. C
20. B
21. C
22. B
23. C
24. B
25. C
26. B
27. B
28. A
29. D
30. D
31. A
32. C
33. B
34. D
35. C
36. B
37. A
38. A
39. A
40. B
41. C
42. D
43. C
44. B
45. B
46. D
47. D
48. A
49. A
50. B
51. B
52. D
53. A
54. C
55. C
56. B
57. A
58. B
59. C
60. D
61.

Quantitative

61. B
62. C
63. A
64. B
65. C
66. A
67. B
68. A
69. C
70. D
71. B
72. C
73. D
74. D
75. D
76. D
77. B
78. D
79. C
80. B
81. B
82. A
83. A
84. D
85. B
86. A
87. C
88. D
89. B
90. A
91. C
92. A
93. C
94. D
95. C
96. A
97. B
98. A
99. D
100. C
101. D
102. C
103. B
104. D
105. A
106. C
107. A
108. B
109. B
110. D
111. B
112. C

Reading

113. B
114. A
115. C
116. D
117. C
118. C
119. A
120. C
121. D
122. B
123. C
124. B
125. D
126. A
127. C
128. A
129. C
130. A
131. D
132. D
133. D
134. B
135. A
136. C
137. C
138. D
139. B
140. D
141. C
142. A
143. C
144. A
145. D
146. C
147. C
148. B
149. A
150. B
151. B
152. A
153. B
154. D
155. C
156. B
157. A
158. C
159. D
160. B
161. C
162. A
163. D
164. B
165. A
166. D
167. C
168. B
169. D
170. A
171. C
172. B
173. C
174. A

Math

175. B
176. B
177. A
178. B
179. D
180. A
181. D
182. C
183. C
184. C
185. A
186. B
187. D
188. B
189. A
190. C
191. B
192. D
193. C
194. C
195. D
196. C
197. C
198. A
199. B
200. A
201. B
202. B
203. B
204. D
205. C
206. D
207. B
208. B
209. A
210. C
211. A
212. D
213. B
214. B
215. B
216. D
217. B
218. C
219. B
220. A
221. D
222. A
223. A
224. B
225. C
226. C
227. D
228. A
229. D
230. B
231. C
232. D
233. A
234. B
235. A
236. C
237. D
238. A

Language

239. B
240. C
241. A
242. A
243. B
244. B
245. c
246. c
247. a
248. a
249. B
250. A
251. C
252. B
253. C
254. A
255. A
256. D
257. A
258. B
259. C
260. D
261. A
262. C
263. A
264. B
265. D
266. A
267. A
268. C
269. B
270. D
271. C
272. A
273. B
274. D
275. A
276. C
277. C
278. B
279. B
280. C
281. D
282. B
283. C
284. C
285. A
286. B
287. B
288. A
289. D
290. B
291. D
292. B
293. C
294. D
295. A
296. C
297. C
298. A

Blank Answer Sheets

Test 1 Answer Sheet

Verbal

1. Ⓐ Ⓑ Ⓒ Ⓓ
2. Ⓐ Ⓑ Ⓒ Ⓓ
3. Ⓐ Ⓑ Ⓒ Ⓓ
4. Ⓐ Ⓑ Ⓒ Ⓓ
5. Ⓐ Ⓑ Ⓒ Ⓓ
6. Ⓐ Ⓑ Ⓒ Ⓓ
7. Ⓐ Ⓑ Ⓒ Ⓓ
8. Ⓐ Ⓑ Ⓒ Ⓓ
9. Ⓐ Ⓑ Ⓒ Ⓓ
10. Ⓐ Ⓑ Ⓒ Ⓓ
11. Ⓐ Ⓑ Ⓒ Ⓓ
12. Ⓐ Ⓑ Ⓒ Ⓓ
13. Ⓐ Ⓑ Ⓒ Ⓓ
14. Ⓐ Ⓑ Ⓒ Ⓓ
15. Ⓐ Ⓑ Ⓒ Ⓓ
16. Ⓐ Ⓑ Ⓒ Ⓓ
17. Ⓐ Ⓑ Ⓒ Ⓓ
18. Ⓐ Ⓑ Ⓒ Ⓓ
19. Ⓐ Ⓑ Ⓒ Ⓓ
20. Ⓐ Ⓑ Ⓒ Ⓓ
21. Ⓐ Ⓑ Ⓒ Ⓓ
22. Ⓐ Ⓑ Ⓒ Ⓓ
23. Ⓐ Ⓑ Ⓒ Ⓓ
24. Ⓐ Ⓑ Ⓒ Ⓓ
25. Ⓐ Ⓑ Ⓒ Ⓓ
26. Ⓐ Ⓑ Ⓒ Ⓓ
27. Ⓐ Ⓑ Ⓒ Ⓓ
28. Ⓐ Ⓑ Ⓒ Ⓓ
29. Ⓐ Ⓑ Ⓒ Ⓓ
30. Ⓐ Ⓑ Ⓒ Ⓓ
31. Ⓐ Ⓑ Ⓒ Ⓓ
32. Ⓐ Ⓑ Ⓒ Ⓓ
33. Ⓐ Ⓑ Ⓒ Ⓓ
34. Ⓐ Ⓑ Ⓒ Ⓓ
35. Ⓐ Ⓑ Ⓒ Ⓓ
36. Ⓐ Ⓑ Ⓒ Ⓓ
37. Ⓐ Ⓑ Ⓒ Ⓓ
38. Ⓐ Ⓑ Ⓒ Ⓓ
39. Ⓐ Ⓑ Ⓒ Ⓓ
40. Ⓐ Ⓑ Ⓒ Ⓓ
41. Ⓐ Ⓑ Ⓒ Ⓓ
42. Ⓐ Ⓑ Ⓒ Ⓓ
43. Ⓐ Ⓑ Ⓒ Ⓓ
44. Ⓐ Ⓑ Ⓒ Ⓓ
45. Ⓐ Ⓑ Ⓒ Ⓓ
46. Ⓐ Ⓑ Ⓒ Ⓓ
47. Ⓐ Ⓑ Ⓒ Ⓓ
48. Ⓐ Ⓑ Ⓒ Ⓓ
49. Ⓐ Ⓑ Ⓒ Ⓓ
50. Ⓐ Ⓑ Ⓒ Ⓓ
51. Ⓐ Ⓑ Ⓒ Ⓓ
52. Ⓐ Ⓑ Ⓒ Ⓓ
53. Ⓐ Ⓑ Ⓒ Ⓓ
54. Ⓐ Ⓑ Ⓒ Ⓓ
55. Ⓐ Ⓑ Ⓒ Ⓓ
56. Ⓐ Ⓑ Ⓒ Ⓓ
57. Ⓐ Ⓑ Ⓒ Ⓓ
58. Ⓐ Ⓑ Ⓒ Ⓓ
59. Ⓐ Ⓑ Ⓒ Ⓓ
60. Ⓐ Ⓑ Ⓒ Ⓓ

Quantitative

61. Ⓐ Ⓑ Ⓒ Ⓓ
62. Ⓐ Ⓑ Ⓒ Ⓓ
63. Ⓐ Ⓑ Ⓒ Ⓓ
64. Ⓐ Ⓑ Ⓒ Ⓓ
65. Ⓐ Ⓑ Ⓒ Ⓓ
66. Ⓐ Ⓑ Ⓒ Ⓓ
67. Ⓐ Ⓑ Ⓒ Ⓓ
68. Ⓐ Ⓑ Ⓒ Ⓓ
69. Ⓐ Ⓑ Ⓒ Ⓓ
70. Ⓐ Ⓑ Ⓒ Ⓓ
71. Ⓐ Ⓑ Ⓒ Ⓓ
72. Ⓐ Ⓑ Ⓒ Ⓓ
73. Ⓐ Ⓑ Ⓒ Ⓓ
74. Ⓐ Ⓑ Ⓒ Ⓓ
75. Ⓐ Ⓑ Ⓒ Ⓓ
76. Ⓐ Ⓑ Ⓒ Ⓓ
77. Ⓐ Ⓑ Ⓒ Ⓓ
78. Ⓐ Ⓑ Ⓒ Ⓓ
79. Ⓐ Ⓑ Ⓒ Ⓓ
80. Ⓐ Ⓑ Ⓒ Ⓓ
81. Ⓐ Ⓑ Ⓒ Ⓓ
82. Ⓐ Ⓑ Ⓒ Ⓓ
83. Ⓐ Ⓑ Ⓒ Ⓓ
84. Ⓐ Ⓑ Ⓒ Ⓓ
85. Ⓐ Ⓑ Ⓒ Ⓓ
86. Ⓐ Ⓑ Ⓒ Ⓓ
87. Ⓐ Ⓑ Ⓒ Ⓓ
88. Ⓐ Ⓑ Ⓒ Ⓓ
89. Ⓐ Ⓑ Ⓒ Ⓓ
90. Ⓐ Ⓑ Ⓒ Ⓓ
91. Ⓐ Ⓑ Ⓒ Ⓓ
92. Ⓐ Ⓑ Ⓒ Ⓓ
93. Ⓐ Ⓑ Ⓒ Ⓓ
94. Ⓐ Ⓑ Ⓒ Ⓓ
95. Ⓐ Ⓑ Ⓒ Ⓓ
96. Ⓐ Ⓑ Ⓒ Ⓓ
97. Ⓐ Ⓑ Ⓒ Ⓓ
98. Ⓐ Ⓑ Ⓒ Ⓓ
99. Ⓐ Ⓑ Ⓒ Ⓓ
100. Ⓐ Ⓑ Ⓒ Ⓓ
101. Ⓐ Ⓑ Ⓒ Ⓓ
102. Ⓐ Ⓑ Ⓒ Ⓓ
103. Ⓐ Ⓑ Ⓒ Ⓓ
104. Ⓐ Ⓑ Ⓒ Ⓓ
105. Ⓐ Ⓑ Ⓒ Ⓓ
106. Ⓐ Ⓑ Ⓒ Ⓓ
107. Ⓐ Ⓑ Ⓒ Ⓓ
108. Ⓐ Ⓑ Ⓒ Ⓓ
109. Ⓐ Ⓑ Ⓒ Ⓓ
110. Ⓐ Ⓑ Ⓒ Ⓓ
111. Ⓐ Ⓑ Ⓒ Ⓓ
112. Ⓐ Ⓑ Ⓒ Ⓓ

Reading

113. Ⓐ Ⓑ Ⓒ Ⓓ
114. Ⓐ Ⓑ Ⓒ Ⓓ
115. Ⓐ Ⓑ Ⓒ Ⓓ
116. Ⓐ Ⓑ Ⓒ Ⓓ
117. Ⓐ Ⓑ Ⓒ Ⓓ
118. Ⓐ Ⓑ Ⓒ Ⓓ
119. Ⓐ Ⓑ Ⓒ Ⓓ
120. Ⓐ Ⓑ Ⓒ Ⓓ
121. Ⓐ Ⓑ Ⓒ Ⓓ
122. Ⓐ Ⓑ Ⓒ Ⓓ
123. Ⓐ Ⓑ Ⓒ Ⓓ
124. Ⓐ Ⓑ Ⓒ Ⓓ
125. Ⓐ Ⓑ Ⓒ Ⓓ
126. Ⓐ Ⓑ Ⓒ Ⓓ
127. Ⓐ Ⓑ Ⓒ Ⓓ
128. Ⓐ Ⓑ Ⓒ Ⓓ
129. Ⓐ Ⓑ Ⓒ Ⓓ
130. Ⓐ Ⓑ Ⓒ Ⓓ
131. Ⓐ Ⓑ Ⓒ Ⓓ
132. Ⓐ Ⓑ Ⓒ Ⓓ
133. Ⓐ Ⓑ Ⓒ Ⓓ
134. Ⓐ Ⓑ Ⓒ Ⓓ
135. Ⓐ Ⓑ Ⓒ Ⓓ
136. Ⓐ Ⓑ Ⓒ Ⓓ
137. Ⓐ Ⓑ Ⓒ Ⓓ
138. Ⓐ Ⓑ Ⓒ Ⓓ
139. Ⓐ Ⓑ Ⓒ Ⓓ
140. Ⓐ Ⓑ Ⓒ Ⓓ
141. Ⓐ Ⓑ Ⓒ Ⓓ
142. Ⓐ Ⓑ Ⓒ Ⓓ
143. Ⓐ Ⓑ Ⓒ Ⓓ
144. Ⓐ Ⓑ Ⓒ Ⓓ
145. Ⓐ Ⓑ Ⓒ Ⓓ
146. Ⓐ Ⓑ Ⓒ Ⓓ
147. Ⓐ Ⓑ Ⓒ Ⓓ
148. Ⓐ Ⓑ Ⓒ Ⓓ
149. Ⓐ Ⓑ Ⓒ Ⓓ
150. Ⓐ Ⓑ Ⓒ Ⓓ
151. Ⓐ Ⓑ Ⓒ Ⓓ
152. Ⓐ Ⓑ Ⓒ Ⓓ
153. Ⓐ Ⓑ Ⓒ Ⓓ
154. Ⓐ Ⓑ Ⓒ Ⓓ
155. Ⓐ Ⓑ Ⓒ Ⓓ
156. Ⓐ Ⓑ Ⓒ Ⓓ
157. Ⓐ Ⓑ Ⓒ Ⓓ
158. Ⓐ Ⓑ Ⓒ Ⓓ
159. Ⓐ Ⓑ Ⓒ Ⓓ
160. Ⓐ Ⓑ Ⓒ Ⓓ
161. Ⓐ Ⓑ Ⓒ Ⓓ
162. Ⓐ Ⓑ Ⓒ Ⓓ
163. Ⓐ Ⓑ Ⓒ Ⓓ
164. Ⓐ Ⓑ Ⓒ Ⓓ
165. Ⓐ Ⓑ Ⓒ Ⓓ
166. Ⓐ Ⓑ Ⓒ Ⓓ
167. Ⓐ Ⓑ Ⓒ Ⓓ
168. Ⓐ Ⓑ Ⓒ Ⓓ
169. Ⓐ Ⓑ Ⓒ Ⓓ
170. Ⓐ Ⓑ Ⓒ Ⓓ
171. Ⓐ Ⓑ Ⓒ Ⓓ
172. Ⓐ Ⓑ Ⓒ Ⓓ
173. Ⓐ Ⓑ Ⓒ Ⓓ
174. Ⓐ Ⓑ Ⓒ Ⓓ

Math

175. Ⓐ Ⓑ Ⓒ Ⓓ
176. Ⓐ Ⓑ Ⓒ Ⓓ
177. Ⓐ Ⓑ Ⓒ Ⓓ
178. Ⓐ Ⓑ Ⓒ Ⓓ
179. Ⓐ Ⓑ Ⓒ Ⓓ
180. Ⓐ Ⓑ Ⓒ Ⓓ
181. Ⓐ Ⓑ Ⓒ Ⓓ
182. Ⓐ Ⓑ Ⓒ Ⓓ
183. Ⓐ Ⓑ Ⓒ Ⓓ
184. Ⓐ Ⓑ Ⓒ Ⓓ
185. Ⓐ Ⓑ Ⓒ Ⓓ
186. Ⓐ Ⓑ Ⓒ Ⓓ
187. Ⓐ Ⓑ Ⓒ Ⓓ
188. Ⓐ Ⓑ Ⓒ Ⓓ
189. Ⓐ Ⓑ Ⓒ Ⓓ
190. Ⓐ Ⓑ Ⓒ Ⓓ
191. Ⓐ Ⓑ Ⓒ Ⓓ
192. Ⓐ Ⓑ Ⓒ Ⓓ
193. Ⓐ Ⓑ Ⓒ Ⓓ
194. Ⓐ Ⓑ Ⓒ Ⓓ
195. Ⓐ Ⓑ Ⓒ Ⓓ
196. Ⓐ Ⓑ Ⓒ Ⓓ
197. Ⓐ Ⓑ Ⓒ Ⓓ
198. Ⓐ Ⓑ Ⓒ Ⓓ
199. Ⓐ Ⓑ Ⓒ Ⓓ
200. Ⓐ Ⓑ Ⓒ Ⓓ
201. Ⓐ Ⓑ Ⓒ Ⓓ
202. Ⓐ Ⓑ Ⓒ Ⓓ
203. Ⓐ Ⓑ Ⓒ Ⓓ
204. Ⓐ Ⓑ Ⓒ Ⓓ
205. Ⓐ Ⓑ Ⓒ Ⓓ
206. Ⓐ Ⓑ Ⓒ Ⓓ
207. Ⓐ Ⓑ Ⓒ Ⓓ
208. Ⓐ Ⓑ Ⓒ Ⓓ
209. Ⓐ Ⓑ Ⓒ Ⓓ
210. Ⓐ Ⓑ Ⓒ Ⓓ
211. Ⓐ Ⓑ Ⓒ Ⓓ
212. Ⓐ Ⓑ Ⓒ Ⓓ
213. Ⓐ Ⓑ Ⓒ Ⓓ
214. Ⓐ Ⓑ Ⓒ Ⓓ
215. Ⓐ Ⓑ Ⓒ Ⓓ
216. Ⓐ Ⓑ Ⓒ Ⓓ
217. Ⓐ Ⓑ Ⓒ Ⓓ
218. Ⓐ Ⓑ Ⓒ Ⓓ
219. Ⓐ Ⓑ Ⓒ Ⓓ
220. Ⓐ Ⓑ Ⓒ Ⓓ
221. Ⓐ Ⓑ Ⓒ Ⓓ
222. Ⓐ Ⓑ Ⓒ Ⓓ
223. Ⓐ Ⓑ Ⓒ Ⓓ
224. Ⓐ Ⓑ Ⓒ Ⓓ
225. Ⓐ Ⓑ Ⓒ Ⓓ
226. Ⓐ Ⓑ Ⓒ Ⓓ
227. Ⓐ Ⓑ Ⓒ Ⓓ
228. Ⓐ Ⓑ Ⓒ Ⓓ
229. Ⓐ Ⓑ Ⓒ Ⓓ
230. Ⓐ Ⓑ Ⓒ Ⓓ
231. Ⓐ Ⓑ Ⓒ Ⓓ
232. Ⓐ Ⓑ Ⓒ Ⓓ
233. Ⓐ Ⓑ Ⓒ Ⓓ
234. Ⓐ Ⓑ Ⓒ Ⓓ
235. Ⓐ Ⓑ Ⓒ Ⓓ
236. Ⓐ Ⓑ Ⓒ Ⓓ
237. Ⓐ Ⓑ Ⓒ Ⓓ
238. Ⓐ Ⓑ Ⓒ Ⓓ

Language

239. Ⓐ Ⓑ Ⓒ Ⓓ
240. Ⓐ Ⓑ Ⓒ Ⓓ
241. Ⓐ Ⓑ Ⓒ Ⓓ
242. Ⓐ Ⓑ Ⓒ Ⓓ
243. Ⓐ Ⓑ Ⓒ Ⓓ
244. Ⓐ Ⓑ Ⓒ Ⓓ
245. Ⓐ Ⓑ Ⓒ Ⓓ
246. Ⓐ Ⓑ Ⓒ Ⓓ
247. Ⓐ Ⓑ Ⓒ Ⓓ
248. Ⓐ Ⓑ Ⓒ Ⓓ
249. Ⓐ Ⓑ Ⓒ Ⓓ
250. Ⓐ Ⓑ Ⓒ Ⓓ
251. Ⓐ Ⓑ Ⓒ Ⓓ
252. Ⓐ Ⓑ Ⓒ Ⓓ
253. Ⓐ Ⓑ Ⓒ Ⓓ
254. Ⓐ Ⓑ Ⓒ Ⓓ
255. Ⓐ Ⓑ Ⓒ Ⓓ
256. Ⓐ Ⓑ Ⓒ Ⓓ
257. Ⓐ Ⓑ Ⓒ Ⓓ
258. Ⓐ Ⓑ Ⓒ Ⓓ
259. Ⓐ Ⓑ Ⓒ Ⓓ
260. Ⓐ Ⓑ Ⓒ Ⓓ
261. Ⓐ Ⓑ Ⓒ Ⓓ
262. Ⓐ Ⓑ Ⓒ Ⓓ
263. Ⓐ Ⓑ Ⓒ Ⓓ
264. Ⓐ Ⓑ Ⓒ Ⓓ
265. Ⓐ Ⓑ Ⓒ Ⓓ
266. Ⓐ Ⓑ Ⓒ Ⓓ
267. Ⓐ Ⓑ Ⓒ Ⓓ
268. Ⓐ Ⓑ Ⓒ Ⓓ
269. Ⓐ Ⓑ Ⓒ Ⓓ
270. Ⓐ Ⓑ Ⓒ Ⓓ
271. Ⓐ Ⓑ Ⓒ Ⓓ
272. Ⓐ Ⓑ Ⓒ Ⓓ
273. Ⓐ Ⓑ Ⓒ Ⓓ
274. Ⓐ Ⓑ Ⓒ Ⓓ
275. Ⓐ Ⓑ Ⓒ Ⓓ
276. Ⓐ Ⓑ Ⓒ Ⓓ
277. Ⓐ Ⓑ Ⓒ Ⓓ
278. Ⓐ Ⓑ Ⓒ Ⓓ
279. Ⓐ Ⓑ Ⓒ Ⓓ
280. Ⓐ Ⓑ Ⓒ Ⓓ
281. Ⓐ Ⓑ Ⓒ Ⓓ
282. Ⓐ Ⓑ Ⓒ Ⓓ
283. Ⓐ Ⓑ Ⓒ Ⓓ
284. Ⓐ Ⓑ Ⓒ Ⓓ
285. Ⓐ Ⓑ Ⓒ Ⓓ
286. Ⓐ Ⓑ Ⓒ Ⓓ
287. Ⓐ Ⓑ Ⓒ Ⓓ
288. Ⓐ Ⓑ Ⓒ Ⓓ
289. Ⓐ Ⓑ Ⓒ Ⓓ
290. Ⓐ Ⓑ Ⓒ Ⓓ
291. Ⓐ Ⓑ Ⓒ Ⓓ
292. Ⓐ Ⓑ Ⓒ Ⓓ
293. Ⓐ Ⓑ Ⓒ Ⓓ
294. Ⓐ Ⓑ Ⓒ Ⓓ
295. Ⓐ Ⓑ Ⓒ Ⓓ
296. Ⓐ Ⓑ Ⓒ Ⓓ
297. Ⓐ Ⓑ Ⓒ Ⓓ
298. Ⓐ Ⓑ Ⓒ Ⓓ

Test 2 Answer Sheet

Verbal

1. Ⓐ Ⓑ Ⓒ Ⓓ
2. Ⓐ Ⓑ Ⓒ Ⓓ
3. Ⓐ Ⓑ Ⓒ Ⓓ
4. Ⓐ Ⓑ Ⓒ Ⓓ
5. Ⓐ Ⓑ Ⓒ Ⓓ
6. Ⓐ Ⓑ Ⓒ Ⓓ
7. Ⓐ Ⓑ Ⓒ Ⓓ
8. Ⓐ Ⓑ Ⓒ Ⓓ
9. Ⓐ Ⓑ Ⓒ Ⓓ
10. Ⓐ Ⓑ Ⓒ Ⓓ
11. Ⓐ Ⓑ Ⓒ Ⓓ
12. Ⓐ Ⓑ Ⓒ Ⓓ
13. Ⓐ Ⓑ Ⓒ Ⓓ
14. Ⓐ Ⓑ Ⓒ Ⓓ
15. Ⓐ Ⓑ Ⓒ Ⓓ
16. Ⓐ Ⓑ Ⓒ Ⓓ
17. Ⓐ Ⓑ Ⓒ Ⓓ
18. Ⓐ Ⓑ Ⓒ Ⓓ
19. Ⓐ Ⓑ Ⓒ Ⓓ
20. Ⓐ Ⓑ Ⓒ Ⓓ
21. Ⓐ Ⓑ Ⓒ Ⓓ
22. Ⓐ Ⓑ Ⓒ Ⓓ
23. Ⓐ Ⓑ Ⓒ Ⓓ
24. Ⓐ Ⓑ Ⓒ Ⓓ
25. Ⓐ Ⓑ Ⓒ Ⓓ
26. Ⓐ Ⓑ Ⓒ Ⓓ
27. Ⓐ Ⓑ Ⓒ Ⓓ
28. Ⓐ Ⓑ Ⓒ Ⓓ
29. Ⓐ Ⓑ Ⓒ Ⓓ
30. Ⓐ Ⓑ Ⓒ Ⓓ
31. Ⓐ Ⓑ Ⓒ Ⓓ
32. Ⓐ Ⓑ Ⓒ Ⓓ
33. Ⓐ Ⓑ Ⓒ Ⓓ
34. Ⓐ Ⓑ Ⓒ Ⓓ
35. Ⓐ Ⓑ Ⓒ Ⓓ
36. Ⓐ Ⓑ Ⓒ Ⓓ
37. Ⓐ Ⓑ Ⓒ Ⓓ
38. Ⓐ Ⓑ Ⓒ Ⓓ
39. Ⓐ Ⓑ Ⓒ Ⓓ
40. Ⓐ Ⓑ Ⓒ Ⓓ
41. Ⓐ Ⓑ Ⓒ Ⓓ
42. Ⓐ Ⓑ Ⓒ Ⓓ
43. Ⓐ Ⓑ Ⓒ Ⓓ
44. Ⓐ Ⓑ Ⓒ Ⓓ
45. Ⓐ Ⓑ Ⓒ Ⓓ
46. Ⓐ Ⓑ Ⓒ Ⓓ
47. Ⓐ Ⓑ Ⓒ Ⓓ
48. Ⓐ Ⓑ Ⓒ Ⓓ
49. Ⓐ Ⓑ Ⓒ Ⓓ
50. Ⓐ Ⓑ Ⓒ Ⓓ
51. Ⓐ Ⓑ Ⓒ Ⓓ
52. Ⓐ Ⓑ Ⓒ Ⓓ
53. Ⓐ Ⓑ Ⓒ Ⓓ
54. Ⓐ Ⓑ Ⓒ Ⓓ
55. Ⓐ Ⓑ Ⓒ Ⓓ
56. Ⓐ Ⓑ Ⓒ Ⓓ
57. Ⓐ Ⓑ Ⓒ Ⓓ
58. Ⓐ Ⓑ Ⓒ Ⓓ
59. Ⓐ Ⓑ Ⓒ Ⓓ
60. Ⓐ Ⓑ Ⓒ Ⓓ

Quantitative

61. Ⓐ Ⓑ Ⓒ Ⓓ
62. Ⓐ Ⓑ Ⓒ Ⓓ
63. Ⓐ Ⓑ Ⓒ Ⓓ
64. Ⓐ Ⓑ Ⓒ Ⓓ
65. Ⓐ Ⓑ Ⓒ Ⓓ
66. Ⓐ Ⓑ Ⓒ Ⓓ
67. Ⓐ Ⓑ Ⓒ Ⓓ
68. Ⓐ Ⓑ Ⓒ Ⓓ
69. Ⓐ Ⓑ Ⓒ Ⓓ
70. Ⓐ Ⓑ Ⓒ Ⓓ
71. Ⓐ Ⓑ Ⓒ Ⓓ
72. Ⓐ Ⓑ Ⓒ Ⓓ
73. Ⓐ Ⓑ Ⓒ Ⓓ
74. Ⓐ Ⓑ Ⓒ Ⓓ
75. Ⓐ Ⓑ Ⓒ Ⓓ
76. Ⓐ Ⓑ Ⓒ Ⓓ
77. Ⓐ Ⓑ Ⓒ Ⓓ
78. Ⓐ Ⓑ Ⓒ Ⓓ
79. Ⓐ Ⓑ Ⓒ Ⓓ
80. Ⓐ Ⓑ Ⓒ Ⓓ
81. Ⓐ Ⓑ Ⓒ Ⓓ
82. Ⓐ Ⓑ Ⓒ Ⓓ
83. Ⓐ Ⓑ Ⓒ Ⓓ
84. Ⓐ Ⓑ Ⓒ Ⓓ
85. Ⓐ Ⓑ Ⓒ Ⓓ
86. Ⓐ Ⓑ Ⓒ Ⓓ
87. Ⓐ Ⓑ Ⓒ Ⓓ
88. Ⓐ Ⓑ Ⓒ Ⓓ
89. Ⓐ Ⓑ Ⓒ Ⓓ
90. Ⓐ Ⓑ Ⓒ Ⓓ
91. Ⓐ Ⓑ Ⓒ Ⓓ
92. Ⓐ Ⓑ Ⓒ Ⓓ
93. Ⓐ Ⓑ Ⓒ Ⓓ
94. Ⓐ Ⓑ Ⓒ Ⓓ
95. Ⓐ Ⓑ Ⓒ Ⓓ
96. Ⓐ Ⓑ Ⓒ Ⓓ
97. Ⓐ Ⓑ Ⓒ Ⓓ
98. Ⓐ Ⓑ Ⓒ Ⓓ
99. Ⓐ Ⓑ Ⓒ Ⓓ
100. Ⓐ Ⓑ Ⓒ Ⓓ
101. Ⓐ Ⓑ Ⓒ Ⓓ
102. Ⓐ Ⓑ Ⓒ Ⓓ
103. Ⓐ Ⓑ Ⓒ Ⓓ
104. Ⓐ Ⓑ Ⓒ Ⓓ
105. Ⓐ Ⓑ Ⓒ Ⓓ
106. Ⓐ Ⓑ Ⓒ Ⓓ
107. Ⓐ Ⓑ Ⓒ Ⓓ
108. Ⓐ Ⓑ Ⓒ Ⓓ
109. Ⓐ Ⓑ Ⓒ Ⓓ
110. Ⓐ Ⓑ Ⓒ Ⓓ
111. Ⓐ Ⓑ Ⓒ Ⓓ
112. Ⓐ Ⓑ Ⓒ Ⓓ

Reading

113. Ⓐ Ⓑ Ⓒ Ⓓ
114. Ⓐ Ⓑ Ⓒ Ⓓ
115. Ⓐ Ⓑ Ⓒ Ⓓ
116. Ⓐ Ⓑ Ⓒ Ⓓ
117. Ⓐ Ⓑ Ⓒ Ⓓ
118. Ⓐ Ⓑ Ⓒ Ⓓ
119. Ⓐ Ⓑ Ⓒ Ⓓ
120. Ⓐ Ⓑ Ⓒ Ⓓ
121. Ⓐ Ⓑ Ⓒ Ⓓ
122. Ⓐ Ⓑ Ⓒ Ⓓ
123. Ⓐ Ⓑ Ⓒ Ⓓ
124. Ⓐ Ⓑ Ⓒ Ⓓ
125. Ⓐ Ⓑ Ⓒ Ⓓ
126. Ⓐ Ⓑ Ⓒ Ⓓ
127. Ⓐ Ⓑ Ⓒ Ⓓ
128. Ⓐ Ⓑ Ⓒ Ⓓ
129. Ⓐ Ⓑ Ⓒ Ⓓ
130. Ⓐ Ⓑ Ⓒ Ⓓ
131. Ⓐ Ⓑ Ⓒ Ⓓ
132. Ⓐ Ⓑ Ⓒ Ⓓ
133. Ⓐ Ⓑ Ⓒ Ⓓ
134. Ⓐ Ⓑ Ⓒ Ⓓ
135. Ⓐ Ⓑ Ⓒ Ⓓ
136. Ⓐ Ⓑ Ⓒ Ⓓ
137. Ⓐ Ⓑ Ⓒ Ⓓ
138. Ⓐ Ⓑ Ⓒ Ⓓ
139. Ⓐ Ⓑ Ⓒ Ⓓ
140. Ⓐ Ⓑ Ⓒ Ⓓ
141. Ⓐ Ⓑ Ⓒ Ⓓ
142. Ⓐ Ⓑ Ⓒ Ⓓ
143. Ⓐ Ⓑ Ⓒ Ⓓ
144. Ⓐ Ⓑ Ⓒ Ⓓ
145. Ⓐ Ⓑ Ⓒ Ⓓ
146. Ⓐ Ⓑ Ⓒ Ⓓ
147. Ⓐ Ⓑ Ⓒ Ⓓ
148. Ⓐ Ⓑ Ⓒ Ⓓ
149. Ⓐ Ⓑ Ⓒ Ⓓ
150. Ⓐ Ⓑ Ⓒ Ⓓ
151. Ⓐ Ⓑ Ⓒ Ⓓ
152. Ⓐ Ⓑ Ⓒ Ⓓ
153. Ⓐ Ⓑ Ⓒ Ⓓ
154. Ⓐ Ⓑ Ⓒ Ⓓ
155. Ⓐ Ⓑ Ⓒ Ⓓ
156. Ⓐ Ⓑ Ⓒ Ⓓ
157. Ⓐ Ⓑ Ⓒ Ⓓ
158. Ⓐ Ⓑ Ⓒ Ⓓ
159. Ⓐ Ⓑ Ⓒ Ⓓ
160. Ⓐ Ⓑ Ⓒ Ⓓ
161. Ⓐ Ⓑ Ⓒ Ⓓ
162. Ⓐ Ⓑ Ⓒ Ⓓ
163. Ⓐ Ⓑ Ⓒ Ⓓ
164. Ⓐ Ⓑ Ⓒ Ⓓ
165. Ⓐ Ⓑ Ⓒ Ⓓ
166. Ⓐ Ⓑ Ⓒ Ⓓ
167. Ⓐ Ⓑ Ⓒ Ⓓ
168. Ⓐ Ⓑ Ⓒ Ⓓ
169. Ⓐ Ⓑ Ⓒ Ⓓ
170. Ⓐ Ⓑ Ⓒ Ⓓ
171. Ⓐ Ⓑ Ⓒ Ⓓ
172. Ⓐ Ⓑ Ⓒ Ⓓ
173. Ⓐ Ⓑ Ⓒ Ⓓ
174. Ⓐ Ⓑ Ⓒ Ⓓ

Math

175. Ⓐ Ⓑ Ⓒ Ⓓ	188. Ⓐ Ⓑ Ⓒ Ⓓ	201. Ⓐ Ⓑ Ⓒ Ⓓ	214. Ⓐ Ⓑ Ⓒ Ⓓ	227. Ⓐ Ⓑ Ⓒ Ⓓ
176. Ⓐ Ⓑ Ⓒ Ⓓ	189. Ⓐ Ⓑ Ⓒ Ⓓ	202. Ⓐ Ⓑ Ⓒ Ⓓ	215. Ⓐ Ⓑ Ⓒ Ⓓ	228. Ⓐ Ⓑ Ⓒ Ⓓ
177. Ⓐ Ⓑ Ⓒ Ⓓ	190. Ⓐ Ⓑ Ⓒ Ⓓ	203. Ⓐ Ⓑ Ⓒ Ⓓ	216. Ⓐ Ⓑ Ⓒ Ⓓ	229. Ⓐ Ⓑ Ⓒ Ⓓ
178. Ⓐ Ⓑ Ⓒ Ⓓ	191. Ⓐ Ⓑ Ⓒ Ⓓ	204. Ⓐ Ⓑ Ⓒ Ⓓ	217. Ⓐ Ⓑ Ⓒ Ⓓ	230. Ⓐ Ⓑ Ⓒ Ⓓ
179. Ⓐ Ⓑ Ⓒ Ⓓ	192. Ⓐ Ⓑ Ⓒ Ⓓ	205. Ⓐ Ⓑ Ⓒ Ⓓ	218. Ⓐ Ⓑ Ⓒ Ⓓ	231. Ⓐ Ⓑ Ⓒ Ⓓ
180. Ⓐ Ⓑ Ⓒ Ⓓ	193. Ⓐ Ⓑ Ⓒ Ⓓ	206. Ⓐ Ⓑ Ⓒ Ⓓ	219. Ⓐ Ⓑ Ⓒ Ⓓ	232. Ⓐ Ⓑ Ⓒ Ⓓ
181. Ⓐ Ⓑ Ⓒ Ⓓ	194. Ⓐ Ⓑ Ⓒ Ⓓ	207. Ⓐ Ⓑ Ⓒ Ⓓ	220. Ⓐ Ⓑ Ⓒ Ⓓ	233. Ⓐ Ⓑ Ⓒ Ⓓ
182. Ⓐ Ⓑ Ⓒ Ⓓ	195. Ⓐ Ⓑ Ⓒ Ⓓ	208. Ⓐ Ⓑ Ⓒ Ⓓ	221. Ⓐ Ⓑ Ⓒ Ⓓ	234. Ⓐ Ⓑ Ⓒ Ⓓ
183. Ⓐ Ⓑ Ⓒ Ⓓ	196. Ⓐ Ⓑ Ⓒ Ⓓ	209. Ⓐ Ⓑ Ⓒ Ⓓ	222. Ⓐ Ⓑ Ⓒ Ⓓ	235. Ⓐ Ⓑ Ⓒ Ⓓ
184. Ⓐ Ⓑ Ⓒ Ⓓ	197. Ⓐ Ⓑ Ⓒ Ⓓ	210. Ⓐ Ⓑ Ⓒ Ⓓ	223. Ⓐ Ⓑ Ⓒ Ⓓ	236. Ⓐ Ⓑ Ⓒ Ⓓ
185. Ⓐ Ⓑ Ⓒ Ⓓ	198. Ⓐ Ⓑ Ⓒ Ⓓ	211. Ⓐ Ⓑ Ⓒ Ⓓ	224. Ⓐ Ⓑ Ⓒ Ⓓ	237. Ⓐ Ⓑ Ⓒ Ⓓ
186. Ⓐ Ⓑ Ⓒ Ⓓ	199. Ⓐ Ⓑ Ⓒ Ⓓ	212. Ⓐ Ⓑ Ⓒ Ⓓ	225. Ⓐ Ⓑ Ⓒ Ⓓ	238. Ⓐ Ⓑ Ⓒ Ⓓ
187. Ⓐ Ⓑ Ⓒ Ⓓ	200. Ⓐ Ⓑ Ⓒ Ⓓ	213. Ⓐ Ⓑ Ⓒ Ⓓ	226. Ⓐ Ⓑ Ⓒ Ⓓ	

Language

239. Ⓐ Ⓑ Ⓒ Ⓓ	252. Ⓐ Ⓑ Ⓒ Ⓓ	265. Ⓐ Ⓑ Ⓒ Ⓓ	278. Ⓐ Ⓑ Ⓒ Ⓓ	291. Ⓐ Ⓑ Ⓒ Ⓓ
240. Ⓐ Ⓑ Ⓒ Ⓓ	253. Ⓐ Ⓑ Ⓒ Ⓓ	266. Ⓐ Ⓑ Ⓒ Ⓓ	279. Ⓐ Ⓑ Ⓒ Ⓓ	292. Ⓐ Ⓑ Ⓒ Ⓓ
241. Ⓐ Ⓑ Ⓒ Ⓓ	254. Ⓐ Ⓑ Ⓒ Ⓓ	267. Ⓐ Ⓑ Ⓒ Ⓓ	280. Ⓐ Ⓑ Ⓒ Ⓓ	293. Ⓐ Ⓑ Ⓒ Ⓓ
242. Ⓐ Ⓑ Ⓒ Ⓓ	255. Ⓐ Ⓑ Ⓒ Ⓓ	268. Ⓐ Ⓑ Ⓒ Ⓓ	281. Ⓐ Ⓑ Ⓒ Ⓓ	294. Ⓐ Ⓑ Ⓒ Ⓓ
243. Ⓐ Ⓑ Ⓒ Ⓓ	256. Ⓐ Ⓑ Ⓒ Ⓓ	269. Ⓐ Ⓑ Ⓒ Ⓓ	282. Ⓐ Ⓑ Ⓒ Ⓓ	295. Ⓐ Ⓑ Ⓒ Ⓓ
244. Ⓐ Ⓑ Ⓒ Ⓓ	257. Ⓐ Ⓑ Ⓒ Ⓓ	270. Ⓐ Ⓑ Ⓒ Ⓓ	283. Ⓐ Ⓑ Ⓒ Ⓓ	296. Ⓐ Ⓑ Ⓒ Ⓓ
245. Ⓐ Ⓑ Ⓒ Ⓓ	258. Ⓐ Ⓑ Ⓒ Ⓓ	271. Ⓐ Ⓑ Ⓒ Ⓓ	284. Ⓐ Ⓑ Ⓒ Ⓓ	297. Ⓐ Ⓑ Ⓒ Ⓓ
246. Ⓐ Ⓑ Ⓒ Ⓓ	259. Ⓐ Ⓑ Ⓒ Ⓓ	272. Ⓐ Ⓑ Ⓒ Ⓓ	285. Ⓐ Ⓑ Ⓒ Ⓓ	298. Ⓐ Ⓑ Ⓒ Ⓓ
247. Ⓐ Ⓑ Ⓒ Ⓓ	260. Ⓐ Ⓑ Ⓒ Ⓓ	273. Ⓐ Ⓑ Ⓒ Ⓓ	286. Ⓐ Ⓑ Ⓒ Ⓓ	
248. Ⓐ Ⓑ Ⓒ Ⓓ	261. Ⓐ Ⓑ Ⓒ Ⓓ	274. Ⓐ Ⓑ Ⓒ Ⓓ	287. Ⓐ Ⓑ Ⓒ Ⓓ	
249. Ⓐ Ⓑ Ⓒ Ⓓ	262. Ⓐ Ⓑ Ⓒ Ⓓ	275. Ⓐ Ⓑ Ⓒ Ⓓ	288. Ⓐ Ⓑ Ⓒ Ⓓ	
250. Ⓐ Ⓑ Ⓒ Ⓓ	263. Ⓐ Ⓑ Ⓒ Ⓓ	276. Ⓐ Ⓑ Ⓒ Ⓓ	289. Ⓐ Ⓑ Ⓒ Ⓓ	
251. Ⓐ Ⓑ Ⓒ Ⓓ	264. Ⓐ Ⓑ Ⓒ Ⓓ	277. Ⓐ Ⓑ Ⓒ Ⓓ	290. Ⓐ Ⓑ Ⓒ Ⓓ	

Test 3 Answer Sheet

Verbal

1. Ⓐ Ⓑ Ⓒ Ⓓ
2. Ⓐ Ⓑ Ⓒ Ⓓ
3. Ⓐ Ⓑ Ⓒ Ⓓ
4. Ⓐ Ⓑ Ⓒ Ⓓ
5. Ⓐ Ⓑ Ⓒ Ⓓ
6. Ⓐ Ⓑ Ⓒ Ⓓ
7. Ⓐ Ⓑ Ⓒ Ⓓ
8. Ⓐ Ⓑ Ⓒ Ⓓ
9. Ⓐ Ⓑ Ⓒ Ⓓ
10. Ⓐ Ⓑ Ⓒ Ⓓ
11. Ⓐ Ⓑ Ⓒ Ⓓ
12. Ⓐ Ⓑ Ⓒ Ⓓ
13. Ⓐ Ⓑ Ⓒ Ⓓ
14. Ⓐ Ⓑ Ⓒ Ⓓ
15. Ⓐ Ⓑ Ⓒ Ⓓ
16. Ⓐ Ⓑ Ⓒ Ⓓ
17. Ⓐ Ⓑ Ⓒ Ⓓ
18. Ⓐ Ⓑ Ⓒ Ⓓ
19. Ⓐ Ⓑ Ⓒ Ⓓ
20. Ⓐ Ⓑ Ⓒ Ⓓ
21. Ⓐ Ⓑ Ⓒ Ⓓ
22. Ⓐ Ⓑ Ⓒ Ⓓ
23. Ⓐ Ⓑ Ⓒ Ⓓ
24. Ⓐ Ⓑ Ⓒ Ⓓ
25. Ⓐ Ⓑ Ⓒ Ⓓ
26. Ⓐ Ⓑ Ⓒ Ⓓ
27. Ⓐ Ⓑ Ⓒ Ⓓ
28. Ⓐ Ⓑ Ⓒ Ⓓ
29. Ⓐ Ⓑ Ⓒ Ⓓ
30. Ⓐ Ⓑ Ⓒ Ⓓ
31. Ⓐ Ⓑ Ⓒ Ⓓ
32. Ⓐ Ⓑ Ⓒ Ⓓ
33. Ⓐ Ⓑ Ⓒ Ⓓ
34. Ⓐ Ⓑ Ⓒ Ⓓ
35. Ⓐ Ⓑ Ⓒ Ⓓ
36. Ⓐ Ⓑ Ⓒ Ⓓ
37. Ⓐ Ⓑ Ⓒ Ⓓ
38. Ⓐ Ⓑ Ⓒ Ⓓ
39. Ⓐ Ⓑ Ⓒ Ⓓ
40. Ⓐ Ⓑ Ⓒ Ⓓ
41. Ⓐ Ⓑ Ⓒ Ⓓ
42. Ⓐ Ⓑ Ⓒ Ⓓ
43. Ⓐ Ⓑ Ⓒ Ⓓ
44. Ⓐ Ⓑ Ⓒ Ⓓ
45. Ⓐ Ⓑ Ⓒ Ⓓ
46. Ⓐ Ⓑ Ⓒ Ⓓ
47. Ⓐ Ⓑ Ⓒ Ⓓ
48. Ⓐ Ⓑ Ⓒ Ⓓ
49. Ⓐ Ⓑ Ⓒ Ⓓ
50. Ⓐ Ⓑ Ⓒ Ⓓ
51. Ⓐ Ⓑ Ⓒ Ⓓ
52. Ⓐ Ⓑ Ⓒ Ⓓ
53. Ⓐ Ⓑ Ⓒ Ⓓ
54. Ⓐ Ⓑ Ⓒ Ⓓ
55. Ⓐ Ⓑ Ⓒ Ⓓ
56. Ⓐ Ⓑ Ⓒ Ⓓ
57. Ⓐ Ⓑ Ⓒ Ⓓ
58. Ⓐ Ⓑ Ⓒ Ⓓ
59. Ⓐ Ⓑ Ⓒ Ⓓ
60. Ⓐ Ⓑ Ⓒ Ⓓ

Quantitative

61. Ⓐ Ⓑ Ⓒ Ⓓ
62. Ⓐ Ⓑ Ⓒ Ⓓ
63. Ⓐ Ⓑ Ⓒ Ⓓ
64. Ⓐ Ⓑ Ⓒ Ⓓ
65. Ⓐ Ⓑ Ⓒ Ⓓ
66. Ⓐ Ⓑ Ⓒ Ⓓ
67. Ⓐ Ⓑ Ⓒ Ⓓ
68. Ⓐ Ⓑ Ⓒ Ⓓ
69. Ⓐ Ⓑ Ⓒ Ⓓ
70. Ⓐ Ⓑ Ⓒ Ⓓ
71. Ⓐ Ⓑ Ⓒ Ⓓ
72. Ⓐ Ⓑ Ⓒ Ⓓ
73. Ⓐ Ⓑ Ⓒ Ⓓ
74. Ⓐ Ⓑ Ⓒ Ⓓ
75. Ⓐ Ⓑ Ⓒ Ⓓ
76. Ⓐ Ⓑ Ⓒ Ⓓ
77. Ⓐ Ⓑ Ⓒ Ⓓ
78. Ⓐ Ⓑ Ⓒ Ⓓ
79. Ⓐ Ⓑ Ⓒ Ⓓ
80. Ⓐ Ⓑ Ⓒ Ⓓ
81. Ⓐ Ⓑ Ⓒ Ⓓ
82. Ⓐ Ⓑ Ⓒ Ⓓ
83. Ⓐ Ⓑ Ⓒ Ⓓ
84. Ⓐ Ⓑ Ⓒ Ⓓ
85. Ⓐ Ⓑ Ⓒ Ⓓ
86. Ⓐ Ⓑ Ⓒ Ⓓ
87. Ⓐ Ⓑ Ⓒ Ⓓ
88. Ⓐ Ⓑ Ⓒ Ⓓ
89. Ⓐ Ⓑ Ⓒ Ⓓ
90. Ⓐ Ⓑ Ⓒ Ⓓ
91. Ⓐ Ⓑ Ⓒ Ⓓ
92. Ⓐ Ⓑ Ⓒ Ⓓ
93. Ⓐ Ⓑ Ⓒ Ⓓ
94. Ⓐ Ⓑ Ⓒ Ⓓ
95. Ⓐ Ⓑ Ⓒ Ⓓ
96. Ⓐ Ⓑ Ⓒ Ⓓ
97. Ⓐ Ⓑ Ⓒ Ⓓ
98. Ⓐ Ⓑ Ⓒ Ⓓ
99. Ⓐ Ⓑ Ⓒ Ⓓ
100. Ⓐ Ⓑ Ⓒ Ⓓ
101. Ⓐ Ⓑ Ⓒ Ⓓ
102. Ⓐ Ⓑ Ⓒ Ⓓ
103. Ⓐ Ⓑ Ⓒ Ⓓ
104. Ⓐ Ⓑ Ⓒ Ⓓ
105. Ⓐ Ⓑ Ⓒ Ⓓ
106. Ⓐ Ⓑ Ⓒ Ⓓ
107. Ⓐ Ⓑ Ⓒ Ⓓ
108. Ⓐ Ⓑ Ⓒ Ⓓ
109. Ⓐ Ⓑ Ⓒ Ⓓ
110. Ⓐ Ⓑ Ⓒ Ⓓ
111. Ⓐ Ⓑ Ⓒ Ⓓ
112. Ⓐ Ⓑ Ⓒ Ⓓ

Reading

113. Ⓐ Ⓑ Ⓒ Ⓓ
114. Ⓐ Ⓑ Ⓒ Ⓓ
115. Ⓐ Ⓑ Ⓒ Ⓓ
116. Ⓐ Ⓑ Ⓒ Ⓓ
117. Ⓐ Ⓑ Ⓒ Ⓓ
118. Ⓐ Ⓑ Ⓒ Ⓓ
119. Ⓐ Ⓑ Ⓒ Ⓓ
120. Ⓐ Ⓑ Ⓒ Ⓓ
121. Ⓐ Ⓑ Ⓒ Ⓓ
122. Ⓐ Ⓑ Ⓒ Ⓓ
123. Ⓐ Ⓑ Ⓒ Ⓓ
124. Ⓐ Ⓑ Ⓒ Ⓓ
125. Ⓐ Ⓑ Ⓒ Ⓓ
126. Ⓐ Ⓑ Ⓒ Ⓓ
127. Ⓐ Ⓑ Ⓒ Ⓓ
128. Ⓐ Ⓑ Ⓒ Ⓓ
129. Ⓐ Ⓑ Ⓒ Ⓓ
130. Ⓐ Ⓑ Ⓒ Ⓓ
131. Ⓐ Ⓑ Ⓒ Ⓓ
132. Ⓐ Ⓑ Ⓒ Ⓓ
133. Ⓐ Ⓑ Ⓒ Ⓓ
134. Ⓐ Ⓑ Ⓒ Ⓓ
135. Ⓐ Ⓑ Ⓒ Ⓓ
136. Ⓐ Ⓑ Ⓒ Ⓓ
137. Ⓐ Ⓑ Ⓒ Ⓓ
138. Ⓐ Ⓑ Ⓒ Ⓓ
139. Ⓐ Ⓑ Ⓒ Ⓓ
140. Ⓐ Ⓑ Ⓒ Ⓓ
141. Ⓐ Ⓑ Ⓒ Ⓓ
142. Ⓐ Ⓑ Ⓒ Ⓓ
143. Ⓐ Ⓑ Ⓒ Ⓓ
144. Ⓐ Ⓑ Ⓒ Ⓓ
145. Ⓐ Ⓑ Ⓒ Ⓓ
146. Ⓐ Ⓑ Ⓒ Ⓓ
147. Ⓐ Ⓑ Ⓒ Ⓓ
148. Ⓐ Ⓑ Ⓒ Ⓓ
149. Ⓐ Ⓑ Ⓒ Ⓓ
150. Ⓐ Ⓑ Ⓒ Ⓓ
151. Ⓐ Ⓑ Ⓒ Ⓓ
152. Ⓐ Ⓑ Ⓒ Ⓓ
153. Ⓐ Ⓑ Ⓒ Ⓓ
154. Ⓐ Ⓑ Ⓒ Ⓓ
155. Ⓐ Ⓑ Ⓒ Ⓓ
156. Ⓐ Ⓑ Ⓒ Ⓓ
157. Ⓐ Ⓑ Ⓒ Ⓓ
158. Ⓐ Ⓑ Ⓒ Ⓓ
159. Ⓐ Ⓑ Ⓒ Ⓓ
160. Ⓐ Ⓑ Ⓒ Ⓓ
161. Ⓐ Ⓑ Ⓒ Ⓓ
162. Ⓐ Ⓑ Ⓒ Ⓓ
163. Ⓐ Ⓑ Ⓒ Ⓓ
164. Ⓐ Ⓑ Ⓒ Ⓓ
165. Ⓐ Ⓑ Ⓒ Ⓓ
166. Ⓐ Ⓑ Ⓒ Ⓓ
167. Ⓐ Ⓑ Ⓒ Ⓓ
168. Ⓐ Ⓑ Ⓒ Ⓓ
169. Ⓐ Ⓑ Ⓒ Ⓓ
170. Ⓐ Ⓑ Ⓒ Ⓓ
171. Ⓐ Ⓑ Ⓒ Ⓓ
172. Ⓐ Ⓑ Ⓒ Ⓓ
173. Ⓐ Ⓑ Ⓒ Ⓓ
174. Ⓐ Ⓑ Ⓒ Ⓓ

Math

175. Ⓐ Ⓑ Ⓒ Ⓓ
176. Ⓐ Ⓑ Ⓒ Ⓓ
177. Ⓐ Ⓑ Ⓒ Ⓓ
178. Ⓐ Ⓑ Ⓒ Ⓓ
179. Ⓐ Ⓑ Ⓒ Ⓓ
180. Ⓐ Ⓑ Ⓒ Ⓓ
181. Ⓐ Ⓑ Ⓒ Ⓓ
182. Ⓐ Ⓑ Ⓒ Ⓓ
183. Ⓐ Ⓑ Ⓒ Ⓓ
184. Ⓐ Ⓑ Ⓒ Ⓓ
185. Ⓐ Ⓑ Ⓒ Ⓓ
186. Ⓐ Ⓑ Ⓒ Ⓓ
187. Ⓐ Ⓑ Ⓒ Ⓓ
188. Ⓐ Ⓑ Ⓒ Ⓓ
189. Ⓐ Ⓑ Ⓒ Ⓓ
190. Ⓐ Ⓑ Ⓒ Ⓓ
191. Ⓐ Ⓑ Ⓒ Ⓓ
192. Ⓐ Ⓑ Ⓒ Ⓓ
193. Ⓐ Ⓑ Ⓒ Ⓓ
194. Ⓐ Ⓑ Ⓒ Ⓓ
195. Ⓐ Ⓑ Ⓒ Ⓓ
196. Ⓐ Ⓑ Ⓒ Ⓓ
197. Ⓐ Ⓑ Ⓒ Ⓓ
198. Ⓐ Ⓑ Ⓒ Ⓓ
199. Ⓐ Ⓑ Ⓒ Ⓓ
200. Ⓐ Ⓑ Ⓒ Ⓓ
201. Ⓐ Ⓑ Ⓒ Ⓓ
202. Ⓐ Ⓑ Ⓒ Ⓓ
203. Ⓐ Ⓑ Ⓒ Ⓓ
204. Ⓐ Ⓑ Ⓒ Ⓓ
205. Ⓐ Ⓑ Ⓒ Ⓓ
206. Ⓐ Ⓑ Ⓒ Ⓓ
207. Ⓐ Ⓑ Ⓒ Ⓓ
208. Ⓐ Ⓑ Ⓒ Ⓓ
209. Ⓐ Ⓑ Ⓒ Ⓓ
210. Ⓐ Ⓑ Ⓒ Ⓓ
211. Ⓐ Ⓑ Ⓒ Ⓓ
212. Ⓐ Ⓑ Ⓒ Ⓓ
213. Ⓐ Ⓑ Ⓒ Ⓓ
214. Ⓐ Ⓑ Ⓒ Ⓓ
215. Ⓐ Ⓑ Ⓒ Ⓓ
216. Ⓐ Ⓑ Ⓒ Ⓓ
217. Ⓐ Ⓑ Ⓒ Ⓓ
218. Ⓐ Ⓑ Ⓒ Ⓓ
219. Ⓐ Ⓑ Ⓒ Ⓓ
220. Ⓐ Ⓑ Ⓒ Ⓓ
221. Ⓐ Ⓑ Ⓒ Ⓓ
222. Ⓐ Ⓑ Ⓒ Ⓓ
223. Ⓐ Ⓑ Ⓒ Ⓓ
224. Ⓐ Ⓑ Ⓒ Ⓓ
225. Ⓐ Ⓑ Ⓒ Ⓓ
226. Ⓐ Ⓑ Ⓒ Ⓓ
227. Ⓐ Ⓑ Ⓒ Ⓓ
228. Ⓐ Ⓑ Ⓒ Ⓓ
229. Ⓐ Ⓑ Ⓒ Ⓓ
230. Ⓐ Ⓑ Ⓒ Ⓓ
231. Ⓐ Ⓑ Ⓒ Ⓓ
232. Ⓐ Ⓑ Ⓒ Ⓓ
233. Ⓐ Ⓑ Ⓒ Ⓓ
234. Ⓐ Ⓑ Ⓒ Ⓓ
235. Ⓐ Ⓑ Ⓒ Ⓓ
236. Ⓐ Ⓑ Ⓒ Ⓓ
237. Ⓐ Ⓑ Ⓒ Ⓓ
238. Ⓐ Ⓑ Ⓒ Ⓓ

Language

239. Ⓐ Ⓑ Ⓒ Ⓓ
240. Ⓐ Ⓑ Ⓒ Ⓓ
241. Ⓐ Ⓑ Ⓒ Ⓓ
242. Ⓐ Ⓑ Ⓒ Ⓓ
243. Ⓐ Ⓑ Ⓒ Ⓓ
244. Ⓐ Ⓑ Ⓒ Ⓓ
245. Ⓐ Ⓑ Ⓒ Ⓓ
246. Ⓐ Ⓑ Ⓒ Ⓓ
247. Ⓐ Ⓑ Ⓒ Ⓓ
248. Ⓐ Ⓑ Ⓒ Ⓓ
249. Ⓐ Ⓑ Ⓒ Ⓓ
250. Ⓐ Ⓑ Ⓒ Ⓓ
251. Ⓐ Ⓑ Ⓒ Ⓓ
252. Ⓐ Ⓑ Ⓒ Ⓓ
253. Ⓐ Ⓑ Ⓒ Ⓓ
254. Ⓐ Ⓑ Ⓒ Ⓓ
255. Ⓐ Ⓑ Ⓒ Ⓓ
256. Ⓐ Ⓑ Ⓒ Ⓓ
257. Ⓐ Ⓑ Ⓒ Ⓓ
258. Ⓐ Ⓑ Ⓒ Ⓓ
259. Ⓐ Ⓑ Ⓒ Ⓓ
260. Ⓐ Ⓑ Ⓒ Ⓓ
261. Ⓐ Ⓑ Ⓒ Ⓓ
262. Ⓐ Ⓑ Ⓒ Ⓓ
263. Ⓐ Ⓑ Ⓒ Ⓓ
264. Ⓐ Ⓑ Ⓒ Ⓓ
265. Ⓐ Ⓑ Ⓒ Ⓓ
266. Ⓐ Ⓑ Ⓒ Ⓓ
267. Ⓐ Ⓑ Ⓒ Ⓓ
268. Ⓐ Ⓑ Ⓒ Ⓓ
269. Ⓐ Ⓑ Ⓒ Ⓓ
270. Ⓐ Ⓑ Ⓒ Ⓓ
271. Ⓐ Ⓑ Ⓒ Ⓓ
272. Ⓐ Ⓑ Ⓒ Ⓓ
273. Ⓐ Ⓑ Ⓒ Ⓓ
274. Ⓐ Ⓑ Ⓒ Ⓓ
275. Ⓐ Ⓑ Ⓒ Ⓓ
276. Ⓐ Ⓑ Ⓒ Ⓓ
277. Ⓐ Ⓑ Ⓒ Ⓓ
278. Ⓐ Ⓑ Ⓒ Ⓓ
279. Ⓐ Ⓑ Ⓒ Ⓓ
280. Ⓐ Ⓑ Ⓒ Ⓓ
281. Ⓐ Ⓑ Ⓒ Ⓓ
282. Ⓐ Ⓑ Ⓒ Ⓓ
283. Ⓐ Ⓑ Ⓒ Ⓓ
284. Ⓐ Ⓑ Ⓒ Ⓓ
285. Ⓐ Ⓑ Ⓒ Ⓓ
286. Ⓐ Ⓑ Ⓒ Ⓓ
287. Ⓐ Ⓑ Ⓒ Ⓓ
288. Ⓐ Ⓑ Ⓒ Ⓓ
289. Ⓐ Ⓑ Ⓒ Ⓓ
290. Ⓐ Ⓑ Ⓒ Ⓓ
291. Ⓐ Ⓑ Ⓒ Ⓓ
292. Ⓐ Ⓑ Ⓒ Ⓓ
293. Ⓐ Ⓑ Ⓒ Ⓓ
294. Ⓐ Ⓑ Ⓒ Ⓓ
295. Ⓐ Ⓑ Ⓒ Ⓓ
296. Ⓐ Ⓑ Ⓒ Ⓓ
297. Ⓐ Ⓑ Ⓒ Ⓓ
298. Ⓐ Ⓑ Ⓒ Ⓓ

Test 4 Answer Sheet

Verbal

1. (A) (B) (C) (D)
2. (A) (B) (C) (D)
3. (A) (B) (C) (D)
4. (A) (B) (C) (D)
5. (A) (B) (C) (D)
6. (A) (B) (C) (D)
7. (A) (B) (C) (D)
8. (A) (B) (C) (D)
9. (A) (B) (C) (D)
10. (A) (B) (C) (D)
11. (A) (B) (C) (D)
12. (A) (B) (C) (D)
13. (A) (B) (C) (D)
14. (A) (B) (C) (D)
15. (A) (B) (C) (D)
16. (A) (B) (C) (D)
17. (A) (B) (C) (D)
18. (A) (B) (C) (D)
19. (A) (B) (C) (D)
20. (A) (B) (C) (D)
21. (A) (B) (C) (D)
22. (A) (B) (C) (D)
23. (A) (B) (C) (D)
24. (A) (B) (C) (D)
25. (A) (B) (C) (D)
26. (A) (B) (C) (D)
27. (A) (B) (C) (D)
28. (A) (B) (C) (D)
29. (A) (B) (C) (D)
30. (A) (B) (C) (D)
31. (A) (B) (C) (D)
32. (A) (B) (C) (D)
33. (A) (B) (C) (D)
34. (A) (B) (C) (D)
35. (A) (B) (C) (D)
36. (A) (B) (C) (D)
37. (A) (B) (C) (D)
38. (A) (B) (C) (D)
39. (A) (B) (C) (D)
40. (A) (B) (C) (D)
41. (A) (B) (C) (D)
42. (A) (B) (C) (D)
43. (A) (B) (C) (D)
44. (A) (B) (C) (D)
45. (A) (B) (C) (D)
46. (A) (B) (C) (D)
47. (A) (B) (C) (D)
48. (A) (B) (C) (D)
49. (A) (B) (C) (D)
50. (A) (B) (C) (D)
51. (A) (B) (C) (D)
52. (A) (B) (C) (D)
53. (A) (B) (C) (D)
54. (A) (B) (C) (D)
55. (A) (B) (C) (D)
56. (A) (B) (C) (D)
57. (A) (B) (C) (D)
58. (A) (B) (C) (D)
59. (A) (B) (C) (D)
60. (A) (B) (C) (D)

Quantitative

61. (A) (B) (C) (D)
62. (A) (B) (C) (D)
63. (A) (B) (C) (D)
64. (A) (B) (C) (D)
65. (A) (B) (C) (D)
66. (A) (B) (C) (D)
67. (A) (B) (C) (D)
68. (A) (B) (C) (D)
69. (A) (B) (C) (D)
70. (A) (B) (C) (D)
71. (A) (B) (C) (D)
72. (A) (B) (C) (D)
73. (A) (B) (C) (D)
74. (A) (B) (C) (D)
75. (A) (B) (C) (D)
76. (A) (B) (C) (D)
77. (A) (B) (C) (D)
78. (A) (B) (C) (D)
79. (A) (B) (C) (D)
80. (A) (B) (C) (D)
81. (A) (B) (C) (D)
82. (A) (B) (C) (D)
83. (A) (B) (C) (D)
84. (A) (B) (C) (D)
85. (A) (B) (C) (D)
86. (A) (B) (C) (D)
87. (A) (B) (C) (D)
88. (A) (B) (C) (D)
89. (A) (B) (C) (D)
90. (A) (B) (C) (D)
91. (A) (B) (C) (D)
92. (A) (B) (C) (D)
93. (A) (B) (C) (D)
94. (A) (B) (C) (D)
95. (A) (B) (C) (D)
96. (A) (B) (C) (D)
97. (A) (B) (C) (D)
98. (A) (B) (C) (D)
99. (A) (B) (C) (D)
100. (A) (B) (C) (D)
101. (A) (B) (C) (D)
102. (A) (B) (C) (D)
103. (A) (B) (C) (D)
104. (A) (B) (C) (D)
105. (A) (B) (C) (D)
106. (A) (B) (C) (D)
107. (A) (B) (C) (D)
108. (A) (B) (C) (D)
109. (A) (B) (C) (D)
110. (A) (B) (C) (D)
111. (A) (B) (C) (D)
112. (A) (B) (C) (D)

Reading

113. (A) (B) (C) (D)
114. (A) (B) (C) (D)
115. (A) (B) (C) (D)
116. (A) (B) (C) (D)
117. (A) (B) (C) (D)
118. (A) (B) (C) (D)
119. (A) (B) (C) (D)
120. (A) (B) (C) (D)
121. (A) (B) (C) (D)
122. (A) (B) (C) (D)
123. (A) (B) (C) (D)
124. (A) (B) (C) (D)
125. (A) (B) (C) (D)
126. (A) (B) (C) (D)
127. (A) (B) (C) (D)
128. (A) (B) (C) (D)
129. (A) (B) (C) (D)
130. (A) (B) (C) (D)
131. (A) (B) (C) (D)
132. (A) (B) (C) (D)
133. (A) (B) (C) (D)
134. (A) (B) (C) (D)
135. (A) (B) (C) (D)
136. (A) (B) (C) (D)
137. (A) (B) (C) (D)
138. (A) (B) (C) (D)
139. (A) (B) (C) (D)
140. (A) (B) (C) (D)
141. (A) (B) (C) (D)
142. (A) (B) (C) (D)
143. (A) (B) (C) (D)
144. (A) (B) (C) (D)
145. (A) (B) (C) (D)
146. (A) (B) (C) (D)
147. (A) (B) (C) (D)
148. (A) (B) (C) (D)
149. (A) (B) (C) (D)
150. (A) (B) (C) (D)
151. (A) (B) (C) (D)
152. (A) (B) (C) (D)
153. (A) (B) (C) (D)
154. (A) (B) (C) (D)
155. (A) (B) (C) (D)
156. (A) (B) (C) (D)
157. (A) (B) (C) (D)
158. (A) (B) (C) (D)
159. (A) (B) (C) (D)
160. (A) (B) (C) (D)
161. (A) (B) (C) (D)
162. (A) (B) (C) (D)
163. (A) (B) (C) (D)
164. (A) (B) (C) (D)
165. (A) (B) (C) (D)
166. (A) (B) (C) (D)
167. (A) (B) (C) (D)
168. (A) (B) (C) (D)
169. (A) (B) (C) (D)
170. (A) (B) (C) (D)
171. (A) (B) (C) (D)
172. (A) (B) (C) (D)
173. (A) (B) (C) (D)
174. (A) (B) (C) (D)

Math

175. Ⓐ Ⓑ Ⓒ Ⓓ	188. Ⓐ Ⓑ Ⓒ Ⓓ	201. Ⓐ Ⓑ Ⓒ Ⓓ	214. Ⓐ Ⓑ Ⓒ Ⓓ	227. Ⓐ Ⓑ Ⓒ Ⓓ
176. Ⓐ Ⓑ Ⓒ Ⓓ	189. Ⓐ Ⓑ Ⓒ Ⓓ	202. Ⓐ Ⓑ Ⓒ Ⓓ	215. Ⓐ Ⓑ Ⓒ Ⓓ	228. Ⓐ Ⓑ Ⓒ Ⓓ
177. Ⓐ Ⓑ Ⓒ Ⓓ	190. Ⓐ Ⓑ Ⓒ Ⓓ	203. Ⓐ Ⓑ Ⓒ Ⓓ	216. Ⓐ Ⓑ Ⓒ Ⓓ	229. Ⓐ Ⓑ Ⓒ Ⓓ
178. Ⓐ Ⓑ Ⓒ Ⓓ	191. Ⓐ Ⓑ Ⓒ Ⓓ	204. Ⓐ Ⓑ Ⓒ Ⓓ	217. Ⓐ Ⓑ Ⓒ Ⓓ	230. Ⓐ Ⓑ Ⓒ Ⓓ
179. Ⓐ Ⓑ Ⓒ Ⓓ	192. Ⓐ Ⓑ Ⓒ Ⓓ	205. Ⓐ Ⓑ Ⓒ Ⓓ	218. Ⓐ Ⓑ Ⓒ Ⓓ	231. Ⓐ Ⓑ Ⓒ Ⓓ
180. Ⓐ Ⓑ Ⓒ Ⓓ	193. Ⓐ Ⓑ Ⓒ Ⓓ	206. Ⓐ Ⓑ Ⓒ Ⓓ	219. Ⓐ Ⓑ Ⓒ Ⓓ	232. Ⓐ Ⓑ Ⓒ Ⓓ
181. Ⓐ Ⓑ Ⓒ Ⓓ	194. Ⓐ Ⓑ Ⓒ Ⓓ	207. Ⓐ Ⓑ Ⓒ Ⓓ	220. Ⓐ Ⓑ Ⓒ Ⓓ	233. Ⓐ Ⓑ Ⓒ Ⓓ
182. Ⓐ Ⓑ Ⓒ Ⓓ	195. Ⓐ Ⓑ Ⓒ Ⓓ	208. Ⓐ Ⓑ Ⓒ Ⓓ	221. Ⓐ Ⓑ Ⓒ Ⓓ	234. Ⓐ Ⓑ Ⓒ Ⓓ
183. Ⓐ Ⓑ Ⓒ Ⓓ	196. Ⓐ Ⓑ Ⓒ Ⓓ	209. Ⓐ Ⓑ Ⓒ Ⓓ	222. Ⓐ Ⓑ Ⓒ Ⓓ	235. Ⓐ Ⓑ Ⓒ Ⓓ
184. Ⓐ Ⓑ Ⓒ Ⓓ	197. Ⓐ Ⓑ Ⓒ Ⓓ	210. Ⓐ Ⓑ Ⓒ Ⓓ	223. Ⓐ Ⓑ Ⓒ Ⓓ	236. Ⓐ Ⓑ Ⓒ Ⓓ
185. Ⓐ Ⓑ Ⓒ Ⓓ	198. Ⓐ Ⓑ Ⓒ Ⓓ	211. Ⓐ Ⓑ Ⓒ Ⓓ	224. Ⓐ Ⓑ Ⓒ Ⓓ	237. Ⓐ Ⓑ Ⓒ Ⓓ
186. Ⓐ Ⓑ Ⓒ Ⓓ	199. Ⓐ Ⓑ Ⓒ Ⓓ	212. Ⓐ Ⓑ Ⓒ Ⓓ	225. Ⓐ Ⓑ Ⓒ Ⓓ	238. Ⓐ Ⓑ Ⓒ Ⓓ
187. Ⓐ Ⓑ Ⓒ Ⓓ	200. Ⓐ Ⓑ Ⓒ Ⓓ	213. Ⓐ Ⓑ Ⓒ Ⓓ	226. Ⓐ Ⓑ Ⓒ Ⓓ	

Language

239. Ⓐ Ⓑ Ⓒ Ⓓ	252. Ⓐ Ⓑ Ⓒ Ⓓ	265. Ⓐ Ⓑ Ⓒ Ⓓ	278. Ⓐ Ⓑ Ⓒ Ⓓ	291. Ⓐ Ⓑ Ⓒ Ⓓ
240. Ⓐ Ⓑ Ⓒ Ⓓ	253. Ⓐ Ⓑ Ⓒ Ⓓ	266. Ⓐ Ⓑ Ⓒ Ⓓ	279. Ⓐ Ⓑ Ⓒ Ⓓ	292. Ⓐ Ⓑ Ⓒ Ⓓ
241. Ⓐ Ⓑ Ⓒ Ⓓ	254. Ⓐ Ⓑ Ⓒ Ⓓ	267. Ⓐ Ⓑ Ⓒ Ⓓ	280. Ⓐ Ⓑ Ⓒ Ⓓ	293. Ⓐ Ⓑ Ⓒ Ⓓ
242. Ⓐ Ⓑ Ⓒ Ⓓ	255. Ⓐ Ⓑ Ⓒ Ⓓ	268. Ⓐ Ⓑ Ⓒ Ⓓ	281. Ⓐ Ⓑ Ⓒ Ⓓ	294. Ⓐ Ⓑ Ⓒ Ⓓ
243. Ⓐ Ⓑ Ⓒ Ⓓ	256. Ⓐ Ⓑ Ⓒ Ⓓ	269. Ⓐ Ⓑ Ⓒ Ⓓ	282. Ⓐ Ⓑ Ⓒ Ⓓ	295. Ⓐ Ⓑ Ⓒ Ⓓ
244. Ⓐ Ⓑ Ⓒ Ⓓ	257. Ⓐ Ⓑ Ⓒ Ⓓ	270. Ⓐ Ⓑ Ⓒ Ⓓ	283. Ⓐ Ⓑ Ⓒ Ⓓ	296. Ⓐ Ⓑ Ⓒ Ⓓ
245. Ⓐ Ⓑ Ⓒ Ⓓ	258. Ⓐ Ⓑ Ⓒ Ⓓ	271. Ⓐ Ⓑ Ⓒ Ⓓ	284. Ⓐ Ⓑ Ⓒ Ⓓ	297. Ⓐ Ⓑ Ⓒ Ⓓ
246. Ⓐ Ⓑ Ⓒ Ⓓ	259. Ⓐ Ⓑ Ⓒ Ⓓ	272. Ⓐ Ⓑ Ⓒ Ⓓ	285. Ⓐ Ⓑ Ⓒ Ⓓ	298. Ⓐ Ⓑ Ⓒ Ⓓ
247. Ⓐ Ⓑ Ⓒ Ⓓ	260. Ⓐ Ⓑ Ⓒ Ⓓ	273. Ⓐ Ⓑ Ⓒ Ⓓ	286. Ⓐ Ⓑ Ⓒ Ⓓ	
248. Ⓐ Ⓑ Ⓒ Ⓓ	261. Ⓐ Ⓑ Ⓒ Ⓓ	274. Ⓐ Ⓑ Ⓒ Ⓓ	287. Ⓐ Ⓑ Ⓒ Ⓓ	
249. Ⓐ Ⓑ Ⓒ Ⓓ	262. Ⓐ Ⓑ Ⓒ Ⓓ	275. Ⓐ Ⓑ Ⓒ Ⓓ	288. Ⓐ Ⓑ Ⓒ Ⓓ	
250. Ⓐ Ⓑ Ⓒ Ⓓ	263. Ⓐ Ⓑ Ⓒ Ⓓ	276. Ⓐ Ⓑ Ⓒ Ⓓ	289. Ⓐ Ⓑ Ⓒ Ⓓ	
251. Ⓐ Ⓑ Ⓒ Ⓓ	264. Ⓐ Ⓑ Ⓒ Ⓓ	277. Ⓐ Ⓑ Ⓒ Ⓓ	290. Ⓐ Ⓑ Ⓒ Ⓓ	

Test 5 Answer Sheet

Verbal

1. Ⓐ Ⓑ Ⓒ Ⓓ
2. Ⓐ Ⓑ Ⓒ Ⓓ
3. Ⓐ Ⓑ Ⓒ Ⓓ
4. Ⓐ Ⓑ Ⓒ Ⓓ
5. Ⓐ Ⓑ Ⓒ Ⓓ
6. Ⓐ Ⓑ Ⓒ Ⓓ
7. Ⓐ Ⓑ Ⓒ Ⓓ
8. Ⓐ Ⓑ Ⓒ Ⓓ
9. Ⓐ Ⓑ Ⓒ Ⓓ
10. Ⓐ Ⓑ Ⓒ Ⓓ
11. Ⓐ Ⓑ Ⓒ Ⓓ
12. Ⓐ Ⓑ Ⓒ Ⓓ
13. Ⓐ Ⓑ Ⓒ Ⓓ
14. Ⓐ Ⓑ Ⓒ Ⓓ
15. Ⓐ Ⓑ Ⓒ Ⓓ
16. Ⓐ Ⓑ Ⓒ Ⓓ
17. Ⓐ Ⓑ Ⓒ Ⓓ
18. Ⓐ Ⓑ Ⓒ Ⓓ
19. Ⓐ Ⓑ Ⓒ Ⓓ
20. Ⓐ Ⓑ Ⓒ Ⓓ
21. Ⓐ Ⓑ Ⓒ Ⓓ
22. Ⓐ Ⓑ Ⓒ Ⓓ
23. Ⓐ Ⓑ Ⓒ Ⓓ
24. Ⓐ Ⓑ Ⓒ Ⓓ
25. Ⓐ Ⓑ Ⓒ Ⓓ
26. Ⓐ Ⓑ Ⓒ Ⓓ
27. Ⓐ Ⓑ Ⓒ Ⓓ
28. Ⓐ Ⓑ Ⓒ Ⓓ
29. Ⓐ Ⓑ Ⓒ Ⓓ
30. Ⓐ Ⓑ Ⓒ Ⓓ
31. Ⓐ Ⓑ Ⓒ Ⓓ
32. Ⓐ Ⓑ Ⓒ Ⓓ
33. Ⓐ Ⓑ Ⓒ Ⓓ
34. Ⓐ Ⓑ Ⓒ Ⓓ
35. Ⓐ Ⓑ Ⓒ Ⓓ
36. Ⓐ Ⓑ Ⓒ Ⓓ
37. Ⓐ Ⓑ Ⓒ Ⓓ
38. Ⓐ Ⓑ Ⓒ Ⓓ
39. Ⓐ Ⓑ Ⓒ Ⓓ
40. Ⓐ Ⓑ Ⓒ Ⓓ
41. Ⓐ Ⓑ Ⓒ Ⓓ
42. Ⓐ Ⓑ Ⓒ Ⓓ
43. Ⓐ Ⓑ Ⓒ Ⓓ
44. Ⓐ Ⓑ Ⓒ Ⓓ
45. Ⓐ Ⓑ Ⓒ Ⓓ
46. Ⓐ Ⓑ Ⓒ Ⓓ
47. Ⓐ Ⓑ Ⓒ Ⓓ
48. Ⓐ Ⓑ Ⓒ Ⓓ
49. Ⓐ Ⓑ Ⓒ Ⓓ
50. Ⓐ Ⓑ Ⓒ Ⓓ
51. Ⓐ Ⓑ Ⓒ Ⓓ
52. Ⓐ Ⓑ Ⓒ Ⓓ
53. Ⓐ Ⓑ Ⓒ Ⓓ
54. Ⓐ Ⓑ Ⓒ Ⓓ
55. Ⓐ Ⓑ Ⓒ Ⓓ
56. Ⓐ Ⓑ Ⓒ Ⓓ
57. Ⓐ Ⓑ Ⓒ Ⓓ
58. Ⓐ Ⓑ Ⓒ Ⓓ
59. Ⓐ Ⓑ Ⓒ Ⓓ
60. Ⓐ Ⓑ Ⓒ Ⓓ

Quantitative

61. Ⓐ Ⓑ Ⓒ Ⓓ
62. Ⓐ Ⓑ Ⓒ Ⓓ
63. Ⓐ Ⓑ Ⓒ Ⓓ
64. Ⓐ Ⓑ Ⓒ Ⓓ
65. Ⓐ Ⓑ Ⓒ Ⓓ
66. Ⓐ Ⓑ Ⓒ Ⓓ
67. Ⓐ Ⓑ Ⓒ Ⓓ
68. Ⓐ Ⓑ Ⓒ Ⓓ
69. Ⓐ Ⓑ Ⓒ Ⓓ
70. Ⓐ Ⓑ Ⓒ Ⓓ
71. Ⓐ Ⓑ Ⓒ Ⓓ
72. Ⓐ Ⓑ Ⓒ Ⓓ
73. Ⓐ Ⓑ Ⓒ Ⓓ
74. Ⓐ Ⓑ Ⓒ Ⓓ
75. Ⓐ Ⓑ Ⓒ Ⓓ
76. Ⓐ Ⓑ Ⓒ Ⓓ
77. Ⓐ Ⓑ Ⓒ Ⓓ
78. Ⓐ Ⓑ Ⓒ Ⓓ
79. Ⓐ Ⓑ Ⓒ Ⓓ
80. Ⓐ Ⓑ Ⓒ Ⓓ
81. Ⓐ Ⓑ Ⓒ Ⓓ
82. Ⓐ Ⓑ Ⓒ Ⓓ
83. Ⓐ Ⓑ Ⓒ Ⓓ
84. Ⓐ Ⓑ Ⓒ Ⓓ
85. Ⓐ Ⓑ Ⓒ Ⓓ
86. Ⓐ Ⓑ Ⓒ Ⓓ
87. Ⓐ Ⓑ Ⓒ Ⓓ
88. Ⓐ Ⓑ Ⓒ Ⓓ
89. Ⓐ Ⓑ Ⓒ Ⓓ
90. Ⓐ Ⓑ Ⓒ Ⓓ
91. Ⓐ Ⓑ Ⓒ Ⓓ
92. Ⓐ Ⓑ Ⓒ Ⓓ
93. Ⓐ Ⓑ Ⓒ Ⓓ
94. Ⓐ Ⓑ Ⓒ Ⓓ
95. Ⓐ Ⓑ Ⓒ Ⓓ
96. Ⓐ Ⓑ Ⓒ Ⓓ
97. Ⓐ Ⓑ Ⓒ Ⓓ
98. Ⓐ Ⓑ Ⓒ Ⓓ
99. Ⓐ Ⓑ Ⓒ Ⓓ
100. Ⓐ Ⓑ Ⓒ Ⓓ
101. Ⓐ Ⓑ Ⓒ Ⓓ
102. Ⓐ Ⓑ Ⓒ Ⓓ
103. Ⓐ Ⓑ Ⓒ Ⓓ
104. Ⓐ Ⓑ Ⓒ Ⓓ
105. Ⓐ Ⓑ Ⓒ Ⓓ
106. Ⓐ Ⓑ Ⓒ Ⓓ
107. Ⓐ Ⓑ Ⓒ Ⓓ
108. Ⓐ Ⓑ Ⓒ Ⓓ
109. Ⓐ Ⓑ Ⓒ Ⓓ
110. Ⓐ Ⓑ Ⓒ Ⓓ
111. Ⓐ Ⓑ Ⓒ Ⓓ
112. Ⓐ Ⓑ Ⓒ Ⓓ

Reading

113. Ⓐ Ⓑ Ⓒ Ⓓ
114. Ⓐ Ⓑ Ⓒ Ⓓ
115. Ⓐ Ⓑ Ⓒ Ⓓ
116. Ⓐ Ⓑ Ⓒ Ⓓ
117. Ⓐ Ⓑ Ⓒ Ⓓ
118. Ⓐ Ⓑ Ⓒ Ⓓ
119. Ⓐ Ⓑ Ⓒ Ⓓ
120. Ⓐ Ⓑ Ⓒ Ⓓ
121. Ⓐ Ⓑ Ⓒ Ⓓ
122. Ⓐ Ⓑ Ⓒ Ⓓ
123. Ⓐ Ⓑ Ⓒ Ⓓ
124. Ⓐ Ⓑ Ⓒ Ⓓ
125. Ⓐ Ⓑ Ⓒ Ⓓ
126. Ⓐ Ⓑ Ⓒ Ⓓ
127. Ⓐ Ⓑ Ⓒ Ⓓ
128. Ⓐ Ⓑ Ⓒ Ⓓ
129. Ⓐ Ⓑ Ⓒ Ⓓ
130. Ⓐ Ⓑ Ⓒ Ⓓ
131. Ⓐ Ⓑ Ⓒ Ⓓ
132. Ⓐ Ⓑ Ⓒ Ⓓ
133. Ⓐ Ⓑ Ⓒ Ⓓ
134. Ⓐ Ⓑ Ⓒ Ⓓ
135. Ⓐ Ⓑ Ⓒ Ⓓ
136. Ⓐ Ⓑ Ⓒ Ⓓ
137. Ⓐ Ⓑ Ⓒ Ⓓ
138. Ⓐ Ⓑ Ⓒ Ⓓ
139. Ⓐ Ⓑ Ⓒ Ⓓ
140. Ⓐ Ⓑ Ⓒ Ⓓ
141. Ⓐ Ⓑ Ⓒ Ⓓ
142. Ⓐ Ⓑ Ⓒ Ⓓ
143. Ⓐ Ⓑ Ⓒ Ⓓ
144. Ⓐ Ⓑ Ⓒ Ⓓ
145. Ⓐ Ⓑ Ⓒ Ⓓ
146. Ⓐ Ⓑ Ⓒ Ⓓ
147. Ⓐ Ⓑ Ⓒ Ⓓ
148. Ⓐ Ⓑ Ⓒ Ⓓ
149. Ⓐ Ⓑ Ⓒ Ⓓ
150. Ⓐ Ⓑ Ⓒ Ⓓ
151. Ⓐ Ⓑ Ⓒ Ⓓ
152. Ⓐ Ⓑ Ⓒ Ⓓ
153. Ⓐ Ⓑ Ⓒ Ⓓ
154. Ⓐ Ⓑ Ⓒ Ⓓ
155. Ⓐ Ⓑ Ⓒ Ⓓ
156. Ⓐ Ⓑ Ⓒ Ⓓ
157. Ⓐ Ⓑ Ⓒ Ⓓ
158. Ⓐ Ⓑ Ⓒ Ⓓ
159. Ⓐ Ⓑ Ⓒ Ⓓ
160. Ⓐ Ⓑ Ⓒ Ⓓ
161. Ⓐ Ⓑ Ⓒ Ⓓ
162. Ⓐ Ⓑ Ⓒ Ⓓ
163. Ⓐ Ⓑ Ⓒ Ⓓ
164. Ⓐ Ⓑ Ⓒ Ⓓ
165. Ⓐ Ⓑ Ⓒ Ⓓ
166. Ⓐ Ⓑ Ⓒ Ⓓ
167. Ⓐ Ⓑ Ⓒ Ⓓ
168. Ⓐ Ⓑ Ⓒ Ⓓ
169. Ⓐ Ⓑ Ⓒ Ⓓ
170. Ⓐ Ⓑ Ⓒ Ⓓ
171. Ⓐ Ⓑ Ⓒ Ⓓ
172. Ⓐ Ⓑ Ⓒ Ⓓ
173. Ⓐ Ⓑ Ⓒ Ⓓ
174. Ⓐ Ⓑ Ⓒ Ⓓ

Math

175. ⒶⒷⒸⒹ
176. ⒶⒷⒸⒹ
177. ⒶⒷⒸⒹ
178. ⒶⒷⒸⒹ
179. ⒶⒷⒸⒹ
180. ⒶⒷⒸⒹ
181. ⒶⒷⒸⒹ
182. ⒶⒷⒸⒹ
183. ⒶⒷⒸⒹ
184. ⒶⒷⒸⒹ
185. ⒶⒷⒸⒹ
186. ⒶⒷⒸⒹ
187. ⒶⒷⒸⒹ
188. ⒶⒷⒸⒹ
189. ⒶⒷⒸⒹ
190. ⒶⒷⒸⒹ
191. ⒶⒷⒸⒹ
192. ⒶⒷⒸⒹ
193. ⒶⒷⒸⒹ
194. ⒶⒷⒸⒹ
195. ⒶⒷⒸⒹ
196. ⒶⒷⒸⒹ
197. ⒶⒷⒸⒹ
198. ⒶⒷⒸⒹ
199. ⒶⒷⒸⒹ
200. ⒶⒷⒸⒹ
201. ⒶⒷⒸⒹ
202. ⒶⒷⒸⒹ
203. ⒶⒷⒸⒹ
204. ⒶⒷⒸⒹ
205. ⒶⒷⒸⒹ
206. ⒶⒷⒸⒹ
207. ⒶⒷⒸⒹ
208. ⒶⒷⒸⒹ
209. ⒶⒷⒸⒹ
210. ⒶⒷⒸⒹ
211. ⒶⒷⒸⒹ
212. ⒶⒷⒸⒹ
213. ⒶⒷⒸⒹ
214. ⒶⒷⒸⒹ
215. ⒶⒷⒸⒹ
216. ⒶⒷⒸⒹ
217. ⒶⒷⒸⒹ
218. ⒶⒷⒸⒹ
219. ⒶⒷⒸⒹ
220. ⒶⒷⒸⒹ
221. ⒶⒷⒸⒹ
222. ⒶⒷⒸⒹ
223. ⒶⒷⒸⒹ
224. ⒶⒷⒸⒹ
225. ⒶⒷⒸⒹ
226. ⒶⒷⒸⒹ
227. ⒶⒷⒸⒹ
228. ⒶⒷⒸⒹ
229. ⒶⒷⒸⒹ
230. ⒶⒷⒸⒹ
231. ⒶⒷⒸⒹ
232. ⒶⒷⒸⒹ
233. ⒶⒷⒸⒹ
234. ⒶⒷⒸⒹ
235. ⒶⒷⒸⒹ
236. ⒶⒷⒸⒹ
237. ⒶⒷⒸⒹ
238. ⒶⒷⒸⒹ

Language

239. ⒶⒷⒸⒹ
240. ⒶⒷⒸⒹ
241. ⒶⒷⒸⒹ
242. ⒶⒷⒸⒹ
243. ⒶⒷⒸⒹ
244. ⒶⒷⒸⒹ
245. ⒶⒷⒸⒹ
246. ⒶⒷⒸⒹ
247. ⒶⒷⒸⒹ
248. ⒶⒷⒸⒹ
249. ⒶⒷⒸⒹ
250. ⒶⒷⒸⒹ
251. ⒶⒷⒸⒹ
252. ⒶⒷⒸⒹ
253. ⒶⒷⒸⒹ
254. ⒶⒷⒸⒹ
255. ⒶⒷⒸⒹ
256. ⒶⒷⒸⒹ
257. ⒶⒷⒸⒹ
258. ⒶⒷⒸⒹ
259. ⒶⒷⒸⒹ
260. ⒶⒷⒸⒹ
261. ⒶⒷⒸⒹ
262. ⒶⒷⒸⒹ
263. ⒶⒷⒸⒹ
264. ⒶⒷⒸⒹ
265. ⒶⒷⒸⒹ
266. ⒶⒷⒸⒹ
267. ⒶⒷⒸⒹ
268. ⒶⒷⒸⒹ
269. ⒶⒷⒸⒹ
270. ⒶⒷⒸⒹ
271. ⒶⒷⒸⒹ
272. ⒶⒷⒸⒹ
273. ⒶⒷⒸⒹ
274. ⒶⒷⒸⒹ
275. ⒶⒷⒸⒹ
276. ⒶⒷⒸⒹ
277. ⒶⒷⒸⒹ
278. ⒶⒷⒸⒹ
279. ⒶⒷⒸⒹ
280. ⒶⒷⒸⒹ
281. ⒶⒷⒸⒹ
282. ⒶⒷⒸⒹ
283. ⒶⒷⒸⒹ
284. ⒶⒷⒸⒹ
285. ⒶⒷⒸⒹ
286. ⒶⒷⒸⒹ
287. ⒶⒷⒸⒹ
288. ⒶⒷⒸⒹ
289. ⒶⒷⒸⒹ
290. ⒶⒷⒸⒹ
291. ⒶⒷⒸⒹ
292. ⒶⒷⒸⒹ
293. ⒶⒷⒸⒹ
294. ⒶⒷⒸⒹ
295. ⒶⒷⒸⒹ
296. ⒶⒷⒸⒹ
297. ⒶⒷⒸⒹ
298. ⒶⒷⒸⒹ

Test 6 Answer Sheet

Verbal

1. Ⓐ Ⓑ Ⓒ Ⓓ
2. Ⓐ Ⓑ Ⓒ Ⓓ
3. Ⓐ Ⓑ Ⓒ Ⓓ
4. Ⓐ Ⓑ Ⓒ Ⓓ
5. Ⓐ Ⓑ Ⓒ Ⓓ
6. Ⓐ Ⓑ Ⓒ Ⓓ
7. Ⓐ Ⓑ Ⓒ Ⓓ
8. Ⓐ Ⓑ Ⓒ Ⓓ
9. Ⓐ Ⓑ Ⓒ Ⓓ
10. Ⓐ Ⓑ Ⓒ Ⓓ
11. Ⓐ Ⓑ Ⓒ Ⓓ
12. Ⓐ Ⓑ Ⓒ Ⓓ
13. Ⓐ Ⓑ Ⓒ Ⓓ
14. Ⓐ Ⓑ Ⓒ Ⓓ
15. Ⓐ Ⓑ Ⓒ Ⓓ
16. Ⓐ Ⓑ Ⓒ Ⓓ
17. Ⓐ Ⓑ Ⓒ Ⓓ
18. Ⓐ Ⓑ Ⓒ Ⓓ
19. Ⓐ Ⓑ Ⓒ Ⓓ
20. Ⓐ Ⓑ Ⓒ Ⓓ
21. Ⓐ Ⓑ Ⓒ Ⓓ
22. Ⓐ Ⓑ Ⓒ Ⓓ
23. Ⓐ Ⓑ Ⓒ Ⓓ
24. Ⓐ Ⓑ Ⓒ Ⓓ
25. Ⓐ Ⓑ Ⓒ Ⓓ
26. Ⓐ Ⓑ Ⓒ Ⓓ
27. Ⓐ Ⓑ Ⓒ Ⓓ
28. Ⓐ Ⓑ Ⓒ Ⓓ
29. Ⓐ Ⓑ Ⓒ Ⓓ
30. Ⓐ Ⓑ Ⓒ Ⓓ
31. Ⓐ Ⓑ Ⓒ Ⓓ
32. Ⓐ Ⓑ Ⓒ Ⓓ
33. Ⓐ Ⓑ Ⓒ Ⓓ
34. Ⓐ Ⓑ Ⓒ Ⓓ
35. Ⓐ Ⓑ Ⓒ Ⓓ
36. Ⓐ Ⓑ Ⓒ Ⓓ
37. Ⓐ Ⓑ Ⓒ Ⓓ
38. Ⓐ Ⓑ Ⓒ Ⓓ
39. Ⓐ Ⓑ Ⓒ Ⓓ
40. Ⓐ Ⓑ Ⓒ Ⓓ
41. Ⓐ Ⓑ Ⓒ Ⓓ
42. Ⓐ Ⓑ Ⓒ Ⓓ
43. Ⓐ Ⓑ Ⓒ Ⓓ
44. Ⓐ Ⓑ Ⓒ Ⓓ
45. Ⓐ Ⓑ Ⓒ Ⓓ
46. Ⓐ Ⓑ Ⓒ Ⓓ
47. Ⓐ Ⓑ Ⓒ Ⓓ
48. Ⓐ Ⓑ Ⓒ Ⓓ
49. Ⓐ Ⓑ Ⓒ Ⓓ
50. Ⓐ Ⓑ Ⓒ Ⓓ
51. Ⓐ Ⓑ Ⓒ Ⓓ
52. Ⓐ Ⓑ Ⓒ Ⓓ
53. Ⓐ Ⓑ Ⓒ Ⓓ
54. Ⓐ Ⓑ Ⓒ Ⓓ
55. Ⓐ Ⓑ Ⓒ Ⓓ
56. Ⓐ Ⓑ Ⓒ Ⓓ
57. Ⓐ Ⓑ Ⓒ Ⓓ
58. Ⓐ Ⓑ Ⓒ Ⓓ
59. Ⓐ Ⓑ Ⓒ Ⓓ
60. Ⓐ Ⓑ Ⓒ Ⓓ

Quantitative

61. Ⓐ Ⓑ Ⓒ Ⓓ
62. Ⓐ Ⓑ Ⓒ Ⓓ
63. Ⓐ Ⓑ Ⓒ Ⓓ
64. Ⓐ Ⓑ Ⓒ Ⓓ
65. Ⓐ Ⓑ Ⓒ Ⓓ
66. Ⓐ Ⓑ Ⓒ Ⓓ
67. Ⓐ Ⓑ Ⓒ Ⓓ
68. Ⓐ Ⓑ Ⓒ Ⓓ
69. Ⓐ Ⓑ Ⓒ Ⓓ
70. Ⓐ Ⓑ Ⓒ Ⓓ
71. Ⓐ Ⓑ Ⓒ Ⓓ
72. Ⓐ Ⓑ Ⓒ Ⓓ
73. Ⓐ Ⓑ Ⓒ Ⓓ
74. Ⓐ Ⓑ Ⓒ Ⓓ
75. Ⓐ Ⓑ Ⓒ Ⓓ
76. Ⓐ Ⓑ Ⓒ Ⓓ
77. Ⓐ Ⓑ Ⓒ Ⓓ
78. Ⓐ Ⓑ Ⓒ Ⓓ
79. Ⓐ Ⓑ Ⓒ Ⓓ
80. Ⓐ Ⓑ Ⓒ Ⓓ
81. Ⓐ Ⓑ Ⓒ Ⓓ
82. Ⓐ Ⓑ Ⓒ Ⓓ
83. Ⓐ Ⓑ Ⓒ Ⓓ
84. Ⓐ Ⓑ Ⓒ Ⓓ
85. Ⓐ Ⓑ Ⓒ Ⓓ
86. Ⓐ Ⓑ Ⓒ Ⓓ
87. Ⓐ Ⓑ Ⓒ Ⓓ
88. Ⓐ Ⓑ Ⓒ Ⓓ
89. Ⓐ Ⓑ Ⓒ Ⓓ
90. Ⓐ Ⓑ Ⓒ Ⓓ
91. Ⓐ Ⓑ Ⓒ Ⓓ
92. Ⓐ Ⓑ Ⓒ Ⓓ
93. Ⓐ Ⓑ Ⓒ Ⓓ
94. Ⓐ Ⓑ Ⓒ Ⓓ
95. Ⓐ Ⓑ Ⓒ Ⓓ
96. Ⓐ Ⓑ Ⓒ Ⓓ
97. Ⓐ Ⓑ Ⓒ Ⓓ
98. Ⓐ Ⓑ Ⓒ Ⓓ
99. Ⓐ Ⓑ Ⓒ Ⓓ
100. Ⓐ Ⓑ Ⓒ Ⓓ
101. Ⓐ Ⓑ Ⓒ Ⓓ
102. Ⓐ Ⓑ Ⓒ Ⓓ
103. Ⓐ Ⓑ Ⓒ Ⓓ
104. Ⓐ Ⓑ Ⓒ Ⓓ
105. Ⓐ Ⓑ Ⓒ Ⓓ
106. Ⓐ Ⓑ Ⓒ Ⓓ
107. Ⓐ Ⓑ Ⓒ Ⓓ
108. Ⓐ Ⓑ Ⓒ Ⓓ
109. Ⓐ Ⓑ Ⓒ Ⓓ
110. Ⓐ Ⓑ Ⓒ Ⓓ
111. Ⓐ Ⓑ Ⓒ Ⓓ
112. Ⓐ Ⓑ Ⓒ Ⓓ

Reading

113. Ⓐ Ⓑ Ⓒ Ⓓ
114. Ⓐ Ⓑ Ⓒ Ⓓ
115. Ⓐ Ⓑ Ⓒ Ⓓ
116. Ⓐ Ⓑ Ⓒ Ⓓ
117. Ⓐ Ⓑ Ⓒ Ⓓ
118. Ⓐ Ⓑ Ⓒ Ⓓ
119. Ⓐ Ⓑ Ⓒ Ⓓ
120. Ⓐ Ⓑ Ⓒ Ⓓ
121. Ⓐ Ⓑ Ⓒ Ⓓ
122. Ⓐ Ⓑ Ⓒ Ⓓ
123. Ⓐ Ⓑ Ⓒ Ⓓ
124. Ⓐ Ⓑ Ⓒ Ⓓ
125. Ⓐ Ⓑ Ⓒ Ⓓ
126. Ⓐ Ⓑ Ⓒ Ⓓ
127. Ⓐ Ⓑ Ⓒ Ⓓ
128. Ⓐ Ⓑ Ⓒ Ⓓ
129. Ⓐ Ⓑ Ⓒ Ⓓ
130. Ⓐ Ⓑ Ⓒ Ⓓ
131. Ⓐ Ⓑ Ⓒ Ⓓ
132. Ⓐ Ⓑ Ⓒ Ⓓ
133. Ⓐ Ⓑ Ⓒ Ⓓ
134. Ⓐ Ⓑ Ⓒ Ⓓ
135. Ⓐ Ⓑ Ⓒ Ⓓ
136. Ⓐ Ⓑ Ⓒ Ⓓ
137. Ⓐ Ⓑ Ⓒ Ⓓ
138. Ⓐ Ⓑ Ⓒ Ⓓ
139. Ⓐ Ⓑ Ⓒ Ⓓ
140. Ⓐ Ⓑ Ⓒ Ⓓ
141. Ⓐ Ⓑ Ⓒ Ⓓ
142. Ⓐ Ⓑ Ⓒ Ⓓ
143. Ⓐ Ⓑ Ⓒ Ⓓ
144. Ⓐ Ⓑ Ⓒ Ⓓ
145. Ⓐ Ⓑ Ⓒ Ⓓ
146. Ⓐ Ⓑ Ⓒ Ⓓ
147. Ⓐ Ⓑ Ⓒ Ⓓ
148. Ⓐ Ⓑ Ⓒ Ⓓ
149. Ⓐ Ⓑ Ⓒ Ⓓ
150. Ⓐ Ⓑ Ⓒ Ⓓ
151. Ⓐ Ⓑ Ⓒ Ⓓ
152. Ⓐ Ⓑ Ⓒ Ⓓ
153. Ⓐ Ⓑ Ⓒ Ⓓ
154. Ⓐ Ⓑ Ⓒ Ⓓ
155. Ⓐ Ⓑ Ⓒ Ⓓ
156. Ⓐ Ⓑ Ⓒ Ⓓ
157. Ⓐ Ⓑ Ⓒ Ⓓ
158. Ⓐ Ⓑ Ⓒ Ⓓ
159. Ⓐ Ⓑ Ⓒ Ⓓ
160. Ⓐ Ⓑ Ⓒ Ⓓ
161. Ⓐ Ⓑ Ⓒ Ⓓ
162. Ⓐ Ⓑ Ⓒ Ⓓ
163. Ⓐ Ⓑ Ⓒ Ⓓ
164. Ⓐ Ⓑ Ⓒ Ⓓ
165. Ⓐ Ⓑ Ⓒ Ⓓ
166. Ⓐ Ⓑ Ⓒ Ⓓ
167. Ⓐ Ⓑ Ⓒ Ⓓ
168. Ⓐ Ⓑ Ⓒ Ⓓ
169. Ⓐ Ⓑ Ⓒ Ⓓ
170. Ⓐ Ⓑ Ⓒ Ⓓ
171. Ⓐ Ⓑ Ⓒ Ⓓ
172. Ⓐ Ⓑ Ⓒ Ⓓ
173. Ⓐ Ⓑ Ⓒ Ⓓ
174. Ⓐ Ⓑ Ⓒ Ⓓ

Math

175. Ⓐ Ⓑ Ⓒ Ⓓ
176. Ⓐ Ⓑ Ⓒ Ⓓ
177. Ⓐ Ⓑ Ⓒ Ⓓ
178. Ⓐ Ⓑ Ⓒ Ⓓ
179. Ⓐ Ⓑ Ⓒ Ⓓ
180. Ⓐ Ⓑ Ⓒ Ⓓ
181. Ⓐ Ⓑ Ⓒ Ⓓ
182. Ⓐ Ⓑ Ⓒ Ⓓ
183. Ⓐ Ⓑ Ⓒ Ⓓ
184. Ⓐ Ⓑ Ⓒ Ⓓ
185. Ⓐ Ⓑ Ⓒ Ⓓ
186. Ⓐ Ⓑ Ⓒ Ⓓ
187. Ⓐ Ⓑ Ⓒ Ⓓ
188. Ⓐ Ⓑ Ⓒ Ⓓ
189. Ⓐ Ⓑ Ⓒ Ⓓ
190. Ⓐ Ⓑ Ⓒ Ⓓ
191. Ⓐ Ⓑ Ⓒ Ⓓ
192. Ⓐ Ⓑ Ⓒ Ⓓ
193. Ⓐ Ⓑ Ⓒ Ⓓ
194. Ⓐ Ⓑ Ⓒ Ⓓ
195. Ⓐ Ⓑ Ⓒ Ⓓ
196. Ⓐ Ⓑ Ⓒ Ⓓ
197. Ⓐ Ⓑ Ⓒ Ⓓ
198. Ⓐ Ⓑ Ⓒ Ⓓ
199. Ⓐ Ⓑ Ⓒ Ⓓ
200. Ⓐ Ⓑ Ⓒ Ⓓ
201. Ⓐ Ⓑ Ⓒ Ⓓ
202. Ⓐ Ⓑ Ⓒ Ⓓ
203. Ⓐ Ⓑ Ⓒ Ⓓ
204. Ⓐ Ⓑ Ⓒ Ⓓ
205. Ⓐ Ⓑ Ⓒ Ⓓ
206. Ⓐ Ⓑ Ⓒ Ⓓ
207. Ⓐ Ⓑ Ⓒ Ⓓ
208. Ⓐ Ⓑ Ⓒ Ⓓ
209. Ⓐ Ⓑ Ⓒ Ⓓ
210. Ⓐ Ⓑ Ⓒ Ⓓ
211. Ⓐ Ⓑ Ⓒ Ⓓ
212. Ⓐ Ⓑ Ⓒ Ⓓ
213. Ⓐ Ⓑ Ⓒ Ⓓ
214. Ⓐ Ⓑ Ⓒ Ⓓ
215. Ⓐ Ⓑ Ⓒ Ⓓ
216. Ⓐ Ⓑ Ⓒ Ⓓ
217. Ⓐ Ⓑ Ⓒ Ⓓ
218. Ⓐ Ⓑ Ⓒ Ⓓ
219. Ⓐ Ⓑ Ⓒ Ⓓ
220. Ⓐ Ⓑ Ⓒ Ⓓ
221. Ⓐ Ⓑ Ⓒ Ⓓ
222. Ⓐ Ⓑ Ⓒ Ⓓ
223. Ⓐ Ⓑ Ⓒ Ⓓ
224. Ⓐ Ⓑ Ⓒ Ⓓ
225. Ⓐ Ⓑ Ⓒ Ⓓ
226. Ⓐ Ⓑ Ⓒ Ⓓ
227. Ⓐ Ⓑ Ⓒ Ⓓ
228. Ⓐ Ⓑ Ⓒ Ⓓ
229. Ⓐ Ⓑ Ⓒ Ⓓ
230. Ⓐ Ⓑ Ⓒ Ⓓ
231. Ⓐ Ⓑ Ⓒ Ⓓ
232. Ⓐ Ⓑ Ⓒ Ⓓ
233. Ⓐ Ⓑ Ⓒ Ⓓ
234. Ⓐ Ⓑ Ⓒ Ⓓ
235. Ⓐ Ⓑ Ⓒ Ⓓ
236. Ⓐ Ⓑ Ⓒ Ⓓ
237. Ⓐ Ⓑ Ⓒ Ⓓ
238. Ⓐ Ⓑ Ⓒ Ⓓ

Language

239. Ⓐ Ⓑ Ⓒ Ⓓ
240. Ⓐ Ⓑ Ⓒ Ⓓ
241. Ⓐ Ⓑ Ⓒ Ⓓ
242. Ⓐ Ⓑ Ⓒ Ⓓ
243. Ⓐ Ⓑ Ⓒ Ⓓ
244. Ⓐ Ⓑ Ⓒ Ⓓ
245. Ⓐ Ⓑ Ⓒ Ⓓ
246. Ⓐ Ⓑ Ⓒ Ⓓ
247. Ⓐ Ⓑ Ⓒ Ⓓ
248. Ⓐ Ⓑ Ⓒ Ⓓ
249. Ⓐ Ⓑ Ⓒ Ⓓ
250. Ⓐ Ⓑ Ⓒ Ⓓ
251. Ⓐ Ⓑ Ⓒ Ⓓ
252. Ⓐ Ⓑ Ⓒ Ⓓ
253. Ⓐ Ⓑ Ⓒ Ⓓ
254. Ⓐ Ⓑ Ⓒ Ⓓ
255. Ⓐ Ⓑ Ⓒ Ⓓ
256. Ⓐ Ⓑ Ⓒ Ⓓ
257. Ⓐ Ⓑ Ⓒ Ⓓ
258. Ⓐ Ⓑ Ⓒ Ⓓ
259. Ⓐ Ⓑ Ⓒ Ⓓ
260. Ⓐ Ⓑ Ⓒ Ⓓ
261. Ⓐ Ⓑ Ⓒ Ⓓ
262. Ⓐ Ⓑ Ⓒ Ⓓ
263. Ⓐ Ⓑ Ⓒ Ⓓ
264. Ⓐ Ⓑ Ⓒ Ⓓ
265. Ⓐ Ⓑ Ⓒ Ⓓ
266. Ⓐ Ⓑ Ⓒ Ⓓ
267. Ⓐ Ⓑ Ⓒ Ⓓ
268. Ⓐ Ⓑ Ⓒ Ⓓ
269. Ⓐ Ⓑ Ⓒ Ⓓ
270. Ⓐ Ⓑ Ⓒ Ⓓ
271. Ⓐ Ⓑ Ⓒ Ⓓ
272. Ⓐ Ⓑ Ⓒ Ⓓ
273. Ⓐ Ⓑ Ⓒ Ⓓ
274. Ⓐ Ⓑ Ⓒ Ⓓ
275. Ⓐ Ⓑ Ⓒ Ⓓ
276. Ⓐ Ⓑ Ⓒ Ⓓ
277. Ⓐ Ⓑ Ⓒ Ⓓ
278. Ⓐ Ⓑ Ⓒ Ⓓ
279. Ⓐ Ⓑ Ⓒ Ⓓ
280. Ⓐ Ⓑ Ⓒ Ⓓ
281. Ⓐ Ⓑ Ⓒ Ⓓ
282. Ⓐ Ⓑ Ⓒ Ⓓ
283. Ⓐ Ⓑ Ⓒ Ⓓ
284. Ⓐ Ⓑ Ⓒ Ⓓ
285. Ⓐ Ⓑ Ⓒ Ⓓ
286. Ⓐ Ⓑ Ⓒ Ⓓ
287. Ⓐ Ⓑ Ⓒ Ⓓ
288. Ⓐ Ⓑ Ⓒ Ⓓ
289. Ⓐ Ⓑ Ⓒ Ⓓ
290. Ⓐ Ⓑ Ⓒ Ⓓ
291. Ⓐ Ⓑ Ⓒ Ⓓ
292. Ⓐ Ⓑ Ⓒ Ⓓ
293. Ⓐ Ⓑ Ⓒ Ⓓ
294. Ⓐ Ⓑ Ⓒ Ⓓ
295. Ⓐ Ⓑ Ⓒ Ⓓ
296. Ⓐ Ⓑ Ⓒ Ⓓ
297. Ⓐ Ⓑ Ⓒ Ⓓ
298. Ⓐ Ⓑ Ⓒ Ⓓ

Test 7 Answer Sheet

Verbal

1. Ⓐ Ⓑ Ⓒ Ⓓ
2. Ⓐ Ⓑ Ⓒ Ⓓ
3. Ⓐ Ⓑ Ⓒ Ⓓ
4. Ⓐ Ⓑ Ⓒ Ⓓ
5. Ⓐ Ⓑ Ⓒ Ⓓ
6. Ⓐ Ⓑ Ⓒ Ⓓ
7. Ⓐ Ⓑ Ⓒ Ⓓ
8. Ⓐ Ⓑ Ⓒ Ⓓ
9. Ⓐ Ⓑ Ⓒ Ⓓ
10. Ⓐ Ⓑ Ⓒ Ⓓ
11. Ⓐ Ⓑ Ⓒ Ⓓ
12. Ⓐ Ⓑ Ⓒ Ⓓ
13. Ⓐ Ⓑ Ⓒ Ⓓ
14. Ⓐ Ⓑ Ⓒ Ⓓ
15. Ⓐ Ⓑ Ⓒ Ⓓ
16. Ⓐ Ⓑ Ⓒ Ⓓ
17. Ⓐ Ⓑ Ⓒ Ⓓ
18. Ⓐ Ⓑ Ⓒ Ⓓ
19. Ⓐ Ⓑ Ⓒ Ⓓ
20. Ⓐ Ⓑ Ⓒ Ⓓ
21. Ⓐ Ⓑ Ⓒ Ⓓ
22. Ⓐ Ⓑ Ⓒ Ⓓ
23. Ⓐ Ⓑ Ⓒ Ⓓ
24. Ⓐ Ⓑ Ⓒ Ⓓ
25. Ⓐ Ⓑ Ⓒ Ⓓ
26. Ⓐ Ⓑ Ⓒ Ⓓ
27. Ⓐ Ⓑ Ⓒ Ⓓ
28. Ⓐ Ⓑ Ⓒ Ⓓ
29. Ⓐ Ⓑ Ⓒ Ⓓ
30. Ⓐ Ⓑ Ⓒ Ⓓ
31. Ⓐ Ⓑ Ⓒ Ⓓ
32. Ⓐ Ⓑ Ⓒ Ⓓ
33. Ⓐ Ⓑ Ⓒ Ⓓ
34. Ⓐ Ⓑ Ⓒ Ⓓ
35. Ⓐ Ⓑ Ⓒ Ⓓ
36. Ⓐ Ⓑ Ⓒ Ⓓ
37. Ⓐ Ⓑ Ⓒ Ⓓ
38. Ⓐ Ⓑ Ⓒ Ⓓ
39. Ⓐ Ⓑ Ⓒ Ⓓ
40. Ⓐ Ⓑ Ⓒ Ⓓ
41. Ⓐ Ⓑ Ⓒ Ⓓ
42. Ⓐ Ⓑ Ⓒ Ⓓ
43. Ⓐ Ⓑ Ⓒ Ⓓ
44. Ⓐ Ⓑ Ⓒ Ⓓ
45. Ⓐ Ⓑ Ⓒ Ⓓ
46. Ⓐ Ⓑ Ⓒ Ⓓ
47. Ⓐ Ⓑ Ⓒ Ⓓ
48. Ⓐ Ⓑ Ⓒ Ⓓ
49. Ⓐ Ⓑ Ⓒ Ⓓ
50. Ⓐ Ⓑ Ⓒ Ⓓ
51. Ⓐ Ⓑ Ⓒ Ⓓ
52. Ⓐ Ⓑ Ⓒ Ⓓ
53. Ⓐ Ⓑ Ⓒ Ⓓ
54. Ⓐ Ⓑ Ⓒ Ⓓ
55. Ⓐ Ⓑ Ⓒ Ⓓ
56. Ⓐ Ⓑ Ⓒ Ⓓ
57. Ⓐ Ⓑ Ⓒ Ⓓ
58. Ⓐ Ⓑ Ⓒ Ⓓ
59. Ⓐ Ⓑ Ⓒ Ⓓ
60. Ⓐ Ⓑ Ⓒ Ⓓ

Quantitative

61. Ⓐ Ⓑ Ⓒ Ⓓ
62. Ⓐ Ⓑ Ⓒ Ⓓ
63. Ⓐ Ⓑ Ⓒ Ⓓ
64. Ⓐ Ⓑ Ⓒ Ⓓ
65. Ⓐ Ⓑ Ⓒ Ⓓ
66. Ⓐ Ⓑ Ⓒ Ⓓ
67. Ⓐ Ⓑ Ⓒ Ⓓ
68. Ⓐ Ⓑ Ⓒ Ⓓ
69. Ⓐ Ⓑ Ⓒ Ⓓ
70. Ⓐ Ⓑ Ⓒ Ⓓ
71. Ⓐ Ⓑ Ⓒ Ⓓ
72. Ⓐ Ⓑ Ⓒ Ⓓ
73. Ⓐ Ⓑ Ⓒ Ⓓ
74. Ⓐ Ⓑ Ⓒ Ⓓ
75. Ⓐ Ⓑ Ⓒ Ⓓ
76. Ⓐ Ⓑ Ⓒ Ⓓ
77. Ⓐ Ⓑ Ⓒ Ⓓ
78. Ⓐ Ⓑ Ⓒ Ⓓ
79. Ⓐ Ⓑ Ⓒ Ⓓ
80. Ⓐ Ⓑ Ⓒ Ⓓ
81. Ⓐ Ⓑ Ⓒ Ⓓ
82. Ⓐ Ⓑ Ⓒ Ⓓ
83. Ⓐ Ⓑ Ⓒ Ⓓ
84. Ⓐ Ⓑ Ⓒ Ⓓ
85. Ⓐ Ⓑ Ⓒ Ⓓ
86. Ⓐ Ⓑ Ⓒ Ⓓ
87. Ⓐ Ⓑ Ⓒ Ⓓ
88. Ⓐ Ⓑ Ⓒ Ⓓ
89. Ⓐ Ⓑ Ⓒ Ⓓ
90. Ⓐ Ⓑ Ⓒ Ⓓ
91. Ⓐ Ⓑ Ⓒ Ⓓ
92. Ⓐ Ⓑ Ⓒ Ⓓ
93. Ⓐ Ⓑ Ⓒ Ⓓ
94. Ⓐ Ⓑ Ⓒ Ⓓ
95. Ⓐ Ⓑ Ⓒ Ⓓ
96. Ⓐ Ⓑ Ⓒ Ⓓ
97. Ⓐ Ⓑ Ⓒ Ⓓ
98. Ⓐ Ⓑ Ⓒ Ⓓ
99. Ⓐ Ⓑ Ⓒ Ⓓ
100. Ⓐ Ⓑ Ⓒ Ⓓ
101. Ⓐ Ⓑ Ⓒ Ⓓ
102. Ⓐ Ⓑ Ⓒ Ⓓ
103. Ⓐ Ⓑ Ⓒ Ⓓ
104. Ⓐ Ⓑ Ⓒ Ⓓ
105. Ⓐ Ⓑ Ⓒ Ⓓ
106. Ⓐ Ⓑ Ⓒ Ⓓ
107. Ⓐ Ⓑ Ⓒ Ⓓ
108. Ⓐ Ⓑ Ⓒ Ⓓ
109. Ⓐ Ⓑ Ⓒ Ⓓ
110. Ⓐ Ⓑ Ⓒ Ⓓ
111. Ⓐ Ⓑ Ⓒ Ⓓ
112. Ⓐ Ⓑ Ⓒ Ⓓ

Reading

113. Ⓐ Ⓑ Ⓒ Ⓓ
114. Ⓐ Ⓑ Ⓒ Ⓓ
115. Ⓐ Ⓑ Ⓒ Ⓓ
116. Ⓐ Ⓑ Ⓒ Ⓓ
117. Ⓐ Ⓑ Ⓒ Ⓓ
118. Ⓐ Ⓑ Ⓒ Ⓓ
119. Ⓐ Ⓑ Ⓒ Ⓓ
120. Ⓐ Ⓑ Ⓒ Ⓓ
121. Ⓐ Ⓑ Ⓒ Ⓓ
122. Ⓐ Ⓑ Ⓒ Ⓓ
123. Ⓐ Ⓑ Ⓒ Ⓓ
124. Ⓐ Ⓑ Ⓒ Ⓓ
125. Ⓐ Ⓑ Ⓒ Ⓓ
126. Ⓐ Ⓑ Ⓒ Ⓓ
127. Ⓐ Ⓑ Ⓒ Ⓓ
128. Ⓐ Ⓑ Ⓒ Ⓓ
129. Ⓐ Ⓑ Ⓒ Ⓓ
130. Ⓐ Ⓑ Ⓒ Ⓓ
131. Ⓐ Ⓑ Ⓒ Ⓓ
132. Ⓐ Ⓑ Ⓒ Ⓓ
133. Ⓐ Ⓑ Ⓒ Ⓓ
134. Ⓐ Ⓑ Ⓒ Ⓓ
135. Ⓐ Ⓑ Ⓒ Ⓓ
136. Ⓐ Ⓑ Ⓒ Ⓓ
137. Ⓐ Ⓑ Ⓒ Ⓓ
138. Ⓐ Ⓑ Ⓒ Ⓓ
139. Ⓐ Ⓑ Ⓒ Ⓓ
140. Ⓐ Ⓑ Ⓒ Ⓓ
141. Ⓐ Ⓑ Ⓒ Ⓓ
142. Ⓐ Ⓑ Ⓒ Ⓓ
143. Ⓐ Ⓑ Ⓒ Ⓓ
144. Ⓐ Ⓑ Ⓒ Ⓓ
145. Ⓐ Ⓑ Ⓒ Ⓓ
146. Ⓐ Ⓑ Ⓒ Ⓓ
147. Ⓐ Ⓑ Ⓒ Ⓓ
148. Ⓐ Ⓑ Ⓒ Ⓓ
149. Ⓐ Ⓑ Ⓒ Ⓓ
150. Ⓐ Ⓑ Ⓒ Ⓓ
151. Ⓐ Ⓑ Ⓒ Ⓓ
152. Ⓐ Ⓑ Ⓒ Ⓓ
153. Ⓐ Ⓑ Ⓒ Ⓓ
154. Ⓐ Ⓑ Ⓒ Ⓓ
155. Ⓐ Ⓑ Ⓒ Ⓓ
156. Ⓐ Ⓑ Ⓒ Ⓓ
157. Ⓐ Ⓑ Ⓒ Ⓓ
158. Ⓐ Ⓑ Ⓒ Ⓓ
159. Ⓐ Ⓑ Ⓒ Ⓓ
160. Ⓐ Ⓑ Ⓒ Ⓓ
161. Ⓐ Ⓑ Ⓒ Ⓓ
162. Ⓐ Ⓑ Ⓒ Ⓓ
163. Ⓐ Ⓑ Ⓒ Ⓓ
164. Ⓐ Ⓑ Ⓒ Ⓓ
165. Ⓐ Ⓑ Ⓒ Ⓓ
166. Ⓐ Ⓑ Ⓒ Ⓓ
167. Ⓐ Ⓑ Ⓒ Ⓓ
168. Ⓐ Ⓑ Ⓒ Ⓓ
169. Ⓐ Ⓑ Ⓒ Ⓓ
170. Ⓐ Ⓑ Ⓒ Ⓓ
171. Ⓐ Ⓑ Ⓒ Ⓓ
172. Ⓐ Ⓑ Ⓒ Ⓓ
173. Ⓐ Ⓑ Ⓒ Ⓓ
174. Ⓐ Ⓑ Ⓒ Ⓓ

Math

175. Ⓐ Ⓑ Ⓒ Ⓓ
176. Ⓐ Ⓑ Ⓒ Ⓓ
177. Ⓐ Ⓑ Ⓒ Ⓓ
178. Ⓐ Ⓑ Ⓒ Ⓓ
179. Ⓐ Ⓑ Ⓒ Ⓓ
180. Ⓐ Ⓑ Ⓒ Ⓓ
181. Ⓐ Ⓑ Ⓒ Ⓓ
182. Ⓐ Ⓑ Ⓒ Ⓓ
183. Ⓐ Ⓑ Ⓒ Ⓓ
184. Ⓐ Ⓑ Ⓒ Ⓓ
185. Ⓐ Ⓑ Ⓒ Ⓓ
186. Ⓐ Ⓑ Ⓒ Ⓓ
187. Ⓐ Ⓑ Ⓒ Ⓓ
188. Ⓐ Ⓑ Ⓒ Ⓓ
189. Ⓐ Ⓑ Ⓒ Ⓓ
190. Ⓐ Ⓑ Ⓒ Ⓓ
191. Ⓐ Ⓑ Ⓒ Ⓓ
192. Ⓐ Ⓑ Ⓒ Ⓓ
193. Ⓐ Ⓑ Ⓒ Ⓓ
194. Ⓐ Ⓑ Ⓒ Ⓓ
195. Ⓐ Ⓑ Ⓒ Ⓓ
196. Ⓐ Ⓑ Ⓒ Ⓓ
197. Ⓐ Ⓑ Ⓒ Ⓓ
198. Ⓐ Ⓑ Ⓒ Ⓓ
199. Ⓐ Ⓑ Ⓒ Ⓓ
200. Ⓐ Ⓑ Ⓒ Ⓓ
201. Ⓐ Ⓑ Ⓒ Ⓓ
202. Ⓐ Ⓑ Ⓒ Ⓓ
203. Ⓐ Ⓑ Ⓒ Ⓓ
204. Ⓐ Ⓑ Ⓒ Ⓓ
205. Ⓐ Ⓑ Ⓒ Ⓓ
206. Ⓐ Ⓑ Ⓒ Ⓓ
207. Ⓐ Ⓑ Ⓒ Ⓓ
208. Ⓐ Ⓑ Ⓒ Ⓓ
209. Ⓐ Ⓑ Ⓒ Ⓓ
210. Ⓐ Ⓑ Ⓒ Ⓓ
211. Ⓐ Ⓑ Ⓒ Ⓓ
212. Ⓐ Ⓑ Ⓒ Ⓓ
213. Ⓐ Ⓑ Ⓒ Ⓓ
214. Ⓐ Ⓑ Ⓒ Ⓓ
215. Ⓐ Ⓑ Ⓒ Ⓓ
216. Ⓐ Ⓑ Ⓒ Ⓓ
217. Ⓐ Ⓑ Ⓒ Ⓓ
218. Ⓐ Ⓑ Ⓒ Ⓓ
219. Ⓐ Ⓑ Ⓒ Ⓓ
220. Ⓐ Ⓑ Ⓒ Ⓓ
221. Ⓐ Ⓑ Ⓒ Ⓓ
222. Ⓐ Ⓑ Ⓒ Ⓓ
223. Ⓐ Ⓑ Ⓒ Ⓓ
224. Ⓐ Ⓑ Ⓒ Ⓓ
225. Ⓐ Ⓑ Ⓒ Ⓓ
226. Ⓐ Ⓑ Ⓒ Ⓓ
227. Ⓐ Ⓑ Ⓒ Ⓓ
228. Ⓐ Ⓑ Ⓒ Ⓓ
229. Ⓐ Ⓑ Ⓒ Ⓓ
230. Ⓐ Ⓑ Ⓒ Ⓓ
231. Ⓐ Ⓑ Ⓒ Ⓓ
232. Ⓐ Ⓑ Ⓒ Ⓓ
233. Ⓐ Ⓑ Ⓒ Ⓓ
234. Ⓐ Ⓑ Ⓒ Ⓓ
235. Ⓐ Ⓑ Ⓒ Ⓓ
236. Ⓐ Ⓑ Ⓒ Ⓓ
237. Ⓐ Ⓑ Ⓒ Ⓓ
238. Ⓐ Ⓑ Ⓒ Ⓓ

Language

239. Ⓐ Ⓑ Ⓒ Ⓓ
240. Ⓐ Ⓑ Ⓒ Ⓓ
241. Ⓐ Ⓑ Ⓒ Ⓓ
242. Ⓐ Ⓑ Ⓒ Ⓓ
243. Ⓐ Ⓑ Ⓒ Ⓓ
244. Ⓐ Ⓑ Ⓒ Ⓓ
245. Ⓐ Ⓑ Ⓒ Ⓓ
246. Ⓐ Ⓑ Ⓒ Ⓓ
247. Ⓐ Ⓑ Ⓒ Ⓓ
248. Ⓐ Ⓑ Ⓒ Ⓓ
249. Ⓐ Ⓑ Ⓒ Ⓓ
250. Ⓐ Ⓑ Ⓒ Ⓓ
251. Ⓐ Ⓑ Ⓒ Ⓓ
252. Ⓐ Ⓑ Ⓒ Ⓓ
253. Ⓐ Ⓑ Ⓒ Ⓓ
254. Ⓐ Ⓑ Ⓒ Ⓓ
255. Ⓐ Ⓑ Ⓒ Ⓓ
256. Ⓐ Ⓑ Ⓒ Ⓓ
257. Ⓐ Ⓑ Ⓒ Ⓓ
258. Ⓐ Ⓑ Ⓒ Ⓓ
259. Ⓐ Ⓑ Ⓒ Ⓓ
260. Ⓐ Ⓑ Ⓒ Ⓓ
261. Ⓐ Ⓑ Ⓒ Ⓓ
262. Ⓐ Ⓑ Ⓒ Ⓓ
263. Ⓐ Ⓑ Ⓒ Ⓓ
264. Ⓐ Ⓑ Ⓒ Ⓓ
265. Ⓐ Ⓑ Ⓒ Ⓓ
266. Ⓐ Ⓑ Ⓒ Ⓓ
267. Ⓐ Ⓑ Ⓒ Ⓓ
268. Ⓐ Ⓑ Ⓒ Ⓓ
269. Ⓐ Ⓑ Ⓒ Ⓓ
270. Ⓐ Ⓑ Ⓒ Ⓓ
271. Ⓐ Ⓑ Ⓒ Ⓓ
272. Ⓐ Ⓑ Ⓒ Ⓓ
273. Ⓐ Ⓑ Ⓒ Ⓓ
274. Ⓐ Ⓑ Ⓒ Ⓓ
275. Ⓐ Ⓑ Ⓒ Ⓓ
276. Ⓐ Ⓑ Ⓒ Ⓓ
277. Ⓐ Ⓑ Ⓒ Ⓓ
278. Ⓐ Ⓑ Ⓒ Ⓓ
279. Ⓐ Ⓑ Ⓒ Ⓓ
280. Ⓐ Ⓑ Ⓒ Ⓓ
281. Ⓐ Ⓑ Ⓒ Ⓓ
282. Ⓐ Ⓑ Ⓒ Ⓓ
283. Ⓐ Ⓑ Ⓒ Ⓓ
284. Ⓐ Ⓑ Ⓒ Ⓓ
285. Ⓐ Ⓑ Ⓒ Ⓓ
286. Ⓐ Ⓑ Ⓒ Ⓓ
287. Ⓐ Ⓑ Ⓒ Ⓓ
288. Ⓐ Ⓑ Ⓒ Ⓓ
289. Ⓐ Ⓑ Ⓒ Ⓓ
290. Ⓐ Ⓑ Ⓒ Ⓓ
291. Ⓐ Ⓑ Ⓒ Ⓓ
292. Ⓐ Ⓑ Ⓒ Ⓓ
293. Ⓐ Ⓑ Ⓒ Ⓓ
294. Ⓐ Ⓑ Ⓒ Ⓓ
295. Ⓐ Ⓑ Ⓒ Ⓓ
296. Ⓐ Ⓑ Ⓒ Ⓓ
297. Ⓐ Ⓑ Ⓒ Ⓓ
298. Ⓐ Ⓑ Ⓒ Ⓓ

Test 8 Answer Sheet

Verbal

1. Ⓐ Ⓑ Ⓒ Ⓓ
2. Ⓐ Ⓑ Ⓒ Ⓓ
3. Ⓐ Ⓑ Ⓒ Ⓓ
4. Ⓐ Ⓑ Ⓒ Ⓓ
5. Ⓐ Ⓑ Ⓒ Ⓓ
6. Ⓐ Ⓑ Ⓒ Ⓓ
7. Ⓐ Ⓑ Ⓒ Ⓓ
8. Ⓐ Ⓑ Ⓒ Ⓓ
9. Ⓐ Ⓑ Ⓒ Ⓓ
10. Ⓐ Ⓑ Ⓒ Ⓓ
11. Ⓐ Ⓑ Ⓒ Ⓓ
12. Ⓐ Ⓑ Ⓒ Ⓓ
13. Ⓐ Ⓑ Ⓒ Ⓓ
14. Ⓐ Ⓑ Ⓒ Ⓓ
15. Ⓐ Ⓑ Ⓒ Ⓓ
16. Ⓐ Ⓑ Ⓒ Ⓓ
17. Ⓐ Ⓑ Ⓒ Ⓓ
18. Ⓐ Ⓑ Ⓒ Ⓓ
19. Ⓐ Ⓑ Ⓒ Ⓓ
20. Ⓐ Ⓑ Ⓒ Ⓓ
21. Ⓐ Ⓑ Ⓒ Ⓓ
22. Ⓐ Ⓑ Ⓒ Ⓓ
23. Ⓐ Ⓑ Ⓒ Ⓓ
24. Ⓐ Ⓑ Ⓒ Ⓓ
25. Ⓐ Ⓑ Ⓒ Ⓓ
26. Ⓐ Ⓑ Ⓒ Ⓓ
27. Ⓐ Ⓑ Ⓒ Ⓓ
28. Ⓐ Ⓑ Ⓒ Ⓓ
29. Ⓐ Ⓑ Ⓒ Ⓓ
30. Ⓐ Ⓑ Ⓒ Ⓓ
31. Ⓐ Ⓑ Ⓒ Ⓓ
32. Ⓐ Ⓑ Ⓒ Ⓓ
33. Ⓐ Ⓑ Ⓒ Ⓓ
34. Ⓐ Ⓑ Ⓒ Ⓓ
35. Ⓐ Ⓑ Ⓒ Ⓓ
36. Ⓐ Ⓑ Ⓒ Ⓓ
37. Ⓐ Ⓑ Ⓒ Ⓓ
38. Ⓐ Ⓑ Ⓒ Ⓓ
39. Ⓐ Ⓑ Ⓒ Ⓓ
40. Ⓐ Ⓑ Ⓒ Ⓓ
41. Ⓐ Ⓑ Ⓒ Ⓓ
42. Ⓐ Ⓑ Ⓒ Ⓓ
43. Ⓐ Ⓑ Ⓒ Ⓓ
44. Ⓐ Ⓑ Ⓒ Ⓓ
45. Ⓐ Ⓑ Ⓒ Ⓓ
46. Ⓐ Ⓑ Ⓒ Ⓓ
47. Ⓐ Ⓑ Ⓒ Ⓓ
48. Ⓐ Ⓑ Ⓒ Ⓓ
49. Ⓐ Ⓑ Ⓒ Ⓓ
50. Ⓐ Ⓑ Ⓒ Ⓓ
51. Ⓐ Ⓑ Ⓒ Ⓓ
52. Ⓐ Ⓑ Ⓒ Ⓓ
53. Ⓐ Ⓑ Ⓒ Ⓓ
54. Ⓐ Ⓑ Ⓒ Ⓓ
55. Ⓐ Ⓑ Ⓒ Ⓓ
56. Ⓐ Ⓑ Ⓒ Ⓓ
57. Ⓐ Ⓑ Ⓒ Ⓓ
58. Ⓐ Ⓑ Ⓒ Ⓓ
59. Ⓐ Ⓑ Ⓒ Ⓓ
60. Ⓐ Ⓑ Ⓒ Ⓓ

Quantitative

61. Ⓐ Ⓑ Ⓒ Ⓓ
62. Ⓐ Ⓑ Ⓒ Ⓓ
63. Ⓐ Ⓑ Ⓒ Ⓓ
64. Ⓐ Ⓑ Ⓒ Ⓓ
65. Ⓐ Ⓑ Ⓒ Ⓓ
66. Ⓐ Ⓑ Ⓒ Ⓓ
67. Ⓐ Ⓑ Ⓒ Ⓓ
68. Ⓐ Ⓑ Ⓒ Ⓓ
69. Ⓐ Ⓑ Ⓒ Ⓓ
70. Ⓐ Ⓑ Ⓒ Ⓓ
71. Ⓐ Ⓑ Ⓒ Ⓓ
72. Ⓐ Ⓑ Ⓒ Ⓓ
73. Ⓐ Ⓑ Ⓒ Ⓓ
74. Ⓐ Ⓑ Ⓒ Ⓓ
75. Ⓐ Ⓑ Ⓒ Ⓓ
76. Ⓐ Ⓑ Ⓒ Ⓓ
77. Ⓐ Ⓑ Ⓒ Ⓓ
78. Ⓐ Ⓑ Ⓒ Ⓓ
79. Ⓐ Ⓑ Ⓒ Ⓓ
80. Ⓐ Ⓑ Ⓒ Ⓓ
81. Ⓐ Ⓑ Ⓒ Ⓓ
82. Ⓐ Ⓑ Ⓒ Ⓓ
83. Ⓐ Ⓑ Ⓒ Ⓓ
84. Ⓐ Ⓑ Ⓒ Ⓓ
85. Ⓐ Ⓑ Ⓒ Ⓓ
86. Ⓐ Ⓑ Ⓒ Ⓓ
87. Ⓐ Ⓑ Ⓒ Ⓓ
88. Ⓐ Ⓑ Ⓒ Ⓓ
89. Ⓐ Ⓑ Ⓒ Ⓓ
90. Ⓐ Ⓑ Ⓒ Ⓓ
91. Ⓐ Ⓑ Ⓒ Ⓓ
92. Ⓐ Ⓑ Ⓒ Ⓓ
93. Ⓐ Ⓑ Ⓒ Ⓓ
94. Ⓐ Ⓑ Ⓒ Ⓓ
95. Ⓐ Ⓑ Ⓒ Ⓓ
96. Ⓐ Ⓑ Ⓒ Ⓓ
97. Ⓐ Ⓑ Ⓒ Ⓓ
98. Ⓐ Ⓑ Ⓒ Ⓓ
99. Ⓐ Ⓑ Ⓒ Ⓓ
100. Ⓐ Ⓑ Ⓒ Ⓓ
101. Ⓐ Ⓑ Ⓒ Ⓓ
102. Ⓐ Ⓑ Ⓒ Ⓓ
103. Ⓐ Ⓑ Ⓒ Ⓓ
104. Ⓐ Ⓑ Ⓒ Ⓓ
105. Ⓐ Ⓑ Ⓒ Ⓓ
106. Ⓐ Ⓑ Ⓒ Ⓓ
107. Ⓐ Ⓑ Ⓒ Ⓓ
108. Ⓐ Ⓑ Ⓒ Ⓓ
109. Ⓐ Ⓑ Ⓒ Ⓓ
110. Ⓐ Ⓑ Ⓒ Ⓓ
111. Ⓐ Ⓑ Ⓒ Ⓓ
112. Ⓐ Ⓑ Ⓒ Ⓓ

Reading

113. Ⓐ Ⓑ Ⓒ Ⓓ
114. Ⓐ Ⓑ Ⓒ Ⓓ
115. Ⓐ Ⓑ Ⓒ Ⓓ
116. Ⓐ Ⓑ Ⓒ Ⓓ
117. Ⓐ Ⓑ Ⓒ Ⓓ
118. Ⓐ Ⓑ Ⓒ Ⓓ
119. Ⓐ Ⓑ Ⓒ Ⓓ
120. Ⓐ Ⓑ Ⓒ Ⓓ
121. Ⓐ Ⓑ Ⓒ Ⓓ
122. Ⓐ Ⓑ Ⓒ Ⓓ
123. Ⓐ Ⓑ Ⓒ Ⓓ
124. Ⓐ Ⓑ Ⓒ Ⓓ
125. Ⓐ Ⓑ Ⓒ Ⓓ
126. Ⓐ Ⓑ Ⓒ Ⓓ
127. Ⓐ Ⓑ Ⓒ Ⓓ
128. Ⓐ Ⓑ Ⓒ Ⓓ
129. Ⓐ Ⓑ Ⓒ Ⓓ
130. Ⓐ Ⓑ Ⓒ Ⓓ
131. Ⓐ Ⓑ Ⓒ Ⓓ
132. Ⓐ Ⓑ Ⓒ Ⓓ
133. Ⓐ Ⓑ Ⓒ Ⓓ
134. Ⓐ Ⓑ Ⓒ Ⓓ
135. Ⓐ Ⓑ Ⓒ Ⓓ
136. Ⓐ Ⓑ Ⓒ Ⓓ
137. Ⓐ Ⓑ Ⓒ Ⓓ
138. Ⓐ Ⓑ Ⓒ Ⓓ
139. Ⓐ Ⓑ Ⓒ Ⓓ
140. Ⓐ Ⓑ Ⓒ Ⓓ
141. Ⓐ Ⓑ Ⓒ Ⓓ
142. Ⓐ Ⓑ Ⓒ Ⓓ
143. Ⓐ Ⓑ Ⓒ Ⓓ
144. Ⓐ Ⓑ Ⓒ Ⓓ
145. Ⓐ Ⓑ Ⓒ Ⓓ
146. Ⓐ Ⓑ Ⓒ Ⓓ
147. Ⓐ Ⓑ Ⓒ Ⓓ
148. Ⓐ Ⓑ Ⓒ Ⓓ
149. Ⓐ Ⓑ Ⓒ Ⓓ
150. Ⓐ Ⓑ Ⓒ Ⓓ
151. Ⓐ Ⓑ Ⓒ Ⓓ
152. Ⓐ Ⓑ Ⓒ Ⓓ
153. Ⓐ Ⓑ Ⓒ Ⓓ
154. Ⓐ Ⓑ Ⓒ Ⓓ
155. Ⓐ Ⓑ Ⓒ Ⓓ
156. Ⓐ Ⓑ Ⓒ Ⓓ
157. Ⓐ Ⓑ Ⓒ Ⓓ
158. Ⓐ Ⓑ Ⓒ Ⓓ
159. Ⓐ Ⓑ Ⓒ Ⓓ
160. Ⓐ Ⓑ Ⓒ Ⓓ
161. Ⓐ Ⓑ Ⓒ Ⓓ
162. Ⓐ Ⓑ Ⓒ Ⓓ
163. Ⓐ Ⓑ Ⓒ Ⓓ
164. Ⓐ Ⓑ Ⓒ Ⓓ
165. Ⓐ Ⓑ Ⓒ Ⓓ
166. Ⓐ Ⓑ Ⓒ Ⓓ
167. Ⓐ Ⓑ Ⓒ Ⓓ
168. Ⓐ Ⓑ Ⓒ Ⓓ
169. Ⓐ Ⓑ Ⓒ Ⓓ
170. Ⓐ Ⓑ Ⓒ Ⓓ
171. Ⓐ Ⓑ Ⓒ Ⓓ
172. Ⓐ Ⓑ Ⓒ Ⓓ
173. Ⓐ Ⓑ Ⓒ Ⓓ
174. Ⓐ Ⓑ Ⓒ Ⓓ

Math

175. Ⓐ Ⓑ Ⓒ Ⓓ
176. Ⓐ Ⓑ Ⓒ Ⓓ
177. Ⓐ Ⓑ Ⓒ Ⓓ
178. Ⓐ Ⓑ Ⓒ Ⓓ
179. Ⓐ Ⓑ Ⓒ Ⓓ
180. Ⓐ Ⓑ Ⓒ Ⓓ
181. Ⓐ Ⓑ Ⓒ Ⓓ
182. Ⓐ Ⓑ Ⓒ Ⓓ
183. Ⓐ Ⓑ Ⓒ Ⓓ
184. Ⓐ Ⓑ Ⓒ Ⓓ
185. Ⓐ Ⓑ Ⓒ Ⓓ
186. Ⓐ Ⓑ Ⓒ Ⓓ
187. Ⓐ Ⓑ Ⓒ Ⓓ
188. Ⓐ Ⓑ Ⓒ Ⓓ
189. Ⓐ Ⓑ Ⓒ Ⓓ
190. Ⓐ Ⓑ Ⓒ Ⓓ
191. Ⓐ Ⓑ Ⓒ Ⓓ
192. Ⓐ Ⓑ Ⓒ Ⓓ
193. Ⓐ Ⓑ Ⓒ Ⓓ
194. Ⓐ Ⓑ Ⓒ Ⓓ
195. Ⓐ Ⓑ Ⓒ Ⓓ
196. Ⓐ Ⓑ Ⓒ Ⓓ
197. Ⓐ Ⓑ Ⓒ Ⓓ
198. Ⓐ Ⓑ Ⓒ Ⓓ
199. Ⓐ Ⓑ Ⓒ Ⓓ
200. Ⓐ Ⓑ Ⓒ Ⓓ
201. Ⓐ Ⓑ Ⓒ Ⓓ
202. Ⓐ Ⓑ Ⓒ Ⓓ
203. Ⓐ Ⓑ Ⓒ Ⓓ
204. Ⓐ Ⓑ Ⓒ Ⓓ
205. Ⓐ Ⓑ Ⓒ Ⓓ
206. Ⓐ Ⓑ Ⓒ Ⓓ
207. Ⓐ Ⓑ Ⓒ Ⓓ
208. Ⓐ Ⓑ Ⓒ Ⓓ
209. Ⓐ Ⓑ Ⓒ Ⓓ
210. Ⓐ Ⓑ Ⓒ Ⓓ
211. Ⓐ Ⓑ Ⓒ Ⓓ
212. Ⓐ Ⓑ Ⓒ Ⓓ
213. Ⓐ Ⓑ Ⓒ Ⓓ
214. Ⓐ Ⓑ Ⓒ Ⓓ
215. Ⓐ Ⓑ Ⓒ Ⓓ
216. Ⓐ Ⓑ Ⓒ Ⓓ
217. Ⓐ Ⓑ Ⓒ Ⓓ
218. Ⓐ Ⓑ Ⓒ Ⓓ
219. Ⓐ Ⓑ Ⓒ Ⓓ
220. Ⓐ Ⓑ Ⓒ Ⓓ
221. Ⓐ Ⓑ Ⓒ Ⓓ
222. Ⓐ Ⓑ Ⓒ Ⓓ
223. Ⓐ Ⓑ Ⓒ Ⓓ
224. Ⓐ Ⓑ Ⓒ Ⓓ
225. Ⓐ Ⓑ Ⓒ Ⓓ
226. Ⓐ Ⓑ Ⓒ Ⓓ
227. Ⓐ Ⓑ Ⓒ Ⓓ
228. Ⓐ Ⓑ Ⓒ Ⓓ
229. Ⓐ Ⓑ Ⓒ Ⓓ
230. Ⓐ Ⓑ Ⓒ Ⓓ
231. Ⓐ Ⓑ Ⓒ Ⓓ
232. Ⓐ Ⓑ Ⓒ Ⓓ
233. Ⓐ Ⓑ Ⓒ Ⓓ
234. Ⓐ Ⓑ Ⓒ Ⓓ
235. Ⓐ Ⓑ Ⓒ Ⓓ
236. Ⓐ Ⓑ Ⓒ Ⓓ
237. Ⓐ Ⓑ Ⓒ Ⓓ
238. Ⓐ Ⓑ Ⓒ Ⓓ

Language

239. Ⓐ Ⓑ Ⓒ Ⓓ
240. Ⓐ Ⓑ Ⓒ Ⓓ
241. Ⓐ Ⓑ Ⓒ Ⓓ
242. Ⓐ Ⓑ Ⓒ Ⓓ
243. Ⓐ Ⓑ Ⓒ Ⓓ
244. Ⓐ Ⓑ Ⓒ Ⓓ
245. Ⓐ Ⓑ Ⓒ Ⓓ
246. Ⓐ Ⓑ Ⓒ Ⓓ
247. Ⓐ Ⓑ Ⓒ Ⓓ
248. Ⓐ Ⓑ Ⓒ Ⓓ
249. Ⓐ Ⓑ Ⓒ Ⓓ
250. Ⓐ Ⓑ Ⓒ Ⓓ
251. Ⓐ Ⓑ Ⓒ Ⓓ
252. Ⓐ Ⓑ Ⓒ Ⓓ
253. Ⓐ Ⓑ Ⓒ Ⓓ
254. Ⓐ Ⓑ Ⓒ Ⓓ
255. Ⓐ Ⓑ Ⓒ Ⓓ
256. Ⓐ Ⓑ Ⓒ Ⓓ
257. Ⓐ Ⓑ Ⓒ Ⓓ
258. Ⓐ Ⓑ Ⓒ Ⓓ
259. Ⓐ Ⓑ Ⓒ Ⓓ
260. Ⓐ Ⓑ Ⓒ Ⓓ
261. Ⓐ Ⓑ Ⓒ Ⓓ
262. Ⓐ Ⓑ Ⓒ Ⓓ
263. Ⓐ Ⓑ Ⓒ Ⓓ
264. Ⓐ Ⓑ Ⓒ Ⓓ
265. Ⓐ Ⓑ Ⓒ Ⓓ
266. Ⓐ Ⓑ Ⓒ Ⓓ
267. Ⓐ Ⓑ Ⓒ Ⓓ
268. Ⓐ Ⓑ Ⓒ Ⓓ
269. Ⓐ Ⓑ Ⓒ Ⓓ
270. Ⓐ Ⓑ Ⓒ Ⓓ
271. Ⓐ Ⓑ Ⓒ Ⓓ
272. Ⓐ Ⓑ Ⓒ Ⓓ
273. Ⓐ Ⓑ Ⓒ Ⓓ
274. Ⓐ Ⓑ Ⓒ Ⓓ
275. Ⓐ Ⓑ Ⓒ Ⓓ
276. Ⓐ Ⓑ Ⓒ Ⓓ
277. Ⓐ Ⓑ Ⓒ Ⓓ
278. Ⓐ Ⓑ Ⓒ Ⓓ
279. Ⓐ Ⓑ Ⓒ Ⓓ
280. Ⓐ Ⓑ Ⓒ Ⓓ
281. Ⓐ Ⓑ Ⓒ Ⓓ
282. Ⓐ Ⓑ Ⓒ Ⓓ
283. Ⓐ Ⓑ Ⓒ Ⓓ
284. Ⓐ Ⓑ Ⓒ Ⓓ
285. Ⓐ Ⓑ Ⓒ Ⓓ
286. Ⓐ Ⓑ Ⓒ Ⓓ
287. Ⓐ Ⓑ Ⓒ Ⓓ
288. Ⓐ Ⓑ Ⓒ Ⓓ
289. Ⓐ Ⓑ Ⓒ Ⓓ
290. Ⓐ Ⓑ Ⓒ Ⓓ
291. Ⓐ Ⓑ Ⓒ Ⓓ
292. Ⓐ Ⓑ Ⓒ Ⓓ
293. Ⓐ Ⓑ Ⓒ Ⓓ
294. Ⓐ Ⓑ Ⓒ Ⓓ
295. Ⓐ Ⓑ Ⓒ Ⓓ
296. Ⓐ Ⓑ Ⓒ Ⓓ
297. Ⓐ Ⓑ Ⓒ Ⓓ
298. Ⓐ Ⓑ Ⓒ Ⓓ

Made in the USA
Monee, IL
12 September 2019